NEW

Language
LEADER

ADVANCED

COURSEBOOK

COTTON | FALVEY | KENT | LEBEAU | REES

CONTENTS

Listening	Speaking / Pronunciation	Scenario	Study Skills / Writing	Video
A radio programme about education; reacting to the text (1.1) A job interview (1.3)	Discussing education (1.1) The qualities of successful people (1.2) Jobs and CVs (1.3)	Scenario: choosing an intern Key language: stating requirements, saying what is essential and desirable Task: choosing an intern	Justifying opinions (1.2) A CV (1.3) Study skills: Self-awareness Writing skills: A covering letter (1.5)	Meet the expert: an interview with Helen Kempster, a careers consultant, about job hunting and interviews (1.3)
An interview with the director of a conservation charity; predicting (2.2)	Important factors for tourists; Specialised tourism (2.1) Discussing threats to the natural and built environment (2.2) Talk about the rules at a beach (2.3)	Scenario: Granville Island Key language: stating your position, clarifying Task: participating in a meeting	A notice of rules for a beach (2.3) Study skills: Planning and organising essays Writing skills: A problem–solution essay (2.5)	Meet the expert: an interview with Noirin Hegarty from Lonely Planet, about the work of a travel publisher (2.3)
A radio interview with an ambassador's partner; inferring attitude (3.3)	Discussing stereotypes; Reflecting on your culture (3.1) Discussing international collaboration (3.2) Making criticisms (3.3)	Scenario: The oil spill crisis Key language: Stating objectives, giving strong advice Task: Devising an action plan	Using subordinate clauses (3.2) Study skills: Active listening Writing skills: A speech	Meet the expert: an interview with Brendan Paddy from the Disasters Emergency Committee, about international aid (3.2)
A speech about healthcare provision; identifying the author's purpose (4.2) A speech by a VIP at a graduation ceremony for nurses (4.3)	Talking about health and fitness; discussing health quotes (4.1) Discussing spending on healthcare; describe and evaluate the healthcare system in your country (4.2) Working in healthcare (4.3)	Scenario: Change your ways Key language: Justifying opinions Task: Choosing and planning a publicity campaign	An essay about the healthcare system in your country (4.2) Study skills: Analysing visual information Writing skills: Describing visual information	Meet the expert: an interview with Neil Shah, Director of the Stress Management Society (4.1)
An extract from a radio programme about Japan; expanding the topic (5.1) A radio programme about fashion and social responsibility; identifying support for main argument (5.3)	A debate about materialism (5.1) Talking about design classics (5.2) Debating topics related to the fashion industry (5.3)	Scenario: Retail revamp Key language: Discussing hypothetical ideas Task: Developing a recovery strategy	A description of one of your possessions (5.2) Study skills: Reading complex texts effectively Writing skills: Summarising	Meet the expert: an interview with fashion designers Francesca Rosella and Ryan Genz, about their company Cutecircuit (5.3)
A presentation; a question and answer session (6.4)	Talking about advances in technology (6.1) Talking about technological change (6.2) Discussing DNA testing (6.3)	Scenario: A radio debate Key language: Persuading, criticising, accepting criticism, offering counter-arguments Task: Participating in a debate	A message board text about technological advances (6.1) Improving written texts (6.3) Study skills: Intercultural awareness Writing skills: Reporting a survey	Study skills video: a talk about studying in another country. (6.5)

CONTENTS

Listening	Speaking / Pronunciation	Scenario	Study Skills / Writing	Video
A lecture about creativity (7.1) A radio programme about Keynes and Aristotle; evaluating a summary (7.2)	Talking about creative and lateral thinking; thinking of new uses for everyday objects (7.1) Talking about great thinkers (7.2) Identifying outcomes (7.3)	Scenario: Camomila Key language: Approving ideas, expressing doubt/objections Task: A new plan for Camomila	Study Skills: Critical thinking Writing skills: An opinion-led essay	Meet the expert: an interview with Mairi Ryan from the Royal Society of Arts, about their public events programme (7.2)
Six people talking about their jobs; justifying choices (8.1) A journalist talking to students (8.2) A talk about an astronaut (8.3) Five people talking about media (8.3)	Talking about the media; Discussing headlines for a news programme (8.1) Talking about journalism (8.2) Talking about social media (8.3) Discussing the effectiveness of media; evaluating effectiveness (8.3)	Scenario: Sailing close to the wind Key language: Being cautious Task: Resolving ethical dilemmas	Study skills: Style and register Writing skills: Formal, neutral and informal emails	Meet the expert: an interview with Dr Nell Haynes, an anthropologist, about the impact of social media (8.3)
Five extracts from a book (9.1) A talk on teenagers; evaluating with criteria (9.2) A talk about international migration (9.3)	Talking about social issues (9.1) Talking about juvenile crime and punishment (9.2) Talking about migration (9.3)	Scenario: Lawmakers Key language: Balancing an argument Task: Amending and modifying the law	Writing about migration; write a poem (9.3) Study skills: Synthesising information Writing skills: A synthesis	Meet the expert: an interview with Nik Peachey, an educational consultant, about body language in different cultures (9.1)
Interviews with people who attended events (10.1) Musical extracts (10.2) A webcast about using the internet (10.3)	Talking about the popularity of the arts; Describing an event (10.1) Discussing music; How music changes lives (10.2) Discussing technology and entertainment (10.3)	Scenario: Global village Key language: An informal talk Task: Informal presentation	A review for an event (10.1) A press release for a concert (10.2) Study skills: Seminar/Discussion skills Writing skills: Critical reflective writing	Study skills video: a seminar about the language of drama (10.5)
A radio programme about microfinance (11.2)	Talking about successful businesses; deciding and justifying priorities (11.1) Talking about Fairtrade; evaluating evidence (11.2) Talking about negotiating, considering alternative views (11.3)	Scenario: Saving lives at sea Key language: Setting the agenda, responding to offers Task: Negotiating a contract	A summary of a budget (11.1) The first paragraph of an essay about microfinance (11.2) Study skills: Making a business presentation, introduction, conclusion Writing skills: A tactful business email	Study skills video: a presentation about the launch of a new product (11.5)
Three people talk about setting up a human colony on Mars (12.1) A podcast about plastic (12.2)	Talking about space exploration and setting up a human colony on Mars (12.1) Reducing the consumption of plastic (12.2) Talking about insects and food production (12.3)	Scenario: Ask the panel Key language: Referring to what other people have said Task: Taking part in a panel discussion	Writing about setting up a human colony on Mars (12.1) Writing about reducing consumption of plastic (12.2) Study skills: Examination skills Writing skills: A personal statement	Meet the expert: an interview with professors Richard Kitney and Paul Freemont, about synthetic biology (12.2)

Audioscripts (p165–182)

1 Education and employment

1.1 ISSUES IN EDUCATION

Education costs money, but then so does ignorance. Claus Moser (b. 1922), German-born British academic

SPEAKING AND VOCABULARY

1a Complete the opinions with the words in the box.

assessment	curriculum	dumbing down	elitism
interpersonal skills	plagiarism	streaming	

1   'The most important aspect of education is the _____, or subjects which are taught.'
2   'Frequent examinations are a much more reliable and useful way of measuring performance than continuous _____.'
3   '_____ is an excellent idea because it enables students with a similar ability to work at the same pace.'
4   'Education is not about developing your _____, but about learning facts.'
5   'Private education creates _____ and encourages inequality in society, which is absolutely disgusting.'
6   'Copying someone else's ideas, _____, cheating and buying qualifications is sometimes necessary.'
7   'It's easier to get good grades nowadays because education is _____. Qualifications are worth less than in the past.'

1b Which opinions do you agree or disagree with? Work with a partner and discuss your ideas.

2 Work with a partner and discuss the following.

1   the advantages and disadvantages of your country's education system
2   the positive and negative aspects of your own educational experiences

READING

3 Which of the following are important to learn at school?

1   important dates in history, e.g. battles
2   the names of capital cities
3   times tables, e.g. 4 x 7 = 28
4   scientific formulae, e.g. $E = mc^2$
5   spelling
6   mental arithmetic, e.g. adding up numbers in your head
7   poems and excerpts from literature

4 What techniques do you have for learning any of the above? Tell a partner.

5 What do you understand by the term 'rote learning'? Scan the article to check your answer.

6 Read the article. In which paragraph does the writer:

1   **argue** that it is pointless to memorise significant historical facts?
2   **claim** that rote learning is often used by professionals?
3   **comment** that there is an educational split in the world?
4   **conclude** that putting knowledge into practice is the most important thing?
5   **deny** that there are no positive aspects to rote learning?
6   **point out** that rote learning is considered old-fashioned?
7   **suggest** that learning alone is often boring?

7 Is the writer positive, negative or undecided about rote learning? Do you agree with the writer? Why?/Why not?

Education blog ▶   Recent posts ▶

Learning by rote in the digital age

When it comes to education, there's a divide between East and West. Eastern nations' education systems have historically favoured rote learning – that is, memorisation – compared with Western schooling, which often cites creativity and innovation as key goals of a rounded education. Rote learning has become seen as an antiquated method of teaching. The dictionary defines learning 'by rote' as: 'from memory, without thought of the meaning; in a mechanical way'.

The decline of rote learning in the West has been facilitated by technology. No one needs to memorise friends' phone numbers or email addresses because such data is conveniently stored and accessible electronically – our phones have become databases, while the internet can answer any question to which there exists an answer. So why remember the date of the Treaty of Versailles when you can find the answer on Google in about six seconds?

But now there are rumblings in the UK of a need to return to rote learning, which has stirred controversy in the media. You'd be forgiven for thinking the whole thing was a terrible idea. But there are benefits to memorising stuff.

In fact, memorising key data is fundamental to learning any skill. Doctoring requires knowledge of the anatomy, lawyering requires knowledge of cases and statutes, learning languages requires grammar and even new alphabets in some cases. Of course, being able to recall things will not further your understanding of those things, but without memorising these foundation elements, you cannot progress to a deeper understanding of a subject.

While the internet and computers have undermined the need for us to remember things, it may well be that mobile learning can help revive this style of learning by making it more convenient, more accessible and more fun.

Drilling yourself – with flashcards or by brute repetition – is hard work (and usually tedious), which is why most people need their multiplication tables to be drilled into them by teachers or parents. Rote learning without a willing third party can be a battle of discipline and motivation. But mobile learning can make those flashcards and drills more appropriate to individual study; our devices can challenge and inform us at the same time and also keep us motivated, whether through game-like structures or recording our progress.

Learning by rote does have limited use. Once you've acquired the fundamentals of a subject, the need to memorise data usually diminishes and it becomes the application of knowledge which is important.

VOCABULARY
REPORTING WHAT OTHERS SAY

8 Match the verbs in bold in Exercise 6 with their meanings.

a   say that something is not true
b   make a point strongly, giving reasons/ evidence
c   decide that something is true after consideration
d   express an opinion
e   state that something is true
f   put forward an idea in a tentative way
g   bring to the reader's attention

LISTENING

9a `1.1` Listen to three people on a radio programme talking about the purpose of education. Where are they from and what do they do?

9b Listen again and make notes on the speakers' views.

1   How do their opinions differ?
2   What suggestions do they make?
3   Who is the most persuasive speaker? Why?

9c Compare your notes with a partner.

10 Reacting to the text **Work in small groups and discuss the questions.**

1   What is your reaction to the views you heard on the radio programme? How common do you think they are?
2   Which is closest to the view of the writer of the article in Exercise 6?
3   What similarities are there between the views expressed on the radio programme and the education system in your country?

SPEAKING

11 Work in small groups and discuss the statements and questions.

1   'You get what you pay for.' Do you think this is true for education in your country?
2   Males and females should be educated separately.
3   What do you think are the key goals of education?
4   What are the advantages and disadvantages of school uniforms?

12 Work with a student from another group. Tell him/her about your group's ideas. Listen and make notes on what he/she tells you.

13 Report back to your group about what the student told you in Exercise 12, using your notes. Are the ideas similar or different to your group's ideas?

SPEAKING

1a Think of three successful people in these fields: business, the arts, science. Why do you think they are successful (e.g. education, hard work, talent, good luck)? Tell a partner.

1b Which qualities do the people you described share?

READING

2 Read the profiles of three successful people quickly. In what way are they successful?

3 Look at some common characteristics of successful people. Which of them apply to the people you read about?

1	hard-working	4	creative
2	innovative	5	business-minded
3	highly educated	6	self-disciplined

4 Read the profiles again and answer the questions.

1 What do you think of Nooyi's management style?
2 How do you think Kim's earlier career could have helped her achieve her later success?
3 What difficulties did Greider have to overcome and how did she do so?
4 Which of the three people are you most impressed by? Tell a partner.

VOCABULARY
SUFFIXES (ADJECTIVES)

5a Find adjectives in the profiles which are formed from the nouns in the box.

allergy	infection	influence
passion	persuasion	power	success

5b What suffixes are used to form these adjectives?

allergy – allergic

6a Make adjectives from the nouns in the box. Use the correct suffixes.

affection	ambition	education
empathy	fiction	logic	speculation

6b Answer the questions.

1 Who is the most successful person you know? Give reasons.
2 Who is your favourite fictional character? Why?
3 What is the most powerful piece of art or film that you have seen?
4 What educational background is needed to become a teacher in your country?

Indra Nooyi

In 2010 Indra Nooyi was named the most powerful businesswoman in the world by *Fortune* magazine. She has been working as Chairperson and Chief Executive Officer of PepsiCo since 2006. Born in India, she has a Bachelor of Science degree, an MBA from the Indian Institute of Management and a Master's degree in Public and Private Management from Yale University.

Nooyi has a reputation for being very persuasive and has the ability to rouse an audience. She also has a very informal style in meetings and openly solicits the opinions of her staff. At one investors' conference, Nooyi sat down with the delegates and conducted the business equivalent of a fireside chat.

Nooyi is constantly reinventing her business model. 'The minute you've decided a new business model, it's extinct because somebody is going to copy it.' For years she's been talking about the importance of healthier products and education about nutrition. She works 18–20 hours a day and is currently serving on the board of several organisations.

Angela Jia Kim

Angela Jia Kim is a successful entrepreneur, having already founded two companies.

Her first piano teacher was her mother and later she graduated from the Eastman School of Music. Her classical refinement and passionate performances have delighted audiences worldwide.

One day just as she was about to perform on stage, she had an allergic reaction to a body lotion. As a result of this, she decided to develop her own line of skincare products. 'I was paying attention to what I was eating,' she says. 'Shouldn't I pay attention to what I was putting on my body?' She started experimenting to find non-toxic creams and eventually launched Om Aroma & Co., an organic skincare line.

Carol Greider

Carol Greider won the Nobel Prize in Medicine in 2009 after making a breakthrough in DNA and cancer research. However, Carol struggled at elementary school. She found it difficult to pronounce words and to read out loud. She was put into remedial spelling class and this led to problems with self-esteem. She thought of herself as stupid until she was diagnosed with dyslexia.

She had to memorise words to spell them, but then began to enjoy reading for pleasure. Then she found it easy to remember things in Biology and History. She enjoyed working hard. However, she still struggled to get into graduate school and received many rejection letters due to poor scores in the Graduate Recorded Exam.

Eventually, she was offered a place by the California Institute of Technology and UC Berkeley. She chose UC Berkeley as she wanted to work with Elizabeth Blackburn, whose enthusiasm for DNA and chromosome research she found infectious. In 2004 she became Department Director at Johns Hopkins University School of Medicine. Carol eventually won the Nobel Prize with Blackburn. She always credits all her colleagues who have been influential in her scientific journey.

Her degree was in Music, not Business, so she sought advice from respected businesswomen who were going through similar experiences. She went on to create Savor the Success, an online community for female entrepreneurs. She says her success in business is due to her training as a concert pianist and, of course, hard work.

GRAMMAR
THE CONTINUOUS ASPECT

7a Read the profiles of Indra Nooyi and Angela Jia Kim again and find examples of these tenses.

1 present continuous
2 past continuous
3 present perfect continuous

7b Which of the tenses you found are used to talk about:

1 an action that was in progress at an earlier time?
2 an action that is currently in progress?
3 an action which began in the past and is still continuing or has just finished?

➡ Language reference and extra practice, pages 126–127

8 Explain the difference in meaning between the sentences in each pair.

1 a I work in Madrid, but I live in a village forty kilometres away.
  b I'm working in Madrid, but I'm moving to Barcelona next year.
2 a I've worked in London, Paris and Rome, but now I work in Tokyo.
  b I've been working in Tokyo for a year and expect to continue to do so for some time.
3 a I worked in Oslo in 2013.
  b I was working in Oslo when my father fell ill.
4 a I'll work when you get home if you look after the children.
  b I'll be working when you get home, so please try to keep quiet.
5 a When her car broke down, she was driving to Moscow for a conference.
  b When her car broke down, she went the rest of the way by bus.
6 a We are renting an apartment until our house is ready.
  b We rent an apartment by the sea most summers.

9 Correct the mistakes in the use of tenses in the text.

comes
I really respect my best friend. He ~~is coming~~ from Poland and is speaking four languages. He is living in London since 1998 and I've been knowing him for ten years. We met on holiday when we hitchhike through Spain. One day while we walk through the Cantabrian Mountains, he told me that even though he had been leaving school at fifteen, he was going to be very successful. He joined his company when it is having difficulties. He was working his way up to the top since then. He is only working there for seven years and he is already being the Director.

WRITING

10 Justifying opinions Write a short paragraph giving and justifying your opinion on one of these statements.

1 A good education is the key to a successful life.
2 Luck and family connections are more important than a good education.
3 Success is ten percent inspiration and ninety percent perspiration.

SPEAKING

1 Work in small groups and discuss the questions.

1 How do you find out about jobs in your country?
2 What jobs have you had/would you like to have?
3 Have you ever written a CV/résumé? When?
4 Is there a standard format for CVs/résumés in your country?

READING

2 Which of the following do you think are essential to mention in your CV?

1 website addresses of companies you have worked for
2 details of pre-university qualifications
3 a photograph
4 date of birth
5 postal address
6 telephone number and email address
7 names of referees
8 internships/work placements
9 software used
10 charity work
11 interests
12 positions of responsibility
13 title, e.g. *Mr/Miss/Ms*
14 achievements
15 interpersonal skills

3a Evaluating effectiveness Read Vadim Kufenko's CV quickly. Do you think it is a good CV? Is there anything you would do differently?

3b Read the CV again and answer the questions.

1 What do you notice about the way the profile is written?
2 Which exchange programme might he have found the most difficult? Why?
3 What kinds of job do you think he might be suitable for?

4 Vadim is applying for a job in the marketing department of a British company that exports British products to Russia. They require a fluent Russian speaker, with advanced English and experience in finance and marketing. Rewrite Vadim's profile to help him get this job.

CV

Name: Vadim Kufenko
Date of birth: 8 May 1986
Email address: kufenko.vadim3@online.ru

PROFILE

An enthusiastic and dedicated professional with excellent analytical abilities in the field of finance. Exceptional numerical skills. Quick to grasp new ideas and concepts and able to work on his own initiative. Has a logical approach to challenges and is able to meet tight deadlines. Strong project management skills. A good team player with outstanding interpersonal skills.

WORK EXPERIENCE

December 2008–October 2013
Financial Analyst at the Bank of Foreign Trade, St Petersburg. Responsibilities: daily financial analysis, preparing financial statements, data processing and marketing surveys

EDUCATION

December 2013–present
PhD in Economics and Finance, St Petersburg State University of Economics and Finance

September 2007–July 2008
MA in Economics, specialising in Finance and Credit, St Petersburg State University of Economics and Finance

September 2003–June 2007
BA in Economics, St Petersburg State University of Economics and Finance

1998–1999
Southwest Junior High School, Lawrence, Kansas, USA

1993–2003
School #157, St Petersburg

INTERNSHIPS AND EXCHANGE PROGRAMMES

September–December 2007
Exchange programme at the University of Jyväskylä, Finland Programmes: Finance, Business Networks, Family Business, Marketing (in English), Finnish language

April 2007
Short internship at the Bank of Foreign Trade, St Petersburg

April–July 2006
Exchange programme at the Berlin School of Economics, Germany Programmes (in German): International Economic Relations, International Marketing, German language

ADDITIONAL SKILLS

Languages: English (advanced IELTS 8.0, BULATS), German (intermediate), Finnish (elementary)

HOBBIES

Trading in stocks and shares, swimming and jogging

VOCABULARY
ABBREVIATIONS

5 Work in small groups and match the abbreviations with the descriptions.

1	PhD	3	MBA	5	BULATS	7	TOEFL
2	MSc	4	BA	6	IELTS		

a   a first degree in the Humanities
b   a postgraduate degree in a science subject
c   a postgraduate degree, which entitles the holder to the title *Dr*
d   a postgraduate business qualification
e   a qualification in Business English
f   a test of reading, writing, listening and speaking, often used by British and Australian universities
g   a test of comprehension in written and spoken English, often used by American universities

LISTENING

6a **1.2** Listen to part of Vadim's job interview and answer the questions.

1   Why does the interviewer mention when the interview will finish?
2   What regret does Vadim mention?
3   What advice does the interviewer give Vadim?
4   How does Vadim turn a possible weakness into a strength?
5   Why does Vadim want the advertised job?
6   What mistake does the interviewer make?

6b Listen again and evaluate the interview. Answer the questions.

1   Do you think what Vadim said highlights his strengths?
2   How would you describe the interviewer's attitude towards Vadim?
3   How do you think the interview is going so far?

GRAMMAR
THE PERFECT ASPECT

7 Look at Audio script 1.2 on page 165 and find examples of the following.

1   present perfect simple
2   present perfect continuous
3   past perfect
4   future perfect
5   perfect infinitive
6   *having* + past participle

8 The perfect aspect links two times together. Which two times (present, past or future) are being linked together in each sentence?

1   Hopefully, we'll have finished the interview by 3 p.m.
2   I'd applied for a number of work placements before I got the one in the bank.
3   I've been on two exchange programmes: one in Finland and one in Germany.
4   Having read your CV, we'd like to know more about your internship and exchange programmes.
5   I seem to have lost your references.
6   Since December 2013 I've been writing my doctoral thesis.

➡ Language reference and extra practice, pages 126–127

9 Complete the sentences with the correct perfect form of the verbs in brackets.

1   I intended to come for just a couple of months, but next September I _____ (be) here for five years.
2   When I interviewed him, he _____ (already/be) out of work for over a year.
3   My sister _____ (be) the head of a PR company for the last ten years.
4   We _____ (interview) five people since 9 a.m., but I don't think any of them meet the requirements.
5   It's no use sending your CV now. They _____ (choose) a candidate by the end of today.
6   I was hoping _____ (finish) by now.
7   _____ (complete) my training, I am now looking for a job in finance.

WRITING

10a Choose a job that you would like to be interviewed for. Write a short CV to help you get the job.

10b Swap CVs with a partner and tell each other what jobs they are for. Suggest improvements to your partner's CV.

▶ MEET THE EXPERT

Watch an interview with Helen Kempster, a careers consultant, about job hunting and interviews.
Turn to page 150 for video activities.

SITUATION

Anderson University is a private university in the United Kingdom. Many of its students want to do internships of three to six months with companies or international organisations. They generally pay a fee and use the services of Morton Associates, a firm that specialises in arranging internships.

Morton Associates is looking for a suitable candidate for an internship with the international organisation UNESCO.

1a Read the situation, the description of UNESCO and the duties of the intern.

1b Work in pairs or small groups and discuss what kind of person would be suitable for this internship. Think about the candidate's educational qualifications, personal qualities, experience, skills and interests.

2 Discuss your profile of the ideal candidate with another pair or group.

3 `1.3` Listen to Lisa and Howard, two members of Morton Associates, talking about the requirements for candidates applying for an internship at UNESCO. Work with a partner and make notes under these headings.

- Qualifications
- Work experience
- Interests
- Languages
- Computer skills

KEY LANGUAGE
STATING REQUIREMENTS, SAYING WHAT IS
ESSENTIAL AND DESIRABLE

4 Read the extracts in Exercise 5 and try to predict what words are missing.

5 `1.4` Listen to extracts from the conversation in Exercise 3 and complete the gaps. Do not use more than two words for each gap.

1 L: It's _____ that candidates are doing a postgraduate degree.
2 H: What about languages?
   L: Well, they _____ an excellent knowledge of one of the working languages of the organisation – that means really good English or French, oral and written.
   H: Right, so that's _____.
3 H: How about work experience?
   L: Well, they don't mention that specifically, but it's obviously _____ to have some work experience.
4 H: You haven't mentioned computer skills.
   L: Well, candidates _____ to be able to use office-related software.
5 H: Anything else?
   L: No, but we'll be _____ some evidence of a special cultural or scientific interest.

6 Look at Audio script 1.3 on page 165. Underline all the phrases which are used to state requirements, and say whether each one is essential or desirable.

UNESCO activities

UNESCO promotes international cooperation among its 195 Member States and eight Associate Members in the fields of education, science, culture and communication. It has a wide range of programmes, which will appeal to students from diverse disciplines.

Aims:
- to mobilise for education so that every child, boy or girl, has access to education as a fundamental human right
- to build international understanding through protection of heritage and support for cultural diversity
- to pursue scientific cooperation
- to protect freedom of expression

Duties of the intern

- to assist in administrative duties as assigned by the director
- to assist in the research and writing of department publications
- to assist with the creation of PowerPoint presentations and maintenance of databases
- to help coordinate special events and conferences
- to take part in the development of student educational programmes

TASK
CHOOSING AN INTERN

7a Work in groups of three. You are members of Morton Associates. You are going to recommend one intern for the internship at UNESCO. There is only one vacancy at the moment. Read the profiles and underline the strong points of each candidate. Make a note of any points you think the candidate lacks.

Student A: read the profile of Pilar Martinez.
Student B: read the profile of Anette Frieberg.
Student C: read the profile of Kenneth Watana.

7b In your groups, discuss the candidates. Talk about their strengths and weaknesses and why they should/shouldn't get the internship.

7c Rank the candidates in order of their suitability for the internship (1 = most suitable, 3 = least suitable).

7d Choose the best candidate to recommend for the internship. Then compare your choice with other groups.

Profile

Qualifications *Final year PhD in Fine Art*

Languages *Fluent Spanish, intermediate level English and French*

Pilar Martinez

Computer skills *Basic knowledge of office programs and software*

Experience *Holiday work with a picture restorer at National Museum of Art*

Attitude *Very articulate. Passionate about art conservation. Not at all interested in current affairs. Seemed rather naïve and unsophisticated about world affairs. Has travelled all over the world. Made interesting comments about cross-cultural problems.*

Other information *Dressed fashionably. Recommendation from art professor: 'Pilar is single-minded. Art is her life. She is open to new ideas – that's her best quality.' Wants to work in picture conservation all over the world after she graduates.*

Profile

Qualifications *Final year PhD. Topic: language policies in Swedish schools*

Languages *Bilingual English–Swedish*

Computer skills *Extensive knowledge of computer programs and software*

Anette Frieberg

Experience *Worked during two summers for a 'travel by teaching' organisation. Gained a good knowledge of Asian cultures.*

Attitude *An extrovert. Seemed extremely confident. Expressed her opinions on social issues forcefully. Possibly not very open-minded. She didn't appear to be a good listener.*

Other information *Dressed rather casually for the interview. Recommendation from a lecturer: 'Anette's greatest strength is as a team leader. She expects a lot from members of her team.' Is President of the University International Society. Would like to work for an organisation which promotes women's and children's rights.*

Profile

Qualifications *Final year MA in Museum and Artefact Studies*

Languages *Thai, fairly good English and French (upper-intermediate level). Is learning German in evening class.*

Kenneth Watana

Computer skills *Competent using common software programs*

Experience *One-month part-time work at a local Railway Museum. Visitor information, communication with public.*

Attitude *Quiet, reflective person. Hesitated frequently before answering questions.*
Extremely polite during the interview. Seemed unwilling to give his views on current affairs.

Other information *Smart appearance. Is editor of the university newspaper. Also active in the Drama Society – recently gave talk on Asian Theatre and Rituals. Recommendation from tutor: 'James is a team player rather than a leader. He has exceptional research skills.' Very interested in underwater cultural heritage and social media. His hobby is snorkelling. Goes to Turkey every summer to do some snorkelling.*

USEFUL PHRASES

Talking about strengths and weaknesses

One of his/her strongest points is …
His/Her best quality is …
What impresses me about him/her is …
His/Her biggest asset is …
One of his/her major weaknesses is …
I think he/she lacks …
I'm worried/concerned about his/her age/experience/qualifications …
What concerns me about the candidate is …

STUDY SKILLS
SELF-AWARENESS

1a What is self-awareness? How can it influence your ability to learn something new?

1b Think of something you have tried to learn recently. Work with a partner and discuss the questions.

1 How did you learn the new skill?
2 Were you successful? Why?/Why not?
3 What did you learn about yourself?

1c Work in small groups and share your experiences. What were the most common reasons for the success or failure of your learning? Your motivation or lack of it? Ease or difficulty of the task? Good/Bad teaching? Another reason?

2 Motivation Discuss the questions in your groups.

1 What is your main motivation for improving your English?
2 What else is motivating you to improve your English language proficiency?
3 Why are you more likely to succeed if you are highly motivated?

3a **1.5** Two students are being interviewed by a linguist who is researching the motivation of learners of English. Read the descriptions of two types of motivation. Then listen to the students, Anna and Hayato, and decide which type of motivation they have.

> **Instrumental motivation:** The person is learning the language to achieve a definite goal, e.g. to get a better job, to be promoted, to pass an external examination.
>
> **Integrative motivation:** The person is learning the language to communicate with people from another culture that speak the language. The person wants to identify with the target language group and fit in with it.

3b Which student, Anna or Hayato, expresses the following ideas? Listen again and check.

He/She …

1 needs to communicate better in English for work reasons. H
2 is a flexible person when travelling. A
3 will make more money by improving his/her English. H
4 wants to learn more about the literature of the country. A
5 does not want to learn a lot about English culture. H
6 learnt about English culture at an early age. A
7 wants to achieve native speaker proficiency. A
8 is learning English in a company environment. H

4 Learning style It is important to be aware of your learning style as this will indicate not only your strengths, but also areas you need to develop. Read about four approaches to learning on page 159. Then work in groups and discuss the questions.

1 Which style do you think best describes your personality?
2 Are you a mix of the styles? If so, in what way?
3 Is one learning style predominant in your group? Talk to your group about their learning styles. Do you think your teachers need to know about this? Why?/Why not?

5a Note down the qualities and skills you have which would impress a potential employer. Then work in groups and compare your lists.

5b In your groups, discuss what you should or should not do to improve your English. Think about your personality or character, your motivation and your learning styles.

WRITING SKILLS
A COVERING LETTER

6 When to use a covering letter Complete the text with the words in the box. Three of the words are not used.

convincing	essentially	impact	inspiration
motivate	speculative	targeted	vacancy	vital

> A covering letter should always be included when you send out a CV or an application form. It should create interest and [1]_____ the employer to get to know more about you. There are two types of covering letter. In a(n) [2]_____ covering letter, the writer is responding to a specific advertised [3]_____. However, in a(n) [4]_____ covering letter, the writer aims at a specific employer or a number of companies or organisations he/she is interested in joining. A covering letter is [5]_____ if your application is speculative because the employer will only read it and look at your CV if your letter is really [6]_____.

7 How to structure a covering letter Put the information in the order (1–5) it would normally appear in a covering letter.

a Highlight your strong points, your understanding of the work and why you are suited to it.

b End the letter with an appropriate sentence.

c Indicate your availability for interview.

d Explain why you are interested in the job.

e State what the vacancy is and how you heard about it. If the covering letter is speculative, say what kind of work you are interested in.

8 [1.6] **What to do in a covering letter** Listen to a talk by Naomi Lloyd, a communications consultant, and make notes on what she says about the following.

- introduction
- length of the letter
- ending the letter
- strengths
- applying for different jobs

9 Look at Audio script 1.6 on page 166 and check your answers.

10a Vadim Kufenko is also applying for the position of Research Assistant with *Euronews Magazine*. The magazine provides readers with information on trends in international banking, foreign exchange investment and capital markets. Read the covering letter Vadim includes with his CV. Do you think he has followed the rules of writing a covering letter? Work with a partner and discuss your ideas.

Dear Ms Sommer,

Re: Research Assistant

(1) I am writing to apply for the above position advertised in the graduate section of *The Chronicle*, dated 5 June. I enclose my Curriculum Vitae for your consideration.

(2) Having read your company literature, I am very interested in joining your organisation. I am convinced that the position of Research Assistant would be well suited to my qualifications and experience. It would also provide me with an interesting challenge.

(3) My role as Financial Analyst in the Bank of Foreign Trade in St Petersburg has given me invaluable experience of working in teams on research projects. It has also enabled me to develop key skills such as analysing financial statements, undertaking marketing surveys and writing concise reports, which are all relevant to this position. Of course, I am used to working to tight deadlines.

(4) During my holidays, I have travelled widely in Europe and have gained useful cross-cultural skills. As a result, I feel I would be able to fit comfortably into the multinational teams which I know are an important feature of your organisation.

(5) If I am fortunate enough to be selected for the position, you will be employing an enthusiastic, highly motivated and loyal member of staff, who will be an asset to your organisation. I am available for interview at any time and look forward to hearing from you.

Yours sincerely,

Vadim Kufenko

10b Read the letter again. Each paragraph contains a *topic sentence* and one or more supporting ideas. With your partner, study the example, then analyse paragraphs 3 and 4 in the same way.

A *topic sentence* contains the main idea upon which a paragraph is developed. It often appears at the beginning of a paragraph, introducing the main idea.

Example: paragraph 2

Topic sentence: *Having read your company literature, I am very interested in joining your organisation.*

Supporting ideas: (the reasons why Vadim thinks he would be an asset to the company): He thinks the job suits his qualifications and experience and offers a suitable challenge.

---

11 Certain phrases are common in covering letters. Find words and phrases in the letter with these meanings.

1 which I hope you will study carefully (paragraph 1)
2 descriptions of your organisation's activities (paragraph 2)
3 something that needs skill and energy to achieve (paragraph 2)
4 extremely useful (paragraph 3)
5 short and clear (paragraph 3)
6 getting work done very quickly and on time (paragraph 3)
7 have obtained (paragraph 4)
8 someone of value (paragraph 5)

12 You have already written a CV. Now write an impressive covering letter for the job below, so that you will be invited for an interview.

Volunteers wanted

We are looking for volunteers with a wide range of skills and experience to participate in projects (such as building a school) in more than thirty of the world's poorest countries.

You *can* make a difference.

Send your CV to:

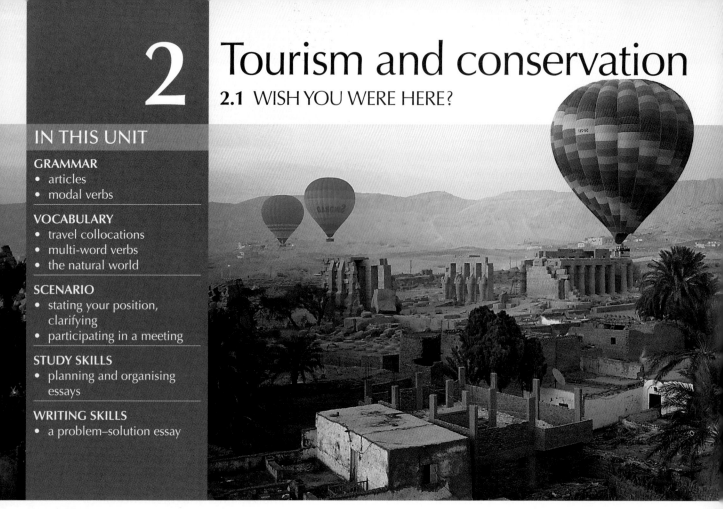

2 Tourism and conservation

2.1 WISH YOU WERE HERE?

IN THIS UNIT

GRAMMAR
- articles
- modal verbs

VOCABULARY
- travel collocations
- multi-word verbs
- the natural world

SCENARIO
- stating your position, clarifying
- participating in a meeting

STUDY SKILLS
- planning and organising essays

WRITING SKILLS
- a problem–solution essay

Travel makes a wise man better, but a fool worse. Thomas Fuller (1654–1734), English physician and writer

SPEAKING

1 Work with a partner and discuss how important the following are for tourists. Put them in order of importance (1–8).
- weather
- cost
- food
- ease of travel
- accommodation
- sights
- activities
- environmental considerations

2 What are popular holiday destinations for people from your country? How have these changed in the last ten years?

VOCABULARY
TRAVEL COLLOCATIONS

3a Match 1–8 with a–h to make collocations. Then check your answers in the holiday brochure extracts opposite.

1	budget	a	deal
2	boutique	b	delicacy
3	carbon	c	monuments
4	last-minute	d	footprint
5	local	e	airline
6	ancient	f	temperatures
7	organised	g	hotel
8	baking	h	excursions

3b Match the collocations in Exercise 3a with the categories in Exercise 1.

3c What other collocations can you add to each category?

accommodation: luxury hotel

READING

4a Read the holiday brochure extracts A–F and match them with the holiday types in the box. You do not need all of the words in the box.

adventure holiday   backpacking   city break
cruise   resort holiday   safari   self-catering holiday
sightseeing tour   working holiday

4b What other holiday types can you think of?

5a Which of the holidays in the extracts would be suitable for the following people? Work with a partner and discuss your ideas.

1. an adventurous ecology graduate travelling alone
2. a sporty group of friends in their twenties looking for fun and excitement
3. a young urban professional couple who want plenty to do
4. a cultured holidaymaker interested in the environment
5. a wealthy couple looking for a relaxing holiday
6. four student friends with a limited budget who want to escape after the exams

5b Which holiday would you choose? Why?

A Spend seven nights exploring the Caribbean aboard a state-of-the-art vessel: *The Palladium.* Offering the ultimate on-board experience and boasting eleven decks, it still retains a unique and intimate atmosphere. Select a stateroom with a balcony for awe-inspiring ocean views or share a cabin for four. With five restaurants to choose from, each meal is a gastronomic delight. In the evenings, choose from a comprehensive range of entertainment options: from cabaret to DJs and live bands. Pamper yourself with a wide variety of treatments available in the Palm Court Spa. Or why not try indoor rock-climbing? Fully escorted organised excursions are available at each port of call. This is an experience not to be missed. Call now on …

Last-minute deals

B Romantic specials. Weekends for two in Paris.
Explore the famous sights of the city of love – the Eiffel Tower, the Louvre, Montmartre – and then sample the culinary skills of renowned Parisian chefs. Stylish boutique hotel in the heart of this chic, bustling capital. Unbeatable prices. For more info, go to **Earlybird.biz.**

C Feeling restless? Itchy feet? Active budget holidays in New Zealand. The holiday includes a week of escorted trekking with breathtaking views, the opportunity to bungee jump and try paragliding. Experience a variety of exotic landscapes with a visit to a volcano, glacier hiking and whitewater rafting. Local specialities and hospitality as you've never experienced before. All flights and internal transfers included. Book now at **DownUnder.net.**

D Thai Odyssey. Fully guided holidays to explore the spectacular ancient monuments of a country rich in history.
Enjoy magnificent scenery, baking temperatures and indulge in mouth-watering local delicacies. Our 'green' under-canvas 'hotels' encourage visitors to calculate carbon emissions and will arrange for guests to plant trees if they want to offset their carbon footprint. Holidays for the discerning and sophisticated traveller with an interest in sustainable development. An experience to savour. Flights not included. Single supplements apply. For further details, visit **Exped.biz.**

E Explore the picturesque Greek island of Kefalonia.
Help out restoring isolated cottages or work on an archaeological dig. Explore the island on foot. Experience the outstanding views and secluded beaches and unwind in this off-the-beaten-track location, far from the stresses and strains of the rat race. Steer clear of the tourist traps, recharge your batteries and return completely refreshed. Ideal for groups. All-inclusive budget deal. Special offer price includes flight (budget airline) and basic s/c accommodation (upgrades available). Optional Jeep hire. **Athena Travel.**

F The holiday of a lifetime in the Badumbas National Park. See the big game and get back to nature and make new friends. Staying at the exclusive Masai Game Lodge with three-star facilities, you will also spend time under canvas out in the bush. Stunning flora and fauna. A visual feast of wildlife, all experienced at close quarters, including lions, elephants and rhinos. All travel is in air-conditioned off-road vehicles. New company. Special introductory offer. Unbeatable fifty percent discount. No single supplements apply. For more info, go to **ZebraTourZ.**

6a Analysing a genre Find examples in the extracts of typical language for travel brochures. Write them under these headings.

Positive adjectives (and collocations): *comprehensive range*
Imperatives: *Call now*
Other expressions: *… why not try … ?*

6b Write a one-paragraph brochure entry about your local area or the area you are studying in.

VOCABULARY
MULTI-WORD VERBS

7a Some tourists are talking about what they like to do on holiday. Complete the sentences with the words in the box.

around	away	back	down	in
of	off (x2)	up (x2)		

1 'A holiday is all about getting _____ from it all.'
2 'I just want time away from work when I feel I can really let my hair _____.'
3 'I just love going somewhere new and soaking _____ the atmosphere.'
4 'We live in a big city, although I grew up in the country, so getting _____ to nature is important.'
5 'I love to really live it _____ on holiday. I like to blow what money I have in a short time. I save all year and then have a really good time.'
6 'We're keen on finding unusual places – going _____ the beaten track.'
7 'Steering clear _____ the tourist traps is our main priority when booking a holiday.'
8 'I don't really like to do very much on holiday. Just lounging _____ by the pool is enough.'
9 'The main thing is to avoid getting ripped _____, so I try not to look like a tourist.'
10 'I love seeing new things and taking _____ the sights.'

7b **2.1** Listen and check your answers. Then practise saying the sentences with the correct stress.

7c Which of the opinions in Exercise 7a are most like your own?

SPEAKING

8 What do you know about the specialised types of tourism below? How do you feel about them? Work in small groups and discuss your ideas.

- battlefield
- culinary
- eco
- disaster
- celebrity
- health/medical (including 'surgery safaris')
- volunteer
- space

READING

1a Work in groups and brainstorm everything you know about the Galapagos Islands.

1b Read the text quickly and check your ideas in Exercise 1a.

2a Work with a partner. Student A, read the first two paragraphs of the text and write three quiz questions. Student B, read the last two paragraphs and write three quiz questions.

2b With your partner, ask and answer each other's questions from Exercise 2a.

3a Read the text again. Write a heading for each paragraph.

3b Where would you expect to find this text? Why?
- online news website
- travel company website
- online encyclopedia

3c Which fact or facts in the text did you find most interesting? Why?

4 What do the highlighted words in the text refer to?

The Galapagos Islands

Located about 926 km off the coast of Ecuador in the Pacific Ocean and just a short flight from Quito, the capital, the Galapagos Islands are a small chain of islands spread out over 220 km and known for their vast number of endemic species. There are eighteen major islands in the chain, five of which are inhabited, and more than 100 smaller islands covering a total land area of about 8,000 km^2. The largest island is Isabela, which makes up three-quarters of the total land area and rises to a height of 1,707 m. The islands are surrounded by the Galapagos Marine Reserve, stretching over 137,269 km^2.

The Galapagos archipelago is distributed on either side of the equator and sits on a tectonic plate which is moving towards the South American continent at a rate of over 6 cm a year. The first islands were formed by volcanoes that rose out of the ocean at least 8,000,000 years ago. Lava built up underwater, forming undersea mountains which broke through the water and formed islands. While the oldest islands have now sunk back beneath the sea, new ones are still being formed by volcanic eruptions, the most recent of which was in 2009.

The islands, discovered in 1535, are among the most scientifically important and biologically outstanding places on the planet. According to zoologists and botanists, they are home to some of the most beautiful sights in nature. Almost all the reptiles and half the species are not found anywhere else. Marine iguanas, flightless cormorants, mocking birds and thirteen species of finches are all endemic to the islands, which are also famous for their giant tortoises, blue-footed boobies and the only living tropical penguins.

There are a number of environmental threats, the main one being the plants and animals, such as feral goats, cats and cattle, brought to the islands by humans. An eradication plan only partially succeeded in ridding the islands of introduced species. The island's biodiversity is also under threat from the human population, which is growing at an unsustainable rate. In the 1950s, the population was 1,000, whereas it is now over 26,000. Furthermore, the Galapagos Marine Reserve and whole ecosystem is under threat from illegal fishing activities, while the growth of tourism also threatens the wildlife of the archipelago.

VOCABULARY
THE NATURAL WORLD

5 Find words or phrases in the text with these meanings.

1 native or restricted to a certain place
2 an area for animals and birds where they are protected
3 a chain of islands
4 a huge slab of rock that makes up the top layer of the Earth
5 molten rock that flows from volcanoes
6 escaped from domestication and become wild
7 a variety of different life forms living in the area
8 all the animals and plants that live in a particular area

LISTENING

6a **2.2** Listen to the first part of an interview with Dr Graham Watkins, the Executive Director of a conservation charity and an expert on the Galapagos Islands. Are the statements about him true or false? Correct the false statements.

1 His father was a conservationist. *F agricultural scientist*
2 Dr Watkins studied Biology at Oxford University. *F Zoology*
3 He worked as a guide in the Galapagos Islands. *T 18 months*
4 He studied Zoology and Evolution at the University of Pennsylvania. *F 6 years*
5 His first job after leaving the University of Pennsylvania was in the field of conservation biology. *T evaporated into charge*

6b **2.3** Listen to the second part of the interview and answer the questions.

1 Does Dr Watkins think tourism is a bad thing? Why?/Why not?
2 Give examples of negative consequences of tourism that are
   a direct.   **b** hidden.
3 What are invasive species?

7a Predicting In the third part of the interview, Dr Watkins is asked whether we should stay away from conservation areas. Predict what he will say.

7b **2.4** Listen and check your predictions. Then answer the questions.

1 How can the impact of tourism be minimised?
2 What are the best forms of tourism?
3 What is sustainable development?
4 How do you feel about Dr Watkins' final statement?

GRAMMAR
ARTICLES

8a Match the uses of articles a–k with the underlined examples in the text on page 18.

1 **Definite article**
a common knowledge – we know/can tell from the context what is being referred to
b repetition – this is not the first mention of the person or thing
c uniqueness – the only one of its kind in the world or in this context
d with a superlative phrase
e with names of countries, federations or groups of islands which are plural
f with names of rivers, oceans and seas

2 **Zero article**
g with uncountable nouns, when speaking about the noun in general
h with the names of most cities, streets, countries and continents
i with plural countable nouns, when speaking about the noun in general
j with most numbers (except *a half*, *a hundred*, *a thousand*)

3 **Indefinite article**
k with a singular countable noun mentioned for the first time

8b Match the correct article (*a/an*, *the* or zero) with the uses 1–3.

1 to introduce what is new or something the reader is unaware of
2 to indicate 'common ground' (e.g. to refer forwards, backwards or to our shared experience or general knowledge)
3 to make generalisations (with plural and uncountable nouns)

8c *Off the coast* and *a number of* are fixed expressions, where the article is always the same. Complete the fixed expressions below with *a* or *the*.

1 _____ bit of   3 off _____ record
2 in _____ hurry   4 make _____ start

➡ Language reference and extra practice, pages 128–129

8d Complete the extracts from the listening, adding articles where appropriate.

1 I became conservationist in part because of my family background. My father was agricultural scientist and travelled throughout world. One of my brothers was born in Africa. I was born in British Guiana.

2 I went to University of Oxford to study Zoology. I finished my first degree there. After that, I was lucky enough to become guide in Galapagos Islands. I did that for about eighteen months and as a result of that experience, which was really quite life-changing experience, I went to University of Pennsylvania to study Ecology and Evolution.

3 I think first thing to say about tourism is that in many situations it's very positive thing. It can help conservation quite substantially, but there are also many examples in world, for example in Caribbean, where tourism also causes problems and has direct impact on environment. Many of reefs in Caribbean have serious problems as result of pollution.

SPEAKING

9 Work in groups. Choose one of the following that you would like to protect in your country. Discuss the threats facing it and how you would protect it.

1 a natural feature
2 a historical building
3 an endangered species

READING

1 Work in groups and discuss the advantages and disadvantages of going to:

1   an isolated, unspoilt beach with no amenities.
2   a resort beach with sun loungers, waiter service and full water sports facilities.

2 Read the article quickly and choose the best title.

A   THE BEACH THAT TURNED BACK THE COMMERCIAL TIDE

B   MEXICAN COMMUNITY STOPS DEVELOPERS

3 Complete the introduction to the article with a possible ending.

> Robert L. White reports on how a determined group of locals in Mexico …

4 Read the article again and match the paragraphs A–G with the topics 1–4. A topic can go with more than one paragraph. One paragraph has no match.

1   resorts for the wealthy
2   the campaign to save the beach
3   an unspoilt beach
4   the fate of other beaches

5 Compare paragraphs A and B of the article. What do you notice about the writer's language?

6 Find two-word phrases in the article with these meanings.

1   a series of actions by ordinary people intended to achieve a result
2   an official organisation that has power to make decisions for a particular area
3   a long, hard fight
4   problems concerning the people and things around you
5   facts relating to human society that you think about
6   a group of companies working together

7 Answer the questions.

1   Do you agree that the destruction of many of the world's idyllic places is inevitable? Why?/Why not?
2   In which ways do you think this story is an example of a significant or general change in attitude towards tourism development?

8 Evaluating advantages and disadvantages Work with a partner and do the tasks.

1   List the advantages and disadvantages of developing Balandra, as described in the article.
2   Add your own ideas about the advantages and disadvantages of this type of development, from the viewpoint of different interest groups.
3   Evaluate the advantages and disadvantages. Was the right decision made?

A Picture a perfect beach. From an expanse of flawless white sand, implausibly turquoise water shelves out over a stoneless seabed to a clear horizon. Overhead, pelicans wheel lazily in search of fish. One suddenly folds its wings, like a prehistoric umbrella, and hurtles downward. The splashdown is the first sound you can remember hearing for several minutes.

B Now imagine a whacking great hotel plonked on all this; plus a golf course and a few jet skis, of course, just to keep the decibel levels up. This is the fate that has befallen so many of the world's idyllic places that there seems something almost inevitable about it. Thanks to a determined and organised grassroots campaign, however, it won't be happening on this particular Mexican strand.

C Balandra beach, outside the city of La Paz, state capital of Baja California Sur, has been spared from future development after residents, civil society groups and environmentalists organised themselves into a collective, amassing a petition of 18,440 signatures calling on the regional authorities to protect the area. On 25 March, after a protracted struggle by the Colectivo Balandra, state officials finally designated a total of 2,131 hectares of land and sea a natural protected area, in a move that could signal a shift in Mexico's approach to tourism and conservation.

D Environmental issues were, naturally, one of the main planks of the collective's campaign. As the group warned on its website, 'The landscapes of the rest of the beaches of La Paz have already been modified with various types of constructions and installations; Balandra is the only one that remains to us.'

E But there were social considerations at stake here, too, because Balandra is essentially a beach for the people of La Paz, where tourism is of the unobtrusive variety. In stark contrast to the super-rich celebrity playground of Cabo San Lucas, just down the road, this is not a place that exists to service the appetites of deck shoe-wearing management consultants from LA.

F The threat came, specifically, from a business consortium headed by the son of a former state governor of Veracruz, whose family own land in the area. Miguel Alemán Magnani's hotel-and-golf vision involved international capital, according to the Mexican newspaper *El Universal*, and the group had been trying since at least 2005 to get the go-ahead for the project.

G Development of Balandra would surely have brought jobs: margaritas would have been served, tour parties guided and pets pampered. But the people of La Paz have looked into that particular future and dared to choose another path. They have shown that it is possible to take on the inevitable – and win.

GRAMMAR
MODAL VERBS

9 Read a leaflet encouraging people to sign a petition to save a beach and underline the modal verbs. Then match the modal verbs with these functions. A modal verb can go with more than one function.

1   lack of obligation   *We don't have to let them win.*
2   obligation not to do something   6   future possibility
3   advice   7   obligation
4   refusal   8   deduction
5   ability

➡ Language reference and extra practice, pages 128–129

SAVE OUR BEACH!
You might have seen reports that developers are planning to destroy our beach.

We mustn't let them do that. We don't have to let them win. It might mean fewer tourists in the short term, but we believe it is worth fighting for. With your help, we can win this campaign and we may be able to change the government's attitude to the environment.

You should sign the petition on the back now. Your signature could help us make a difference. You have to be eighteen to sign this petition. We won't stop until the developers stop!

10 Complete the sentences with modal verbs.

1   The developers _____ do that. I'm absolutely sure it's against the regulations.
2   That _____ be the Mayor. He's in Balandra.
3   I _____ go to La Paz this afternoon. I have a meeting there at 4.30 p.m.
4   We _____ leave for La Paz yet. We've got lots of time.
5   The developers _____ asked for a meeting with the citizens of La Paz first.
6   We _____ speak to the reporters until we are absolutely clear what our message is.
7   I can't meet you tomorrow. I _____ work on the environmental campaign.
8   Sorry, but I _____ come to the residents' meeting. I'm too busy then.

SPEAKING AND WRITING

11a Work in groups. You are responsible for looking after a local beach. Talk about the rules that users of the beach will have to follow.

11b Write a notice with your list of rules to be placed at the entrance to the beach.

▶ MEET THE EXPERT
Watch an interview with Noirin Hegarty from Lonely Planet, about the work of a travel publisher.
Turn to page 150 for video activities.

SITUATION

Granville Island is a fairly large island in the Caribbean with a population of 780,000. Its main sources of income are fruit, fish and tourism. Five years ago a hurricane devastated the capital city and nearby towns, as well as the fruit plantations. As a result, the unemployment rate on the island has risen to 20 percent. Now foreign property companies are coming to Granville Island to develop its economy and rebuild its tourist facilities. This has led local environmental groups to accuse the authorities of sacrificing Granville's natural habitats in order to develop a seaside resort.

Ricardo Hernandez

Born in Cuba, Hernandez entered the United States as a political refugee. He made a fortune in real estate in New York refurbishing old apartment buildings, then moved to Florida, where he made another fortune constructing hotels. A billionaire, now of American nationality, he is thought to be in the top five of America's richest men.

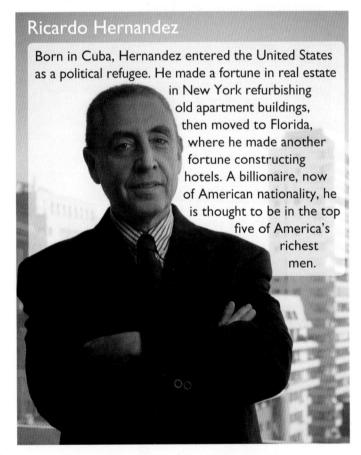

1 Read the situation and the information about Ricardo Hernandez above and answer the questions.

1 How might the authorities be sacrificing Granville's natural habitats?
2 What is special about Ricardo Hernandez?

2a ▐2.5▐ Listen to an excerpt from the local radio news and make notes under these headings.
- Reason for buying the Roberts Estate
- Planned facilities
- Possible problems

2b Work in groups and discuss the possible advantages and disadvantages of Hernandez's project.

KEY LANGUAGE
STATING YOUR POSITION, CLARIFYING

3a ▐2.6▐ Listen to a conversation between Ricardo Hernandez and Louisa Bradshaw, the Mayor of the community where Hernandez would like to develop a golf course. Answer the questions.

1 What is Hernandez's position concerning the length of the golf course?
2 What supporting arguments does he use to persuade the Mayor to accept his point of view?
3 What will Hernandez do if his project is not accepted?

3b Listen again and complete the sentences from the recording.

1 I'd like to make _____ about this.
2 The size of the course _____, I'm afraid.
3 It _____ to shorten its length. It's my dream to build the _____ golf course in the world here on this island.
4 But I _____ if I have to build a shorter course.
5 You see, _____ a full-length, eighteen-hole course if you want to attract the top golfers in the world to play here.
6 I hope you _____.
7 Exactly. A full-length course _____.
8 I couldn't go ahead _____ on that.

3c Work with a partner and practise saying the sentences in Exercise 3b.

4 Look at Audio script 2.6 on page 167. Find examples of seeking and giving clarification.
Scale down? What do you mean exactly?

5 Paraphrase each of the examples you found in Exercise 4.
Could you clarify what you mean by 'scale down'?

TASK
PARTICIPATING IN A MEETING

> The Mayor decides to hold an informal meeting to allow Ricardo Hernandez to talk about his project and for other group representatives to express their opinion and ask questions.
>
> After the meeting, the Mayor will decide whether to recommend the project to the local council.

6 Work in groups of five. You are going to attend the informal meeting. Read your role cards and prepare for the meeting. You can add your own ideas.

Student A: Mayor: look at page 155.
Student B: Ricardo Hernandez: look at page 156.
Student C: Head of the Wildlife Society: look at page 157.
Student D: Journalist: look at page 158.
Student E: Chamber of Commerce representative: look at page 158.

7a Hold the meeting. Ask your questions and give your opinions. Try to persuade the other people at the meeting to accept your ideas.

7b The Mayor announces whether he/she will recommend that the local council supports the project.

USEFUL PHRASES

Supporting the project

There's no doubt it'll bring great benefits to our community.
The resort is clearly in everyone's interests.
The project will revitalise the area.

Rejecting the project

The project simply isn't feasible.
It's not the right thing for this area.
You haven't thought it through.

Asking polite questions

Could I (just) ask you, what else will you do for our community?
I'd like to ask you a question. How does this project help young people?

Checking understanding

So what you're saying is …
Do you mean … ?
If I understand you correctly, you're saying …

Showing you don't understand

Sorry, I'm not (quite) sure what you mean.
Could you explain that point again, please?

Expressing reservations

I'm not sure this is the right project for this area.
I think this needs further thought.
Let's think about the implications.
There could be several harmful effects. For example, …

Challenging the argument

I think there's a flaw in this argument.
I'm not totally convinced by what you say.
It sounds like a good idea, but …

STUDY SKILLS
PLANNING AND ORGANISING ESSAYS

1a There are some fundamental steps involved in writing essays. Put these steps in the correct order (1–10).

a Establish your argument or point of view.

b Analyse the question and define key terms.

c Brainstorm ideas.

d Complete and check your references and bibliography.

e Research and take notes on the topic, using books, journals, the internet and other credible academic sources.

f Write your plan and organise your ideas.

g Write a first draft to include your introduction, main body and conclusion.

h Prepare the final draft.

i Redraft and edit your essay.

j Have a friend or colleague read your final draft.

1b Work with a partner and compare your answers to Exercise 1a.

2 Analysing the question To answer an essay question effectively, it is essential to understand the verb which gives the key instruction. Look at these essay questions. Work with a partner and discuss the meaning of the verbs in bold.

1 **Discuss** the advantages and disadvantages of ecotourism.

   'Discuss' means you are being asked to write about the advantages and disadvantages of ecotourism in detail, considering different ideas and opinions.

2 **Define** the term 'ecotourism', giving examples.

3 **Account for** the decrease in the whale population during the last twenty years.

4 Critically **evaluate** the role of tourism in protecting the environment.

5 **Outline** the steps taken by your local community to recycle waste.

6 **Analyse** the threats to the world's coral reefs.

7 **Assess** the effects of illegal logging on wildlife in Mexico.

8 **Compare** the measures taken by Kenya and Uganda to protect wildlife.

3a **2.7** **Brainstorming is an effective activity for generating new ideas about an essay topic. Listen to a university lecturer giving advice to a student, Erika, about three approaches to brainstorming. Make notes under these headings.**

- Free association
- Visual thinking
- Question and answer

3b Work with a partner and compare your notes. Which approach do you prefer?

WRITING SKILLS
A PROBLEM–SOLUTION ESSAY

4a Study this pattern of organisation, which is often found in academic texts that present problems and explore what can be done about them.

1 Situation

2 Problem(s)

3 Solution(s)

4 Evaluation (assessing the solution and implications)

4b Read the problem–solution essay opposite. Match the paragraphs (A–F) with topics 1–4 in Exercise 4a. Some paragraphs may go with more than one topic.

5 Underline linking words or phrases in the essay which:

1 add something.   4 show cause and effect.

2 give an example.   5 indicate a good result.

3 make a contrast.

6 Work in groups. Read the essay question and brainstorm ideas for the topic.

The elephant is an endangered species. Discuss what action can be taken to protect elephants and save them from extinction.

7a In your groups, match the information from your brainstorming with topics 1–4 in Exercise 4a.

7b What is the best way to deal with the problem in the essay question? What are the implications of the solutions you propose?

8 **2.8** **Listen to a wildlife expert describing the situation of the elephant population of Africa and make notes on the main points.**

9a Write the first paragraph of the essay. Use a maximum of 70 words.

9b Work with a partner. Read each other's paragraph and comment on its content and language.

10 Write a problem–solution essay on one of these topics. Use the structure in Exercise 4a.

1 an animal which is under threat of extinction, e.g. the elephant, rhinoceros, cheetah, gorilla, tiger or whale

2 an environmental problem, e.g. the harmful effects of tourism

Discuss the reasons why the Antarctic is under threat and suggest how its environment can be protected.

A   The natural wilderness of the Antarctic is under threat because of the increasing number of tourists who are visiting the area. As many as 30,000 are expected to come to Antarctica this year to observe penguins, seals and seabirds.

B   Scientists worry that this curiosity to see the Antarctic area before the ice melts away will only hasten its deterioration. They believe that the growth in tourism could increase the risk to the marine environment and land ecosystems.

C   A major concern is that cruise ships are increasingly visiting the area and if there was an accident, they could cause major pollution. For instance, a Norwegian cruise ship recently ran aground on Antarctica's Deception Island, spilling diesel fuel.

D   Fortunately, the Norwegian ship was ice-strengthened and it only spilled a small amount of fuel, which quickly dispersed in water. On the other hand, some bigger cruise ships do not have super-strengthened hulls and use heavy fuel oil. This would be very difficult to clean up in the event of a serious accident and thousands of penguins and other marine life could become coated in oil.

E   As a result of the Norwegian accident, there have been several proposals for dealing with the problem. One idea is that there should be a ban on ships which have not been specially strengthened to deal with sea ice. Another suggestion is that there should be a buddy system for large ships so that if one gets into trouble, there would always be another vessel nearby, which it could call for help. A more radical suggestion is that only small research vessels should be allowed into the Antarctic area.

F   Whatever the solutions, any action would be difficult to implement because, unlike in the Arctic region, there are no state or international laws governing tourism practices in the Antarctic. Moreover, the owners of the cruise ships do not seem to be able to agree on what sort of checks and controls are needed in the region.

3 International relations

3.1 NATIONAL TRAITS

IN THIS UNIT

GRAMMAR
- subordinate clauses
- modal perfect

VOCABULARY
- dependent prepositions
- adjectives of character
- international organisations
- international relations

SCENARIO
- stating objectives, giving strong advice
- devising an action plan

STUDY SKILLS
- active listening

WRITING SKILLS
- a speech

Nations are always making mistakes because they do not understand each other's psychology.
Edward Grey (1862–1933), British Liberal statesman

SPEAKING AND READING

1 Work in groups and discuss the questions.

1 What views do you think people from other countries have about people from your country?
2 How do you think people from your country see themselves? What is important to them?
3 Do you think it is possible to talk about 'national characteristics'?
4 Are people more defined by their nationality, their local community or their family? Give reasons for your answer.

2a Read these statements, sometimes made about British people. Which do you think are true and which are false?

The British are …
1 serious.
2 reluctant to express their feelings.
3 extravagant shoppers.
4 calm, patient drivers.
5 home lovers.
6 open and direct communicators.
7 interested in social status.
8 excessively polite.

2b Work with a partner and compare your ideas. Then read the article opposite and check your answers.

3 Which character traits of the British surprised you most? Why?

4 Which of the character traits listed are the same for your culture/nationality?

5 Complete the phrases with prepositions. Then find the phrases in the article and check your answers.

1 have a passion _____
2 have a love _____
3 have an obsession _____
4 have a fascination _____
5 have a reluctance _____
6 have the ability _____
7 be proud _____
8 be great _____

6a Write sentences about your own culture or people's views of your own culture. Use the phrases in Exercise 5.

A lot of people think we have an obsession with food, but in fact, we have an obsession with …

A lot of people think we have an obsession with food, and it's true.

6b Work with a partner and compare your sentences.

VOCABULARY
ADJECTIVES OF CHARACTER

7 Match the adjectives in the box with their meanings.

aloof   charismatic   cultured   devious
dogmatic   emotional   hospitable
meticulous   pragmatic   self-effacing

1 unable to keep your feelings under control
2 rarely boasting about yourself and playing down
   your achievements
3 knowledgeable about art, music and literature
4 approaching problems in a rational, practical way
5 always certain your beliefs are right
6 having a magnetic personality
7 distant and unfriendly
8 attentive to detail
9 using clever tricks and manipulation to get what
   you want
10 welcoming and generous to visitors

8a Are the adjectives in Exercise 7 positive, negative or neutral?

8b To what extent could any of the qualities be applied to your own culture?

SPEAKING

9a Reflecting on your culture Work in groups and discuss the following in relation to your own culture. How do people feel about them? How important are they?

1 greetings
2 silence
3 small talk
4 punctuality
5 personal space
6 gestures
7 etiquette and manners

9b What differences have you found when meeting people from other cultures?

Traits of the nation

Top Traits

Our top national characteristic is talking about the weather, just ahead of a passion for queuing, but other qualities in the top ten are not so endearing; sarcasm, a love of television soaps and curtain twitching were all identified as central to the British identity.

Obsession with class was also high on the list, along with more modern ills such as road rage.

Working long hours, fascination with property prices and the love of bargains also made it into the top fifty.

But it was not all bad news. Stiff upper lip came out high in the poll, with respondents also choosing a reluctance to complain, a good sense of humour and the ability to laugh at ourselves. The results were based on a study of 5,000 adults who were asked to pick out the things – good and bad – they believe make us unique as a nation.

A spokesman for global research company OnePoll.com, which conducted the survey, said that despite some of the negative traits identified, Britons were still extremely proud of their country.

'This is a brilliant list of characteristics and some of the observations are absolutely spot on,' he said. 'You can't go anywhere or do anything in Britain without someone talking about the weather and we're almost proud of the fact that we get more rain than anywhere else. What this poll demonstrates really well is how proud we are to be British – more than two-thirds of respondents said they felt honoured to be a part of this country.'

1 talking about the weather
2 great at queuing
3 sarcasm
4 watching soap operas
5 a love of bargains
6 a love of curtain twitching
7 stiff upper lip
8 moaning
9 obsession with class
10 inability to complain
11 working long hours
12 clever sense of humour
13 obsession with property values
14 road rage
15 being proud of where we live
16 not saying what we mean
17 the ability to laugh at ourselves
18 jealousy of wealth and success
19 being overly polite
20 an inability to express our emotions
21 love of rambling through the countryside
22 leaving things to the last minute
23 keeping our homes neat and tidy
24 achieving against all odds

SPEAKING

1 What examples of international collaboration can you think of? How successful were they? Think about emergencies and disasters, space programmes, scientific research, etc.

READING

2a Read the article opposite quickly. Work with a partner and discuss whether you agree with the title. Give reasons for your answer.

2b Read the article again. Are the sentences true, false or not given?

1   CERN was originally a Swiss/French laboratory. *Not given*
2   CERN has four main experiments. *T*
3   People often work long hours at CERN. *T*
4   Most people at CERN seem very happy with their family and social life. *T*
5   People have very specific jobs at CERN. *F*
6   CERN is organised with traditional structures. *F*

3a Word sets Find words in the article which are connected with:

1   passion.
2   speed.
3   working together.

3b Work with a partner and compare your answers.

4 Work in groups and discuss the questions.

1   Which information about CERN did you find most interesting? Why?
2   The work at CERN requires huge international investment. Do you think this money is well spent?

GRAMMAR
SUBORDINATE CLAUSES

5a Look at the title of the article and answer the questions.

(Part A) *After the Higgs hype,* (Part B) *CERN still has as much purpose and passion as ever.*

Which part (A or B):
1   does not make sense on its own? *A*
2   is a main clause? *B*
3   is a subordinate clause? *A*

5b Look at four more sentences from the article and identify the subordinate clause in each sentence.

1   As the tram trundles through the suburbs of Geneva, a huge lit-up globe lets me know I have arrived at CERN.
2   Under my feet are the colliders and detectors that are helping us understand what the universe is actually made of.
3   Scientists whose countries are in conflict work together.
4   Even someone like me, who is not really up to speed on quarks, strangeness, mass and gluons, can pick up this terrific buzz.

➡ Language reference and extra practice, pages 130–131

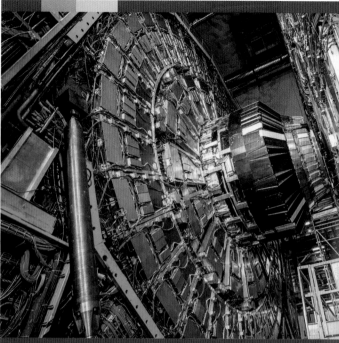

After the Higgs hype, CERN still has as much purpose and passion as ever

You don't need to be a scientist to appreciate the excitement and sense of discovery that pervades CERN, the world's great mecca of particle physics. But what's it like to live and work there?

As the tram trundles through the suburbs of Geneva, a huge lit-up globe lets me know I have arrived at CERN (the European Organisation for Nuclear Research). Most of it looks like a fairly undistinguished campus. 'The money has not been spent on the buildings,' I am repeatedly told. 'The money is all underground.' Underground, of course, are the tunnels where beams of light are smashed into each other. Under my feet are the colliders and detectors that are helping us understand what the universe is actually made of.

CERN, indeed physics itself, has entered popular consciousness in recent years. Geeks are pretty cool and theoretical physics has replaced philosophy as a signifier of intellectual prowess. I have been wondering about CERN since seeing hordes of people cheering when the announcements about the Higgs boson were made and a recalcitrant Peter Higgs getting the Nobel Prize.

CERN, founded in 1954, has twenty member states, with many other countries cooperating. The atmosphere is collegiate but blokey. The ratio of men to women is about 80:20. The problem seems to be getting women into apprenticeships. Once in, though, there appears to be less of an old boys' network than in many professions. 'As long as you drink coffee, you are in.'

Most people here have four or five languages. CERN employs 2,000 people, but another 10,000 pass through, working on the four main experiments (AMS, CMS, Atlas and LHC). To live here requires commitment – the surrounding villages either in France or Switzerland are expensive. But it soon becomes clear that people are here for the work and the line between work and leisure is permeable. They often work sixteen hours a day – because they want to.

When I ask most people what they have given up to be at CERN, they look bewildered. It seems a love of physics goes hand in hand with a love of skiing and snowboarding. They love the fact their children are in local schools and are bilingual.

Right across CERN there is movement between different roles: physicists become engineers. Everyone on an experiment will do overnight shifts in the control room. All this produces a less hierarchical way of working.

It is this flattening out of traditional structures that makes this place special, as well as the daily and huge international cooperation. Scientists whose countries are in conflict work together. The fact that the director is well paid, but not on a mega CEO/banker-type salary, helps this sense of common purpose.

I have never been anywhere where I felt such a sense of shared purpose. It is in the canteen at lunchtime, where folk whizz about with trays of food and seemingly no system, as if they were crazed particles themselves, so that one fears a collision. But there is none – just this sense of charged intensity. People talk passionately in every tongue about the problems they are solving. Everywhere one feels these minds working collectively and intently and even someone like me, who is not really up to speed on quarks, strangeness, mass and gluons, can pick up this terrific buzz.

6a Join the sentences. Use the words in brackets.

1   The scientists use video conferencing facilities. The scientists work together from their labs all over the world. (in order to)
2   The main CERN site has a large computer centre. The computer centre contains very powerful data-processing facilities. (which)
3   CERN is currently famous for the Large Hadron Collider. CERN also gained prestige through its connection with the beginnings of the World Wide Web. (although)
4   In March 2013, CERN made an announcement. They said, 'We confirm that we have discovered the Higgs boson particle'. (announced that)
5   The system was shut down on 19 September 2008. A magnet was found to be faulty. (when)
6   Peter Higgs' Nobel Prize in physics was controversial. Several other physicists were also responsible for developing the mechanism to predict a particle. (because)
7   You could make a personal visit to CERN. You will get a better understanding of its work culture and values. (if)

6b Match your sentences from Exercise 6a with these types of clauses.

a   clause or reason
b   conditional clause
c   clause of contrast
d   clause of purpose
e   clause of time
f   reported speech
g   relative clause

VOCABULARY AND SPEAKING

7a Work in groups and try to work out what these abbreviations for international organisations stand for.

1   IMF   2   IOC   3   UNESCO

7b **3.1** Listen and check your answers. Then look at Audio script 3.1 on page 168 and check again.

7c Work in groups and choose words from the box to write what the abbreviations for international organisations stand for. You can use some words more than once.

administration	aeronautics	Asian	association	Atlantic
aviation	civil	countries	European	exporting	health
international	national	nations	north	organisation
petroleum	south-east	space	trade	treaty	union	world

1   WHO   3   ASEAN   5   EU   7   ICAO
2   OPEC   4   NATO   6   WTO   8   NASA

8a What functions do the organisations in Exercise 7c perform?

8b Prioritising Which organisations are the most important? What are the reasons why you prioritised as you did? Work in groups and discuss your ideas.

WRITING

9 Write a short paragraph about one of the organisations in Exercise 7c. Include subordinate clauses.

▶ MEET THE EXPERT

Watch an interview with Brendan Paddy from the Disasters Emergency Committee, about international aid.
Turn to page 151 for video activities.

SPEAKING AND READING

1 What are the three most/least desirable characteristics in an ambassador? Choose from the words in the box.

aloof   analytical   articulate   assertive   charming
committed   corrupt   devious   dignified
diligent   energetic   good at solving problems
impulsive   indiscrete   observant   outgoing
passionate   provocative   respectful   sensitive
strong   stuffy   willing to learn

2 Read the extracts from interviews with ambassadors. Which of the characteristics from Exercise 1 are mentioned?

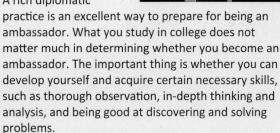

Ambassador Wang

A **Q:** _____

A: I'm a career diplomat. I had been engaged in diplomatic work for more than twenty years before becoming an ambassador. A rich diplomatic practice is an excellent way to prepare for being an ambassador. What you study in college does not matter much in determining whether you become an ambassador. The important thing is whether you can develop yourself and acquire certain necessary skills, such as thorough observation, in-depth thinking and analysis, and being good at discovering and solving problems.

B **Q:** _____

A: Being strong and healthy is very important as an ambassador. You must be able to endure the long meetings and conferences at the United Nations and be energetic all the time. It is a great honour to be an ambassador. I'm very proud to represent a country that is the birthplace of a 5,000-year-old civilisation, now home to one-fifth of the world's population and whose economy has been developing at a rapid pace over the past two decades, which is rarely seen in the world today.

C **Q:** _____

A: One's knowledge is always limited, no matter how intelligent one is. There are 193 member states in the United Nations. Each country has its own different history and culture. So it is hard to know each culture very well. But I think the important thing is to be modest and eager to learn when you get along with people from a different culture. When you respect others and treat them as equals, you will surely be respected and find it easy to make friends.

Ambassador Bristol

D **Q:** _____

A: All independent countries of the world seek to foster good relations with each other and for that reason they appoint citizens to represent the country's interests abroad. For the most part, all nations have the same interests – trade, national security, health, education and so on. But not all of them share the same point of view. This is where an ambassador is called upon to be a diplomat – to be sensitive in her handling of discussions and negotiations on matters which could be of vital interest to her country, while being careful to maintain good relations between her country and others.

E **Q:** _____

A: Being an ambassador is a job about relationships, so one of the most obvious qualities would be an outgoing personality – someone who is charming, articulate and can think quickly on her feet. Being willing to learn constantly is another very important quality. Representing a small nation brings its own degree of difficulty, so an ambassador for such a nation, like my own Grenada, has also to know how to balance sensitivity to the positions of others while being assertive of her own country's interests. Presenting yourself with dignity and poise – without being stuffy – is indispensable for creating the kind of impression that commands respectful attention. Need I add committed, passionate and diligent?

F **Q:** _____

A: There is very little not to enjoy about serving one's country and fellow citizens. The reward of assisting others on an individual basis, raising your country's profile within the community of nations or delivering an international agreement that boosts your national economy, gives an ambassador immeasurable satisfaction.

3 Read the extracts again. Match the questions (1–6) with the ambassadors' answers (A–F).

1   What steps did you take to become an ambassador?
2   What personal qualities do you need?
3   What is the job of an ambassador?
4   I would really be interested in knowing what it is like to be an ambassador. You must get very stressed out. Do you often get sick?
5   What did you most/least enjoy about being an ambassador?
6   How do you know what the proper etiquette is when dealing with different cultures?

4 What was most surprising about the ambassadors' answers?

VOCABULARY
INTERNATIONAL RELATIONS

5a Match words from box A with words from box B to make as many collocations about the world of diplomacy as possible.

A cultural diplomatic international overseas summit

B awareness conflict community crisis immunity incident meeting negotiations posting

5b Write your own sentences using some of the collocations in Exercise 5a.

LISTENING

6a [3.2] An ambassador's partner often accompanies his/her wife/husband on overseas postings. Listen to an excerpt from a radio interview in which an ambassador's wife talks about her life. How do you think the speaker feels about her role as the partner of an ambassador?

6b Listen again and make notes under these headings.
- Problems with overseas postings
- Regrets

6c Inferring attitude *Inferring* means 'reaching a conclusion based on reasoning and what you already know, rather than explicit statements'. Based on what you know about Elizabeth, what do you think she would like about a more regular life in one place? What would she miss about her current roaming lifestyle?

6d What would you enjoy/dislike about moving from country to country or staying in one place?

GRAMMAR
MODAL PERFECT

7a [3.3] Listen to the extracts from the interview in Exercise 6a and complete the sentences.
1 I know I _____ some Russian before we went out there, but I didn't have time.
2 I suppose I _____ a local Russian to give me lessons, but I just didn't have the motivation at that point.

7b Look at sentences 1 and 2 in Exercise 7a and at sentences 3–6 below. Match them with functions a–g. Some sentences may go with more than one function.
3 The Ambassador needn't have gone through customs.
4 You ought to have mentioned that earlier.
5 The Ambassador can't have written this.
6 She must have lost her passport.

a possibility
b certainty
c impossibility
d criticism
e absence of necessity
f necessity
g regret

8 Answer the questions about the sentences in Exercises 7a and 7b.
1 Which sentences refer to things that did happen?
2 Which sentences refer to things that did not happen?
3 In which sentences don't we know?

➡ Language reference and extra practice, pages 130–131

9 Rewrite the sentences using modals. Sometimes more than one answer is possible.
1 I'm sure you left your passport on the plane.
You must have left your passport on the plane.
2 He was wrong not to pass on the information to the president.
3 I'm sure the ambassador didn't say that.
4 I finished the report by 5 p.m., but it wasn't necessary.
5 It wasn't necessary for me to tell the head of security.
6 Maybe the ambassador missed the plane.
7 It was a mistake for us to leave the ambassador's reception.
8 I'm sure the ambassador enjoyed the reception.

SPEAKING

10a Work in groups. You are all part of the organising committee for a diplomatic reception that was a disaster. Make a list of all the things that went wrong (e.g. the catering, the guest list, an embarrassing incident, cultural mistakes, entertainment).

10b Criticise each other using *should have, shouldn't have, ought to have, ought not to have.*
You should have sent out more invitations.

SITUATION

Four days ago, the oil tanker *Poseidon Marquis* was travelling a few kilometres off the coast of Northern Africa when there was an unexpected explosion in its engine room. The tanker's hull was damaged and a huge amount of oil spilled into the sea. The oil slick covers over 200 km² and is spreading all the time. The oil spill will have an immediate harmful impact on the coasts of Libya, Egypt and Algeria and will, in the longer term, affect other Mediterranean countries unless swift action is taken.

1 Read the situation. Work with a partner and list some harmful effects which will probably result from the oil spill.

2 Read some comments by various people who will be affected by the oil spill and answer these questions.

1 Do the comments match the harmful effects that you listed in Exercise 1?
2 Which are the three most serious effects, in your opinion? Give reasons for your answer.

1 'It could take ten years for the coastline to recover. We'll need to bring in a number of international organisations to provide help, expertise and finance. We've no experience of dealing with this type of problem. Our country does not have the capacity to deal with a disaster of this magnitude.' (Minister of the Environment)

2 'There'll be no fishing along the coast for some time. There'll be no fish to catch. Many of us will lose our jobs.' (a local fisherman)

3 'The effect of the oil slick on marine life will be devastating.' (Representative – International Wildlife Association)

4 'The spill could cause a dramatic increase in cancers and other diseases in the affected areas.' (a local medical officer)

5 'The cost of dealing with the damage could bankrupt the Poseidon Oil Company.' (a local resident)

6 'Newspaper reporting of the oil slick will obviously have a negative impact on our tourism industry.' (Minister for Tourism)

7 'It's probably the most beautiful beach on the coastline. Now it's covered with oil. I wouldn't dream of taking the children there – they'd probably start playing with it!' (a local resident)

8 'The spill will do irreparable damage to our reputation as an ethical oil company if we don't act quickly to clean up the sea.' (Director, Poseidon Oil Company)

9 'This will result in massive unemployment for workers who depend on coastal activities.' (a financial journalist)

10 'The international lawyers will be happy – they'll make a fortune from this disaster.' (a company director)

KEY LANGUAGE
STATING OBJECTIVES, GIVING STRONG ADVICE

3a `3.4` Listen to a conversation between the Chairperson of the Poseidon Oil Company, Julia Leiterman, and a United Nations official. What major objectives does the Chairperson mention in the conversation?

3b Listen again. Tick the expressions the speakers use to state objectives.

1 Our main objective now is to develop a strategy …
2 Your target must be to contain the oil spill.
3 So one of our main goals will be to involve the international community.
4 That should be a key objective …
5 We would like to set up regular meetings.

3c Look at Audio script 3.4 on page 168 and find expressions the speakers use to give strong advice.

TASK
DEVISING AN ACTION PLAN

4 Work in groups and make a list of the action (short- and long-term) that must be taken to deal with the oil spill.

The company must raise money to finance the work of the clean-up operation.

5a Work in two new groups, A and B. Look at your lists from Exercise 4 and work out an action plan to deal with the oil spill. The action plan will be presented at a forthcoming press conference. It should have three phases.

Phase 1: action to be taken in the next month
Phase 2: action to be taken in the next three months
Phase 3: action to be taken in the next year

In Phase 1, you should include only the action which you think should be prioritised (i.e. the company needs to take urgent action within a month).

5b Present your action plans to each other.

6a As a class, agree on a joint action plan, which the Chairperson will present at the press conference.

6b Discuss who will carry out each action in your plan and who should pay for its cost.

USEFUL PHRASES

Accepting

That sounds like a good idea.
I think it's the right way to go.
Yes, it's the best way forward.

Rejecting

I'm not sure it's the right thing to do.
I'm afraid I don't think it'll work.
I don't think it's feasible.

STUDY SKILLS
ACTIVE LISTENING

1 Complete the text with the words in the box.

careful	conscious	distracted	total

The best way to improve your listening skills is to practise active listening. Active listening requires you to make a ¹_____ effort to hear not only the words that someone speaks, but also to try to understand the ²_____ message being sent. To do this, you must pay ³_____ attention to the speaker and not be ⁴_____.

2a Prepare a two-minute talk on this topic.
In which overseas country would you like to spend a year studying or working? Give reasons for your answer.

2b Work with a partner. Listen to each other's talk and take notes. Give an oral summary of your partner's talk. Your partner listens and corrects any incorrect information.

3 Work with a partner and discuss.
1 Were your oral summaries completely accurate/almost accurate/inaccurate?
2 If it was not very accurate, what do you think was the reason?
3 What kind of verbal/non-verbal signals did you give to show you were listening (e.g. nodding your head)?
4 Did you interrupt your partner at any time during the presentation? If so, why?
5 Did you concentrate throughout?

4a What do you understand by the term 'active listening'? Work in groups and discuss the ways in which you show that you are an active listener.

4b Make a list of the criteria you will use later to assess your own ability to listen actively.

4c 3.5 Listen to a trainer from a communication skills course giving a short lecture on how to become an active listener. Make notes under these headings.
- Focus on the speaker's message
- Show that you are listening
- Give feedback
- Don't interrupt
- Respond positively

4d Work with a partner and compare your notes.

5a Prepare a three-minute talk on one of these topics.
1 An international leader, living or dead, that you particularly admire. Say what he/she has accomplished and explain why you admire him/her.
2 An international organisation that you particularly admire. Say what it has accomplished and explain why you admire it.

5b Work with a partner and listen to each other's talks.

5c Give your partner feedback on his/her ability to be a good listener. Give reasons for your evaluation.

WRITING SKILLS
A SPEECH

6 Skilled speakers use stylistic devices to help make a speech more interesting, lively and memorable. Match the stylistic devices (1–6) with the extracts from some speeches (a–f).
1 **Tripling:** Three words or phrases which follow each other, so that they make an impact.
2 **Metaphor:** Comparing two things in a figurative sense.
3 **Rhetorical questions:** Questions a speaker asks, but doesn't answer directly. Often used to persuade or emphasise.
4 **Repetition:** Words or phrases that recur throughout a speech to emphasise facts or ideas.
5 **Alliteration:** Repetition of an initial consonant sound. The consonant is usually repeated in two words which come together, but sometimes in words that are not next to each other.
6 **Antithesis:** Emphasising the contrast between two ideas. Often a similar structure is used.

a *That's one small step for man, one giant leap for mankind.* Neil Armstrong, 1969

b *America's faith in freedom and democracy was a rock in a raging sea.* George W. Bush, 2001

c *Marriage is a wonderful institution, but who would want to live in an institution?* anonymous

d *Anyone who trades liberty for security deserves neither liberty nor security.* Benjamin Franklin, 1739

e *A man touched down on the moon, a wall came down in Berlin, a world was connected by our own science and imagination.* Barack Obama, 2008

f *For me, 'revolution' simply means 'radical change'.* Aung San Suu Kyi, 2010

7a Read a short, critical speech about the United Nations which will be made to a group of university students. Make notes about the speaker's main points.

7b Work in groups and think of arguments why the United Nations plays an effective role in international affairs. Make notes. If you have time, research the topic on the internet.

8a Use your notes and research to write a persuasive speech presenting the work of the United Nations in a positive light.

8b Work with a partner and take turns to deliver your speech. Imagine that your audience is a group of university undergraduates.

"

May I start by thanking the President of your society for inviting me to talk on the topic 'How effective is the United Nations in International Affairs?'

I'm afraid I'm going to disappoint many of you when I address this question since I believe the United Nations has been largely ineffective, unimaginative and powerless since it was set up in 1945.

What were the main aims of the United Nations Charter? Surely, they were to create an organisation which would stop wars and create harmony among nations through cooperation, tolerance and fairness. Have they succeeded in those aims? The answer, in my view, is emphatically 'no'.

Since the United Nations was founded, there have been more, not fewer, wars than previously and its debates, resolutions and peacekeeping operations have not done nearly enough to prevent wars and conflicts. Let me give you some striking examples.

The United Nations failed to prevent the genocide of one million people in Rwanda in 1994. It failed also to prevent genocide in Darfur. It failed again to intervene in the Second Congo War. Are further examples necessary to illustrate the inability of the UN to deploy its forces where and when they are needed?

The Security Council, the organisation's main decision-making body, is an undemocratic body and can be likened to a tiger with neither teeth nor claws. It is composed of five permanent members (Russia, China, the UK, the USA and France), all of whom have vested interests, and it excludes powerful nations such as India, which has over a billion people. Because of the power of veto granted to its members, it is often powerless to take action in times of international crisis.

Likewise, in the area of disarmament, the UN has been far from impressive. It has failed to stop the proliferation of arms trading around the world and it has been unable to stop powerful nations developing weapons of mass destruction.

The UN is an incredibly expensive institution to maintain and is extremely bureaucratic. Its staff live well, pay no taxes and have no incentive, therefore, to reform the inefficient organisation.

There is an urgent need to reform the United Nations if it is to be an effective organisation. The answer is probably to place less emphasis on its peacekeeping mission and to focus more on its humanitarian work. The UN can provide invaluable support when responding to natural and man-made disasters, such as droughts, earthquakes and food shortages.

I've presented the United Nations in a poor light to you, but I can assure you I'm simply reflecting many people's opinions. The United Nations, in its present form, is totally unable to achieve its objectives.

"

4 Health and care

4.1 HEALTH AND HAPPINESS

A good laugh and a long sleep are the best cures in the doctor's book. Irish proverb

SPEAKING

1 Work with a partner and discuss these questions.

1 What do you do that is good or bad for your physical health?
2 What do you do that is good or bad for your mental health?
3 Rate your own fitness on a scale of 0–5 (0 = very bad, 5 = excellent). Are you happy with your level? Can/Will you do anything to improve it?
4 Do you think there is a connection between health and happiness?

READING

2 Read the article and answer the questions.

1 Where do you think the article comes from?
2 How would you describe the overall style of the article?
   a humorous
   b serious
   c lively
   d flippant
   e provocative
   f bossy
3 What does it say about the connection between happiness and health?
4 Read the first sentence of the article again. Why do you think that may be the case?

3 Reporting research Read the article again and answer the questions.

1 How many claims are made in the text which are based on scientific research, not just the writer's opinion? What are these claims and what is the evidence?
2 Which phrases are used to introduce these claims?
3 What would you expect to find in the text if these claims were made in a serious scientific article?
4 Can you think of some other scientific research that has been reported recently in the media? Where and how was it reported?

4a Answer the quiz question in the article. Then work in groups and compare your answers. Give reasons for your answers.

4b Read about your choices on page 159. Then read about the other choices you didn't make. Would you like to change any of your original choices? Discuss the comments with your group.

5 Find examples of informal language in the texts on page 37 and 159. What different features of informal language have you found?

VOCABULARY
HEALTH COLLOCATIONS

6a Match the words in the box with the categories. Some words may go in more than one category.

blood pressure	chest pain	flu virus	heart attack
heart surgery	high salt intake	immune system	
infant mortality	life expectancy	maternity ward	
omega-3 oils	premature ageing	tanning salon	

1 types of medical treatment
2 places
3 things we eat
4 children
5 the body's defences against illness
6 health problems
7 causes of illness
8 ways of measuring health

6b Which of the words above are in the article in Exercise 2?

SPEAKING

7 Work in groups and discuss the quotes. What do they mean? Do you agree with these ideas? Why?/ Why not?

1 *Health is the greatest possession.* Lao Tzu, Chinese philosopher (c500 BC)
2 *A human can be healthy without killing animals for food. Therefore, if he eats meat, he participates in taking animal life merely for the sake of his appetite.* Leo Tolstoy, Russian novelist (1828–1910)
3 *Your body hears everything your mind says.* Naomi Judd, singer/songwriter (b. 1946)
4 *Happiness is nothing more than good health and a bad memory.* Albert Schweitzer, German/French physician (1875–1965)

▶ MEET THE EXPERT

Watch an interview with Neil Shah, Director of the Stress Management Society.
Turn to page 151 for video activities.

Your health and happiness

In the daily rush of life we don't always make our own happiness our number one priority. Perhaps we should though, because being happy has clear health benefits. Researchers have discovered that happy people have stronger immune systems than unhappy people; they don't pick up as many colds or get struck down as often by a flu virus. Their blood pressure is lower, and they have better protection against heart attacks and strokes. Happy people also deal better with pain and bounce back faster after an operation. Their life expectancy is longer, too.

Studies also indicate that happy people take better care of their health. They have regular check-ups and do more exercise than unhappy people, and don't forget to put on sunscreen.

But what if you're not naturally the life and soul of the party? Or you don't wake up in the morning grinning from ear to ear?

Not to worry, the good news is that research shows we can all – no matter how gloomy – learn to be happy. The only trouble is, we're often not that good at predicting what will really make us happy. So take our quick quiz to find out the best way for you to achieve bliss – and be healthy.

▶ Quiz

Which of these things would bring you the greatest joy? Choose three.

- moving to the countryside
- getting married
- going to the gym
- supporting a good cause
- a relaxing day fishing
- being slim
- taking an evening class in something you really want to learn
- going on holiday with a group of your best friends
- tidying up your room, flat or house
- winning one million euros

SPEAKING

1 Work with a partner and discuss the questions.

1 Compared with other issues such as unemployment, law and order, taxation and education, is the healthcare system an important political issue in your country?

2 What differences do you think there might be between the healthcare systems in countries like the USA and the UK and countries like Cuba and Venezuela? Consider facilities and technology, financing of and national expenditure on healthcare and international reputations.

LISTENING

2a 4.1 A politician is giving a speech to the National Federation of Medical Practitioners, outlining his argument concerning healthcare provision for the nation. Listen and take notes.

2b Work with a partner. Use your notes to summarise the talk and identify the different stages in the speaker's argument.

2c Listen again. Check your ideas, add to your notes and improve your summary of the speaker's argument. Can you identify the different connections between his points (e.g. causal and contrast links, relevance of examples)?

3 Identifying the author's purpose Look at Audio script 4.1 on page 169 and find short extracts that serve these purposes.

1 countering or weakening an opposing argument
2 introducing factual examples
3 emphasising/exaggerating to support an argument
4 making a claim

READING

4a Read the article and answer the questions.

1 What does the title mean?
2 What is the aim of the journalist in writing this report?
3 What are the key features of the Cuban system?
4 In your opinion, does the journalist think Moore was fair to focus on Cuba as a contrast to the USA?

4b Read the article again and answer the questions.

1 How does the opening paragraph show 'a healthcare system that is extensive, accessible and ropey'?
2 How do life expectancy, infant mortality rates and health expenditure in Cuba and the USA compare?
3 What are the secrets of Cuba's healthcare success?
4 What do we learn about Cuban doctors' sense of vocation?
5 What are your thoughts on the contrast between the healthcare systems in the USA and Cuba?

5 Find words and phrases in the article with these meanings.

1 a continuous or regular flow
2 a smooth mixture
3 a philosophy or set of guiding principles
4 have the right to
5 financially poor
6 equal or similar to
7 designed for
8 a paradise or place of perfection

First-world results on a third-world budget

According to Michael Moore's latest documentary, _Sicko_, Cuba's medical care puts America's to shame. Rory Carroll investigates.

1 As a tropical sun rises over Havana, two dozen pensioners perform a series of stretches and gentle exercises in a small plaza, shaded by palms. Meanwhile, two blocks away, in a small shabby office, two doctors receive a steady stream of phone calls and patients. Although the doctors can deal with most cases, serious ones are referred to the antiquated Calixto García hospital.

2 This snapshot of Havana shows a healthcare system that is extensive, accessible and, at times, ropey. What is unique is the blend of third-world conditions with a progressive ethos and first-world results.

3 Michael Moore's documentary, _Sicko_, holds up Cuba as a model. Whether it is a consultation or open-heart surgery, citizens are entitled to free treatment. As a result, this impoverished Caribbean island has better health indicators than its much wealthier neighbour ninety miles across the Florida Straits.

4 According to the World Health Organisation, a Cuban man can expect to live to seventy-five and a woman to seventy-nine. In addition, the probability of a child dying aged under five is five per 1,000 live births. That is better than the USA and on a par with the UK, yet these world-class results are delivered by an annual expenditure of $260 per person, less than a tenth of Britain's $3,065 and a fraction of America's $6,543.

5 There is no mystery about Cuba's core strategy for averting illness: prevention. From promoting exercise, hygiene and regular check-ups, the system is geared towards averting illnesses and treating them before they become advanced and costly. Other prevention strategies take the form of health advice adverts and tips on fighting mosquitoes.

6 Simple, free access to GPs is a bedrock of healthcare. It is estimated that there is one doctor for every 175 people, compared to 485 in the UK. 'We are told to encourage them to contact us. And they do, all the time, day and night,' says one GP, somewhat ruefully. Cuban doctors have a reputation for dedication. With an average monthly salary of just twenty dollars, they cannot be accused of entering the profession for money. One neurosurgeon spoke of hitchhiking to work and operating on an empty stomach.

7 Cuban healthcare is no utopia. At times, it is ragged and harsh. However, the virtues are no myth. People live as long as they do because the system, overall, works. To be poor and sick in Cuba is tough, but it is not to be forgotten.

GRAMMAR
COHESION 1 (LINKERS)

6a Match the highlighted words in the article with the categories.

a　additive linkers: *Furthermore,*
b　contrastive linkers: *Whereas,*
c　causal linkers: *Since,*
d　temporal linkers: *After,*

6b Which of the linkers in Exercise 6a link ideas:

1　across two separate sentences?
2　across two clauses in a single sentence?

➤ Language reference and extra practice, pages 132–133

7 Look at the linkers in the box and answer the questions.

after that	as	as soon as	as well as this
consequently	even so	even though	for this reason
in contrast	moreover	nevertheless	nonetheless
on the other hand	otherwise	similarly	
therefore	until	while	whilst

1　Match the linkers with the categories in Exercise 6a. Some may go in more than one category.
2　Do the words/phrases link ideas across sentences or clauses?

> **GRAMMAR TIP**
>
> The linkers which connect ideas across two sentences are usually conjunctive adverbs. When you connect ideas in this way, you can use a semi-colon rather than a full stop.
> *Cuba is a relatively poor country; nevertheless, it has an exemplary healthcare system.*

8 Rewrite the sentences using one of the linkers in brackets. Only one of the two linkers is correct.

1　Although the Americans spend the most on healthcare, they don't have the world's best system. (even so, whereas)
2　The Cubans emphasise prevention of illness. In contrast, the Americans emphasise treatment of illness. (as a result, whereas)
3　Cuba is a relatively poor country. Consequently, it makes sense for its government to focus on prevention as this is cheaper. (although, since)
4　While I was reading the article, I realised that while spending a lot of money on healthcare is probably a good idea, it doesn't necessarily lead to the best results. (furthermore, even though)
5　If the government doesn't improve healthcare, people will continue to die unnecessarily and the current approach is also a waste of money. (furthermore, otherwise)

9 Complete these sentences with your own ideas. Then work with a partner and compare your answers.

1　My government helps _____. As well as this, it _____.
2　In my country, _____. As a result, _____.
3　People in my country _____, whereas in the USA they _____.
4　One thing that is great about my home town is _____. Furthermore, _____.
5　I _____, otherwise I _____.

VOCABULARY
HEALTHCARE

10 Explain the differences in meaning between these sets of words.

1　doctor, surgeon, general practitioner (GP), paramedic, pharmacist, consultant
2　doctor's surgery, hospital, pharmacy, hospice
3　see the doctor, have a check-up, have an operation, have a scan/an X-ray
4　lack of funding, outdated equipment, long waiting lists, post-operative infection
5　alternative medicine, palliative care, preventive medicine, conventional medicine

SPEAKING

11 Work in small groups. Describe and evaluate the healthcare system in your country. Use these points to help you.

- organisation
- funding
- positives/negatives
- national reputation
- personal experience
- recent changes/the future

WRITING

12 Write a short essay in about 250 words describing and evaluating the healthcare system in your country. Try to incorporate linkers and vocabulary from this lesson. Use your ideas from Exercise 11.

SPEAKING

1 Work with a partner and discuss the questions.

1 What do you understand by these terms?
   a career
   b profession
   c public service
   d idealism
   e vocation

2 Which jobs might be considered vocations?

LISTENING

2a Work with a partner and discuss the questions.

1 What is your image of a typical nurse? Where does this image come from?
2 What qualities does a nurse need?
3 Why are men a minority of nurses? Do you think more men will be nurses in the future?
4 Do you think all nurses have a strong sense of vocation?

2b `4.2` **Listen to a talk by a VIP at a graduation ceremony for nurses and answer the questions.**

1 What advice does she give?
2 What questions does she ask?
3 How would you answer her questions?

READING

3 The article on the right presents a very different point of view. Read it quickly. What is/are the main problem(s) the writer mentions and what solutions does he propose?

4a Read the article again and answer the questions.

1 What is it that makes the doctor most unhappy during a normal working day?
2 What kind of nurse does the doctor like and respect?
3 What does the doctor think patients should be worried about?
4 As a patient, would you be happy for nurses to carry out these duties?
5 Why do you think the doctor has written this article?

4b Evaluating contrasting arguments
The VIP in the listening and the doctor in the article present different points of view. Which do you find more convincing? Why?

Are nurses angels? I don't think so.

'Many nurses,' he admits, 'are magnificent. But equally,' says this hospital doctor, 'many are <u>lazy</u> and <u>uncaring</u>.' His bitterly outspoken attack is bound to provoke fury, but raises uncomfortable questions about the system he believes has ruined nursing as a vocation. For obvious reasons, he wishes to remain anonymous.

'As a young doctor, I witness many distressing scenes on a day-to-day basis. But there is nothing more upsetting than seeing <u>patients suffer</u> because of basic laziness and incompetence. On each shift, I find myself constantly having to <u>check and check</u> again to ensure the nurses caring for my patients do their job properly.

Of course, I have worked with some admirable nurses who do more than their job description and will skip breaks and work late to ensure their patients are well cared for. But nurses of this calibre are becoming less common and the problem stems from higher up in the system. When the standards in a department are institutionally poor, young, enthusiastic nurses are certain to have their confidence and <u>ambition</u> gradually eroded.

Part of the problem is that nursing has been dumbed down. Compared with the past, nursing is now looked down upon. But, paradoxically, nurses' training today is <u>much more academic</u>, conveying the idea that the hands-on stuff no longer matters as much.

Many nurses no longer have a sense of vocation; instead, it's all about becoming a manager. It seems to me that many nurses enter the profession almost as an afterthought.

But if I was a patient, what would really worry me is the announcement that nurses are to be given the power to prescribe all medicines, as well as having full responsibility for diagnosis, treatment (including surgical operations) and discharge of patients, without supervision from a qualified doctor.

What we really need is for nurses to stay as nurses. We need nurses who really care for their patients and who recognise, as we all should, that the career of caring is one to be highly respected.'

Are nurses really lazy and incompetent or is it doctors who are the problem? Tell us in the reader comments below.

This junior doctor is not to be considered representative and clearly has more to learn about multidisciplinary working. By whingeing about his nursing colleagues, he is likely to further damage the stressful working relationship he is in.

Hospital nurse

I've been nursing for thirty-six years and the majority of nurses remain as committed and passionate about nursing as I do. Having just finished another long day caring for terminally ill patients, I feel quite disheartened and am on the verge of crying.

Sue

Nurses go into the profession knowing the money isn't brilliant, but we enjoy the satisfaction that the care we provide on a daily basis is as holistic and as professional as the system will allow.

Ian, a cardiac nurse for seven years

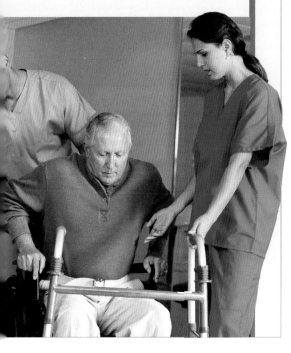

WRITING

5 Read the three replies to the doctor's article. Then write your own reply in one paragraph.

VOCABULARY
THE LANGUAGE OF EMOTION

6a Find words in the article connected with people's feelings (e.g. *exciting, frightened*). Which two words are near-synonyms?

6b Look at the words in the box. Check the meanings of any words you do not know. Then answer the questions.

antagonised	disillusioned	disorientating	exasperating	elated
exhilarating	inspiring	invigorating	relieved	rejuvenated

1 What kind of places do you find disorientating?
   Actually, my local hospital is really disorientating – the place is a maze of corridors!
2 When was the last time you felt elated?
3 What are some things that people do that you find exasperating?
4 What was one of the most exhilarating experiences of your life?
5 Which famous people do you consider inspiring?
6 What kind of physical activity do you find invigorating?

6c Work with a partner and ask each other questions using the remaining words in the box.

GRAMMAR
FUTURE FORMS WITH *BE*

7a Look at these sentences from the listening and reading texts. Then find other examples of future forms with *be* in Audio script 4.2 on page 169 and in the article in Exercise 3.

I'm very likely to need your services one day.
I'm on the verge of crying.

7b Which of the forms is more formal than the others?

7c Answer the questions about the forms in Exercise 7a.

1 Which forms are used when we want to:
   a emphasise that something will happen soon?
   b say that something will definitely happen?
   c say that something is expected to happen at a particular time?
   d say that something will probably happen?
2 Which forms take:
   a the infinitive?
   b *-ing*?

➥ Language reference and extra practice, pages 132–133

SPEAKING

8 Work in groups and discuss the questions.

1 What vocations do people you know have (e.g. your family and friends)? Do you think they made a good choice?
2 Do you think it is more difficult for people to have a vocation today than in the past?
3 What is more important: loving your work or earning a good salary?

SCENARIO
CHANGE YOUR WAYS

SITUATION

The government health department regularly runs health awareness publicity campaigns aimed at members of the general public. Proposals for future campaigns are currently being discussed, with the subject, aims and the publicity strategy all under consideration. One proposal will be selected as the next campaign.

1 Read the situation, look at the posters and discuss the questions.

1   What can you see in each poster?
2   What is the main message and approach of each campaign?
3   What can you remember about similar health campaigns in your country?

2a [4.3] Listen to a meeting where Charlie is making his proposal for a health awareness campaign and complete the notes.

a   subject of the campaign: [1]_____
b   reasons for selecting this subject:
  • [2]_____
  • [3]_____
  • [4]_____
c   main aim of the campaign: [5]_____
d   campaign strategy:
  • [6]_____
  • [7]_____
  • [8]_____
e   publicity campaign:
  • methods: [9]_____
  • style: [10]_____
  • slogan: [11]_____

2b Do you think this is an important campaign to run? What are its strengths and weaknesses? How could the campaign be improved next time?

Your guide to the eatwell plate
helping you eat a healthier diet

Get started now
See inside!

Public Health England in association with Government and the Food...

HM Government

Keep Warm Keep Well

Information for...
Over 60s
Low-income families
People living with a disability

Keep Warm Keep Well

NHS

FACE
HAS THEIR FACE FALLEN ON ONE SIDE? CAN THEY SMILE?

ARMS
CAN THEY RAISE BOTH ARMS AND KEEP THEM THERE?

SPEECH
IS THEIR SPEECH SLURRED?

TIME
TO CALL 999 IF YOU SEE ANY SINGLE ONE OF THESE SIGNS

nhs.uk/actfast · stroke.org.uk

WHEN STROKE STRIKES, ACT F.A.S.T.

KEY LANGUAGE
JUSTIFYING OPINIONS

3 In the meeting, Charlie has to justify his choice of campaign and his approach. Complete the sentences from the listening with language used to justify opinions. Then listen again and check your answers.

1 One _____ this campaign _____ eating too much salt is a significant risk factor in developing high blood pressure.
2 So you can see that this affects a large number of people, _____?
3 By _____ within just four weeks of reducing your salt consumption, your blood pressure will be lower.
4 That's _____ the kind of thing that people want to see.
5 _____ we do these two things, people _____ less salt.
6 The _____ that the problem's so widespread _____ a TV advertising campaign's fully justified.
7 While _____ that'd be expensive, it'd be the most direct way to reach such a large target audience.
8 You may well _____, and the _____ is that salt kills slugs.

4 Match the sentences in Exercise 3 (1–8) with the techniques used when justifying opinions (a–f). Some sentences may go with more than one technique.

a using adverbs to give emphasis and focus
b showing causal and similar direct connections
c asking or answering a rhetorical question
d introducing a key point
e illustrating a key point
f dealing with a possible criticism

5 Which of the phrases or techniques for justifying your opinions do/don't you regularly use in discussions? Why?

TASK
CHOOSING AND PLANNING A PUBLICITY CAMPAIGN

6 Work in groups of three. You all work for the government health department. You have to decide which health issue to focus on and then plan the different elements of the campaign. Read your information and decide why this is an important issue for the government to address with a publicity campaign.

Student A: look at page 155.
Student B: look at page 156.
Student C: look at page 157.

7 Have a meeting with the other members of your group. Follow the instructions.

1 Each person should present the information about his/her health issue and explain why it is important.
2 As a team, choose one of the issues and then plan the campaign. Consider the guidelines and points listed in the memo. You have a maximum budget of €400,000 (see table of campaign media costs, for reference).

MEMO

Health awareness publicity campaign: points to consider

- Which health or fitness issue should be addressed?
- What is the target audience for the campaign?
- What are the two or three key messages of the campaign?
- What is the overall campaign slogan?
- What campaign methods will we use?
- How long should the campaign run for?
- Can all this be done within budget?
- What will the posters or other visual material look like?

Campaign media costs

€200,000	producing a TV advert
€50,000	TV advertising for one month
€20,000	producing a radio advert
€10,000	radio advertising for one month
€20,000	producing a newspaper advert or poster or leaflet
€40,000	advertising in national newspapers for one month
€2,000	distributing 10,000 posters/leaflets (to schools, medical centres, stations, etc.)
€40,000	designing a website
€100,000	organising 100 special events at schools/in workplaces

8 Produce a mock-up of a campaign poster or other visual communication document.

9 Present your campaign to the other groups in the class.

USEFUL PHRASES

Inviting someone to speak

So what's your presentation about?
Let's hear what you have to say.
Tell us about the issue you've read about.

Responding to an argument

That's quite convincing.
It's hard to disagree.
That doesn't sound so important to me.

Making a choice

So which shall we choose?
Any preferences?
Which do you think we should go for?

STUDY SKILLS
ANALYSING VISUAL INFORMATION

1 Work in small groups and discuss the questions.

1   Are some illnesses or diseases becoming more common in your country?
2   What do you understand by *communicable* and *non-communicable diseases*?

2 Look at the chart and answer these questions.

1   Where does the chart come from?
2   Is it a reliable source? Why?/Why not?

3 Match the explanations (1–5) with the terms (A–J) on the right of the chart.

1   very serious diseases caused by bacteria or a virus and related to breathing or your lungs (e.g. pneumonia, avian influenza (bird flu), swine flu)
2   brain diseases caused when the blood supply to the brain is disrupted in some way (e.g. stroke)
3   deaths at or around the time of birth (e.g. stillbirth)
4   diseases of the heart (e.g. heart attack, angina, chest pain)
5   diseases in which waste from the bowels is watery (e.g. cholera)

4 Look at the terms on the right of the chart again. Which describe:
1   communicable diseases?
2   non-communicable diseases?

5 Work with a partner and discuss the questions.
1   Does the chart show every single cause of death?
2   Does the chart give information for every year between 2004 and 2030?
3   Choose one or two of the figures down the left-hand side of the chart. Write the exact number it represents.

6 In one sentence, describe what the chart shows.
This chart shows …

7 What is the main trend in the chart? Explain it in your own words.

8 According to the chart, are the sentences true or false?
1   By 2030, malaria will have become the least significant cause of death.
2   The number of deaths from cancers will show a steady increase over the period 2018–2030.
3   In 2022 there will be about eight million deaths from (ischaemic) heart disease.
4   The percentage of deaths from cerebrovascular diseases will remain almost stable between 2020 and 2024.
5   Deaths from tuberculosis will decrease sharply between 2020 and 2030.
6   Deaths from road accidents will overtake deaths from perinatal causes around 2024.

9 Are you surprised by anything in the chart? Why do you think these changes are expected to take place?

10 In your opinion, is the chart clear? Is there anything missing? Can you think of anything that would have helped you to understand the chart more easily?

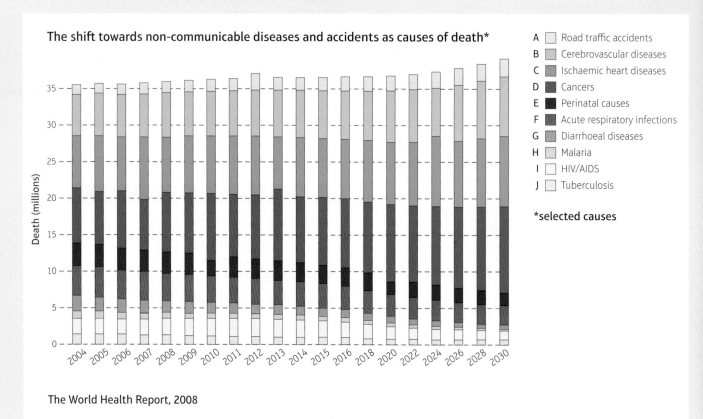

The shift towards non-communicable diseases and accidents as causes of death*

A   Road traffic accidents
B   Cerebrovascular diseases
C   Ischaemic heart diseases
D   Cancers
E   Perinatal causes
F   Acute respiratory infections
G   Diarrhoeal diseases
H   Malaria
I   HIV/AIDS
J   Tuberculosis

*selected causes

The World Health Report, 2008

WRITING SKILLS
DESCRIBING VISUAL INFORMATION

11 Read the writing task and put the stages of the writing process (a–g) in the correct order (1–7).

The chart below shows the causes of death worldwide between 2004 and 2030. Summarise the information by choosing and describing the main features and make comparisons where relevant. Write at least 150 words.

a Check for mistakes (e.g. grammar, spelling, punctuation).
b Look at any other written information on the chart.
c Count how many words you have used.
d Read the title/heading of the chart.
e Plan your answer: decide what the main points are and make notes on them, including key data.
f Look at the words/figures on the vertical and horizontal axes of the chart.
g Write your answer (main points and supporting data). Use linkers.

12 Read the description of the chart and answer the questions.

1 What is the topic of each paragraph?
2 What is the difference between the first and last sentences?

The chart shows the main causes of death worldwide between 2004 and 2030. Overall, the mortality rate is predicted to climb from just over thirty-five million in 2004 to approximately thirty-nine million in 2030.

In 2004, about ten million deaths were attributed to communicable diseases. (This) represented close to thirty percent of the total. By 2030, however, deaths due to these diseases can be expected to have fallen to around five million, representing less than fifteen percent of the total, with a particularly steep decline in deaths caused by diarrhoeal diseases and malaria.

Conversely, deaths will rise for most non-communicable diseases, especially where cancer deaths are concerned. These will nearly double over the period. A further category is fatalities that are the result of road accidents. The latter will go up steadily from roughly one million in 2004 to somewhere in the region of 2.5 million in 2030.

The main trend that emerges from the chart is that deaths from non-communicable diseases and accidents will increase, while deaths from communicable diseases will drop.

13 Find examples of approximation in the description.

just over thirty-five million

14 Find examples of cohesion in the description. Circle all the reference words (words that refer to something mentioned earlier) and say what they refer to.

This = ten million deaths

15 Are these sentences about describing a chart true or false?

1 You can just copy the title/heading of the chart and use it word-for-word in your answer.
2 You should try to give as much detail as possible.
3 As you write, it's a good idea to look back at what you've already written.
4 To avoid repetition, you should vary your vocabulary and sentence structures.
5 Try to include one or two complex sentences.
6 The overview must come at the end, as in the example below.
7 It's fine if your answer is a few words below the minimum length (say, 140 words).

16 Look at the chart on page 160. Write at least 150 words about it, saying what it shows and describing the main points/trends. Don't forget to:

• select information carefully.
• include a few key figures, where necessary.
• avoid excessive detail.
• use approximators where appropriate.

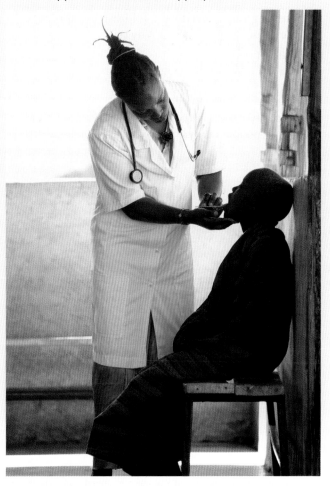

5 Fashion and consumerism

5.1 GLOBAL CONSUMERISM

IN THIS UNIT

GRAMMAR
- future in the past
- emphatic structures

VOCABULARY
- consumer collocations
- compound adjectives formed with nouns
- suffixes (nouns 1)

SCENARIO
- discussing hypothetical ideas
- developing a recovery strategy

STUDY SKILLS
- reading complex texts effectively

WRITING SKILLS
- summarising

So soon as a fashion is universal, it is out of date. Marie von Ebner-Eschenbach (1830–1916), Austrian writer

SPEAKING

1 In small groups, discuss the following statements. Are they true for you? Why?/Why not?

1 I hate shopping.
2 Most of my favourite possessions are things that I've bought for myself.
3 I rarely buy things 'on impulse'.
4 It's really important to have a lot of branded goods.
5 I think people in my country are very materialistic.

READING

2 Read the introduction of a description of a radio series. What three aspects of global consumerism will the programmes explore?

3 Read about the four programmes. In which programme might we hear about:

a the effects of consumerism on demographic changes?
b consumerism as a recent phenomenon?
c narrowing the gulf between the 'haves' and the 'have-nots'?
d the relationship between consumerism and appearances?
e consumer education?
f consumerism that is not simply an urban phenomenon?

GLOBAL CONSUMERISM

This special four–part series investigates consumer trends around the world. What can they tell us about the mindsets of different countries? We visit India, the United Arab Emirates, Botswana and Japan and find that what people buy defines, to an ever greater extent, who they are or who they would like to be. But what's driving our passion to consume? And does it increase our fulfilment?

Episode 1: India

In the first programme of this series looking at consumer issues around the globe, we focus on the gap between rich and poor and how it could be bridged by the construction of new shopping malls, not only in cities, but also in the countryside. In addition, we explore the relationship between the country's new consumerism and its people's mental health.

LISTENING

4a 5.1 **Listen to an extract from the programme about Japan and answer the questions.**

1   What evidence is given to support the idea that Japanese people love brands?
2   Why do brands have such value in Japan?
3   What happened in Japan between the end of the Second World War and the mid-1990s?
4   Why have young women been the single most influential group of consumers in recent years and why is this considered a problem?
5   Do Japanese people think there is a solution to this problem? If so, what is it?

4b Expanding the topic **Work with a partner and discuss the questions.**

1   What is the most interesting piece of information you have learnt about consumerism in Japan?
2   What do you think will happen to Japanese consumer society in the future?
3   Which of the other three programmes would you most like to listen to? Why?
4   What aspects of consumerism might feature in a similar programme about your country?

Episode 2: United Arab Emirates

This programme examines how consumers in the UAE are putting a premium on looking good. According to a recent report, some residents in the country spend as much each year on cosmetics as they do on housing rent. High disposable income levels, a strong shopping culture and a massive influx of tourists are key drivers of this trend. So, too, are the increasing numbers of men who are using personal care products.

Episode 3: Botswana

This is the story of an emerging consumer society. Thanks to the discovery of diamonds in 1966 and a number of years of sound government, Botswana's economy is relatively healthy, creating a new breed of consumer. Yet credit and personal debt are major issues here. So who has responsibility for promoting sensible spending habits? Is it the job of schools, of the banks or of religious organisations?

Episode 4: Japan

In the last programme of this globetrotting series, we look into the reasons why this advanced consumer nation is obsessed with brands. Why is this the only country in the world where people trust brands so much they will buy a car without taking it for a test drive? We also see the impact of consumerism on the shrinking birth rate and on the family.

VOCABULARY
CONSUMER COLLOCATIONS

5a Which of the words in the box form common collocations with *consumer*?

~~advice~~	boom	choice	confidence	demand
desire	goods	group	issues	pain
price index	products	society	spending	
trends	watchdog	wish		

consumer advice

5b Complete the sentences with collocations from Exercise 5a.

1   A _____ makes sure consumers are treated fairly and that products are safe.
2   The _____ was followed by a severe downturn.
3   With so many models on the market, good _____ is essential.
4   We've all heard of the _____, but what does it mean? Well, it's one in which buying goods and services is considered to be very important.

SPEAKING

6 Work in two groups, A and B. Read the information and plan your argument. Then have a debate.

Group A: you belong to a pressure group that wants people in your country to be less materialistic in the future.

1   Think of some reasons (economic, social, environmental, etc.) why your country should be less of a consumer society in the coming years.
2   Look at Group B's information. Try to predict their arguments and consider how you will refute them.

Group B: you know that there is a powerful pressure group that wants your country to be less materialistic.

1   Think of some reasons (economic, social, etc.) why your society should be, or should continue to be, a consumer society in the future.
2   Look at Group A's information. Try to predict their arguments and consider how you will refute them.

SPEAKING

1 Work with a partner and discuss the questions.

1 What do you understand by the term 'design classic'?

2 Which design classics do you know? Which country do they come from? Which do you like, and why? Use these categories to help you.

    a clothes/shoes/accessories   d technology

    b means of transport   e children's toys

    c objects/things in the home

3 How does something become a design classic? What qualities does it need?

READING

2a Read the article about an iconic car and complete the timeline.

Ford Model T launched	Beetle chassis design by Béla Barényi
1908	**1925**

2b Read the article again and answer the questions. Choose no more than two words from the article for each answer.

1 Which group of people in Europe were very interested in Henry Ford's Model T?

2 What could easily be reached from the site of the new factory and city?

3 When did people start working at the factory?

4 Which word connected with children was used dismissively by overseas visitors to describe the car?

5 What did Volkswagen stand for in the period after 1945?

3 Combining sources of information

Work in groups. What factors do you think contributed to the great success of 'the people's car'? Use the information in the text, as well as your own general knowledge.

I'm early for my meeting with Horst Geller, but he's already waiting for me in the lobby of the Golf Hotel. There's a half-consumed latte on the table in front of him. 'Sorry,' he says, 'I was going to wait for you, but I needed a shot of coffee.'

Later he confesses that he needs about five before lunch. We're here to talk about his life-long passion, cars, and his latest research into the history of Volkswagen, today the largest carmaker in the world.

Volkswagen – it means 'people's car' in German. And that's how it started out, back in the 1930s. 'Actually,' Geller explains, 'the Americans got there first; Henry Ford's Model T, launched in 1908, was really the first car for ordinary people.'

Ford's car inspired designers across the pond and in 1925, an eighteen-year-old Hungarian technology student, Béla Barényi, came up with the basic chassis design for what was to become the Volkswagen Beetle.

Fast forward a decade. In 1934, Ferdinand Porsche, an Austrian engineer (Yes, that's Porsche as in the sports car!), was commissioned to develop the 'volkswagen'. It was to be a basic vehicle that could transport two adults and three children at a speed of 100km/h and would cost about 900 Reichsmark – about the price of a small motorcycle. It would be available to ordinary German citizens through a savings plan. The world-renowned Beetle was about to be born.

In 1938, a site was chosen for the factory where the new cars were going to be built. It was centrally located within Germany, there was plenty of space for the plant and it had good access to transport routes.

GRAMMAR
FUTURE IN THE PAST

4a When we talk about the past, we sometimes want to describe what was going to happen in the future from the viewpoint of the past. Find examples of this 'future in the past' in the article.

I was going to wait for you …

4b Which of the forms you have found describe:

1 something that happened later?
2 something that did not happen later?
3 something that happened very soon afterwards?

4c Put the forms in three groups.

1 quite formal
2 quite informal
3 neutral (neither particularly formal nor informal)

This was important if workers were to be attracted to the project. 'A whole new city was founded around the factory. This is present-day Wolfsburg – still the home of the Volkswagen company.' Geller is warming to his theme and orders an Americano.

Eye-catching advertising for the new car made its appearance. However, some of the images were rather misleading, implying that five people would have found the vehicle spacious and comfortable. 'Actually, this was far from the truth.'

In the spring of 1939, the first 1,000 employees were recruited, and 10,000 cars were supposed to be produced by December. But the ensuing chaos of the Second World War meant that not one of the 350,000 people who paid into the savings scheme would ever see their car.

In 1945, with the war-damaged factory under British control, production of the people's car resumed. However, visiting foreign representatives of the motor industry were unimpressed, finding it too ugly and noisy. 'One British delegate called it "a toy not to be taken seriously". Big mistake: it would go on to be the most produced single make of car in history, overtaking the Ford Model T in 1972. In total, over twenty-one million were eventually made.'

'The company itself, back in German hands from 1949, would become an important symbol of German post-war regeneration.' And Geller has somehow lined up a third coffee while I've been absorbed in his tale.

5 Choose the correct form to complete the sentences.

1 The British representatives said the people's car *was to / was likely to* remain popular for only two or three years, if that.
2 The new factory was based on the Ford factory in Detroit, USA, and *was to be / was being* the most modern in Europe.
3 In the 1970s, Volkswagen knew the Beetle couldn't last for ever and they *were going to / were to* have to do something about it.
4 In January 1978, the last Beetle rolled off the assembly line in Wolfsburg, although they *were continuing / would continue* to be manufactured in Mexico until 2003.

6 Complete the sentences with your own ideas. Then read your sentences to a partner. Add more details about what happened.

1 Last year I was going to _____, but _____.
2 Yesterday I was supposed to _____, but _____.
3 This morning I was about to _____ when _____.
4 I thought my friend was likely to _____, but actually _____.

➡ Language reference and extra practice, pages 134–135

VOCABULARY
COMPOUND ADJECTIVES FORMED WITH NOUNS

7a Match the adjectives in the box with the categories.

eye-catching	life-long	present-day	world-renowned

1 noun + adjective   3 noun + past participle
2 noun + present participle   4 adjective + noun

7b Find examples of compound adjectives in the article. Which category do they belong to? Which compound adjective uses a prefix?

7c Match words from box A with words from box B to make compound adjectives. Then decide what they mean and what you could use them to talk about.

A	high	time	hand	smoke

B	made	free	quality	consuming

SPEAKING

8 Work in groups. Choose five objects around you. Describe and evaluate their design. Which are the most attractive or interesting? Are any of them (or will they become) design classics?

WRITING

9 Choose one of your possessions which has an attractive or interesting design and write a description of it in about 100 words.

SPEAKING

1 Work with a partner and discuss the questions.

1 What do the photos on this page show?
2 What do you know about the arguments related to these controversial practices?

READING

2a Look at the newspaper headlines 1–6. What do you think each story is about?

1 Court case puts sweatshops in the spotlight
2 Starving for fashion's sake
3 Discrimination still in fashion
4 This season's colour is more than a shade
5 Protest poses questions for global players
6 Throwaway: the global cost of fast fashion

2b Match the headlines (1–6) with the article extracts (a–f). Ignore the missing words in each extract.

a Animal-rights ¹_____ protested at Milan Fashion Week by jumping onto the catwalk, chanting 'Fur is dead' and waving 'Fur Shame' banners.

b The defendants, like other fashion companies, state that they are not responsible for ²_____ of local regulations concerning pay and working hours committed by foreign factories that supply the clothes.

c Many industries responded to increasing consumer interest in environmental ³_____ by introducing green products and production processes. The rise in consumer eco-⁴_____ has reached a point where, finally, the fashion industry is beginning to follow suit, and green is now all the rage.

d Recent research suggests the increase in eating disorders amongst models may be due to the industry's unrelenting ⁵_____ with size zero* clothing.

e The report claims that the strong demand for cheap and readily available clothes is placing the world under great social and environmental pressure. It asks if the ⁶_____ of this 'fast fashion', which is increasing in ⁷_____, is a price worth paying.

f It is significant that, on the catwalk and in the fashion magazines, the face of fashion still appears to be exclusively white, despite the initial ⁸_____ of black fashion models 40 years ago.

*size zero – the smallest clothes size in America

VOCABULARY
SUFFIXES (NOUNS 1)

3a Match suffixes from box A with words from box B to make as many nouns as possible.

A	-ability	-(n)ce	-ist	-ity
	-ion	-ness		

B	active	conscious	convenient
	emerge	obsess	popular
	sustain	violate	

3b Complete the article extracts in Exercise 2b with the correct form of nouns from Exercise 3a.

3c Compete with a partner. How many nouns can you make from the adjectives and verbs in the article extracts in Exercise 2b? You have three minutes.

LISTENING

4a 5.2 **Listen to the first part of a radio programme about fashion and social responsibility and answer these questions.**

1 Which newspaper stories in Exercise 2b does the radio show refer to?
2 Who do you think will defend the fashion business, Sarah or Diana?

4b 5.3 **Who do you think will make these points, Sarah or Diana? Listen to the second part of the programme and check.**

1 Monitoring conditions in suppliers' factories is not straightforward.
2 Fashion companies aim to increase profits.
3 Thin models have a negative influence on people's self-perception.
4 Designers are artists who want to show their work in the best way possible.

4c Listen again and make notes on the arguments presented by Sarah and Diana.

5a Identifying support for main argument **Work with a partner and compare your notes. What are the main points in each stage of the conversation? Diana and Sarah both make four points. Compare your ideas with the rest of the class and then check with your teacher.**

5b The main points are supported by other information. Look at Audio script 5.3 on page 170 and identify the supporting points for the main points in Exercise 5a.

5c Who do you think makes the strongest case overall? Who do you side with? Why?

GRAMMAR
EMPHATIC STRUCTURES

6a **5.4** Inversion **Complete the sentences from the listening. Then listen and check.**

1 _____ sooner has _____ attached one than he picks up the next from the thousands in the bag.
2 _____ does he realise _____ he is about to spark a huge debate about fashion, models, men and anorexia.
3 At _____ time are _____ aware of the effect this fast fashion is having on the environment.

6b Answer the questions about the sentences in Exercise 6a.

1 What is unusual about the subject–verb word order after the opening phrases?
2 Why does sentence 2 include the word *does*, while the others do not?

7a **5.5** Cleft sentences **Complete the sentences from the listening. Then listen and check.**

1 _____'s the enforcement of these rules that fashion chains have to focus on.
2 _____ the companies _____ is maximise their profits, not improve their workers' lives.
3 I mean, it's _____ that kind of shallow change _____ I'm talking about.
4 _____ you need to do _____ change the whole approach of the industry towards body size.

7b Answer the questions about the sentences in Exercise 7a.

1 How many clauses are there in each sentence?
2 Look at the first clauses. Which ones concern the object of the verb in the second clause? Which concern the verb itself in the second clause?

7c Rewrite the sentences in Exercise 7a. Begin with the words given.

1 The fashion chains _____.
2 The companies _____.
3 I am _____.
4 You need _____.

8 Rewrite the sentences using emphatic structures. Begin with the words given.

1 We seldom see naturally sized models.
   Seldom _____.
2 He has designed clothes for film stars and he has also opened stores all around the world.
   Not _____.
3 We mustn't use child labour under any circumstances.
   Under _____.
4 The press officer denied the accusation about the use of sweatshops.
   It _____.
5 People are concerned about the cost of a product, not its environmental impact.
   It _____.
6 The fashion industry encourages young girls to worry about their body size.
   What _____.
7 The designer created a new style using traditional materials.
   What _____.
8 I think that fashion shows and models should be heavily regulated.
   What _____.

➡ Language reference and extra practice, pages 134–135

SPEAKING

9 Work in small groups and debate these topics.

1 The fashion industry should be compelled to only use models that are of average body size.
2 The use of animal fur to make clothes should be banned.
3 Parents should not encourage children under twelve to choose their own clothes.
4 The customer is to blame for the increasingly throwaway consumer culture.
5 Fashion companies should be directly responsible for working conditions in production factories in other countries.

▶ MEET THE EXPERT

Watch an interview with fashion designers Francesca Rosella and Ryan Genz, about their company Cutecircuit. Turn to page 152 for video activities.

SPEAKING

1 Work in small groups and discuss the questions.

1 Which fashion and clothing shops are successful in your country? Why? Do they employ any of these strategies?

- offering something for everyone
- targeting a particular market
- having a low-price strategy
- having an up-market strategy
- advertising widely; creating a strong internet and social media presence
- good functional website and delivery systems

2 Are there any shops that are not doing very well? Why?

3 As a consumer, what makes you choose one shop over another?

SITUATION

All Seasons is a well-established clothing retailer with fifty national shops and five shops abroad. Sales have been declining and the company is in danger of making a loss. The company sells clothes for the general mainstream market, catering for men, women and children. Most of the shops also sell household products such as kitchenware, bed linen and vases. All products are in the medium to high price range.

A retailer that was once the family choice now struggles to attract people into the shops and to provide the fashion that is desired. A recovery strategy is required.

2 **5.6** Read the situation and listen to the CEO of All Seasons outlining the problems facing the company. Make notes on the main points from the consultant's report.

FOUR MAIN AREAS

1 Shops and facilities
shops:
customer service:
overall:

2 The products
positive points:
look and design:
cost:
accessories and homeware:

3 The market
current target market:
consultant's opinion:

4 The internet and brand identity
current website:

KEY LANGUAGE
DISCUSSING HYPOTHETICAL IDEAS

3a **5.7** During the CEO's presentation, some of the directors discussed possible changes. Listen and complete the extracts.

1 _____ we did have a café, wouldn't that just reduce our sales space? And also, it'd mean that _____ food storage and preparation facilities. Most of our shops are in restricted high-street locations – I'm not sure how feasible _____.

2 Well, if we _____ new designs by major designers rather than use our own in-house designers, _____ more up-to-date. Mind you, we'd need to produce the clothes quickly then, _____ behind the times.

3 Just on that point, I was wondering if we _____ an element of specialisation rather than make a total change.

4 Well, if we had a special range, say one for kids, but _____ a wide general range for customers, _____ ourselves from other stores without losing our current customer base. _____ a chance to market the special range and use this as a way to get people into our shops.

3b Answer the questions.

1 Why do the speakers use this particular language in this kind of discussion?

2 Which words do you know that mean 'if' and 'if we didn't'?

TASK
DEVELOPING A RECOVERY STRATEGY

4 Work in groups of four. You are on the Board of Directors for All Seasons. You are going to decide how to save the company. Before the meeting, prepare your ideas and review your notes from the consultant's report.

Student A: look at page 155.
Student B: look at page 156.
Student C: look at page 157.
Student D: look at page 158.

5 Hold the meeting and discuss the four different proposals. How can All Seasons become a destination store? Use the meeting guidelines to help your discussion.

Meeting guidelines

- Target market: specialised ranges or complete change?
- Shop makeover: appearance? facilities?
- Product range: clothing – design? quality? price?
- The internet: retail site and/or social media?
- Accessories/Homeware: new product lines? close departments?
- Marketing: advertising? re-launch events?

USEFUL PHRASES

Making a proposal

I think the best way forward would be …
There are several reasons why I think this.
Firstly, … . Secondly, …
I've told you about … , so let's move on to …
To conclude, …

Disagreeing

I think it'd be a mistake to concentrate on that.
I'm really not sure that'd be the best way forward.
I'd have to disagree with you on that, I'm afraid.

STUDY SKILLS
READING COMPLEX TEXTS EFFECTIVELY

1 Look at the title of the article and read the first paragraph. Answer the questions.

1 What type of text is it?
2 What are the key words in the title?
3 What are the two things you learn about youth culture?

2a Building an overview Read the article quickly and do the tasks.

1 Read to find the main topic only of each paragraph. (This will often be given in the first sentence of a paragraph.)
2 Make a note of the main topic of the paragraph.

2b Look at your overview notes from Exercise 2a. Which paragraphs are closely connected?

3 Use your overview notes to identify in which paragraph you might find information about:

1 hip-hop culture no longer being an urban phenomenon.
2 youth culture initially being a commercial product.
3 punk influencing the wider fashion industry.

4 Reading for detail Pay attention to complex noun phrases and reference words. Answer the questions about the article.

1 What is:
   a the subject of *led* (line 3)?
   b the object of *led* (line 5)?
2 What do these reference words refer to?
   a *with which* (line 7)
   b *them* (line 12)
   c *This* (line 23)
   d the subject of *is* (line 37)

5 Read the article in detail and add notes about each key point in your overview notes. Identify the supporting points and argument that connect to the topic of each paragraph. Then work with a partner and compare your notes.

6 How would you describe the relationship between youth culture and mainstream fashion in your country? Are there any distinct youth subcultures?

Commerce, punk, hip-hop and manga: the emergence of youth culture and its relationship to the mainstream

In the West, the first distinct youth fashions appeared after the Second World War. Significant economic developments after 1945 led directly to young people making their own decisions concerning taste and style. Principally, there was a huge demand for labour,
5 which led to an elevation in salary levels, particularly for young people, who then had relatively large amounts of disposable income with which they could enjoy their lives in the period between school and marriage (Abrams 1959).

This increase in disposable income meant that these young people
10 became an identifiable consumer market. Consequently, many industries, such as television, fashion and music, produced goods and services that were directly aimed at them. In a sense, youth culture was defined by the products that were produced specifically for young people by industry and commerce.

15 However, not all types of youth culture develop in this way. Whilst much of youth culture has been a result of commercial activity, there are undoubtedly smaller subcultures which are stylistically innovative and which are created by the young people themselves. Punk and hip-hop cultures illustrate this and also reveal further
20 connections between mainstream society and youth culture.

The punk culture of 1970s England may be seen as a direct reaction by young people against the intense commercialisation of youth fashion and music. This subculture was not the result of the commercial targeting of the young by industry, rather it was
25 created independently by young people. However, punk culture went on to form a different connection with the mainstream culture when its style was adopted by the fashion industry, such that models had green hair, clothes were ripped and cosmetics companies sold make-up in vivid colours (Rouse 1989).

30 This adoption of an innovative youth subculture by the mainstream culture is also present in the historical journey of hip-hop culture. Rap music and an urban-look of baggy jeans, sports shoes and baseball caps emerged from a very specific social and geographical sphere, namely, the young black culture of inner city North
35 America. Yet this specific style has now spread amongst young people of all races across the world, from Boston to Beijing, and is as much suburban as it is urban. This has occurred because of the direct marketing of this specific subculture to the wider youth market by companies on a global scale to substantially increase
40 their profits. For example, in 1992, MTV launched a music show entitled *Yo! MTV raps* and by 1993, eighty percent of teenagers 'favoured the [hip-hop] style' (Speigler 1995).

The manga fashion subculture that comes from the world of video gaming and graphic novels is different in its origins to hip-hop and
45 punk, but similar to the latter in its later journey. Manga and video games are commercial in purpose and they provide the source for this subculture, which involves wearing theatrical fashions and costumes. From this youth culture, which developed from a commercial source, there has been a spread to wider fashion
50 culture and high street stores (Fumutaki 2009).

Thus, it can be seen that youth culture is directly connected to mainstream consumer culture, although this relationship is not as simple as may first be assumed.

WRITING SKILLS
SUMMARISING

7a Identifying main points You are going to summarise the article opposite in 150–200 words. Complete the flow chart for the first part of the article with the words in the box.

1945	defined	products	spend

after ¹_____ youth subcultures developed ⟶

young people had more money to ²_____ as they wanted due to elevation of salaries ⟶

businesses targeted young people's disposable income by making special ³_____ for them ⟶

youth culture ⁴_____ by these products

7b Look at the flow chart again. What information has been left out? Why?

8 Avoiding plagiarism As you make notes or a flow chart, use your own words where possible. This is one aspect of avoiding plagiarism in your summary. Analyse the flow chart in Exercise 7a and identify language that has been changed from the original.

9 Rephrase the following ideas in your own words.
1 due to an elevation of salaries
2 disposable income
3 youth culture was defined by these products

10 Make a flow chart for the second part of the article. Then work with a partner and compare your flow charts. Have you left out similar pieces of information? How have you changed the language? Which words and phrases haven't been changed?

11a Compare this first sentence with the first part of the flow chart in Exercise 7a, then with the original text. What are the differences? How many clauses does this sentence have?

Particular fashion and styles for young people emerged after 1945, which was a time when the high demand for labour provided young people with higher salaries and thus more spending money.

11b Write two or three sentences for the rest of the flow chart. Use linkers such as *however*, *as* and *consequently*. Then work with a partner and compare your sentences.

11c Write a summary of the article. Use your flow chart from Exercise 10 to help you.

6 Technology and change

6.1 ATTITUDES TO TECHNOLOGY

We owe a lot to Thomas Edison. If it wasn't for him, we'd be watching television by candlelight.
Milton Berle (1908–2002), American comedian

SPEAKING AND READING

1 Work with a partner and discuss the questions.

1 What do you understand by the word *technology*?
2 How have advances in technology affected your working/studying and social life?
3 What kinds of advances would you like to see in the next twenty years?
4 Is the latest technology always an improvement? Can you give any examples of when it hasn't been?

2 Do the technology quiz on page 160. Then check your answers on page 158.

3 Do you think we rely on technology too much? Why?/Why not? Work with a partner and discuss your ideas.

4 Which item of technology do you think is the most:

1 important?
2 useful?
3 controversial?
4 unpopular?
5 pointless?

VOCABULARY
DESCRIBING TECHNOLOGY

5a Match the words in the box with the headings. Which word does not go with either heading? Why?

out-of-date:
up-to-date:

a museum piece	behind the times	cutting-edge	had its day
innovative	new-fangled	obsolete	outdated	redundant
retro	revolutionary	state-of-the-art	superseded	the last word in

5b Complete the sentences with words from Exercise 5a. Sometimes more than one answer is possible.

1 I don't see the point of those _____ GPS watches. I just want something simple that looks good and tells the time.
2 That device was _____ before it even went on the market. Nobody uses them anymore.
3 This really is a(n) _____ development. It will change the way we communicate forever.
4 It's not exactly _____ technology, but it's still a pretty useful piece of equipment.
5 This phone is huge and it doesn't even have a camera. It's _____.
6 My computer's eight years old, and very slow. I think it's _____.
7 Cassette tapes were _____ by CDs in the 1990s.
8 The factory is ultra-modern. It recently introduced _____ machines in its production process.

READING

6a Read the message board texts and answer the questions.

1 Which of the people are for/against/ undecided about the question?
2 Which points do you agree/disagree with? Which is closest to your own point of view?

6b Summarise each writer's argument in one sentence.

7 Analysing style What do you notice about the way the writers on the message board express their opinions? Is the style:

1 formal or informal?
2 subjective or objective?
3 well-structured or disorganised?
4 emotional or unemotional?

8a Find examples of the following in the message board texts.

1 rhetorical questions
2 colloquial language
3 other formal/informal style features

8b What other stylistic features did you notice? Why do you think they are used?

9 Complete the sentences with prepositions. Then check your answers in the message board texts.

1 What does a fear of technology stem _____, in your opinion?
2 Which item of technology has had the biggest impact _____ your/your parents' life?
3 Does technology contribute _____ the happiness of mankind?
4 Has the rise _____ the popularity of social networking sites resulted _____ better understanding between men and women?
5 Do you think technological advances will lead _____ people living on other planets?
6 Is the expansion _____ robot technologies a good thing?

WRITING

10a Write your opinion for a message board on this question: Have technological advances had a positive effect on people's lives in your country?

10b Swap your writing with a partner and write a response to his/her message.

Technology views

Have technological advances had a positive impact on people's lives?

 SWEDESven All the really fundamental changes have been connected to advances in technology. Think about all the lives which have been saved due to breakthroughs in, for example, medicine. And what about the general extended life expectancy? What about transport and communication? Some people have always been anti-technology. There are always dramatic changes going on, especially now, in terms of communication. The internet is amazing and has had an awesome effect on people's lives.

 NoWayJosé It's true technology has altered people's lives, but I'm not sure it's been for the better. A lot of stress stems from the fact that technology speeds everything up in our already fast-paced world. We're now reachable twenty-four hours a day and we expect instant answers; and this has an impact on people's work-life balance. There are also the dehumanising effects of technology – we've become slaves to machines. What about the dangers of things like GM crops or 'Frankenstein foods'? It's dangerous to mess about with nature. Advances in technology breed laziness and contribute to a sedentary lifestyle. Look at all those kids who would rather play a computer game than kick a ball around.

 AndreaCat SWEDESven's right – technology can fix all society's problems. Even during wars there's a great push for new tech. Cars which cause pollution resulting in global warming are now being superseded by hybrid and electric ones. They'll reduce the carbon footprint. BTW, those of you who think technology is so bad: WHY ARE YOU USING THE INTERNET TO TELL US THIS?!

 Raina23 Not sure you're right, AndreaCat. Technology's a double-edged sword. There have been radical changes brought about by inventions like the telephone, car and the internet. But the important thing is that control of technology is power. It's the way it is used which is important. For example, some technological advances are not always used in a good way. What about the rise in cosmetic surgery, artificial intelligence, cloning, designer babies, people living forever? Where's futuristic technology taking us? This, together with a move towards an ever-greater reliance on technology, is leading us to a nightmare vision of the future.

JaneyJane Technology has a lot to answer for. I'm with you on this, NoWayJosé. Never mind improving people's lives, it accounts for the increase in pollution and exploitation. Lots of people are killed in wars because of so-called technological advances. As for the expansion of access to the internet, there are millions of people in the world who haven't even made a phone call yet! There's a real digital divide. Technological advances because of their uneven distribution actually have a negative effect on people's opportunities. Major technological change is basically destroying the planet. I doubt we can save it in time. It's really all about greed. I guess this is more to do with human nature rather than technology itself, though.

READING

1 Work in groups and rank the following in terms of how much they have changed the world.

a   antibiotics
b   electricity
c   mobile phones
d   the internet
e   the printing press

2a Read the introduction to a blog. What is it about?

2b Work in groups of three. Each read about one person in the blog. Then describe the person's achievements to your group.

3 Read the other two texts and answer the questions.

1   How can the information from mobile phone data in Kenya be used?
2   How did Ng make his free lectures more accessible?
3   Why won't online learning replace face-to-face learning in universities?
4   What was learnt from the Hole in the Wall experiment?

4 Match the words from the texts (1–8) with their meanings (a–h).

1   insight
2   prominent
3   epidemiologist
4   cross-reference (v)
5   artificial intelligence
6   embed
7   autonomously
8   fund (v)

a   provide money for an activity, organisation or event
b   the study of how to make computers do intelligent things that people can do
c   without the control or help of anyone else
d   a medical scientist who studies the control of epidemic diseases
e   a sudden, clear understanding of something, especially a complicated idea
f   provide references to another, related text or data source
g   important and easily seen
h   put firmly and deeply into something else

5 Considering consequences In your groups, discuss which of the three ideas will be most beneficial to mankind. Can you think of any negative consequences?

OPINION
Frances O'Connell, Technology blog

CNN has just published its list of top ten thinkers. The list honours 'people who are changing the world with their insights and innovations.' Here are my three favourites from the fields of science and technology.

To my mind, these three great thinkers are outstanding, not just for their ideas and talents but for the way they have used them to improve the lives of ordinary people – and with life-changing results. I have a feeling we have yet to see the true impact their innovations will have on the world.

Caroline Buckee is prominent in the field of medicine. An epidemiologist at the Harvard School of Public Health in Boston, she has done extensive research into malaria, a disease causing the deaths of more than 600,000 people a year.

In Kenya, Buckee and her co-workers tracked texts and calls from nearly 15 million mobile phones to establish how people move around this vast country. They cross-referenced the data against a malaria prevalence map to show how human travel can contribute to the spread of the disease. The results highlighted regions where health officials needed to focus their efforts. Warnings can now be sent to people going to and from high-risk areas. A text message can remind them to use a bed net or take other safety measures. It will help medical workers all over the world to control not only the spread of malaria but also other deadly diseases.

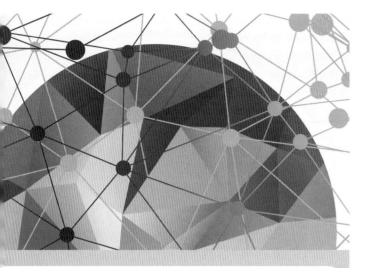

Andrew Ng specialises in the areas of machine learning and artificial intelligence. In 2008, he started a programme which placed a number of Stanford University courses online, for free, including his own course on Machine Learning. It consisted of video lectures by him and student materials used in the Stanford class. He then experimented by producing shorter clips from lectures. Finally, in 2011, he set up two open, online courses. The response was amazing. Over 100,000 students registered for the first course. He followed up by launching, with a partner, an on-line learning site, Coursera. It has become the largest open-online-course company, with 600 free courses and over 7 million registered students.

Andrew Ng does not claim that web-based courses are better than face-to-face learning. It cannot be denied that online courses lack a sense of community and one-on-one relationships with teachers. However, Ng is motivated by a passion to provide more effective online education. He has recently been hired by the giant Chinese search organisation, Baidu, as its chief scientist.

Sugata Mitra is best known for his Hole in the Wall experiment, which was set up in 1999. He embedded a computer into a wall in a New Delhi slum area and children were allowed to use it for free. Many children taught themselves to use the computer and go online, demonstrating children's capacity to learn autonomously. The experiment has since been repeated in many other locations in India, often with the same success. It has received its fair share of criticism, however. In areas without adequate adult supervision, some Holes in the Wall were vandalised, leading critics to claim that the experiment had failed. Yet despite this, many still believe Mitra's findings to be highly significant.

In 2013, Mitra won the TED prize, which awarded one million dollars to an exceptional individual. The money will be used to fund Mitra's dream of building a cloud-based school – a laboratory for children to share knowledge and connect with online mentors.

GRAMMAR
THE PASSIVE

6a Find nine examples of the passive in the texts.

6b What tense is used in each example?

7 Match the sentences (1–7) with the uses of the passive (a–g).

1   The technician was sacked yesterday.
2   The final chapter sums up all the issues that have been discussed throughout the book.
3   The trainees were impressed by the brand-new, state-of-the-art laboratory on the ground floor.
4   Penicillin is one of the most widely used antibiotics. It was discovered by Alexander Fleming in 1928.
5   Mistakes were made.
6   The research will be carried out next year.
7   Safety glasses must be worn in the laboratory at all times.

a   The agent is obvious.
b   The agent is unimportant or we don't know who the agent is.
c   If the subject of a sentence is long, we often make the verb passive so that the long phrase comes at the end.
d   We often make a verb passive so that new information comes at the end.
e   We want to avoid mentioning the agent (so as not to blame someone or to avoid responsibility).
f   We want to focus on issues rather than on the people involved, especially in scientific and academic English.
g   We are describing rules and procedures.

➡ Language reference and extra practice, pages 136–137

8 Work with a partner. Read the text and choose six places where the passive might be more appropriate.

Areha is a good example of a new town. In 1967, Eduardo Raffo designed it. Huge empty spaces and beautiful green landscapes delighted him. The Areha Development Corporation hired Raffo at the start of the project, but in 1969 they sacked him and appointed a young Italian designer instead. The authorities formally designated Areha a new town on 2 February 1972. Areha prospered for many years, but many changes have happened since the recent recession. The two main engineering companies closed down last year. However, the planners deliberately located Areha at a point equidistant from four large towns and people expect it to recover quickly once the recession is over.

SPEAKING

9 Work in groups and discuss the questions.

1   How has the world been spoilt by technology?
2   What has been lost due to technological change?
3   How has literature, the arts and music been affected by technological change?
4   Do you think technological innovation is/has been dominated by men?
5   Do/Would you prefer to learn online or face-to-face?

READING AND SPEAKING

1 Work in groups and discuss what you know about DNA.

2 Scan the first two paragraphs of the article and find:

1 what the following numbers refer to: 2007, 23, 499, 254.
2 three diseases.

3 Read the article quickly and summarise the writer's opinion about DNA testing.

4 Read the article. Take brief notes on the steps you need to go through to get your DNA profile read.

5 Identifying advantages and disadvantages What are the advantages of DNA testing? What are the problems and concerns about DNA testing?

6 Discuss the questions.

1 Would you like to have your DNA tested Why?/Why not?
2 Do you agree that some patients cannot handle information without a doctor?

Should you worry about the state of your genes?

Getting your genomic profile read can highlight medical issues, but it's also fraught with complexity and potential confusion, says Dr Phil Hammond.

Have you had your genomic profile read yet? DNA reading from spit samples has been all the rage in America since 2007 and has only recently hit the buffers.

A company called 23andMe (that's the number of paired chromosomes you have) has been at the head of the pack, charging $499 to identify over half a million code sequences in your DNA. You log into the website, fill in your credit card information and register for a genetic scan. A test tube is then sent to you in the post. You fill it with saliva, then send it back and wait eagerly for the results. After a fortnight, you can click on the website for your profile, which predicts how your genes influence your risk of developing 254 diseases and conditions such as diabetes, cancer and heart disease.

And all without having to go anywhere near a doctor. Having a peek at your genes sounds very empowering if you can afford it. And the theory is that it should allow you to take action to prevent the diseases you're most at risk of. If you have a higher genetic risk of colon cancer, then you might choose to have a colonoscopy early. I like the idea of liberating genetic information for the masses, but as with all medical tests, it can give false results and errors, and create huge anxiety if you can't handle uncertainty and complex data. And researchers are rightly wary that by bypassing proper academic assessment, we don't quite know what we've unleashed on the public.

Some American states have been very concerned that these tests can be ordered without a doctor's instruction. The paternalistic view that patients can't handle this information without a doctor on hand to help interpret it is still prevalent in health systems all over the world. But the bigger issue for me is that we don't yet know what the information means and how reliable it is, so we can't really predict with any accuracy whether the test is worth having yet.

You won't be able to get it from 23andMe at present. The company has always argued that their genetic profiling is not a medical device which is meant to give an accurate diagnosis; rather it says it sells ancestry reports and raw genetic data, without medical diagnosis. The Food and Drug Administration (FDA) in America has now sent 23andMe a warning letter arguing the opposite and claiming the company is offering a diagnostic test without proper approval.

There are lots of other concerns, too. What is the company doing with all this genetic information? Will users become research subjects for something they don't agree with? And how good is the quality control for the testing, much of which is outsourced?

By Dr Phil Hammond

VOCABULARY
COLLOCATIONS

7a Find five nouns in the article that come after the word *genetic*.

7b Find four nouns in the article that come after the word *medical*.

7c Find another adjective in the article that comes before the word *diagnosis*.

8a Match 1–9 with a–i to make collocations. Then check your answers in the article.

1	code	9	a	control
2	test	7	b	test
3	false	2	c	tube
4	complex	6	d	systems
5	academic	5	e	assessment
6	health	4	f	data
7	diagnostic	8	g	subjects
8	research	1	h	sequences
9	quality	3	i	results

8b How many other collocations can you make using the words in Exercise 8a?

GRAMMAR
COMPLEX NOUN PHRASES

9 There are different types of phrase you can use to add information after a noun. Underline the post-modifiers in the noun phrases (1–7). Then match them with the types (a–f).

1 a a diagnostic test without proper approval
2 f an essential skill required by all researchers
3 b it is not a medical device which is meant to give an accurate diagnosis
4 c the scientist talking to the journalist
5 d a suggestion that the genetic testing service should be suspended
6 a over half a million code sequences in your DNA
7 e someone to explain the data after they had taken the test

a a prepositional phrase (2 examples)
b a full relative clause
c a present participle clause
d a *that* clause
e a *to*-infinitive
f a past participle clause

10 Noun phrases can be complex and include extra information before and after the noun. What is the 'main' noun in these phrases? How many pieces of extra information have been added to each one?

1 a newly developed, inexpensive DNA testing kit which can calculate risk factors for a wide range of diseases
2 a small Los-Angeles-based company specialising in cutting-edge medical technology
3 several large-scale European research programmes into the effectiveness of different treatments for tuberculosis

11 In which two cases are you most likely to find this kind of complex noun phrase? Explain your answer.
1 academic writing
2 everyday conversation
3 journalism
4 advertisements
5 instruction manuals
6 informal emails

12 Put the words in brackets in the correct order to make noun phrases that complete the sentences.
1 _____ is to help students learn independently. (purpose / the / website / main / the / of / technology)
2 _____ is the emergence of resistance to drugs such as antibiotics. (fundamental / of / the / one / facing / problems / medicine / modern)
3 _____ is an essential skill for university students intent on academic success. (ability / the / to / decode / create / noun / phrases / complex / and)
4 _____ focuses on Mitochondrial DNA that is passed down the maternal line. (Sykes' / Professor / seminal / work / on / testing / DNA)

➥ Language reference and extra practice, pages 136–137

WRITING

13 Read these two pieces of writing. Do they flow well? If not, how can you improve them?

> modern and interactive
> ① This technology website is modern. It is interactive. It can be accessed by students in the science department. ~~The students in the science department~~ who are interested in independent learning.

> ② ~~XX~~ Even though These young people are highly educated. ~~They are~~ and well qualified, They cannot find well paid work, which would Well-paid work offers them medical insurance. It also offers other cutting basic benefits.

SITUATION

A radio station is going to have a debate in front of an audience on the theme of modern technologies. Listeners were invited to write a short essay in response to the following debating topic:
'The modern technology that has brought the most benefits to mankind, or will do so in the near future, is …'
You are one of four listeners who have been selected to take part in the radio debate. Based on your essay, you will present the case for your technology and defend your arguments before a studio audience. At the end of the programme there will be a vote and the winner will receive a cash prize.

The four topics for the debate are:
- electric cars
- fracking
- 3D printers
- surveillance technology*

*CCTV cameras, telephone tapping, speed cameras, etc.

1 Read the situation. Then work in groups and discuss what you know about each of the topics.

2 To help the four listeners prepare for the debate, the programme organisers have sent them an example presentation about mobile technologies. The presenter puts the case for mobile technologies and then answers questions. Answer these questions.

1 What arguments do you think the presenter will use to persuade his audience that mobile technologies have brought the greatest benefits to mankind?
2 What counter-arguments do you expect the audience to come up with?

KEY LANGUAGE
PERSUADING, CRITICISING, ACCEPTING CRITICISM, OFFERING COUNTER-ARGUMENTS

3a 6.1 Listen to the example presentation and answer the questions.
1 Why does the speaker quote statistics and a statement by an expert commentator?
2 According to the speaker, how does mobile technology help people in developing countries and people in business?

3b Listen again and note down examples of these persuasive techniques.
1 giving an impressive statistic
2 repeating a word or phrase
3 using a rhetorical question
4 using alliteration

3c Work with a partner and compare your ideas. Then look at Audio script 6.1 on page 171 and check your answers.

4a 6.2 Listen to the question and answer session at the end of the presentation. Tick the points the members of the audience make.
1 Mobile phone users behave impolitely.
2 People often steal mobile devices.
3 Users often find it difficult to operate mobile phones.
4 Mobile devices have a harmful effect on children.
5 Parents should not allow children to use mobile phones.

4b Listen again and note down phrases for criticising, accepting criticism and offering counter-arguments. Then look at Audio script 6.2 on page 171 and check your answers.

TASK
PARTICIPATING IN A DEBATE

5a Work in groups of four. Read the titles of the technologies on pages 161–162. Choose a different technology each to present to your group.

5b Read the description of your technology and prepare a three-minute talk about it. Use these points to structure your talk and include some of the key language.
- what the technology is
- what its uses are
- what the benefits of the technology are
- what criticisms have been made of the technology
- conclusion

6a In your groups, take turns to present the case for your technology and answer questions from other students. Each student must ask one question to each speaker.

6b In your groups, decide which technology has brought the most benefits to mankind or will do so in the near future. You cannot vote for your technology. Compare your decision with other groups in the class.

USEFUL PHRASES
Persuading
There's no doubt that …   It's undeniable that …   Surely/Clearly/Obviously, …   You must admit that …
Conceding points
I accept that …   There may be some truth in that argument.   OK, that's fair enough, but …   That's a fair point.

STUDY SKILLS
INTERCULTURAL AWARENESS

1 What does the term *intercultural awareness* mean to you? Work with a partner and discuss your ideas.

2a ▶ 6.1 Watch the first part of a talk about the personal qualities and skills people need when studying abroad. What three key qualities does the speaker talk about?

2b Watch the first part of the talk again and answer the questions.

1 At the beginning of the talk the speaker asks for a show of hands. Why does she do this?
2 What gesture does she use to introduce her three main points? What effect does this have?
3 What phrase does she use to signal that she is about to end this part of her talk?

2c Do you agree with the points the speaker makes? Work with a partner and explain your views.

3a ▶ 6.2 Watch the second part of the talk. What examples does the speaker give of non-verbal interpersonal skills?

3b Watch the second part again. Then work in small groups and discuss the questions.

1 What examples does the speaker give to show that her former student had outstanding interpersonal skills?
2 Do you think that non-verbal interpersonal skills are as important as verbal skills? Why?/Why not?

4 Work in small groups and read the three case studies opposite. Then discuss what mistakes, if any, were made by:

1 the overseas student.
2 the Japanese staff.
3 the British employee.

5a Imagine a situation in your own country involving a foreign visitor. Write a brief description (maximum 80 words) of a cultural mistake the visitor makes.

5b Work in groups and exchange your descriptions. Are your examples of mistakes similar or different?

1 The overseas student

An American student is studying for a year at a prestigious European university. In her university she has been accustomed to seeing a lecturer or the head of the department without making an appointment. The faculty has an open-door policy. During the second week at the European university, she dropped in on the department's professor to discuss changing her study programme. She was unable to see him and was told by his assistant, in a very cold tone, that she needed to send an email for an appointment and would probably have to wait at least two weeks to get one.

2 A merger between an English and Japanese company

A small Japanese financial services company has merged with an English firm. After a few months at the new head office in London, the Japanese employees are surprised to discover that the English staff, who are almost all male, are being paid a lot more than them and seem to change their jobs a lot. The Japanese are also shocked by the jokes the staff play on each other and the vulgar language they sometimes use during working hours. Most of the Japanese staff have been with their company for many years and wouldn't think of changing their jobs in order to get a higher salary. Also, they use very polite language at all times when they talk to their colleagues.

3 Communication with a state organisation

A British employee was working for a state institution attached to a government department in Central Europe. He became frustrated by the delays in getting decisions from the institution. To overcome the problem, he started sending documents directly to a senior official in the government department. The head of the institution found out that he was doing this. He was very angry and insisted that the employee show him all the documents before they were sent to the senior official.

WRITING SKILLS
REPORTING A SURVEY

6 Work in pairs and discuss the questions.

1 Have you ever participated in a survey?
2 Why do people conduct surveys?
3 How is the information used?

7a Read the report. Think of suitable headings for each of the sections and note them down in the report.

7b Compare your headings with other students.

8 Rank the survey items according to how much cultural stress the students experienced.

9a What are the main tenses or forms in sections 2, 4 and 5?

9b Why are these different tenses used?

10 You have been asked to write a report on how to reduce the cultural stress of international students. In a survey, students rated a number of suggestions on a four-point scale: excellent (*E*), good (*G*), worth considering (*WC*) and not worth considering (*NWC*). Study the results on page 162. Then write the report, recommending three actions to reduce cultural stress at the university.

International students' experience of cultural stress at a U.S. university

1 _____

A survey of undergraduate and postgraduate students' experience of culture shock was conducted by the project team, led by Anna Porter. Students completed an email survey examining their feelings of cultural stress. The student sample was fifty percent male and fifty percent female. The majority (sixty-eight percent) were 20–24 years old. Seventy percent were engaged in coursework or research in postgraduate programs. All faculties were represented. A wide range of countries was covered, with Asian countries predominating. Over twenty-eight percent of the students came from China, Thailand and Malaysia.

2 _____

A questionnaire was sent to 300 overseas students. Cultural stress was assessed by six items. These measured students' perceptions of the difficulties they were experiencing living and studying in their new culture. The students rated how six statements applied to them on a four-point scale from 0 (not at all) to 3 (very much/most of the time). Figures refer to percentages. Code: NA = not at all, TSD = to a small degree, TCD = to a considerable degree, VM = very much

3 _____

	NA	TSD	TCD	VM
I miss the way of life in my own country.	9.7	39.9	28.6	21.8
People treat me differently because of my nationality.	17.1	26.2	33.1	23.6
I feel uneasy in the USA.	47.5	40.9	9.5	2.1
I don't feel I really belong to this university.	12.0	31.0	43.9	13.1
I'm very worried about my academic progress.	42.7	32.3	11.2	13.8
I'm not happy about the balance between my studying and other activities.	45.6	18.0	14.7	21.7

4 _____

Responses to the questionnaires showed that the most significant reason for cultural stress was that international students found it hard to be away from their culture and way of life. Just over ninety percent felt distress because of that feeling.

They also had a strong impression that they did not really belong to the university (almost sixty percent). Furthermore, they perceived that people treated them differently because of their nationality (56.7 percent).

Some cultural items caused less concern than might have been expected. A majority of students (seventy-five percent) reported that they were reasonably satisfied with their academic progress. Twenty-five percent expressed anxiety about their performance.

Perhaps the most surprising result was that over eighty-eight percent of international students were reasonably comfortable about living in the USA. Moreover, a large number of the students stated that they had achieved a satisfactory balance between study and other activities.

5 _____

It is clear that cultural stress affects a large number of international students to a greater or lesser degree. They greatly miss their familiar way of life at home. It is a cause for concern that a majority of international students think that they do not belong to the university and that they are treated differently because of their nationality. The study has revealed that cultural stress is a problem at the university. Action needs to be taken to remedy the situation.

7 People and ideas
7.1 CREATIVITY

IN THIS UNIT

GRAMMAR
- quantifiers
- conditionals

VOCABULARY
- idioms with *hand*
- expressions of quantity
- irregular plurals

SCENARIO
- approving ideas, expressing doubt/objections
- a new plan for Camomila

STUDY SKILLS
- critical thinking

WRITING SKILLS
- an opinion-led essay

Creativity comes from a conflict of ideas. Donatella Versace (b. 1955), Italian fashion designer

SPEAKING

1 Work with a partner and discuss the questions.

1 Do you think creative people are born or made?
2 What do you understand by the terms *blue sky thinker*, *lateral thinker* and *someone who thinks outside the box*?
3 How creative do you consider yourself to be? What makes you think so?

2a Answer the questions in the quiz below.

Are you a lateral thinker?
Try the puzzles below
....

1 Where are all men equally attractive?
2 On which side of a cup is it best to have the handle?
3 How might someone be severely injured by being hit by some tomatoes?
4 Where do the biggest carrots grow?
5 What living thing has only one foot?
6 How many birthdays does a typical woman have?
7 A cowboy rode into town on Friday. He spent one night there and left on Friday. How do you explain this?

2b Work with a partner and discuss your ideas. Then check your answers on page 162.

LISTENING

3a You are going to listen to a lecture about creativity. How do you think the speaker will answer these questions?

1 How would you define creativity?
2 How can you recognise a creative person?
3 In which areas of work do you think creativity is a useful quality to have?
4 How is creativity different to innovation?

3b 7.1 Listen to the first part of the lecture and check your answers.

4a 7.2 Listen to the second part of the lecture and put the stages of the model of the creative process in the correct order (1–5).

a illumination
b preparation
c verification
d intimation
e incubation

4b Listen again and make notes on what the stages in Exercise 4a mean.

READING

5a **Look at the photos on page 66 and answer the questions.**

1 Who are the creative people in the photographs?
2 What do you know about them?
3 What do you think they have in common?

5b **Work with a partner and discuss the statements.**

1 More U.S. presidents have been left-handed than right-handed.
2 Left-handed people are better at foreign/second language learning than right-handed people.
3 Left-handed people are likely to win at tennis, boxing and baseball.
4 Left-handed people are generally healthier and wealthier.
5 Left-handed people are more likely to be women.
6 Right-handed people are better at doing more than one thing at the same time.
7 In the past, left-handedness was considered undesirable.

6 **Read the article. Are the statements in Exercise 5b true, false or not given?**

7 Applying ideas from the text **Work with a partner and discuss the questions.**

1 How many left-handed people do you know? Are they male or female?
2 Which ideas in the article do you think are true?
3 Do you think you can 'spot' a left-handed person? How are they 'different'?
4 Look at page 183. Which, if any, of the authors of this book do you think are left-handed? Why?

VOCABULARY
IDIOMS WITH *HAND*

8a **Complete the sentences with the idioms in the box.**

a safe pair of hands	give me a hand	got my hands full
hand in hand	hands are tied	on hand
time on my hands	turn her hand to anything	

1 I have so much work to do. I've really _____!
2 It's amazing how multi-talented she is. She can _____.
3 You can trust him with any task. He's _____.
4 I'm bored. I've got nothing to do. I've got _____.
5 I'd love to help, but I'm afraid I'm not allowed. My _____.
6 If you need anything, just call. I'm always _____ to help.
7 I'm really finding this problem very difficult to solve. Do you think you could _____?
8 Some people say that genius goes _____ with madness.

8b **Work with a partner. Use the idioms in Exercise 8a to give an example of a situation which applies to you.**

SPEAKING

9a **Work with a partner. Choose one of the objects from the box and think of new uses for it. You have two minutes to come up with ideas.**

| book | coffee cup | paperclip | pen | spoon |

9b **Repeat the process with a different object.**

9c **Join up with another pair. Turn to page 162 and discuss your results.**

On the other hand

In another instalment in our series on gifted people, Jane Frank takes a look at a very special group.

If you want a quick insight into someone's abilities, throw a ball and see which hand they catch it with. Left-handedness is relatively uncommon, accounting for around ten percent of the population. However, Chris McManus, in his book *Right Hand, Left Hand*, argues that left-handers as a group have up to now produced an above-average number of high achievers. Interestingly, five out of the last seven U.S. presidents have been left-handed.
Research by Dr Alan Searleman of St Lawrence University has shown that left-handed people are more intellectually gifted, with more of them having IQs of over 140 compared to their right-handed counterparts. They are also more creative, successful and eloquent, with vocabularies

up to a third wider. This is perhaps why there are more left-handers in creative professions such as music, art and writing. However, interestingly, one in four of the Apollo astronauts were left handed. So-called 'lefties' are also often better at sport. Left-handed college graduates in the USA have also been found to be twenty-six percent richer. Perhaps surprisingly, left-handedness is three times more common in males than in females.

So, what differentiates them? Left-handers' brains are said to be structured differently. One theory is that they process information via 'visual simultaneous' methods, where several threads of thought can be processed at the same time, making it easier for them to multi-task and solve problems than for right-handers. The latter, according to the theory, process information using analysis, breaking problems down into

pieces and analysing them one at a time. Left-handers use synthesis, which means they solve a problem by looking at it as a whole.

In spite of all their talents and skills, historically, left-handed people have often faced prejudice and discrimination. The origins of the word *left* have negative connotations in many languages. For example, *gauche*, *sinister* and *awkward* are among translations from French, Latin and German. In English, the word *sinister* became identified with evil or bad luck. Schools in many societies forced children to use their right hands, which seriously affected their development. In contrast, *right* is a synonym for *correct* or *proper* and can stand for authority and justice in English and in many European languages.

In the final analysis, however, it may be that left is, in fact, better than right!

SPEAKING

1 Work in groups. Think of five great thinkers whose ideas have influenced people's lives and rank them in order of importance. Then compare your ideas with another group.

2 What do you know about Confucius, Swami Vivekananda, Sir Isaac Newton and Ibn Sīnā?

READING

3 Read the texts quickly and note down key information about each person.

4 Read the texts again. Who:

1 lived the longest?
2 lived the earliest in history?
3 covered the greatest variety of topics in his writings?
4 had his works studied at tertiary level in Europe?
5 gave a talk asking for acceptance of all religions?

5 Work with a partner and discuss the questions.

1 Which of the people in the texts did you find the most interesting? Why?
2 Who, in your opinion, is/was the most important thinker in your country?

Confucius was a Chinese thinker and social philosopher, whose teachings and philosophy deeply influenced thought and life in a variety of countries, including China, Korea, Japan and Vietnam. He was born in Lu State in 551 BC and died in 497 BC. In China he was better known as 'Master Kong'. A number of academics have compared Confucius' influence on Chinese history with that of Socrates in the West. His social philosophy, recorded in *The Analects*, largely revolved around the concept of *rén*, 'compassion' or 'loving others'. Confucius believed that the ruler lived to serve the people and should have a range of qualities, namely *Lǐ* (observing ritual, propriety and etiquette), *Yì* (righteousness) and *Xìn* (honesty and trustworthiness). He also believed in ancestral worship, strong family loyalty and respect to elders.

Swami Vivekananda, also known as Narendra Nath Datta, was born in Kolkata, India, in 1863 and died in 1902. Vivekananda was one of India's most influential spiritual teachers and helped introduce eastern philosophy, yoga and meditation to the West. He spent a considerable amount of time meditating and taught a philosophy of traditional meditation and selfless service. In 1893 he was invited to speak at the World Parliament of Religions in Chicago, where he called for tolerance and the end of religious fanaticism. He spoke for freedom for Indian women and an end to the worst of the caste system. His books on the four yogas (Raja, Karma, Bhakti and Jnana) remain very influential. His letters were of great literary and spiritual value and he was also considered an outstanding singer and poet.

Sir Isaac Newton was a brilliant physicist and mathematician who invented calculus and formulated the laws of gravity, force and motion. Newton's First Law of Motion stated that the natural state of an object is to remain at rest if it is at rest and to continue to move if it is already moving. His concept of inertia stated that an object with a large amount of inertia will have a large mass and an object with a small amount of inertia will have a small mass. Modern physics really started with Newton because he produced the first fundamental theory of mechanics and gravitation in his book *Principia Mathematica*. He modestly said, 'If I have seen further than others, it is by standing upon the shoulders of giants.' He was born in 1642 in England and died in 1727.

Ibn Sīnā, often known by his Latin name of Avicenna, was a physician and the most famous of the philosopher–scientists of Islam. He was born in Uzbekistan in 980 and died in 1037. He wrote around 450 works on a wide range of subjects, including philosophy, astronomy, psychology, Islamic theology, mathematics and poetry. He was the greatest writer of medicine in the Middle Ages and his book *The Canon of Medicine* was required reading throughout European universities until the seventeenth century. He was a pioneer in the area of mental health, believing that a significant proportion of illnesses were psychosomatic. The Avicenna Directories, a global database of medical schools and health institutions, was named after Ibn Sīnā, demonstrating his lasting influence on the development of medicine and health sciences in the East and the West.

VOCABULARY
EXPRESSIONS OF QUANTITY

6 Look at the expressions of quantity in the box. Then find more expressions in the texts.

a bunch of	a couple of	a great deal of
a large quantity of	a pair of	
a slight majority of	a tiny proportion of	

7 Choose the correct words to complete the sentences.

1 Newton's work attracted *a considerable amount of / a slight majority of* criticism.
2 Ibn Sīnā learnt *a great deal of / a couple of* Arab poetry.
3 Alchemical books made up *a pair of / a significant proportion of* Newton's personal library.
4 Vivekananda travelled widely in the USA lecturing on *a wide range of / a tiny proportion of* subjects.
5 The Confucius Institute offers *a wide variety of / one of* language programmes.

LISTENING

8a **7.3** Listen to a radio programme about the ideas of two more great thinkers, Keynes and Aristotle, and note down the two most interesting things about them.

8b **7.4** Evaluating a summary Listen to the first part of the programme again and choose the best summary of what Professor Kotov said.

> **A** Professor Kotov thinks it is time to re-evaluate the work of economist John Maynard Keynes in these difficult economic days, when he would have advocated more government spending on construction and transport to help the economy grow.

> **B** Professor Kotov said that John Maynard Keynes thought governments should spend more in an economic downturn in order to stimulate the economy. He also said that Keynes' ideas were out of fashion, but now they are back.

8c **7.5** Listen to the second part of the programme again and write your own summary (about 40 words) of what Dr Petrakis said.

GRAMMAR
QUANTIFIERS

9 Look at the quantifiers in bold in Audio script 7.3 on page 172 and write them in the correct place in the table. Then add as many other quantifiers as you can think of.

+ singular noun	+ plural noun	+ uncountable noun
	many	

➡ Language reference and extra practice, pages 138–139

10 Answer the questions.

1 Read these sentences. How does *of the* before a plural or uncountable noun change the meaning? *I need some information. I need some of the information.*

2 What is the difference between:
   a *every, all, each*?
   b *little/a little, few, a few*?

3 What is the difference between these statements?
   a *She had seen neither Aristotle nor Plato at Plato's academy.*
   b *She had not seen either Aristotle or Plato at Plato's academy.*

4 What is the difference between these statements?
   a *I like all classical music.*
   b *I don't like some classical music.*
   c *I don't like any classical music.*

11 Complete the text with quantifiers. Sometimes more than one answer is possible.

Nearly [1]_____ of the problems of philosophy were defined by Socrates, Plato and Aristotle. However, Aristotle is known for being one of the [2]_____ figures in history who studied almost [3]_____ subject possible at the time. He wrote [4]_____ texts on the sciences and the arts. He also wrote [5]_____ texts on ethics, the major one being *Nichomachean Ethics*. His most famous work was [6]_____ *Nichomachean Ethics* or *Politics*.

In *Politics*, Aristotle says: 'Democracy is when those who do not own [7]_____ property, but are poor, have authority in the system of government. [8]_____ men are rich, but [9]_____ are free. Democracy is when [10]_____ free citizen has authority. It is democracy when [11]_____ the citizens can deliberate about everything.'

Very [12]_____ information exists about what Aristotle looked like, but he was known to be a kind-hearted man devoted to his family and his friends. He liked to spend a [13]_____ of time walking with his students discussing philosophical problems.

SPEAKING

12 Work in small groups. Take it in turns to give a short talk about one of the great thinkers you thought of in Exercise 1.

▶ MEET THE EXPERT

Watch an interview with Mairi Ryan from the Royal Society of Arts, about their public events programme.
Turn to page 152 for video activities.

SPEAKING

1a Identifying outcomes **Work in small groups and discuss these ideas. Think of as many positive, negative and interesting outcomes as possible.**

1 making all countries drive on the right rather than the left
2 in hot countries, painting all roofs in cities white to save energy
3 arranging all products in supermarkets alphabetically
4 making all young people join the army for a year
5 making chewing gum illegal
6 wearing facemasks when you have a cold

1b **Which of the ideas in Exercise 1a are good? Which are bad? Why?**

READING

2 **Scan the texts and find:**

1 the most common type of book on the book-swapping website.
2 the writer's criteria for a personal trainer.
3 the inventor of the light bulb.

3 **Read the texts again and answer the questions.**

1 Which text mentions something that:
  a once was only for the elite?
  b has improved since its first appearance?
  c is fundamentally the same as when it first appeared?
  d can be recycled via the internet?
2 Which idea appeals to you the most?

4a **Find words in the texts with these meanings.**

1 the amount of electricity, gas, oil or energy that is used (text A)
2 substances that are sent out into the air (text A)
3 within reach and not too difficult to achieve (text B)
4 limited to particular people or groups (text B)
5 too fat in a way that is dangerous to your health (text B)
6 works well and is the result of clever thinking and new ideas (text C)

4b **Write sentences using the words in Exercise 4a.**

SHARING GOOD IDEAS

(A) **Switching to LED bulbs**

People choose electronic LEDs (light emitting diodes) because they last for ages, never break and reduce your energy bill. Traditional light bulbs haven't changed much since Thomas Edison invented them in the late 1870s. You flip a switch and the bulbs give you light. They are simple, but they are fragile and don't last very long. LEDs light up almost immediately and can take a knock, given their solid construction. They are used in flashlights and miner-style head torches. They are being used more and more in homes due to their falling prices. Originally, there was a problem with their blue-white colour, which was a side effect of a chemical used in their manufacture. Now they give off a warm, yellow light. Conversion to LED lighting would reduce our energy consumption by approximately one third, cut our energy bills and reduce carbon emissions.

(B) **Personal training**

I'd have paid for a personal trainer ages ago if I'd realised how motivating they were. Mine is qualified and meets all the criteria I required (fit, passionate about health and fitness, patient, motivational, flexible, good at setting attainable goals and a good communicator). Personal training used to be an exclusive service to the rich, but it is now accessible to millions of people with many choosing one-to-one fitness advice, more tailored personal programmes and group training sessions over gym workouts. The fitness industry is constantly evolving with new training techniques emerging, such as high-intensity interval training and bodyweight training. With half of the Western world's population predicted to be obese by 2050, there will be no shortage of customers. I've definitely been convinced – if I hadn't signed up for personal training, there's no way I'd be as fit as I am now.

VOCABULARY
IRREGULAR PLURALS

5a Complete the table. Then check your answers in a dictionary.

Singular	Plural
1 criterion	_____
2 phenomenon	_____
3 hypothesis	_____
4 _____	analyses
5 _____	theses

5b Tick the correct sentences. Correct the mistakes in the incorrect sentences.

1 He wrote an excellent doctoral theses.
2 There is a strange phenomena that occurs every year in this part of the world.
3 You still haven't proved this hypothesis.
4 What are the criteria for selecting the best idea?
5 We are carrying out a detailed analyses of the test results.

C Book swapping

If I had a euro for every book I had read once and then dumped on a shelf, I would be a rich woman. Many of us own hundreds of books that will never be read again. Up till now, the only book sharing I have done has been with friends and my book club.

You could try www.readitswapit.com. This is a website that lets you exchange the books you won't read again for books that you do want to read. All users of this ingenious website provide a list of their unwanted books. If you find a book you like, you email its owner. The owner then looks at your list. Hopefully, they will see a book they like. Then you both send each other your books. Simple. Currently, there are a lot of thrillers and mysteries such as *The Da Vinci Code*, but if you look hard enough, you'll find something you like.

GRAMMAR
CONDITIONALS

6a Look at these examples from the texts. Which type of conditional (first, second, third, zero or mixed) are they?

1 I'd have paid for a personal trainer ages ago if I'd realised how motivating they were.
2 If I had a euro for every book I had read once and then dumped on a shelf, I would be a rich woman.
3 If you find a book you like, you email its owner.
4 If you look hard enough, you'll find something you like.
5 If I hadn't signed up for personal training, there's no way I'd be as fit as I am now.

6b Which conditional do we use to talk about:

1 likely conditions (things which are very likely to happen)?
2 unlikely conditions (things which might happen, but probably won't)?
3 impossible conditions (things which are unreal and did not happen)?
4 general conditions (things which can occur at any time and often occur more than once, and their results)?

7a Match 1–8 with a pair of clauses (a–h) to make sentences.

1 If they'd brought a map,
2 If you solve the problem,
3 If I were you,
4 If I had my own car,
5 If I'd worked harder,
6 If you don't leave right now,
7 I'll phone the hospital
8 If the ball touches the line,

a I'll phone the police./you'll regret it.
b it's in, not out./don't blow your whistle.
c I could have gone to college./I'd have passed the exam.
d I'll buy everyone dinner./you'll feel a lot better.
e I'd listen to her very carefully./I wouldn't tell her.
f I'd go away every weekend./you wouldn't have to take me to work.
g if you don't have time./if you want.
h they wouldn't be lost now./they would have arrived on time.

7b Match the sentences in Exercise 7a with their functions.

a advice
b offer
c promise
d instructions/rules
e criticism
f regretting
g threats
h imagining, wishing

➥ Language reference and extra practice, pages 138–139

SITUATION

Camomila is a city in South America. It is situated on flat land and surrounded by mountains. Several rivers and streams run through the city. At times there is heavy rainfall and the summers tend to be very hot and humid. The population has grown rapidly over the years to almost two million because of immigration and its appeal to eco-tourists (it is not far from the Amazon rainforest). There is now a thriving industrial area, with many multinational companies, a growing number of electronics enterprises, and large commerce and service sectors.

The new Mayor of the city, Eduardo Alves, is determined that Camomila will become a model city in South America. However, at present the city has a number of serious problems. As a result, the Mayor has hired a firm of international consultants, JBUP, to come up with ideas for improving the city. He has specified that he wants practical, inexpensive solutions which will involve the participation of the local community as much as possible. As consultants of JBUP, you must find the solutions the Mayor is looking for.

1 Read the situation. What problems do you think have arisen because of:

1 the climate?
2 the rapid increase in population?

2 `7.6` The Mayor, Eduardo Alves, accompanied by the councillor responsible for environmental affairs, Manuela Lopes, is meeting the director of JBUP. Listen to the first part of their conversation and make notes on the problems which have arisen concerning:

1 green spaces.
2 the downtown shopping district.
3 buses.
4 trains and stations.
5 flooding.
6 children.

KEY LANGUAGE
APPROVING IDEAS, EXPRESSING DOUBT/OBJECTIONS

3a `7.7` Carl and Christina from JBUP have joined the group. Listen to the second part of the conversation and answer the questions.

1 What does the Mayor propose to make the city 'greener'?
2 What advantages of his proposal does he mention?

3b Match the extracts from the conversation (1–12) with their functions (a–c).

1 Sounds like a great idea.
2 I'm not too keen on this one.
3 I think there'll be some real problems.
4 It would be a very expensive option.
5 But looking after the trees might not be such a big problem.
6 I think it's a really good suggestion.
7 Some of the projects must be for the long term.
8 Will it really work?
9 I just don't think it's feasible.
10 You have to trust local people and give them responsibility.
11 It's a good project, in my opinion.
12 It may not cost as much money as you think.

a approving ideas
b expressing doubt/objections
c offering counter-arguments

TASK
A NEW PLAN FOR CAMOMILA

4 Work in groups. You are consultants at JBUP. Read JBUP's report and choose 4–6 problems. Brainstorm ideas for solving the problems and note down your solutions.

Report

The federal government has given the city a large grant to finance its urban plan. However, the Mayor and city council will welcome solutions which represent value for money, are relatively inexpensive and involve the local community.

Problems

- traffic jams in the downtown shopping district
- frequent flooding in the city
- lack of green spaces in the city
- small, overcrowded buses
- increased crime on the buses
- not enough places for young and old to meet
- no reliable system of dealing with rubbish; usually left outside houses and buildings
- insufficient hotels for tourists; poor quality and service
- lack of courtesy towards tourists; many complain about bad behaviour of young people at night
- overcrowded housing; shabby, run-down houses and apartments, especially in the highly populated, new-town areas
- a large number of 'street children'
- architects do not create green spaces when they build schools, office blocks, apartment buildings, etc.
- lack of facilities in the city: not enough hospitals, theatres, cinemas, art galleries, museums

5a In your groups, try to agree on a plan for the future development of Camomila.

5b Decide which solutions should be given priority and which could be delayed until a later date.

5c Compare your group's plan with the plans of other groups.

STUDY SKILLS
CRITICAL THINKING

1a Work with a partner and discuss the questions.

1 Why is critical thinking such an important skill?
2 What other skills are important for success in the twenty-first century?

1b 7.8 Listen to a teacher talking about critical thinking. What key points does he make? Make notes. Are they the same points as the ones you discussed in Exercise 1a?

2 Read this essay question and the essay on page 75 and answer the questions.

How relevant are the ideas of Jean-Jacques Rousseau to today's educators? Discuss the question and state your opinion on the topic.

1 What is the writer's opinion concerning the topic?
2 In what part(s) of the essay can the reader find the writer's opinion?
3 What area of education does the essay focus on?

3 Work with a partner and discuss the questions.

1 Which two of Rousseau's ideas does the writer present in the essay?
2 What evidence does the writer give in each case to show that Rousseau's ideas are still relevant to today's educators?
3 What do you think are the strongest pieces of evidence he or she offers? Give reasons for your answers.
4 Has the writer presented his or her arguments in a logical, coherent form? Give reasons for your answer.

4 Find words or phrases in the essay with these meanings.

1 start to use something (paragraph 1)
2 give, communicate (paragraph 2)
3 questioned (paragraph 2)
4 tasks requiring people to work together (paragraph 3)
5 emphasised (paragraph 4)
6 presented a point of view (paragraph 5)
7 the most basic and important part (paragraph 6)
8 cannot be challenged or debated (paragraph 7)
9 having a strong effect on something or someone (paragraph 7)
10 better than (paragraph 7)

5 Read the last paragraph of the essay again. Summarise in one sentence the difference between the child-centred and teacher-centred approaches to education.

6 Read the essay again. In groups, make a list of questions you have about the essay and discuss them.

7 Work with a partner and try to persuade each other that your approach gets the best results.

Student A: Prepare an argument in favour of the child-centred approach to educating children.

Student B: Prepare an argument in favour of the teacher-centred approach to educating children.

8a Tick the ideas that you think Rousseau would have agreed with. Then read the essay again and check your answers.

1 educating children to develop their character and moral sense
2 using education to teach children self-control and to be good human beings
3 including physical training in the curriculum
4 giving children a lot of books to read
5 ensuring the child does not learn anything that he or she is not ready to understand
6 educating children's emotions before their reasoning
7 getting students to memorise facts
8 recommending teachers to do more talking in the classroom than their students
9 paying careful attention to the environment in which children study
10 encouraging children to draw conclusions from their experience
11 teaching young adults a manual skill, such as carpentry, as a means of making a living
12 seeing the role of the teacher as facilitating opportunities for learning
13 allowing questions only at the end of a class
14 setting frequent continuous assessment tests of students' knowledge of a subject

8b Which of the ideas in Exercise 8a do you think should be the aims of educators?

1 **Jean-Jacques Rousseau** was a French philosopher and educationalist writing in the eighteenth century. He set out his ideas on education in a novel entitled *Emile*, published in 1762, which describes the ideal education of the book's main character, Emile. Rousseau's ideas have undoubtedly influenced generations of teachers, and his approach to educating young children, in particular, has been put into practice in primary schools all over the world.

2 According to Rousseau, the main purpose of education was not to impart information, but to bring out what was in each person. He did not believe that children should be stuffed with facts, but rather that they should be able to think for themselves and form their own opinions. Education, therefore, should consist of allowing the child as much freedom as possible. Surely, this idea would not be challenged by modern, progressive teachers. And isn't it even more valid now that young people can obtain facts so easily from the internet?

3 There is no doubt that Rousseau's ideas, which were taken up by later educationalists, have greatly influenced the modern approach to a style of education called 'child-centred learning'. This focuses on the needs of children rather than on those of teachers and administrators. The child-centred teacher creates an environment which will encourage children to discover new skills and knowledge. Such teachers create activity centres in the classroom, encourage peer-tutoring and get children to work together on group projects.

4 The importance of Rousseau's ideas to contemporary teachers was highlighted in John Darling's 1994 book *Child-Centred Education and its Critics* (1994:17). The author argues that the history of modern educational theory is a series of footnotes to Rousseau.

5 Another of Rousseau's important ideas was that things rather than people should be used to train a child. He argued that a teacher or parent should never lecture or preach to a child, and that experience and interaction with things was a more effective teacher. For example, when Emile breaks a window, he finds that he gets cold because the window is not repaired. I would argue that this is a perfect example of what modern educationalists call 'discovery learning'.

6 This idea is also at the very heart of the world-famous Montessori method of teaching children. In Montessori schools, which can be found all over the world, the classrooms are filled with games and equipment which children can use to learn skills and gain knowledge. The essence of Montessori teaching is that children learn by experience rather than being told things by a teacher.

7 It is undeniable that Rousseau has been very influential in promoting a child-centred approach to learning, in which the child is an active, responsible participant in his or her own learning. This approach is surely preferable to the teacher-centred approach, which has the teacher in an active role and the students in a passive, receptive role. Modern teachers owe an enormous debt to Rousseau's revolutionary approach.

WRITING SKILLS
AN OPINION-LED ESSAY

9 **Complete the text with the words in the box.**

evidence	ideas	overall	persuade
reasons	summarised		

An opinion-led essay gives an opinion and supports it with [1]_____. The aim of the writer is to [2]_____ the reader to agree with the opinion and to show [3]_____ for a particular opinion. The introduction gives a(n) [4]_____ view of the essay. In the main body of the essay, evidence is presented that supports the thesis. The most important [5]_____ usually come first. In the conclusion, no new evidence is given. The main idea is [6]_____ and the argument is restated.

10 **Read the statements. Do you agree or disagree?**

In the opening paragraph of an opinion-led essay, you should:

1 introduce the subject of the essay.
2 refer to the main point(s) in the question.
3 copy several phrases from the question.
4 try to paraphrase the question.
5 state clearly your opinion on the topic.
6 indicate the scope of the essay.

11a **Read the essay again. Analyse the structure the writer has used to present his or her ideas in the essay. What information is included in each paragraph?**

11b **Work with a partner and discuss your analysis.**

12a **Essay planning Work in groups. Think of some arguments for and against the opinion expressed in the essay. Try to support each argument with reasons and evidence.**

12b **Choose one of the essay questions and plan your essay using the structure below.**

1 Write an opinion-led essay strongly agreeing or disagreeing with the writer of the essay opposite.
2 Choose an influential thinker and write an opinion-led essay on whether you agree or disagree with his/her ideas.

- introduction (general statement, introduce the subject)
- body (arguments + evidence, most important ideas come first)
- conclusion (summary, restatement of your opinion)

13 **Essay writing Write your essay.**

8 Journalism and media

8.1 BREAKING NEWS

IN THIS UNIT

GRAMMAR
- verb patterns
- prepositional verbs

VOCABULARY
- the media
- dependent prepositions

SCENARIO
- being cautious
- resolving ethical dilemmas

STUDY SKILLS
- style and register

WRITING SKILLS
- formal, neutral and informal emails

For most folks, no news is good news; for the press, good news is not news.   Gloria Borger (b.1952), American journalist

SPEAKING

1 Work in small groups and discuss the questions.

1 'Newspapers will soon be a thing of the past.' Do you agree? Why?/Why not?
2 Where do you get the news from (e.g. TV, newspapers, radio, the internet – traditional sites and social media)? Why?
3 What are the advantages and disadvantages of each? Think about speed, convenience, cost, reliability and any other considerations.

2a Complete the statements with the words in the box.

bias   deadline   privacy   record   scoop
sources   speculation

A good news journalist:

1 never misses a _____.
2 respects the _____ of public figures.
3 deals in facts rather than _____.
4 will do almost anything for a _____ or to break a story.
5 always identifies their _____.
6 allows people to speak off the _____ to protect themselves.
7 reports honestly, objectively and without _____ .

2b Work with a partner and discuss the statements in Exercise 2a. Do you agree? Which are the most important?

3a What are these people's roles in the media? Work with a partner and discuss your ideas.

a reporter
b paparazzo
c editor
d producer
e blogger
f correspondent
g anchor
h moderator
i columnist

3b Do you think working in the news media is an attractive profession? Why?/Why not?

LISTENING

4 8.1 Justifying choices Listen to six people who work in the media talking about their jobs. Which part of the news media do you think each speaker works in? Why?

a print media
b broadcast media (TV/radio)
c online media

5a Listen again. Match each speaker (1–6) with one of the job titles (a–i) in Exercise 3a.

5b What difficulties with their job does each speaker mention?

6 Which job would you most like to do? Why?

VOCABULARY
THE MEDIA

7a Look at some words and phrases from the listening. What do you think they mean?

a sound bite   blogosphere   broadsheets
circulation figures   citizen journalism   go viral
hits   libel laws   the tabloids   trending
spin   viewing figures

7b Check your answers. Match the words and phrases in Exercise 7a with their meanings.

1 the number of newspapers sold
2 the number of people who watch a broadcast
3 official rules governing what you may say about people in print
4 present a positive view of something to influence people
5 a very short part of a speech or statement
6 the 'popular press'
7 quality newspapers, the 'quality press'
8 the number of visits to a website
9 passed from person to person on the internet
10 popular at the moment (especially on social media)
11 when ordinary people gather and spread news
12 personal websites and blogs

READING

8a Read the headlines. What do you think the stories are about?

A GOVT TO CRACK DOWN ON NET CRIME
read more

B TV STARS SPLIT TO WED

C OLYMPIC CHIEF IN VOTE RIGGING ROW
UPDATE

D MINISTER QUITS OVER COVER-UP

E DANCER BACKS PRIVACY LAWS
read more

F NATIONAL SPEED LIMITS SET TO CHANGE

G FOOTBALL BOSS AXED
read more

H MURDER PROBE: POLICE QUIZ MODEL

I NEW SCANDAL HITS DIET GURU

J MOVE TO CURB JUNK FOOD SALES
read more

K PM PLEDGES TAX CUT
UPDATE

L FREAK FLOODS TOLL RISES

M CAT SAVES OWNER FROM BLAZE DRAMA

N UN URGED TO ACT OVER NEW CLASHES
UPDATE

8b Which headlines refer to:
1 losing a job?
2 a rescue?
3 new rules/controls?
4 an investigation?
5 a planned reduction in something?
6 death?
7 a romance?
8 an argument/fighting?
9 an embarrassing situation?

9 Answer the questions.
1 Which tenses/verb forms are used in the headlines?
2 Which time do they refer to?
3 What do you notice about the language used?

10 Rewrite the headlines as full sentences.

A *The government is going to take strong action against crime on the internet.*

SPEAKING

11 Work in groups. You are producers of a thirty-minute news programme with an audience demographic of 18–35-year-olds. The headlines in Exercise 8a are the possible stories for today's edition of the programme. Follow these steps.

1 Discuss the possible content of each story and decide how interesting they would be for your viewers.
2 Choose five stories for your programme. You may also include one extra item of 'breaking news' (your own idea).
3 Decide a running order for the stories.
4 Decide how much time will be spent on each story. Will it contain an interview? If so, who will you interview?
5 Present your ideas to another group.

READING

1a Predicting You are going to read an article by Simon Jenkins, an experienced journalist. Predict the skills and qualities you think he will say are needed for a career in journalism.

1b Read the article quickly to find out how many of your predictions were correct.

2a Read the article again and choose the best introductory paragraph.

> 1 **According to Simon Jenkins, the best journalists are great writers with an extensive knowledge of the English language and a solid training in how to write.**

> 2 **Are journalists born or made? According to Simon Jenkins, while the basics can be taught, first there has to be an intense curiosity about the world and a love of the written word.**

2b Read the article again and answer the questions.

1 What does Jenkins find upsetting in written English these days?
2 What does Jenkins compare learning the technique of writing clear English to?
3 Which parts of speech did Jenkins' sub-editor like and which did he not like?
4 Where did Jenkins learn how to write clear English?
5 What do the best journalists do when they meet an exciting person or visit a beautiful place?
6 What are the most important qualities for journalism?
7 What is more important: a story or journalism?

3 Which of the sub-editor's rules does this paragraph break?

It is interesting to see that the three key problems were punctuality, truancy and bad behaviour. Unfortunately, the police had to be called to the run-down state school on several occasions.

HOT OFF THE PRESS

Simon Jenkins, *The Guardian*

A Journalists are creatures of nature, not nurture. The profession develops from instinct, from a peculiar way of seeing and describing the world. It may be objective in practice, but it is subjective in motivation.

B Journalism is expressed in the written or spoken word, but I have never regarded that as its essence. The technical skill is that of creating clear and succinct sentences, which any profession should inculcate. This can be taught and should be part of any core curriculum. Its absence from so much of written English nowadays, from users' manuals to student exam questions to government white papers, is deplorable. I sometimes think a well-produced newspaper is that last redoubt of clear English. There is no talent for such technique. While some people pick it up quickly, it must be acquired, as must a skill at playing the piano. Like many ingénue journalists, I acquired it first in the trial and error of a student newsroom and then went on to a more formal training, in my case with *The Times* newspapers.

C The latter's educational supplement, then integrated with the main paper, possessed two invaluable bits of equipment. One was a source of stories, the politics of education, to which little harm could be done by my reporting. The other was a ferocious Irish sub-editor. He would score through superfluous words, underline bad grammar and mercilessly spike articles, leaning back in his chair, removing his glasses and asking the classic question of any journalism teacher: 'Now, what is it you are really trying to tell me?'

D I absorbed his maxims like mother's milk. Never begin a paragraph with *it*. Make every paragraph a single idea. Nouns and verbs are the workhorses of a sentence, never qualifiers. Delete every adjective and adverb from your story and reinsert only those that appear essential. Never use sloppy words such as *supply, problem, accommodate* and *interesting*, and try to use concrete, not abstract nouns. The best punctuation is a full stop.

E That training was a privilege greater than anything I acquired at school or university. It was the toolkit for a career, always to be kept oiled and polished. I watched colleagues floundering as they sought to fashion stories in ignorance of its framework.

F I used to ask aspiring journalists whether they kept a diary. What was their instinctive response to meeting an exciting person or visiting a beautiful place, to any highly charged emotion? Did they crave to communicate their experience through the written word? It is the best indicator I know of a natural reporter.

G The qualities essential to journalism thus extend far beyond an ability to write. They are those of curiosity, an uninhibited mind, native cunning and an eagerness to communicate, summed up in the gift to narrate. Such is the raw material on which the story depends and without which there is nothing to say. There can be a story without journalism, but no journalism without a story.

4 Find adjectives in the article with these meanings.

1 based on opinions and feelings rather than on facts (paragraph A)
2 clearly expressed, with no wasted words (paragraph B)
3 very bad (paragraph B)
4 extremely useful (paragraph C)
5 unnecessary (paragraph C)
6 carelessly expressed (paragraph D)
7 hoping to be successful at something (paragraph F)
8 not restrained in any way (paragraph G)

5 Paraphrase the following sentences from the article in simple English.

1 I absorbed his maxims like mother's milk.
2 I watched colleagues floundering as they sought to fashion stories.

LISTENING

6a 8.2 **Listen to an experienced journalist talking to a group of students and answer the questions.**

1 What advice is given to those who want to go into journalism by:
 a Joseph Pulitzer?
 b the speaker?
2 What current topic in journalism is the speaker going to look at towards the end of the talk?
3 To what extent does the speaker agree with Simon Jenkins?

6b Listen again and complete the sentences. Then look at Audio script 8.2 on page 174 and check your answers.

1 I'd like to congratulate you on receiving the 'Best _____.
2 First of all, I'm not going to apologise for being a journalist, even though we are not _____.
3 I can't stand listening to complaints about _____.
4 Put it before them briefly _____, clearly so they will _____, picturesquely so _____ and above all, accurately so they will _____.
5 Always treat the reader with _____ and don't make them feel inadequate.

GRAMMAR
VERB PATTERNS

7a Look at the phrases in bold in Audio script 8.2 on page 174 and match them with these patterns.

1 verb + *to*-infinitive
2 verb (+ object) + *to*-infinitive
3 verb (+ object) + infinitive without *to*
4 verb + *-ing*
5 verb + preposition + *-ing*
6 verb + object + preposition + *-ing*

7b Look at Audio script 8.2 again and find other examples of the patterns in Exercise 7a.

8 What is the difference in meaning between these sentences?

1 You don't want them to stop reading.
2 You don't want them to stop to read.

9 Choose the correct form to complete the sentences.

1 I really want *work / to work* for a national newspaper.
2 He doesn't mind *to work / working* late.
3 My teacher persuaded me *study / to study* journalism at college.
4 My boss wouldn't let me *write / to write* the story about the police and the politician.
5 My boss encourages us *to take / taking* tea breaks during the working day.
6 Do you remember *to go / going* for your first job interview?
7 She promised *to file / filing* the story before midnight.
8 I can't stand *read / reading* about celebrity gossip.
9 She blamed me for *delete / deleting* the file, but it wasn't me!

➥ Language reference and extra practice, pages 140–141

10 Complete the sentences with your own ideas. Use the correct verb patterns. Then work with a partner and compare your answers.

1 I don't mind _____.
2 My parents persuaded _____.
3 I promised _____.
4 Next year I really want _____.
5 My parents always encouraged _____.
6 I can't stand _____.
7 Once I blamed my friend _____.
8 I remember _____ when I was a child.
9 When you go out, you must remember _____.

SPEAKING

11 Work in groups and discuss the statements.

1 Journalists invade people's personal lives and publicise things that people want to keep private.
2 There is no higher claim to journalistic integrity than going to jail to protect a source.
3 Journalists are born, not made.

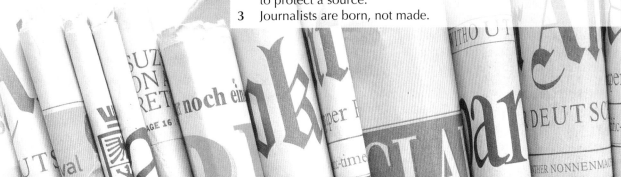

VOCABULARY AND SPEAKING

1a Which social media sites can you think of? Which ones do you use?

1b How many news stories can you think of that started through social media?

2a 8.3 Listen to the introduction to a conference talk. What is the talk about?

2b Listen again and complete the phrases 1–6.

1 I'd like to focus _____ social media
2 to allow time _____ questions
3 please feel free _____ interrupt
4 There won't be any handouts going _____
5 I'd like to begin _____ telling you
6 you thought you were signing _____ for a conference

3 Work in pairs. Brainstorm ideas for a talk on social media. Prepare a short introduction and present it to each other using some of the phrases in Exercise 2b.

READING

4 Scan the transcript of the rest of the talk opposite and answer the questions.

1 How did Chris Hadfield become famous?
2 Which forms of social media did he use?

5a Read the transcript again and answer the questions.

1 What do you think Hadfield wanted to achieve by communicating through social media?
2 What three things does the speaker believe made his campaign a success?

5b What do you think are the most important elements of a successful social media campaign? Compare your ideas.

---

watch   read   participate   about

Transcript

Chris Hadfield
Conquering social media

Well, the two are actually very closely connected. Chris Hadfield is of course the Canadian who spent five months on the International Space Station in 2012 and 2013. He became what many have called the most famous spaceman since Neil Armstrong due to his hugely popular social media campaign, culminating in his zero-gravity version of David Bowie's *Space Oddity*.

Sadly, although Hadfield's Major Tom is no longer available via official channels, his popularity keeps on growing and he now has well over a million Twitter followers, substantially more than the 20,000 or so he had when he left Earth. His media campaign, which was largely run by his sons, focused on using YouTube, Twitter, Facebook, Google+, Tumblr and Reddit – remember his AMA*! – as well as more traditional media outlets, and it offers lasting lessons in understanding how to engender public interest in a subject that could appear dry and boring. And this is why I am talking about him!

So what did he do? It wasn't just that he was online, anyone can do that. In my opinion, there were three important aspects of Hadfield's approach. Firstly, he targeted a specific audience – tech-savvy young people – and captured and kept their attention by posting multiple tweets, photos and videos every day. He didn't bore us with details of scientific data he was collecting, but instead shared stories about day-to-day life in space.

Secondly, because he is a natural and enthusiastic storyteller, these anecdotes – from how to make a sandwich to what happens if you cry in space – succeeded in entertaining as well as informing his audience.

Ah, I see one of you has just tweeted a great question: yes, let me answer that! 'How did he let us know about crying in space?' Well, he uploaded videos of himself on YouTube squirting water into his own eye to show that the water stays in place – it doesn't roll down your face! His answer was aimed at everyone and it's a good example of how he never took himself too seriously. It also made him appear human: he's a spaceman who knows what happens if you cry in space, and we can all connect with that.

So to come back to the third and final point I wanted to make, I believe Hadfield had a clear message that he wanted to share. He didn't say it explicitly, but he demonstrated it persistently in his posts and videos throughout the months he was in space – that is, the idea that space exploration is cool, fascinating and worth spending money on.

So what can we take away from all this? Well, I think the three factors I've described can be applied to all communication via social media, whether you're writing your own blog or planning a corporate social media campaign. If you want to know more, read my blog: 'to get a memorable message across, stay on message and stay human!'

*AMA = ask me anything

GRAMMAR
PREPOSITIONAL VERBS

6a Look at the highlighted prepositional verb in the article and complete the rule.

Prepositional verbs are the combination of a(n) _____ and a(n) _____.

6b Does the verb *look* have the same meaning in these sentences? If not, what changes the meaning?

1   I haven't had time to look at the news on the internet.
2   Police are looking into the disappearance of two children.
3   His dad left him here to look after the business while he's away.

6c Rewrite the sentences replacing the words in bold with the correct form of the prepositional verbs in the box.

come across	come up	get on	get over
look at	look into	look like	look round

1   Anyone who doubts the power of social networking only needs to **observe** the activity on Twitter.
2   How are you **progressing** at work?
3   A free micro-blogging service that started in 2006, Twitter **resembles** an on-screen bulletin.
4   An opportunity has **arisen** for a Twitter correspondent at Sky News.
5   I am resisting an urge to **investigate** Twitter in case it is as addictive as Facebook.
6   If Twitter ever suffers a catastrophic failure it cannot **recover from**, you will still be protected from any data loss.
7   We **inspected** the new office to see if the building was suitable.
8   I've seen a really interesting anecdote on Twitter. I **found** it by chance.

GRAMMAR TIP

We can put adverbs of degree and manner between the verb and preposition, but not between the preposition and object.

He dealt mostly with compelling stories. ✓
He dealt with mostly compelling stories. ✗

➡ Language reference and extra practice, pages 140–141

7 Complete the text with prepositional verbs from Exercise 6c.

Journalists need to be familiar with technical developments in the media. They shouldn't just
¹_____ social networking sites; they need to use them because familiarity with the tools is important. They need to ²_____ their sources from Facebook, MySpace and Twitter and any other type of social media as carefully as they would verify traditional sources. They need to restrict access to private profile information that they don't want the general public to ³_____ by chance. They need to manage their time and their social media efficiently so that they are aware of new stories as soon as they ⁴_____. Although blogging and tweets may ⁵_____ conversation, journalists must be mindful that they represent more than just themselves.

LISTENING AND SPEAKING

8a Evaluating effectiveness How effective are different forms of media for gathering and reporting news? Think about social media, blogs and traditional media such as newspapers and TV.

8b **8.4** Listen to five people talking about different forms of media and answer the questions.

1   Which forms does each speaker mention?
2   Which forms does each speaker prefer? Why?

8c Compare what the speakers said with your own ideas from Exercise 8a.

WRITING

9 Write a short paragraph on one of these statements.

1   It is more important to get news fast than to get it accurately.
2   Social media is replacing mainstream mass media.

▶ MEET THE EXPERT

Watch an interview with Dr Nell Haynes, an anthropologist, about the impact of social media.
Turn to page 153 for video activities.

SITUATION

The *Daily Chronicle* is a daily newspaper in Chicago. Its feature articles focus on scandals in government departments or on misconduct by prominent personalities. The newspaper often sails close to the wind to get its stories and its journalists have been accused of invading people's privacy and showing bias in their reporting. When chasing stories, the newspaper's editor and reporters inevitably face ethical dilemmas.

1 Read the situation. What do you think the phrase *often sails close to the wind* means?

2 Read about a dilemma the newspaper must resolve. Then work with a partner or in small groups and discuss the questions.

The Editor of the sports section of the *Daily Chronicle* has been offered copies of confidential emails sent by the Head Coach of a top baseball team to the owner of a rival team. The source of the emails wishes to be paid $200,000 for the copies. The emails reveal that the Head Coach is considering leaving his present job to coach the rival team. This would be a bombshell in the sporting world and a report in the newspaper about the coach's plans would greatly increase its circulation.

1 What are the advantages and disadvantages of running a story about the Head Coach based on the information in the emails?

2 Should the Sports Editor publish a story about the Head Coach based on what he/she has learnt?

KEY LANGUAGE
BEING CAUTIOUS

3a **8.5** **Listen to the Sports Editor discussing the dilemma with the Chief Editor and answer the questions.**

1 What reason does the Sports Editor give for wanting to buy the emails?
2 What are the Chief Editor's reasons for not wanting to buy the emails?
3 What is the Sports Editor going to do now?

3b **Being cautious** Listen again and complete the sentences.

1 We need to _____ this one _____, Dan. … If you don't get your facts right, he could _____ and get substantial _____.
2 There's a problem with this material. We have no idea how our source got the information. Maybe he did something _____ and if that's the case, we could be in very _____.
3 I don't think our readers will thank us for running the story. It's a very _____ issue. If we get our facts wrong, it'll have a(n) _____ on our reputation. We wouldn't be able to say where we got our information from, so it would look like pure _____ on our part.
4 No, sorry, we need to _____ on this one. I've got a bad feeling about it. It could land us in _____ if the emails are not genuine.

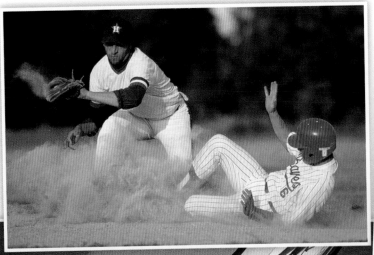

TASK
RESOLVING ETHICAL DILEMMAS

4 Work with a partner and read the descriptions of the ethical dilemmas opposite. Then choose one and discuss the questions.

5 Join up with another pair and summarise briefly the dilemma you chose. Tell them what decision you made, with your reasons. Ask them if they agree with your decision.

6 As a group, discuss what guidelines you could give journalists faced with the kinds of dilemmas described.

USEFUL PHRASES

Considering implications

It could be too risky.
It might damage our reputation.
It may be illegal.
He/She could take us to court.
He/She might take legal action.
They might/could sue us.

Proposing solutions

The best thing to do is …
The answer to this is to …
The best way to deal with it is to …
The best way forward is to …

THE FASHION SHOW

Following the launch of his revolutionary autumn fashions, Emilio Conti gave a present to each journalist that he had invited to the event. They received a bag containing a press kit and a box that the journalists opened after they left the restaurant. Each box contained a Rolex watch worth $30,000, with the journalist's name inscribed on the back. The next day Emilio Conti emailed each journalist, thanking them for attending the launch and ending his message with the words *I look forward to reading your report of our trail-blazing launch*. Articles by influential fashion journalists often determine the success or failure of a fashion collection. What should the journalists do? Accept the gift graciously or take some other action? Consider the implications of your recommended action. Give your reasons.

THE FOREIGN CORRESPONDENT

The foreign correspondent of the *Daily Chronicle* has won many prizes for his outstanding reports from war zones. He is well known for taking high risks in such areas. He is sent to report on a conflict in a very dangerous country. The Chief Editor warns him that he must not take any risks at all to gather information because of the extremely unstable situation in the country. The correspondent ignores the editor's warning because he has heard of a mass killing of citizens near the front line. He goes there to investigate and is kidnapped by some anti-government forces. The kidnappers have threatened to kill the journalist unless the newspaper pays a huge ransom to free him. What should the Chief Editor do? Give your reasons.

A DRAMATIC PHOTO

The Sunday edition of the *Daily Chronicle* is planning to feature an in-depth article on the wars between two rival gangs. The newspaper's photographer has a horrific photo of a police officer walking down a street carrying a young gang member who has been severely wounded by gunshots. Behind them, lying near the pavement, are the dead bodies of two other gang members. There is a lively debate going on in the newsroom as to whether the photo should be put on the front page of the newspaper to accompany the article. What do you think? Should the newspaper use the photo? Give your reasons.

A QUESTION OF CONFIDENTIALITY

A reporter on the *Daily Chronicle* has been contacted by an employee who works for a wealthy businessman. The businessman is well known and highly respected for the huge donations he makes to charities. The employee says that he has knowledge of a dark secret about the businessman's past. He will reveal it to the journalist in return for a suitable payment. He hints that the story will be a huge scoop for the *Daily Chronicle* and that revealing the secret will destroy the reputation of the businessman. Should the reporter agree to meet the employee? If he does, should he pay the contact for his story? Give your reasons.

STUDY SKILLS
STYLE AND REGISTER

1a What is style and register? Why is it important?

1b Look at the genres in the box. Which:
1 tend to be formal?
2 tend to be informal?
3 can be both?

---

academic essay   advertisement
business letter   dissertation   email
personal diary

1c Look at the emails. Decide whether each one is formal or informal. How do you know?

2a Look at these language features. Are they formal (*F*), informal (*I*) or can they be both (*B*)?

1 contractions (e.g. *he's, I'd, we'll, they're*)
2 using single verbs rather than phrasal verbs (e.g. *eliminate* rather than *wipe out*)
3 linkers like *nevertheless, moreover*
4 starting sentences with linkers like *and, but, so, talking about, another thing*
5 personal pronouns (e.g. *I, you, we*)
6 vague language (e.g. *stuff, things, nice*)
7 using tentative, hedging language (e.g. *it is likely to, there is a tendency for*)
8 frequent use of the passive
9 short phrases instead of sentences (e.g. *Got your message. No time to reply.*)
10 dramatic punctuation (e.g. frequent use of question and exclamation marks, dashes and bullet points)
11 complex sentence structures
12 technical language connected with one particular subject

2b Work in groups and discuss what other differences you can think of between formal and informal writing.

3a 8.6 Listen to the first part of a lecture about formal and informal writing. What key points does the speaker make? Make notes. Then compare them with your answers to Exercises 2a and 2b.

3b 8.7 Listen to the second part of the lecture and answer the questions.
1 What is the neutral style of English, according to the speaker?
2 In what situations is it commonly used?

1 NEW MESSAGE
Subject   Article feedback

This is to inform you that your article has been rejected by our editorial team as its style is inappropriate and you have failed to support your point of view with facts and research. If you would like us to reconsider it, we would suggest that you edit it, write it in a more accessible style and refer to previous studies of obesity.

2 NEW MESSAGE

You know that article, the one I've been slaving away at? Yeah, well, you're not going to believe this: I sent it to a newspaper and you know what? They don't want to use it. Thought it was rubbish. Hey, I did my best, it's not the end of the world, but there's no way I'm going to edit it or rewrite it. That's what they suggested. Must be joking! I don't know if I'll send it to anyone else. Guess I'll wait and see.

4 Work in groups. Look at these sentences from essays by Journalism students. In five minutes, write down as many formal alternatives as you can for each word or phrase in bold. The group with the most formal words is the winner.

1 The world of journalism has changed **a lot** in recent years.

2 Journalists are becoming **more and more** aware of the need for high ethical standards.

3 Texting is a new way of **giving** news.

4 Journalists have **come up with** innovative methods of reporting news.

5 All journalists must **weigh up** information from sources to decide if it is reliable.

6 Terrorists rely on the **idea** that they are well trained, but this is not always so.

7 Journalists are often accused of **making up** information.

8 Extensive research has been **done** into the attitudes of Facebook users.

9 Articles **handed in** by journalists are frequently edited.

10 The **bad** effects of the internet are discussed in the report.

11 There have not been **enough** academic studies of social networking language.

12 The industry must **get rid of** phone hacking as a means of getting information.

13 An individual's right to privacy is a **thing** that is often discussed in the press.

14 Journalists often find it difficult to be **fair** when reporting events.

WRITING SKILLS
FORMAL, NEUTRAL AND INFORMAL EMAILS

5 Work with a partner. A student at a school of Journalism has missed the deadline for submitting an essay. Think of some reasons he can give to ask for a deadline extension.

6a Read the email the student sent to his college tutor, Professor Barbara Friedman. Professor Friedman expects students to write fairly formally when they communicate with her. Work in pairs and analyse the good and bad points of the student's email. Comment on both the content and style of the email.

From	Charlie.Smith@my:emails.uk
To	Friedman.B@college.network.uk

Hi Barbara. Well, as you know by now, I didn't get my essay in on time. So sorry, please forgive me. Anyway, I guess you want to know why. You see, it was like this: I had a huge exam on Wednesday in another subject. So I worked day and night to prepare for it. I seemed to spend my whole time drinking cups of black coffee! Anyway, I was totally wiped out after it – couldn't get down to studying the next two days. Like I said, I had zero energy. Hope you understand. Not like me to miss deadlines, is it? How about this? Can you give me more time – say, a week? Like I said, I was tired out, but now I'm raring to go. A week more would be great. It'd give me time to write some really good stuff for the essay. I promise you, you won't be disappointed if you could do that for me. Thanks so much for reading my email. Enjoy your weekend – fab weather at the moment, isn't it? Have fun! Charlie.

6b Rewrite the email in a more formal style.

6c Compare your email with the possible answers on page 163.

7 Do one of the following tasks.

1 Write an email to a Chief Editor of a quality newspaper pitching your own idea for an article.

2 Write a formal email to a professor in your subject area at your college or university, asking the professor if you could work with his research team during your holiday.

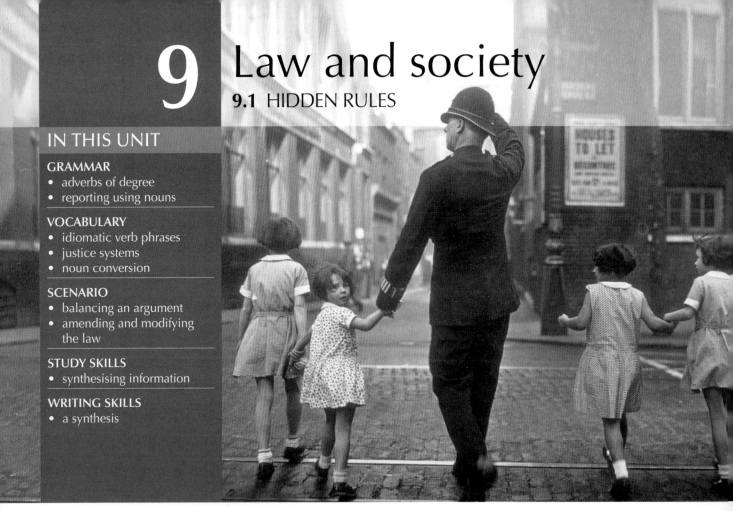

9 Law and society
9.1 HIDDEN RULES

IN THIS UNIT

GRAMMAR
- adverbs of degree
- reporting using nouns

VOCABULARY
- idiomatic verb phrases
- justice systems
- noun conversion

SCENARIO
- balancing an argument
- amending and modifying the law

STUDY SKILLS
- synthesising information

WRITING SKILLS
- a synthesis

Law applied to its extreme is the greatest injustice. Cicero (106–43 BC), Roman lawyer, politician and philosopher

SPEAKING

1a **Complete the statements with the words in the box.**

class	culture	economic	laws	policy	public

1 _____ development causes great social and cultural change.
2 People's friends and relationships are determined by their social _____.
3 Government _____ directly reflects social attitudes.
4 _____ protest is futile as it never achieves its aims.
5 Youth _____ has little impact on mainstream society.
6 Relatively few _____ affect the public's general social behaviour.

1b **Work in groups and discuss your opinion of each of the statements in Exercise 1a.**

READING

2a **Read the extract from *Watching the English* on page 87. What are the book's key topics? Describe the style and register of the language in the extract, giving examples.** semi-formal

2b Identifying claims **Read paragraphs 1 and 2 again and discuss the questions.**

1 Identify all the points the author makes in the first two paragraphs. Is each point a proven fact or an informed claim? How can some of the claims be questioned?
2 Look at the claims you identified again. Which are main topic sentences? Which support or illustrate the main claim?
3 What is your personal evaluation of the claims the author makes? What are your thoughts on the overall topic?

3 **Read paragraphs 3–6 again and discuss the questions.**

1 Which three phrases describe the types of rules under investigation?
2 Which definitions of the word *rule* do these examples match?
a I generally go swimming in the morning.
b You must not eat in the classroom.

LISTENING

4a 9.1 **Listen to five extracts from a radio serialisation of the book and answer the questions.**

1 What social contexts are discussed?
2 What is the underlying principle or rule that she draws out of each example?

4b Listen again and answer the questions.

1 What are the specific examples in each case?
2 What is the author's view of the role privacy plays in social rules?
3 What is the author's opinion of the reputation that drivers have?
4 Why does the author describe the publican or restaurateur as 'poor'?
5 What is the author's claim about humour in other cultures?
6 Which fact do some foreigners think the English are relatively unaware of?

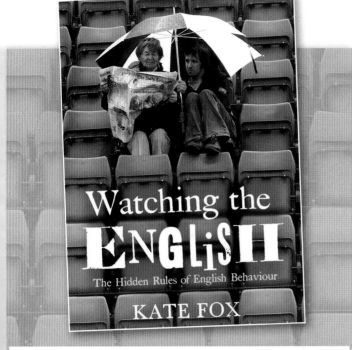

Watching the
ENGLISH
The Hidden Rules of English Behaviour
KATE FOX

1 The human species is addicted to rule making. Every human activity, without exception, is hedged about with complex sets of rules and regulations, dictating precisely when, where, with whom and in what manner the activity may be performed. Animals just do these things; human beings make an almighty song and dance about it. This is known as 'civilisation'.

2 If you think about it, we all use difference in rules as a principal means of distinguishing one culture from another. The first thing we notice when we go on holiday or business abroad is that other cultures have 'different ways of doing things', by which we usually mean that they have rules about, say, food, mealtimes, dress, greetings, hygiene, trade, hospitality, joking, status-differentiation, etc., which are different from our own rules about these practices.

3 The object (of my observational research) was to identify the commonalities in rules governing English behaviour – the unofficial codes of conduct that cut across class, age, sex, region, sub-cultures and other social boundaries.

4 Most people obey the unwritten rules of their society instinctively, without being conscious of doing so. For example, you automatically get dressed in the morning without consciously reminding yourself there is an unspoken rule of etiquette that prohibits going to work in one's pyjamas. But if you had an anthropologist staying with you, she would be asking: 'Why are you changing your clothes?'

5 I am using a rather broad interpretation of a rule, based on four of the definitions allowed by the *Oxford English Dictionary*, namely:
 • a principle, regulation or maxim governing individual conduct
 • a standard of discrimination or estimation; a criterion, a test, a measure
 • an exemplary person or thing; a guiding example
 • a fact, or the statement of a fact, which holds generally good; the normal or usual state of things

6 Thus, my quest to identify the rules of Englishness is not confined to a search for specific codes of conduct, but will include rules in their wider sense of standards, norms, ideals, guiding principles and 'facts' about 'normal or usual' English behaviour.

VOCABULARY
IDIOMATIC VERB PHRASES

5a Match 1–8 with a–h to make verb phrases.

1	mind	a	something for granted
2	make	b	attention to yourself
3	draw	c	something is amiss
4	wash	d	your own business
5	take	e	something to a halt
6	bring	f	your dirty linen in public
7	know	g	your responsibilities
8	shirk	h	a scene

5b Work with a partner. Look at Audio script 9.1 on page 175 and find the verb phrases from Exercise 5a. Then discuss their meanings.

5c Complete the sentences with the correct form of verb phrases from Exercise 5a.

1 She keeps asking me where I got the money from. I wish she would just _____ .
2 If you decide to become team captain, you can't be lazy and _____ .
3 I know you're angry, but please don't _____ – not here in the library.
4 You have to work at a relationship; you can't just _____ love _____ .
5 I _____ , but I'm not sure exactly what. Let's ask Sarah if she knows about any problems.

SPEAKING

6 Think about your society and answer the questions.

1 Discuss any 'unwritten rules' that apply to these contexts:
 • work/business
 • public transport/cars
 • restaurants/food
 • homes/domestic life
 • social/leisure time
 • shopping/street life

2 What happens when people break the rules?
3 Are there any written or explicitly spoken rules concerning social behaviour (e.g. train companies ask passengers to let people off a train before boarding)?
4 Are there any rules that should be written to improve social behaviour?

▶ MEET THE EXPERT

Watch an interview with Nik Peachey, an educational consultant, about body language in different cultures.
Turn to page 153 for video activities.

SPEAKING

1 Work with a partner and discuss the questions.

1 Which of these examples of criminal or antisocial behaviour are commonly associated with teenagers in your country?

- vandalism
- graffiti
- car theft
- online bullying
- shoplifting
- financial fraud
- bank robbery
- street robbery
- playing loud music in public places

2 Do you think your country has a problem with juvenile crime?

2 Most countries have a minimum age of criminal responsibility. What do you think are the minimum ages for these countries? Add the countries to the table. Then check your ideas on page 163.

- the USA (most states)
- Iran (girls only)
- China
- the UK
- Turkey
- the Democratic Republic of the Congo

AGE OF CRIMINAL RESPONSIBILITY
(Below this age, children cannot be dealt with as criminals.)

7	Pakistan, [1]_____
9	Ethiopia, [2]_____
10	Thailand, Ukraine, [3]_____
12	Japan, Belize, the Netherlands, [4]_____
14	Germany, Italy, Russia, [5]_____
15	Iran (boys only)
16	Belgium, [6]_____
18	Argentina

3 Work with a partner and discuss the questions.

1 How does the age of criminal responsibility in your country compare to other countries?
2 Do we need an age of criminal responsibility?
3 What is a suitable minimum age?
4 How does it compare to other legal ages (e.g. age for marriage/driving)?

VOCABULARY
JUSTICE SYSTEMS

4a Complete the abstract for a paper on youth crime with the words in the box. Use a dictionary to help you.

care   community service   courts   custodial
delinquency   deter   deterrent   offenders
punishment   rehabilitation

Youth crime and punishment: a global perspective
Abstract: Despite frequent statistical evidence and perhaps due to political and media claims, the public perceive juvenile [1]_____ to be increasing. This paper describes global approaches to juvenile justice, with a focus on the balance between rehabilitation and [2]_____ when dealing with convicted young [3]_____. Most countries have dedicated youth [4]_____ and juvenile detention centres. A few countries, such as Japan, deal with young offenders solely within the [5]_____ system rather than the justice system. Within justice systems there are two types of sentence: non-custodial and [6]_____. The former includes curfew and control orders, fines and [7]_____. In contrast to adult justice systems, there is often a stronger emphasis on [8]_____ than on simple punishment, although there is a recent trend in some countries, such as the USA, towards harsher punishment, which is justified as being a stronger [9]_____ to potential young criminals. Critics of this trend claim that imprisonment does not [10]_____ as it does not take into account the difficult backgrounds of many criminal adolescents.

4b Work with a partner and discuss the questions.

1 What do you know about the juvenile justice system in your society?
2 Is there a current trend in your country that is similar to that in the USA?
3 Where do you stand on the rehabilitation, punishment and deterrence debate?

READING AND LISTENING

5 Read the brochures opposite and compare two approaches to the treatment of juvenile delinquents in the USA. In what ways do the approaches act as punishment, rehabilitation and deterrence?

6a 9.2 **Listen to the first part of a talk on teenagers by forensic psychologist Diana Kott. What is her argument and what is your opinion of it?**

6b 9.3 **Listen to the second part of the talk and make notes on these psychological traits.**

- fairness
- respect
- encouragement, not punishment
- reject imposed structure
- need guidance
- feel competent and successful
- need to belong
- family

7 Evaluating with criteria **Work with a partner and evaluate the two juvenile punishment programmes with regard to the key teenage psychological traits. Which programme is more appropriate for teenagers?**

8 9.4 **Listen to Diana Kott's evaluation of the two programmes. How similar are her points to yours? Make notes and compare with your partner.**

GRAMMAR
ADVERBS OF DEGREE

9a `9.5` **Complete the sentences with adverbs. Then listen and check your answers.**

1 ... boot camps _____ address juveniles' psychological problems.
2 However, as the teenagers _____ lack the chance to determine the structure ...
3 ... they are _____ certain to see things as unfair.
4 The _____ complex range of tasks and skills required at wilderness camps ...

9b Answer the questions.

1 What types of words do the adverbs in Exercise 9a modify?
2 Which of the adverbs amplify or intensify the meaning of the word they modify?
3 Which of the adverbs decrease or soften the meaning of the word they modify?

9c Look at Audio script 9.4 on page 176 and find more examples of adverbs. Then answer the questions.

1 What is the effect of these adverbs?
2 Can you think of any more similar adverbs?
3 You can say something is *absolutely excellent*, but not *absolutely good*. Why? Which of the other adverbs are similar?

➥ Language reference and extra practice, pages 142–143

SPEAKING

10 Work in groups and discuss the questions.

1 Look at the different types of punishments. What are their advantages and disadvantages when dealing with juvenile crime? Is the seriousness of the crime relevant?
   a imprisonment in a youth detention centre
   b corporal punishment
   c community service, e.g. cleaning streets
   d psychological therapy
   e electronic tagging, curfews and movement restriction
   f fines
2 Is there a difference between the reality of juvenile crime and the public perception of juvenile crime in your country?
3 What is your general view of your country's legal and justice system?

BOSTON BOOT CAMP: DISCIPLINE, STRUCTURE, REFORM

Based on the principles of military training and discipline, Boston Boot Camp gives juvenile delinquents a short, sharp shock that instils respect for authority, rigorous self-discipline and a sense of honor. We change their lives for the better and turn them into respectable members of society.

Teens stay at the camp for thirty to sixty days, removing them from the negative influences of their local community, peers and regular lifestyle. There is no TV, radio or internet. They wear uniforms, live in dormitories and follow an intensive program of physical military training, work, drill exercises and educational experiences.

We operate on a 'Yes, sir! No, sir!' principle. If they obey and follow the rules, they are rewarded. If they break rules or show disobedience, they are punished with further physical exercises. This gives the teens meaningful consequences of their actions.

Our camps are a vital part of the juvenile justice system. We reform disrespectful youths and our methods also act as a deterrent for would-be criminals and recidivists.

Aspen Forest: Wilderness therapy camp

Our camp offers a character-development program for troubled teens that promotes personal growth through living and surviving in the wilderness. The remote setting removes urban distractions and our program's nurturing approach helps students address personal issues, achieve success and develop their leadership potential.

The two-month program consists of two integrated dimensions. One involves learning camp-craft, hiking trips, nature education and physical activity. In order to overcome the challenges that nature presents, communication, teamwork, self-discipline and self-reliance are keys to success and students gain an understanding of actions and consequences.

The other dimension involves counselling, group therapy and reflective writing. The spiritual dimension of life in the wilderness, as a teen watches the sun set over the mountains, can encourage greater insight and personal change than a psychologist's office ever could.

During the final stage, each student takes on leadership responsibilities and assists in teaching new participants. Family involvement is important: parents are in regular contact with their child's counsellor and engage in letter writing to their child.

SPEAKING

1 Work with a partner and discuss.

How do you think a person who has to leave their home country – perhaps for ever – may feel? What do you think he/she would miss most? Think of two possessions he/she might want to take with him/her.

2 Work with a partner and complete the quiz.

HOW MUCH DO YOU KNOW ABOUT INTERNATIONAL MIGRATION?

1 What percentage of the world's population are international migrants?
a 9.4   **b** 3.2   **c** 0.9

2 What is the median age of international migrants?
a 38.4   **b** 32.7   **c** 24.5

3 What percentage are women?
a 48   **b** 36   **c** 27

4 Look at this list of the ten countries which have received the largest number of international migrants. Which do you think are the top three? Australia, Canada, France, Germany, Russia, Saudi Arabia, Spain, the UAE, the UK, the USA

5 The vast majority of migrants move from developing countries to developed countries. True or false?

6 What is the world's largest 'corridor' of migration?
a from India to the UAE
b from Bangladesh to India
c from Mexico to the USA

7 What percentage of migrants are refugees?
a 3%   **b** 7%   **c** 11%

LISTENING

3a 9.6 **Do you think these statements are true or false? Work in groups and discuss. Then listen and check your answers.**

1 International migration is increasing.
2 The majority of international migrants are legal.
3 Migrants can create economic growth in the host country.
4 Migrants are heavy users of public services in the host country.

3b Listen again and make notes on the points in Exercise 3a. Then work with a partner and compare your notes.

GRAMMAR
REPORTING USING NOUNS

4a Look at the examples of nouns used for reporting. Then look at Audio script 9.6 on page 176 and find other examples.

Claims that migrants are taking our jobs … are easy to find …

A very frequent comment people make is that …

4b Look at the sentences you found in Audio script 9.6 and match them with these structures.

1 Their <u>claim is</u> (that) migrants take our jobs. This is false.
2 Their <u>claim that</u> migrants take our jobs <u>is</u> false.

➥ Language reference and extra practice, pages 142–143

5 Make nouns from the verbs in the box. Then use them to report the comments.

accuse	answer	claim	declare	observe	remark

1 'I told you before: I've got dual nationality.' 'But we've discovered you haven't.'
His _____ that he had dual nationality turned out to be false.
2 'We want to stay in this country.' 'I'm afraid you can't.'
They asked for asylum, but the _____ was *no*.
3 'They're really backward.'
Her _____ about the immigrants' customs was offensive.
4 'A lot of them have got really good skills.'
The _____ that many of the migrants were highly skilled was made by several politicians.
5 'It's nonsense to say that border security is lax.'
The government issued a(n) _____ that border security was not lax.
6 'You entered the country illegally.'
The _____ was levelled against him that he had entered the country illegally.

VOCABULARY
NOUN CONVERSION

6a Which of the verbs and adjectives in the box can be used as nouns without adding an affix?

complain	complex	do	hopeful	international
local	mention	must	responsible	trust

6b Complete the sentences with nouns from Exercise 6a.

1 He passed the citizenship test, so we're having a little _____ to celebrate.
2 She arrived in the country aged five and is now a presidential _____.
3 Learning the language is an absolute _____ for new migrants.
4 He was a very talented footballer and the first England _____ who was born abroad.

READING

7 You are going to read two poems about migration. Work in groups and discuss the questions.

1 When was the last time you read a poem?
2 Do you know any poems or lines of poetry by heart?
3 In which situations in life do people sometimes turn to poetry?
4 What do you understand by the terms *metaphor* and *simile*?

8a Read the poems and the texts about the poets. What is your first response to the poems?

8b Interpreting poetic language Work with a partner and discuss the questions.

1 In *Immigrant*, what is the function of the first line of the poem?
2 The non-native pelicans are trying to emulate the native swans. How successful are they in doing this?
3 Why does the poet focus on the pelicans?
4 Marks and Spencer is a very popular clothing store in the UK. Why is she wearing a 'Marks and Spencer's jacket'?
5 Why does she test her accent 'secretly'?
6 What do 'London' and 'home' represent for the poet in *Like a Beacon*?
7 Thinking about the overall shape of the poem *Like a Beacon*, what is the significance of line 8?
8 Find an example of a metaphor and a simile in the poems.
9 Can you see one or two similarities and differences between the poems?
10 Which poem do you like best? Why?

WRITING

9 Choose one of the following writing tasks.

1 Has your country experienced migration recently or in the past? Write three or four paragraphs on what people in your country think about migration. Read your paragraphs to another student. Do you have the same ideas?
2 Write a short poem of your own about migration. Choose any aspect of the topic you like. If necessary, use the poems in Exercise 8a to help you.

LONDON
Poems on the Underground

Fleur Adcock is a New Zealander by birth, but spent part of her childhood in England, returning to live in London in 1963. The influence of her migratory childhood can be traced in her work's exploration of identity. Several of the poems examine roots and rootlessness. Her characteristic tone is restrained, rational, conversational.

Immigrant

November '63: eight months in London.
I pause on the low bridge to watch the pelicans:
they float swanlike, arching their white necks
over only slightly ruffled bundles of wings,
burying awkward beaks in the lake's water.
I clench cold fists in my Marks and Spencer's jacket
and secretly test my accent once again:
St James's Park; St James's Park; St James's Park.

FLEUR ADCOCK (b. 1934)

Grace Nichols was born in Guyana and moved to live in the UK in 1977. Her work has been central to our understanding of the important cultural Caribbean–British connection. The poems are influenced by the history and culture of her homeland and are characterised by an acute attention to the language.

Like a Beacon
In London
every now and then
I get this craving
for my mother's food
I leave art galleries
in search of plantains
saltfish/sweet potatoes

I need this link

I need this touch
of home
swinging my bag
like a beacon
against the cold

GRACE NICHOLS (b. 1950)

SITUATION

There is a new government which intends to unify many of the currently separate state laws. The policy department is currently drafting new laws to fulfil the party's manifesto pledges. The initial proposals have had a poor reception as they were perceived as being too strong and as failing to take into account important exceptions. The policy department has to redraft the laws, maintaining their efficacy whilst eliminating their drawbacks.

1 Read the situation and the extracts from the manifesto and discuss the questions.

1 What laws could be made to meet these manifesto commitments?
2 In your country, which laws relate to these particular issues?

2 Read these current law proposals. Which manifesto commitments have not been addressed?

1 There will be a complete ban on the sale of chocolate and salty snacks to children aged under sixteen, and children will not be allowed to consume more than one sugary fizzy drink per day. Shopkeepers and parents will be liable to fines.
2 There will be a complete ban on the use of plastic shopping bags, enforceable with fines up to $10,000.
3 There will be a complete ban on the carrying of knives in public places.
4 All drivers entering city centres must pay a charge per visit of $75.
5 Parents of children who are absent from school without permission will be punished with fines or imprisonment.

A safer society

We can only have a safe society if we have strong laws that address the current problems. We will introduce new laws to deal with the recent rises in knife crime, aggressive antisocial behaviour and racial intolerance.

A healthier society

At times, the government has to bring in laws that will promote a healthier society for the good of everyone. We will introduce legislation concerning smoking and unhealthy food.

A greener society

The time to act is now, and we are the party that will take that action. We will reduce the use of cars, the use of plastic shopping bags and encourage the use of alternative energy sources.

An educated society

In this information age, we need to ensure that the education of our youth is at the forefront of government policy. We will introduce new laws to reduce truancy and also raise the minimum school-leaving age to seventeen across the nation.

3a 9.7 Listen to a discussion about the re-drafting of one of the laws in Exercise 2 and make notes on these points.

- aim of the law
- strengths
- weaknesses

3b Work with a partner and discuss how you would choose to amend this law.

3c 9.8 Listen to the final decisions and answer the questions.

1 How do the decisions compare to your ideas?
2 What is your opinion of the amended law?
3 Is there anything similar in your country?

KEY LANGUAGE
BALANCING AN ARGUMENT

4a 9.9 Listen to extracts from the discussion in Exercises 3a and 3c and complete the sentences.

1 … lowest achievers. _____, this law is not solely about children.
2 Now, _____ we're here to amend this law, I think that …
3 That's _____, but it's _____ too inflexible …
4 Well, _____ it's important that the law sends out a strong message, _____ think there must be some …
5 Well, _____ that as a fair principle, we mustn't make it …
6 … about fines? _____, imprisonment would be a deterrent, but, overall, I'm not sure …
7 I see _____ one thing I like about the current proposal is that …

4b The phrases you wrote in Exercise 4a are used to balance an argument, in particular, to show that we accept the validity of one point and also accept a contrasting or conflicting point. Answer the questions.

1 Can you remember the arguments that surrounded the phrases in Exercise 4a? Look at Audio script 9.7 on page 177 and check.
2 In each case, can you say which argument the speaker favours?

TASK
AMENDING AND MODIFYING THE LAW

5 You work in the policy department and have to modify the four remaining laws from Exercise 2. Work in two groups and follow the instructions.

Group A: You are responsible for laws 1 and 2.
Group B: You are responsible for laws 3 and 4.

- Discuss the laws you are responsible for and identify their strengths and weaknesses.
- As you criticise the laws, propose amendments.
- As a group, decide which amendments to make and, finally, rephrase the law.

USEFUL PHRASES

Managing a discussion

So, what are your thoughts on this first one?
Look, we've got to make a decision on this. Which do you prefer?
Surely, it's time to move on, isn't it?
Shall we leave this one for a while and come back to it later?
Any other last points to make?

6 Work with a student from the other group. Present your amended laws and the thinking behind the amendments. Evaluate the other student's amended laws. Should further changes be made to any of the laws?

STUDY SKILLS
SYNTHESISING INFORMATION

1 Work in groups and discuss the questions. Make notes on your ideas and report the main points of your discussion to another group.

1 To what extent is unemployment a problem in your country? Is it a particular problem for young people?
2 What are the causes and effects of unemployment? What are the solutions?
3 How much should governments help unemployed people?
4 Martti Ahtisaari, the Finnish winner of the 2008 Nobel Peace Prize, said that youth unemployment is perhaps the greatest challenge in the world. Do you agree?

2 Choose the correct definition for the word *synthesis*.

1 a short statement that gives the main information about something, without giving all the details
2 something that has been made by combining different things, or the process of combining things
3 a statement that expresses in a different (or clearer) way what someone has said or written

3 It is sometimes argued that there are two main types of synthesis: background synthesis and thesis-driven synthesis. Match each type with a description (1 or 2) and an example (a or b).

1 Information is brought together from a variety of sources and organised by topic. Aim: to inform.
2 Information from different sources is used to develop and strengthen an argument. Aim: to persuade

a a lawyer in a court presenting a case for the prosecution or defence
b a website listing flights available with different airlines

4 Think of one or two activities you often do as a student and how they involve synthesis.

WRITING SKILLS
A SYNTHESIS

5 9.10 Hassan is going to write a dissertation on the effects of unemployment on young people. He has downloaded a podcast on writing a literature review. Listen to the podcast and take notes to answer these questions.

1 What is a literature review?
2 What purposes does it serve?

6 Look at the six steps we follow when we write any kind of synthesis. Number them in the correct order.

a Write your synthesis using your own words and citing relevant authors.
b Read material from different sources that will help you do the task.
c Check the synthesis against the original texts to make sure it is accurate.
d Find relationships between the points in your notes. Look for patterns and categories of information, common ideas, similarities, differences, contrasts, contradictions. Mark or highlight links between points using colours, letters or numbers.
e Make notes of key, relevant points for each text in your own words.
f Decide on the best order for the points you will use for your synthesis and write them all on one piece of paper.

7 Look at Hassan's notes for part of his literature review. What kinds of categories, similarities, etc. can you see? Decide how you would synthesise this information, but do not write a synthesis yet.

Patel, H. (2010) Youth unemployment

- negative psychological effects (p.76)
- early experiences of unemployment > further periods out of work later on (young miss out on experience + training while unemployed) (p.142)
- delays age young people leave home/become indep./have family – Australia (p.167)
- detachment from labour market, reduces desire to work; Slacker phenomenon (p.215)

Wilson, J.C. (2013) Unemployment amongst the young in the early 21st century

- rejects claim made by Blanc (2009) that it encourages young people to do further training + 'increase their economic value' (p.45)
- increases crime > increases costs of health services, policing (p.121)
- unemployment early in life > lower earnings, under-employment + unemployment later; scarring effect; 'widespread youth unemployment could create a lost generation' (p.189)

McShane, J. (2012) Wasted: the damaging effects of youth unemployment

- low self-esteem, depression > harder to enter job market (p. 37)
- increases govt. spending on pub. services (p.65)
- nation's economic growth impeded by waste of young talent + energy (p.174)

8 Read Hassan's synthesis. How is the information organised?

A number of recent investigations into youth unemployment find the effects to be overwhelmingly negative.

Patel (2010) and McShane (2012) study the damaging psychological effects. McShane's argument is that unemployment causes low self-esteem and depression in young people, and makes it more difficult for them to find work later.

Patel and Wilson (2013) point out that unemployment early in life is often a predictor of unemployment later on. Patel's explanation is that young people fail to gain experience or be sent on training courses while out of work, reducing their subsequent chances of securing a job.

A further effect noted by Wilson and McShane is the increase in government expenditure on public services such as health and policing. The latter is the result of a rise in crimes committed by unemployed youths.

The only glimmer of hope is that mentioned by Blanc (2009, in Wilson), with the observation that unemployment sometimes encourages young people to do additional training and 'increase their economic value', although this is disputed by Wilson.

9a Read Hassan's synthesis again and find words that are used to report information.

point out

9b Which of the words you found in Exercise 9a could be replaced by these words? Try to match the meanings as closely as you can and use your knowledge of grammar to help you.

1 observed
2 According to X,
3 In X's view,
4 touched on
5 examine

9c Does Hassan use a direct quote anywhere? If so, where?

10a Describe the photo below. When do you think it was taken? Who do you think the people are?

10b Write part of a literature review on *The Great Depression: Consequences*. Look at the notes on page 163 and synthesise the information. Write between 150 and 180 words.

IN THIS UNIT

GRAMMAR
- non-finite clauses
- conversational English

VOCABULARY
- performance reviews
- academic verbs

SCENARIO
- an informal talk
- informal presentation

STUDY SKILLS
- seminar/discussion skills

WRITING SKILLS
- critical reflective writing

Entertainment wants to give you what you want. Art wants to give you what you don't know you want.
David Cronenberg (b. 1943), Canadian filmmaker

SPEAKING

1 Look at the information about arts and entertainment in Scotland. Read the titles of the tables. Where do you think these missing percentages go in each table?

Table 1: 9, 19, 31, 54   **Table 2:** 3, 23, 30, 69

Table 1

Attendance by adults at arts and cultural events in the previous twelve months (2012). Figures as percentages.	
art galleries	
cinema	
classical music/opera	7
dance (incl. ballet)	
literary events/festivals	4
live music	
theatre	31
none	22

Table 2

Participation of adults in arts and entertainment in the previous twelve months (2012). Figures as percentages.	
acting and performance	
art/sculpture	9
creative work on computer, etc.	
dance	12
film/video photography	10
playing a musical instrument	11
reading books	
none	

2 Analysing and responding to data **Work in small groups and discuss the questions.**

1 What do the tables reveal? Put the activities in order of popularity and identify the most and least popular.
2 What parallels and connections can you find between the two tables? How do participation and attendance relate for each activity?
3 Which of the activities have you and your group members attended or participated in during the last twelve months? What are your class's overall figures?
4 How do you think your country would compare?

READING

3a What arts and cultural events have you been to recently? Did you choose any of the events for these reasons?

- recommendations from friends
- reviews in the media
- previously enjoyed similar events or performers
- the chance to see something new and different

3b Read the reviews from the listings magazine *Time Out, London* on page 97. Match the types of events (1–6) with the reviews (A–H). Sometimes more than one answer is possible. Some types of events do not have a match.

1	theatre	4	comedy
2	music	5	dance
3	film	6	art

4 Read the reviews again and answer the questions. Then work with a partner and compare your answers.

1   Which event:
  a   has received an explicitly positive review?
  b   is in a non-central location?
  c   is the first performance in Britain of someone's work?
  d   is described as visually interesting?
  e   probably includes singing?
  f   has performers from the USA?
  g   involves performers manipulating inanimate models?

2   Which events would/wouldn't you like to go to?

Critic's choice

A   On the Waterfront   LIKE | COMMENT
Steven Berkoff returns to the stage in a new adaptation of the Academy Award-winning film about a boxer who takes on the mob.

B   The Phantom of the Opera   LIKE | COMMENT
Critics of this stage musical call it tired, but its lavish and bold set design is still awe-inspiring and it's a touching story of love and desire.

C   Public Service Broadcasting   LIKE | COMMENT
Sample-heavy soundscapes are this excellent London duo's stock-in-trade. Using live guitar and drums, and sometimes piano and banjo, they create eerie, white-knuckle instrumentals with vocal tracks from old radio broadcasts, public information films and archive speeches.

D   Amused Moose   LIKE | COMMENT
Great night out at this award-winning comedy club with a laughter-packed bill.

E   Kenny Wheeler   LIKE | COMMENT
This out-of-the-way venue keeps the quality sky high with another star-studded show featuring legendary UK trumpeter Wheeler and guitar virtuoso Parricelli. Catch this if you can, it should be a corker.

F   Nobody rides the unicorn   LIKE | COMMENT
Puppetcraft present this live music-enhanced tale of a little girl tasked with setting a unicorn free.

G   Haim   LIKE | COMMENT
The three Haim sisters bring their brilliant and breezy West Coast harmonies and epic R&B-influenced pop to the UK. Book now, this will sell out.

H   Thomas Noone   LIKE | COMMENT
UK debut of British-born, Rambert-trained choreographer Thomas Noone and his company performing two pieces based on the complexities of personal relationships.

VOCABULARY
PERFORMANCE REVIEWS

5 Find words and phrases in the reviews with these meanings.

1   when a story from one medium is produced in another
2   a performance group of two people
3   the list of performers appearing during a night at a single place
4   the place where a performance occurs
5   an incredibly talented person, a genius
6   a story
7   a creator of dances
8   a group of actors or performers who work together on different projects

6a Complete the compound adjectives with the words in the box. Then check your answers in the reviews. What do the adjectives mean?

award	awe	British	laughter	live music
out-of	Rambert	R&B	sample	star

a   _____-inspiring   f   _____-enhanced
b   _____-winning   g   _____-heavy
c   _____-packed   h   _____-born
d   _____-the-way   i   _____-trained
e   _____-studded   j   _____-influenced

6b Which three adjectives in Exercise 6a do you think the writer might have created specifically for these reviews and are unlikely to be in dictionaries?

LISTENING

7a 10.1 Listen to interviews done after the events in Exercise 3b. Match the speakers (1–5) with the event (A–H) they attended.

7b What did the speakers think of the events? Listen again and complete the sentences.

1   Well, the music is rather _____ .
2   _____ the cost of the ticket.
3   Experimental music isn't really my _____.
4   Well, it lived up _____ …
5   But that's _____ to say it's _____ worth seeing, just that it's _____ the best.

SPEAKING AND WRITING

8 Work with a partner and describe and review a few performance-based events that you have been to.

9 Write short reviews for your events from Exercise 8 in the style of the reviews on this page (10–50 words per review).

VOCABULARY AND SPEAKING

1a **10.2** Listen to the musical extracts and identify the kinds of music. What instruments can you hear? What other kinds of music do you know?

1b Work in small groups and discuss the questions.

1 What kind(s) of music do you like/dislike?
2 Do you play, or have you ever played, an instrument? If not, which would you like to play?
3 Have your musical tastes changed over the years? If so, how?
4 Is there any music/song you associate with particular events or people in your life?
5 Has music changed your life in any way?

READING

2 Read the press release quickly and find this information.

1 when the press release appeared
2 where the Recycled Orchestra will be performing
3 when the Orchestra was set up
4 where the Orchestra comes from in Paraguay
5 the name of the founder of the Orchestra
6 when MIM first put the eight instruments on display
7 where MIM is located
8 Dr Daniel Piper's job
9 what will be on the menu at Café Allegro
10 when the Family Day will take place

3 Read the press release again. In which paragraph(s) do we read about these things?

1 the relative value of things where the Orchestra comes from
2 the reasons why MIM has invited the Orchestra to perform there
3 the truths that the Orchestra demonstrates
4 the effect the Orchestra has on people

4a Understanding and responding to vocabulary choices How many times does the word *story* appear in the text? Why do you think this is?

4b Underline all the positive words and phrases in the text. Why are there so many?

4c Would you like to attend this event or visit the museum?

GRAMMAR
NON-FINITE CLAUSES

5 Read the sentences from the press release. Look at the underlined non-finite clause in sentence 1 and underline the non-finite clauses in sentences 2 and 3.

1 <u>Founded in 2008</u>, the Recycled Orchestra is … inspiring people around the world …
2 Its members value greatly how music impacts their lives, helping them express creativity, …
3 The museum is bringing the group's members to Phoenix, to share their incredible stories …

Press release

PHOENIX, June 25

Paraguay's Recycled Orchestra set to make U.S. debut at the Musical Instrument Museum 9 and 10 August

'The world sends us garbage. We send back music.' Fabio Chávez

Founded in 2008, La Orchestra de Instrumentos Reciclados de Cateura (the Recycled Orchestra) is already inspiring people around the world with their life-changing story, astonishing musical instruments made from landfill trash, and heart-warming performances. Never before seen in the United States, this youth orchestra will make their U.S. debut with two concerts at the MIM Music Theatre as part of a weeklong artist residency.

Amid a massive landfill in Cateura, Paraguay, children find hope by making music on instruments built from recycled trash. In a shantytown constructed on the landfill, families survive by collecting and reselling garbage. Here, where a violin can cost more than a house, visionary music teacher Fabio Chávez gathered a small team to plunder the landfill for usable materials and create an ensemble of 'recycled' instruments.

6 Match the three main types of non-finite clause (a–c) with the sentences in Exercise 5 (1–3).

a infinitive clauses b past participle clauses
c -ing clauses

7 Read the explanation of a non-finite clause and answer the questions.

A non-finite clause has a lexical verb, but this verb does not indicate tense. We have to understand its reference to time (and person and number) from the context or surrounding clauses. Non-finite clauses are typically subordinate and are usually combined with finite clauses in sentences.

1 In the sentences in Exercise 5, what are the lexical verbs that do not indicate tense?
2 What time does the non-finite clause refer to in each case?

In March MIM installed an exhibit featuring eight of the Recycled Orchestra's innovative instruments, along with video and photography shot in their hometown. In its short time on display, the exhibit dedicated to the group has quickly become a favourite among museum guests. Now, because the Recycled Orchestra's story resonates so strongly with MIM's global mission, the museum is bringing the group's members to Phoenix to share their incredible stories, their passion and their joyful music in an unparalleled weekend of activities.

The Recycled Orchestra is an extraordinary example of a reality we can see around the world and throughout the galleries of MIM: material poverty need not be an obstacle to a life rich in music. Its members value greatly how music impacts their lives, helping them express creativity, build self-confidence and strengthen community. Dr Daniel Piper, MIM's Curator for Latin America and the Caribbean, and the driving force behind bringing the orchestra to MIM, says: 'The exhibit and August residency is MIM's way of recognising their achievements as we invite the community to celebrate youth, social and musical innovation, and the sustaining value of the arts.'

Dr Piper sees strong parallels between the Recycled Orchestra and other stories of hope and resilience told in MIM's galleries. Their story represents the intrinsic need by people around the world to make music. For thousands of years, this need has driven musical innovation and creativity, leading to the incredible variety of instruments we see at MIM, many of which are made with repurposed materials from everyday life.'

Don't miss the opportunity to see the Recycled Orchestra and be part of their unfolding story!

A Paraguayan-inspired menu of white fish stew, grilled beefsteak and rice pudding will be available for lunch at Café Allegro.

CLICK HERE to learn about Family Day with the Recycled Orchestra on Saturday 10 August.

GRAMMAR TIP

Non-finite clauses can occur in a variety of positions within the sentence: at the beginning or end, or embedded in the sentence.

8 Find other examples of the different types of non-finite clause in the press release.

➥ Language reference and extra practice, pages 144–145

9 Complete the sentences (1–6) with the non-finite clauses (a–f). Choose the correct form of the verb in italics and use appropriate punctuation.

1   Certain kinds of music are played in shops _____.
2   The 1985 Live Aid concerts for famine relief in Ethiopia took place in London, Philadelphia and other cities _____ .
3   _____ the rapper was vilified by the media.
4   Tailor-made music programmes have a remarkable effect on some medical patients _____.
5   Cows appreciate calming music _____.
6   In 2013 _____ they formed a band.

a   *blamed / blaming* for an increase in street violence
b   *to reduce / reducing* the need for painkilling drugs by fifty percent
c   *to escape / escaped* the monotony of suburban life
d   *producing / produced* more milk
e   *to watch / watched* by over 400 million people around the world
f   *to stimulate / stimulated* greater spending by customers

SPEAKING

10a Look at some ways music can change people's lives. Discuss the effect they could have on people.

1   learning to play a musical instrument as a child
2   becoming a pop star at the age of eighteen
3   organising a benefit concert

10b Work in groups. Imagine you are going to organise a benefit concert in your town or city with the aim of raising as much money as possible. Decide:

a   which charity/cause/relief effort you would like to support.
b   which venue you would use.
c   which four bands/performers you would invite.

10c Present your ideas to other groups.

WRITING

11 Write a short press release (about 100 words) for the benefit concert in Exercise 10b.

SPEAKING

1 Work in small groups and discuss the questions.

1 a Over the years, how has the internet and digital technology changed entertainment?

   b How do you use the internet for entertainment?

2 What developments might occur in the future regarding digital entertainment?

READING

2 Read the extracts quickly and answer the questions.

1 Which extracts are about:
   a producing entertainment to show or share?
   b consuming entertainment?

2 Match the extracts with their sources.
   i   the abstract of an academic research paper
   ii   a publisher's description of an academic book
   iii a journalist's blog
   iv   a newspaper article

3 Read the extracts again. In which extract are these ideas mentioned?

1 Internet entertainment and communities may be harmful for a nation.

2 Present behaviour is reminiscent of the past.

3 Many online sites and phenomena are short-lived.

4 Digital technology prompts innovation in other areas.

5 Being familiar with the internet enhances personal credibility.

4a Identifying and evaluating main points
Read each extract carefully, identifying and making notes on the various main topics, key ideas and points in each.

4b Work with a partner and compare your notes. Then answer the questions.

1 Do you have knowledge or examples which support ideas in the extracts?

2 Do you have any points to make that may contradict the extracts?

3 Are the developments discussed in the extracts positive, negative or neither?

4 What variations in these situations might there be globally?

5 How do the situations in the extracts compare to your country and your life?

A The traditional living room is now a multi-media space in which households sit together to watch TV, while also using computers, tablets and smartphones, according to the new research report 'State of the Nation', by Ofcom.

The research reveals that families have returned to sitting around a single television set to watch a show together – as was common in much earlier decades. However, when watching the show, half of the people now also spend time online, streaming videos, posting photographs, messaging and social media posting.

The report identified 25% of viewers as 'meshers', using mobile technology and social media to discuss a show that they are watching. A further 50% were categorised as 'media stackers', using phones and tablets when watching a show, but performing unrelated activities on the various devices.

B This time last year I went down to Los Angeles to do a live debate about the merits of user-generated content with a kid called Justin Kan. It was a surreal experience. Kan, a freshly graduated Yale philosophy student, had affixed an always-on video camera on his head. Everything in his life – absolutely everything – is streamed in grainy video onto his website. Back then, Kan was just starting a business called Justin.tv – a user-generated content portal that enabled other self-broadcasting kids like himself to distribute their unedited lives on the internet. Just another ephemeral web 2.0 thing, I concluded. After all, how many kids would be shameless enough to broadcast their entire lives to a voyeuristic world? I was totally wrong. The venture capital-backed Justin.tv is now a significant commercial success.

C The main results of this study about young Shanghainese indicate that the main motivation behind internet café use was entertainment and that internet use in the cafés was ritualistic, habitual and pleasure-seeking. For the urban youth culture, internet cafés provided a space where youngsters could reinforce their identities as trendy, technology-savvy urbanites. The government and public concerns were reflected in the phenomenon as internet cafés have been accused of eroding public morality.

D The past decade has seen an extraordinarily intense period of experimentation with computer technology within the performing arts. Digital media has been increasingly incorporated into live theatre and dance, and new forms of interactive performance have emerged in participatory installations, on CD-ROM and on the web. In *Digital Performance*, Steve Dixon traces the evolution of these practices, presents detailed accounts of key practitioners and performances and analyses the theoretical, artistic and technological contexts of this form of new media art.

VOCABULARY
ACADEMIC VERBS

6a Find verbs in the extracts with these meanings.

1 show that something exists or is true (extract A)
2 provide the means for something to occur (extract B)
3 supply something or spread something over an area (extract B)
4 show that something exists or is true (extract C)
5 support or make stronger (extract C)
6 weaken or reduce in importance (extract C)
7 appear, perhaps developing over time (extract D)
8 look critically and in detail at something (extract D)

6b Complete the sentences with the correct form of verbs from Exercise 6a.

1 Surveys _____ the broadcast industry undervalued the public interest in user-generated content.
2 An attempt was made to _____ global copyright laws in order to protect commercial content more strongly.
3 It is important to _____ the possible factors carefully to be certain why children deceive parents about their levels of internet use.
4 Video and music sharing sites tend to _____ consumers' respect for the rights of media producers.
5 Social networking sites enable users to rapidly _____ information to their peers.
6 My research _____ that privacy is now a primary concern for young adults.
7 The data _____ us to draw clear conclusions concerning the future of entertainment.
8 New forms of art often _____ after both minor and major developments in technology.

LISTENING

7a 10.3 Listen to parts of a conversation between three people about how we use the internet. Number the topics (a–f) in the order you hear them.

a targeted advertising
b distraction
c misinterpreting information
d identity security
e triviality
f dependence

7b Listen again and make notes on topics a–f. To what extent do you agree with what the speakers say? Compare your ideas with a partner.

GRAMMAR
CONVERSATIONAL ENGLISH

8a 10.4 Look at these features of conversational English. Listen to three extracts from the conversation and match them to the features below.

1 Speakers repeat words, especially when restarting a sentence.
2 Simple clause structure – a chain of ideas, linked simply with and, *but, so, then, because*.
3 Speakers interrupt, or talk over, each other.

8b 10.5 Look at these features of conversational English. Listen to four more extracts from the conversation and match them to the features below.

4 Speakers use fillers (*well, you know*) and vague language (*sort of, things like that*) to maintain and organise their speech.
5 Listeners make short supportive comments, without fully interrupting.
6 Sentences are incomplete because the speaker rephrases their idea.
7 Speakers use direct quotes, as if playing a character.

8c Listen to and read Audio script 10.3 on page 178. Find more examples of the features of conversational English in Exercises 8a and b.

➥ Language reference and extra practice, pages 144–145

9a Rewrite the following to appear more similar to conversational English. Use the features in Exercises 8a and b to help you. Compare your ideas with a partner.

1 I asked my mother to use social media; however, she said it was too complicated. She also said that she would keep phoning me. However, I don't like using the phone.

   I told, erm, I asked my mum to use social media, you know, Facebook and things like that, and ...

9b Work in pairs. One student rewrites text 1 below, the other rewrites text 2. Check your partner's ideas.

1 I don't think that parents should stop their children using the internet. One reason is that the children won't learn skills like information searching and deciding which websites to trust. In addition, the internet can help you learn things such as languages and other practical skills. Therefore it is a shame if children can't use it.
2 I used to use social media, such as Facebook, a lot more when I lived abroad in order to keep in touch with people back home and for other similar reasons. However, now that I am back in this country, I would much rather call or text people, or do something similar. Alternatively, I'd rather go and see them.

SPEAKING

10 Work in small groups to discuss the statements below. During each discussion, one student should not speak, but should note the features of conversational English used.

1 There's nothing wrong with parents banning their children from watching TV and/or using the internet.
2 Using the internet for entertainment will remain the preserve of young people.
3 Young people are ignorant of the dangers of revealing their personal data and private lives online.
4 Downloading movies and music for free, without permission, is a criminal act deserving prosecution.

SPEAKING

1 Work in groups and discuss the questions.

1 What formats of reality show are there in your country? Do you watch any of them? Why?/Why not?

2 Why do you think people appear on these shows?

SITUATION

A production company is making a new reality documentary show, *The Global Village*, for online international broadcast. This infotainment show offers interest and fun, as well as revealing and analysing cultural differences in communication and collaboration styles. It will feature twenty-four contestants, all from different countries, who will live on a small, deserted, tropical island for three months. They will work together to build a community – a global village – and survive without any modern conveniences, performing tasks to win food and points. The international public will vote each week to give points to different participants. The contestant with the most points at the end will win a round-the-world trip. There is full online interactivity for the audience, with social media and education resources related to the sociological research of the show. The production company is currently accepting video auditions from the potential participants.

2 Read the situation. What do you think the producers will be looking for in contestants for *The Global Village*? Consider:

- personality traits.
- hobbies and interests.
- practical skills.
- physical appearance.
- singing/acting skills.
- age and health.

3 Read the producer's selection guidelines. Are they similar to your ideas?

RealTV

Selection guidelines

Although a good mix of people is required, the ideal candidates should:

- be interesting, have opinions and something to say; be quick-witted and have a bright personality; have good communication and collaboration skills.
- have useful practical skills – they will fend for themselves, build their homes, cook and improve life on the island.
- be fit and healthy. We must avoid any major health problems during the show, and they will be living in basic conditions and not eating well.
- be entertaining or ready to contribute to the fun. Remember: television is entertainment and some challenges will not be of the survival type, e.g. there will be Tropical Karaoke.
- have an open mind with regard to this new experience and believe it will be a learning experience.

Also, good TV often involves a degree of conflict. Selecting assertive personalities that might clash with other strong personalities would be good, but we don't want complete idiots who can't change. The audience wants to see the journey that these characters make, to see how they learn to live together, how they communicate and collaborate. The participants should be aged twenty-one and above, and an interesting variety of backgrounds would be positive.

4 `10.6` **Listen to two auditions. Which attributes do the candidates claim? Who would/wouldn't you choose to be in the show? Why?**

KEY LANGUAGE
AN INFORMAL TALK

5a Listen again and complete the sentences.

1 _____, all my life I've come top in everything.
2 _____ surviving on the island, well, I reckon that won't be an issue.
3 _____, that doesn't mean that I'm perfect.
4 _____, trying to win *The Global Village* will be a challenge.
5 I'm a builder, which is why I _____ I'd be good to have on the island.
6 I guess you could say that, _____, I'm pretty laid back.
7 So, _____, I reckon I'd be a great choice for *The Global Village*.
8 _____, the island needs a builder.

5b Find the sentences in Exercise 5a in Audio script 10.6 on page 178. Then match the phrases in each sentence with these formal expressions.

a believe
b however
c moving on
d with regard to
e taking everything into consideration
f generally speaking
g as I explained earlier
h to illustrate that

6 Look at Audio script 10.6 on page 178 again. Find more examples of language that would be useful in an informal talk.

7 [10.7] Listen to the producers discussing the two candidates from Exercise 4. Who do they select? Why?

TASK
INFORMAL PRESENTATION

8a You are going to make an audition video for *The Global Village*. First, prepare a short talk for your audition by creating a new character for yourself. Use these questions to help you.

1 What is your nationality? (Choose an English-speaking country.)
2 How old are you? (over twenty-one)
3 What is your family, education and employment background?
4 What interests do you have?
5 How would you describe your personality? (Think about strengths and weaknesses.)
6 What special skills, abilities and qualities do you have?
7 Why should the producers choose you for the show?
8 What do you want to get from the experience?
9 What will you say to end your audition?

8b Compare your ideas with a partner. Which of the criteria in the selection guidelines do your talks refer to or demonstrate? Make further notes. Practise giving your short talk.

8c Work with a partner and make an audio or video recording of your talks (if you have a recording device).

9 Form a group with another pair. Each pair shares their recordings with the other or they audition live. Take notes on each one.

10a Of the four characters, decide individually which two you think the producers would choose. Refer to the criteria in the selection guidelines.

10b As a group, can you agree on two strong candidates for selection for the show? Take notes of your discussion, reasoning and decision.

USEFUL PHRASES
Recalling what someone said
Can you remember what he said about … ? She said that she … , didn't she? What was it he said about … ?
Explaining choices
The main reason I'd choose her is that … What I really liked about him was that … In the end, I'd go for him because …
Making a decision
So, do we all agree that … ? Who's it going to be then? Look, we've got to choose someone; let's go for …

11 Using your notes, write a short report about the selection process and results for the senior management.

STUDY SKILLS
SEMINAR/DISCUSSION SKILLS

1 Discuss the questions.

1 What are the differences between a lecture, a seminar and a tutorial?
2 What are the advantages of seminars for students? Are there any disadvantages?

2 Tick the skills you think could be developed by attending seminars. Then work with a partner and compare your answers.

1 listening actively
2 working with a wide range of different people
3 solving problems
4 communicating effectively by speaking
5 managing differences of opinion and conflict
6 training other people
7 leading a team

3 You are going to watch part of a seminar on the difference between real conversation and conversation in plays, radio and TV drama and films. Work with a partner and discuss the questions.

1 Which plays, films and TV dramas have you seen recently?
2 Think about the language used in the types of drama you've seen. How does it compare with the language of real life?

4a ▶ **10.1** **Watch the first part of the seminar and answer the questions.**

1 Do you think the seminar leader leads the discussion well? Why?
2 How do the students use body language to 'take the floor' (i.e. to get the next turn to speak)?

4b Watch the first part of the seminar again and number these points in the order you hear them.

a The way men and women speak is different.
b Conversation is cooperative.
c Shared background information helps participants understand each other.
d Conversation has a lot of pauses, hesitations, etc.
e Utterances are repetitive and short.

4c Work with a partner. Tell him/her what you can remember about the points from Exercise 4b.

4d ▶ **10.2** **Watch the second part of the seminar and make notes on the main points.**

4e Work with a partner and compare your notes.

5 Look at the phrases in bold in the first paragraph of Video script 10.1 on page 179. Decide which of these functions they perform.

1 checking everyone has understood
2 stating the topic of the seminar
3 identifying your role in the seminar
4 making sure the scope of the topic is understood

6 Work with a partner and choose ten more phrases in bold from Video script 10.1 on page 179. Decide what their function is.

7a Which of these phrases would probably be said by the chair/seminar leader, but not by other participants?

1 I see what you're getting at, but …
2 Sorry, I didn't catch that.
3 On balance, we thought that …
4 Lia, we haven't heard from you yet.
5 Miles put it well when he said that …
6 We're running out of time, so …

7b What is the function of each phrase in Exercise 7a?

8 What can students do to prepare for a seminar? Make a list. Then check your answers on page 163.

9 Work in groups and choose one of these seminar topics or think of your own topic. Prepare for the seminar and practise what you want to say in pairs.

1 Why aren't more young people interested in theatre?
2 Soap operas: a powerful educational tool
3 The predictable nature of TV drama
4 Remakes of films: what's the point?

WRITING SKILLS
CRITICAL REFLECTIVE WRITING

10 What do you think this quote means? Work with a partner and discuss.

The unexamined life is not worth living. Socrates, in Plato's *Apology*

11a Writing about experiences, events, situations or ideas is an important basis for critical reflection and is used in both academic and work contexts. There is no single way to do critical reflection, but a number of three-way models exist. Look at the model on page 105 and match questions 1–3 with each part of the model.

1 What are you going to do next, using the insights you have developed from thinking about the experience?
2 How was this experience similar/different to other experiences? What is important about it, and why? What do you understand now more than before?
3 What happened during this experience? Who was involved? What did they say? What did you say?

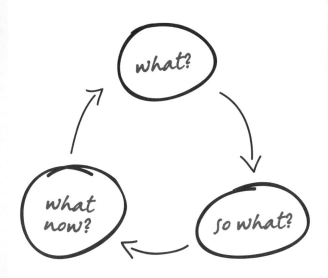

Reflective model in *Reach, Touch and Teach* by Terry Borton, McGraw Hill, Inc. 1970

11b Match the following to each part of the model.

1   analysis   2   description   3   evaluation

12   Based on the model, what do you think is the aim of critical reflection? Choose the correct answer.

1   to blame other people for something that went wrong
2   to understand yourself better
3   to change something about yourself and possibly the world around you
4   to find out why something went wrong on a particular occasion

13   Have you ever done this kind of critical reflective writing? How might it help you?

14   Look at the blog and find one example of writing that is a) descriptive, b) analytical and c) evaluative. Use Exercises 11a and 11b to help you.

15   Look at this list of things you can do in critical reflective writing. Find examples of four of them in the blog.

1   thinking about what happened before the experience (or event) that may have had an impact on it
2   thinking about how you feel or felt
3   thinking about the reasons for your actions
4   asking critical questions about the experience
5   thinking about how you interacted with others involved in the experience
6   thinking about the consequences of your actions
7   thinking about the relationship between your own experience and theory
8   thinking about your strengths and weaknesses
9   thinking about your overall contribution to the experience or event
10   thinking about whether your assumptions or preconceptions have changed
11   thinking about what action you are going to take as a result of this experience

 Tuesday 15 March ▶

Seminar: the language of drama

The previous few days had not been easy for me as I had had to spend a lot of time helping a friend of mine who was experiencing some difficulties. I felt I could not let him down. As a result, I was only able to do the conversation analysis task very quickly the evening before the seminar.

I recorded my sister on my mobile, in the living room. It took me a long time (about two hours) to do the transcription – perhaps because it was my first time. It was very late when I finished the transcription, so I did not have time to analyse it properly. It was also too late to do more than skim through the reading.

These things put me at a distinct disadvantage during the seminar. I was forced to make notes about other students' observations, rather than coming ready with my own notes, and there were terms I was not familiar with. Consequently, I could not contribute very much to the discussion. Overall, I think my preparation was poor. I must organise my time in a more effective way, which allows for unexpected events or emergencies.

During the seminar itself, I was really impressed by the way Shanice chaired for the first time. Earlier in the semester, it seemed that she was reluctant to take on this role, but we saw a completely new side to her – much more confident. On the other hand, I felt quite irritated and upset by the way Ben disagreed with my point about how women speak. I spoke about this with Shanice afterwards and she pointed out that challenging ideas is an important aspect of critical discussion; this made me think that I should try not to take disagreement and criticism so personally.

The most successful part of the seminar for me was when we were talking about the language of Harold Pinter. My extensive experience of theatre-going is very useful for making connections with the ideas of literary critics, and I feel comfortable with these kinds of discussions. Some critics argue that Pinter's very oblique, spare language makes it difficult to read the characters' intentions and understand their motives. I can see what a linguistic debt modern playwrights owe Pinter in this respect. Thinking more about this, I wonder if this is because they want to break down that sense of 'theatricality', the barrier between the stage and 'real life'?

16   Comment on the style of language used in the blog.

17   Write an entry for your own critical reflective blog. Consider these points.

1   You could think and write about:
   a   the subject you are studying.
   b   an event such as a presentation or seminar.
   c   something you've done outside the course/job that has relevance to it.

2   You could include pictures, diagrams, etc.

3   Think about how much you want to 'expose' yourself and others.

4   Try to get a good balance between description, analysis and evaluation.

5   Find a balance between writing in a personal and an objective style.

Business and economics

11.1 UPS AND DOWNS

A business that makes nothing but money is a poor business. Henry Ford (1863–1947), U.S. industrialist and businessman

SPEAKING

1a List three successful businesses. Why do you think the businesses are successful? Work with a partner and compare your ideas.

1b Tick the practices you think apply to the businesses you mentioned in Exercise 1a.

A successful business:

1 constantly innovates, diversifies and takes risks.
2 pays fixed salaries without bonuses or other fringe benefits.
3 makes redundancies to cut costs.
4 keeps overheads down by manufacturing/ outsourcing abroad.
5 makes as much money for shareholders as possible.
6 invests heavily in PR and advertising to create brand awareness.
7 eliminates the competition to gain market share.
8 uses creative accounting to pay less tax.
9 gets customers to pay in advance but pays suppliers as late as possible.

1c Which of the practices in Exercise 1b do you think are common in business?

1d Which practices are the least acceptable to you? Why?

VOCABULARY
BUSINESS AND ECONOMIC TERMS

2a Match words from box A with words from box B to make common business and economic terms. Use *and* to connect the words.

A	assets	boom	creditors	~~imports~~	income
	mergers	mortgages	profit	supply	

B	acquisitions	debtors	demand	expenditure
	~~exports~~	liabilities	loans	loss	slump

imports and exports

2b Match seven of the terms from Exercise 2a with their meanings.

1 the relationship between the goods and services available and what consumers want to buy
2 periods when an economy or business is doing well or badly
3 things owned by a business and things owed by a business
4 the money earned and spent by a government or business
5 changes in the ownership and running of businesses
6 financial products on which interest is charged
7 people or organisations owed money by others or owing money to others

2c Write definitions for the other two terms in Exercise 2a.

READING

3 What sort of information do you expect to find in the business pages of a newspaper/on a news website?

4a Read the stories. Which are 'business bites' and which are 'economic bites'?

A _____ Paradise Place, the struggling luxury travel group, is seeking a substantial cash injection to avoid almost certain bankruptcy after recording further plunging profits this year. Any potential investor would be taking on $56 million of debt. According to a spokesperson, the company could go into administration within weeks unless a buyer is found.

B _____ Trade in counterfeit goods in the UK has escalated. New figures show that the trade in pirate DVDs, fake designer goods and other aspects of the underground economy may have cost the government up to £1.5 billion in lost tax revenue in the past year. With tax revenues decreasing due to the economic slump, there is a real threat to future public spending, a spokesperson announced.

C _____ Still Beautiful, the make-up and beauty products giant, continues to go from strength to strength in a fiercely competitive market. Turnover and profits are well up on this time last year, particularly for its War Paint range. It has just announced a further expansion of its workforce with the creation of 2,000 new jobs and the opening of 350 new retail outlets across Europe over the next two years.

D _____ The Japanese stock market remains volatile. Yesterday was another day of heavy trading with share prices falling again. Although there was a slight recovery towards the end of the day, the forecast is bleak as market confidence remains low due to the effects of the global recession.

E _____ Business is booming for leading internet company Bubble and its subsidiaries in Australia and Southeast Asia. Pre-tax profits rose by 23 percent, according to interim results released this week, and sustained growth is forecast for the rest of the year, which will please shareholders. The reported acquisition of the poorly performing instant messaging app Chat Up could be completed by the end of next month. More good news is that the company's tax liability issues in the UK have now been resolved.

F _____ Another surge in Spanish unemployment figures has been announced today. Predictions are that they will reach a peak in the next three months. There are further gloomy forecasts that industry will be hit hard by the economic slump. Manufacturing output will drop sharply in the next quarter, say analysts, while capital investment by firms will plummet. Meanwhile the inflation rate continues to climb, edging towards 2.5 percent.

G _____ In the USA, falls in the exchange rate have led to a much more positive balance of trade. The trade deficit has been reduced significantly and the government hopes that this will stimulate growth and lead to a small surplus by early next year. There has been further speculation about the introduction of import tariffs and quotas to help the badly hit car industry.

4b Match the headings (1–7) with the stories (A–G).

1 Black market boom
2 Investment fears
3 Paradise lost?
4 Optimistic trade outlook
5 Takeover follows growth
6 Economy suffers downturn
7 Cosmetics firm expands

4c Read the stories again and answer the questions.

1 Which companies are doing well/badly?
2 Which economies are doing well/badly?

5 Find words or phrases in the stories with these meanings.

1 the failure of a business
2 not genuine/original products
3 money earned from sales during a particular period of time
4 shops
5 a period of negative growth
6 companies owned or controlled by a larger company
7 when one company buys another company (or part of one)
8 the general rise in prices
9 the difference between the value of a country's imports and exports
10 a negative balance of trade

6a Find words and phrases in the stories which refer to trends. Do they refer to an upward trend (↑), a downward trend (↓) or another type of trend?

plunging ↓

6b What other phrases referring to trends can you add to the list?

SPEAKING

7a Deciding and justifying priorities
You are responsible for the distribution of the public spending budget for your country (i.e. the income from taxes, loans, etc.). Think about the different areas of spending in the table on page 164 and follow these steps.

1 Fill in the budget for this year to show what you imagine the current situation is.
2 Decide on your priorities for next year.
3 Fill in the budget for next year.

7b Work in groups and present your ideas.

WRITING

8 Write a short summary of the main points of your budget.

SPEAKING AND READING

1 What can be done to help developing countries grow their economies? Do you know any organisations that aim to do this? What do you know about them?

2a Work with a partner. Student A, read the text below and note down the arguments in favour of Fairtrade. Student B, turn to page 164 and note down the arguments against Fairtrade.

2b Work with a partner. Using your notes only, tell each other the arguments for and against Fairtrade.

2c Evaluating evidence Work with a partner and discuss. Which side of the argument do you think is stronger? Give reasons for your answer.

Is Fairtrade fair?
Yes: it puts people back at the heart of trade.

By Harriet Lamb, Fairtrade International

Fairtrade does what it says on the tin: it is about better prices for smallholder farmers and workers in developing countries. Fairtrade addresses the injustices of conventional trade, which too often leaves the poorest, weakest producers earning less than it costs them to grow their crops. It's a bit like a national minimum wage for global trade. Not perfect, not a magic wand, not a panacea for all the problems of poverty, but a step in the right direction.

Free-market economists complain that Fairtrade benefits only a small number of farmers, penalising those outside. This is plain wrong. In fact, the evidence suggests that the opposite is true. Research in Bolivia, for example, found that coffee producers outside Fairtrade were able to negotiate higher prices: Fairtrade had become a price setter. Fairtrade farmers also share their knowledge in trading. For those inside the system, our research shows that through the minimum price guarantee, farmers have more secure and stable incomes. A group of rice farmers in India invested their premium in buying a tractor and a land leveller; productivity increased by 30 percent.

Other critics ask why we are working with retailers or big brands like Cadbury's and Starbucks. Our answer is that only by mainstreaming Fairtrade will we be able to reach more producers. So we are unapologetic in our commitment to scale up. By doing so, moreover, we begin to affect all business behaviour.

A favourite question is why don't we work with UK farmers. We recognise that many farmers in the UK face similar issues to farmers elsewhere, but Fairtrade was established specifically to support the most disadvantaged producers in the world – like the tea-growers of Malawi, who don't even have drinking water in their villages. I always buy my cheese, pears and carrots from my local farmers' market – and enjoy Fairtrade bananas, tea and coffee. It's two sides of the same movement to put people back at the heart of trade. Surely, you cannot say fairer than that.

LISTENING

3a **11.1** Listen to the first part of a radio programme looking at the pros and cons of microfinance. Note down all the pros of microfinance.

3b **11.2** Listen to the second part of the programme and note down all the cons of microfinance.

3c Which speaker did you find easier to follow? Why?

3d What impact do you think the microfinance movement has had on supporting development in some of the world's poorest countries? Work with a partner and discuss.

VOCABULARY
CONFUSING WORDS

4a Look at Audio script 11.1 on pages 179–180. Find words which are often confused with *debt*, *borrow*, *debtors*, *principal* and *effect*.

4b Complete the sentences with one of the words in brackets.

1 We took out a personal _____ to pay for our holiday. (debt, loan)
2 Can you _____ me ten dollars until tomorrow? (lend, borrow)
3 The _____ reason for the farm's failure was the recession. (principle, principal)
4 Our _____ are trying to get their money back. (creditors, debtors)
5 According to the World Bank, the _____ of the latest financial crisis on rural and urban poverty has been dramatic. (affect, effect)

4c Write sentences with the words you did *not* use in Exercise 4b. Use a dictionary to help you.

GRAMMAR
ALTERNATIVES TO *IF*

5 Look at Audio scripts 11.1 and 11.2 on pages 179–180. Find alternatives to *if* and add them to the correct category.

Conditions	
Necessary	*provided that, on (the) condition that, assuming, but for, not … until,* 1 _____
Imaginary	2 _____ */supposing,* 3 _____
Unexpected	4 _____
Alternative	*whether (or not)*
Negative	5 _____

6 What, if any, is the difference in meaning between the sentences in each pair?

1 a If we do not learn lessons from the past, small-scale farmers will lose their jobs.
   b Unless we learn lessons from the past, small-scale farmers will lose their jobs.

2 a They were happy only if they were taking home enormous bonuses.
   b They were happy as long as they were taking home enormous bonuses.

3 a I'll attend the conference in case the Chairman is going.
   b I'll attend the conference if the Chairman is going.

4 a You can get a loan if you are self-employed.
   b You can get a loan even if you are self-employed.

➥ Language reference and extra practice, pages 146–147

7 Rewrite the sentences using the words in brackets.

1 If you hadn't been so generous, the charity would have closed down. (but for)
2 I'm happy to give you a loan, but I need you to make your monthly repayments. (as long as)
3 What would you do if you won the lottery? (supposing)
4 I will agree to those conditions if you increase my commission. (provided that)
5 If we don't win this contract, we'll all lose our jobs. (unless)
6 He will only sign the contract if we give him a pay rise. (unless)
7 Use a lawyer when you negotiate a new contract as you might get bullied. (in case)
8 The search can tell us about his outstanding debts, if he has any. (whether or not)
9 Fairtrade allows documents to be photocopied for personal use, but insists that copyright and sources are also copied. (on the condition that)
10 How are you going to finance your studies if you get a place at university? (assuming)

WRITING

8a Work with a partner and brainstorm ideas for the first paragraphs of this essay.

Evaluate the impact that the microfinance and Fairtrade movements can have in supporting development in some of the world's poorest countries.

8b Write the first paragraph.

8c Work with a partner. Share your paragraphs with each other and make constructive suggestions about how you can improve them.

SPEAKING AND READING

1a Work in groups and give some examples of times when you have had to negotiate (e.g. with noisy neighbours).

1b Discuss the questions.

1 Are you afraid of negotiating? Why?/ Why not?
2 When you negotiate, do you usually concede more than you should?
3 Do you get caught up in arguments when negotiating?
4 Do you think of negotiating in terms of winners and losers?

2a You are going to read some advice on negotiating. Think of five pieces of advice that might appear in the text.

2b Read the advice sheet and check which of your predictions were mentioned.

3 Read the advice sheet again. Which do you think are the five most useful pieces of advice? Why?

VOCABULARY
SUFFIXES (NOUNS 2)

4 Make nouns from the verbs in the box using the suffixes *-tion* and *-sion* and making any other necessary changes. Check the spelling and meaning of any words you do not know in a dictionary.

abstain	admit	clarify	collide	confuse	decide	discriminate
eliminate	extend	indicate	instigate	negotiate	permit	

5 Complete the sentences with nouns from Exercise 4.

1 Rising house prices are a(n) _____ of confidence in the economy.
2 She was sure that _____ was the reason she was not getting promoted as quickly as her male colleagues.
3 The CEO's _____ that she had lied shocked the shareholders.
4 The union has entered into _____ with the management.
5 Alicia's been given a(n) _____ to finish her report.
6 Some further _____ of your position is needed.
7 No final _____ has been taken, but a merger between the two companies seems likely.
8 The inquiry was set up at the _____ of the chairman.

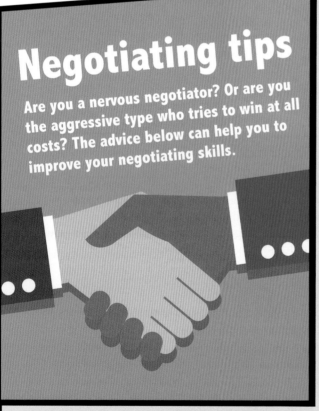

Negotiating tips

Are you a nervous negotiator? Or are you the aggressive type who tries to win at all costs? The advice below can help you to improve your negotiating skills.

- First of all, find out everything you can about the other party. Preparation is vital. Clarify your priorities and be ready to concede less important points. Keep your negotiating strategy simple and flexible.
- Plan ahead for what you are willing to give up. Know your bottom line or BATNA (Best Alternative To A Negotiated Agreement). This represents the point you turn down their offer and stop negotiating.

- Create the right ambience for a win-win negotiation. Try to put yourself in the other party's shoes. Think about what they really need. Stress the need for agreement from the outset and only engage in constructive arguments.
- If you are negotiating in a foreign country, be prepared to fit in with their style of negotiating. Planning is crucial. Learn about the customs, values and practices of the people you are going to negotiate with.
- Set the negotiations up so there won't be time pressures on anyone. If the other party try to bring up a completely new issue, then call for an adjournment. Also, if you are making no progress on a very difficult point, suggest you come back to it later.
- Identify who the decision-maker is. Make sure you know who you're talking to. But don't be intimidated by status.
- Control your emotions when negotiating. Don't give yourself away. Hide short tempers and frustration and never walk out in a rage. Never show fear or anger in face of intimidation. Remember, it's not personal. As soon as emotion enters into the negotiation you are likely to lose.
- Be assertive, not aggressive. Focus on issues, not emotions.
- Be the best listener you can be. Wait for the other party to finish their proposal before responding. Listen to the tone of voice as well as the words.
- Watch out for body language that might give you some indication of how the other side is feeling or indicate a shift in position.
- When you've made an important concession, you should point it out and emphasise that each concession is a serious loss for you. Don't concede ground unless you receive something in return.
- After you've closed the deal, don't go on talking. Shut up. Stand up. Shake hands. And leave.

Be polite, be persistent and keep your focus.

GRAMMAR
PHRASAL VERBS

6 Match the highlighted phrasal verbs in the advice sheet with their meanings.

1 mention/introduce a topic
2 get information
3 show your feelings
4 let go, lose
5 explain, highlight
6 arrange, organise
7 refuse
8 return
9 work well with others in a group
10 continue
11 be quiet
12 rise to your feet
13 be careful because of danger

7 Read the grammar tip above. Then look at these phrasal verbs and answer the questions.

Stand up …
… you should point it out …
This represents the point you turn down their offer …

1 Which phrasal verbs are transitive and which are intransitive?
2 What is the difference in the structures of the phrasal verbs?

8a Choose the best answer to complete the rule. Sometimes more than one answer is possible.

1 With transitive phrasal verbs, if the object is a noun, we can put it:
   a between the verb and the particle.
   b after the particle.
   c before the verb.
2 With transitive phrasal verbs, if the object is a pronoun, we can put it:
   a between the verb and the particle.
   b after the particle.
   c before the verb.

8b Look at the other highlighted phrasal verbs in the advice sheet. Which are transitive and which are intransitive in this context?

GRAMMAR TIP

With transitive phrasal verbs:
• we cannot put an adverb between the verb and particle or between the particle and object.

I turned reluctantly down the offer. ✗
I turned down reluctantly the offer. ✗
I turned the offer down reluctantly. ✓
Reluctantly, I turned the offer down. ✓

• We cannot put a relative pronoun immediately before or after the particle.

That's the offer which turned I down. ✗
That's the offer which I turned down. ✓

---

9 Put the words in brackets in the correct order to complete the sentences.

1 I was in a hurry, so (I / the / out / problem / quickly / pointed).
2 The Chairman wants the meeting in the morning, so (I've / ten / it / set / for / up / o'clock).
3 That's the colleague (gave / last / smoking / who / up / week).
4 The topic was controversial, so (I / it / up / carefully / brought).
5 Unfortunately, it was the secret (which / found / out / I / had).
6 Golf was too expensive, so (I / gave / immediately / up / it).
7 She made me a good offer, but (I've / turned / down / it).

10 Work with a partner and take it in turns to answer the questions.

1 Have you ever turned a job down?
2 Have you ever filled in a form and then regretted it?
3 What is the best thing you have set up?
4 Have you ever found out an important secret?
5 Did you fit in well with your classmates when you were younger?
6 Do you like to have your mistakes pointed out to you?
7 Have you ever given anything up?
8 Do you know when to shut up or do you tend to go on talking?

➡ Language reference and extra practice, pages 146–147

SPEAKING

11 Considering alternative views Work with a partner and prepare for a negotiation. Think about the situation from the other person's point of view.

Student A: turn to page 155.
Student B: turn to page 156.

SITUATION

Kenneth and Ingrid Carter own a company called Marine Instruments. They have recently developed a marine product, an alarm device which helps sailors to locate a member of their crew who has fallen overboard. They need finance to launch the product and to cover their initial marketing costs. They have contacted two investment firms who may be able to help them: Neptune Investments and Ariel Capital. Both firms provide capital and advice for start-up companies and in return expect to share in the profits of the company. This is usually in the form of a percentage stake (shareholding) in the company. Neptune and Ariel like to invest in companies run by enthusiastic, motivated people who have exciting products to develop.

Kenneth and Ingrid have arranged to meet Neptune Investments first. Neptune directors will question Kenneth and Ingrid about their product and if all goes well, will negotiate a deal with them.

Details of the marine product are given opposite.

The MLSD (Marine Life-Saving Device) helps to locate and search for crew members who have fallen overboard from a boat or yacht. The device is attached to the clothing of crew members. If someone falls into the sea, it automatically emits a signal which gives the exact location of the person who has gone overboard to someone on the boat. It also sends a signal to other boats in the area. As a result, crew members who fall into the water can be quickly recovered either by their own boat or other boats which are nearby.

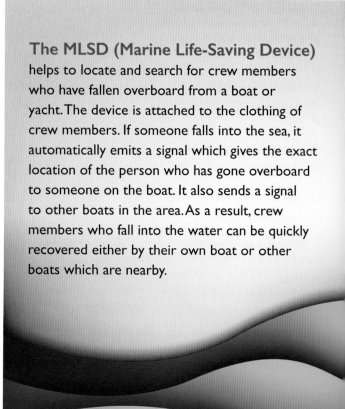

1 Read the situation and the description of the product. Work with a partner and discuss the questions.

1 What kind of companies do the investment firms finance?
2 How do the investment firms get a return on their money?
3 How does the MLSD save lives?
4 Do you think the MLSD is a marketable product? Give reasons for your answer.

2 If you were directors of one of the investment companies, what questions would you ask the inventors of the device? Make a list.

3 11.3 Kenneth and Ingrid meet directors from Neptune Investments. Listen to the first part of their conversation and make notes on these points.

- unique features of the MLSD
- tests
- target consumer
- patents
- production
- plans for the future

KEY LANGUAGE
SETTING THE AGENDA, RESPONDING TO OFFERS

4a `11.4` **Listen to the second part of the discussion and answer the questions.**

1 What financial terms do Kenneth and Ingrid offer Neptune?
2 Why do the two sides fail to make a deal?

4b Complete the extracts from the discussion. Then listen again and check your answers.

1 **W:** Let's talk about the agenda for this afternoon. I propose we discuss three specific _____: the amount of our _____ in your business, the _____ you can offer us and other _____ you're working on. How about that?
   K: Sounds OK to me.
   I: Yeah, that's _____.

2 **W:** Well, I'm sorry, but that's not _____. Investing half a million for a fifteen-percent stake wouldn't _____ us.

3 **I:** If I can come in here, let me remind you of the _____ you'll get from investing in our device. Don't forget it's a(n) _____ product and several marine associations have _____ it and found that it works. Also, it's got an international _____.

4 **W:** Maybe. But we're not _____ about the terms you offer. We're not _____ to invest in the project unless you improve your offer.
   K: How about if we _____ you a bigger stake? Would you be _____ to give us $500,000?

5 **K:** _____ we give you a twenty-percent stake for the full amount, what do you say?
   W: I'm sorry. We were _____ for a much higher stake.
   K: Well, that's our final offer. It looks as if we can't _____ a deal.

5a The extracts in Exercise 4b demonstrate four different ways of responding to proposals. Match the extracts (1–5) with the functions (a–d).

a accepting a proposal
b using persuasive arguments
c rejecting a proposal
d bargaining

5b Which sentence in the extracts refers to the points that will be negotiated?

TASK
NEGOTIATING A CONTRACT

6 Having failed to make a deal with Neptune Investments, the two inventors have now set up a meeting with two directors from Ariel Capital. They are ready to negotiate a contract, providing they can agree on the terms.

Group A: turn to page 155.
Group B: turn to page 157.

7 Begin the negotiation. Try to make a deal that will satisfy both parties.

8 Now work as a class and discuss the questions.

1 What strategy and tactics did you use in your negotiation? How successful were they?
2 How do you feel about the outcome of the negotiation? Was everyone happy with the result? If not, what went wrong?

USEFUL PHRASES

Making concessions

We're prepared to … if you'll …
We'll increase our offer provided/as long as you …
Suppose we … , would you be willing to … ?

Accepting an offer

Fine!
OK!
Right!
Sounds good to me.
OK, that's acceptable to us.

Rejecting an offer

I'm afraid it's not acceptable.
Sorry, but we can't agree to that.
We were hoping/expecting …

STUDY SKILLS
MAKING A BUSINESS PRESENTATION

1 Work in groups and discuss the questions.

1 What makes a good presentation? Make a list of guidelines for presenters.
2 'A presentation is a performance.' Do you agree? Give reasons for your answer.
3 What kinds of presentations are common in business?

2a ▶ **11.1** Introduction In an introduction, you welcome your audience and explain the structure of the talk. Watch the first part of a presentation and complete the introduction with the words and phrases in the box.

after that	by the end of our talk	finally	purpose
first, I'll comment		we'll be happy to answer	

> " Good afternoon, everyone, I think most of you already know me, but for those who don't, my name's Rachel Park and I'm Business Manager of First Service, and I'm sure you've all met our Marketing Manager, John Emerson. The ¹_____ of our presentation today is to familiarise you with our exciting new product, our Winner-100 tennis racket, and to outline our marketing strategy.
>
> ²_____ briefly on the results of some research we've done. Next, I'll describe the unique features of the product. Then, I'll hand over to John. He'll give you a profile of our target consumer. ³_____, he'll talk about our plans for launching the product.
>
> ⁴_____, I'll summarise our key points and, ⁵_____, you should have enough information to start planning how you'll sell the new racket. ⁶_____ any questions when we've finished our talk. "

2b Work with a partner and practise delivering the introduction.

3a ▶ **11.2** Watch the second part of the presentation and answer the questions.

1 Where was most of the research carried out?
2 What are the racket's unique selling points?
3 Who is the new racket aimed at?
4 What promotional support will the salespeople receive?

3b Presenters use signalling language to structure their information. Watch the second part of the presentation again and number these phrases in the order you hear them.

a I'll come back to this point later.
b First of all, I'll talk briefly about the research we carried out to develop the Winner-100.
c What does this mean for our marketing and sales approach? It means you'll be promoting a new racket that gives players what they want.
d Moving on now to the product's unique features.
e To sum up, the Winner-100 is an exciting, innovative product.
f For instance, they reported increased power and control when testing the new racket.
g I'll show you the video clip of the players using the racket.
h But first, are there any questions?
i Back to you, Rachel.

3c Match the functions (1–9) with the signalling language used in the sentences (a–i) in Exercise 3b.

1 giving an example
2 introducing your first point
3 analysing a point
4 referring to a visual aid
5 summarising
6 starting another subject
7 asking for a response from the audience
8 indicating you will give further information about a point later
9 referring to a co-presenter

3d Work with a partner and practise saying the signalling language.

4a Conclusion **Look at these descriptions of how to conclude a presentation. Which did the presenter use in her talk?**

a Restate the main point, but say it a little differently.
b Finish with an impressive quotation.
c Sum up, make a recommendation, thank the audience.
d End by telling a human-interest story.
e Say something that reminds the audience of your original objective.
f Conclude with a positive statement which encourages the audience to take action.
g Say something inspiring which will stick in the audience's mind.

4b Write an alternative conclusion to the presentation using one of the ideas in Exercise 4a.

5 Practise making a presentation about a new piece of sports or fitness equipment which your company has just launched. Answer any questions your colleagues wish to ask.

WRITING SKILLS
A TACTFUL BUSINESS EMAIL

6 Why is it necessary to take extra care with the language you use when sending emails at work? Work in small groups and discuss.

7 Read the feedback on a presentation by Karl Meyer, a new Sales Manager. Rank the complaints according to how serious they are.

Here are some typical comments from the feedback forms:

1 'He arrived late and was very nervous. I don't think he'd prepared his talk properly.'
2 'I was sitting at the back of the room. None of the back row could hear what he said.'
3 'What a boring voice! I switched off after a couple of minutes. And I wasn't the only one.'
4 'He didn't seem to have any plan for his talk. It was like an improvised monologue – no structure at all.'
5 'He forgot to mention the most important thing: the unique selling points of the new product.'
6 'He read most of his presentation. There wasn't much eye contact. He had no rapport with his audience.'
7 'His PowerPoint didn't work properly. He got his slides mixed up and looked really embarrassed. He kept apologising, which annoyed me.'
8 'I asked some straightforward questions, but he couldn't answer them. How can I sell the product if I can't answer my customers' queries?'
9 'He ran out of time, so he raced through the last ten minutes of his talk.'
10 'It was one of the worst presentations I've ever attended!'

8a Paraphrasing **Match these paraphrases (a–f) of some of the complaints in Exercise 7 to the original complaints (1–6).**

a A member of the audience mentioned that your voice was rather quiet.
b It was suggested that you arrived late and seemed a little nervous.
c Varying the tone and pitch of your voice would improve the delivery of your presentation.
d Unfortunately, you failed to mention the unique selling points of the product.
e Several participants felt that your talk lacked a clear structure.
f It's probably not a good idea to read a presentation because you need to keep eye contact with your audience.

8b What words or phrases in each paraphrase help to express the participants' opinions in a tactful way? Try to explain how the words/phrases do this.

8c Paraphrase complaints 7–10 from Exercise 7 so the opinions are expressed in a tactful way.

9 As Karl Meyer's boss, write a tactful email to him, giving feedback on his presentation and advising him on how to improve his performance.

Dear Karl,
I've received some feedback from members of the audience who attended your recent presentation to our local distributors. Unfortunately, there were some negative comments about your presentation. …

10 Compare your answer with the model answer on page 164.

12 Science and nature

12.1 THE RED PLANET

Nothing in life is to be feared. It is only to be understood. Marie Curie (1867–1934), Polish scientist

SPEAKING

1a Work with a partner and discuss the questions.

1 How important is it for humans to explore space?
2 Do you know any current or future projects to explore space?
3 Which planet in our solar system most interests you? Why?

1b Compare Earth and Mars. Which planet do you think:

1 is bigger?
2 is warmer?
3 orbits the Sun faster?
4 has a longer day?
5 has more gravity?
6 has more moons?
7 has more nitrogen in its atmosphere?

1c Check your answers on page 164.

VOCABULARY
GEOLOGICAL TERMS

2a Work with a partner. Take turns to choose a word you know from the box and explain its meaning to your partner, without saying the word. Your partner tries to guess the word.

canyon	crater	erosion	flash flood	geyser	ice cap
meteor	reservoir	subsurface	tsunami		

2b When you have explained all the words you know, look up any unknown words in a dictionary or check with your teacher.

2c Which of the words have a strong connection with water?

READING

3a Read the article and choose the best heading for paragraphs A–F. You do not need four of the headings.

1 Characteristics shared with Earth
2 The possibility of life on Mars
3 More thrilling discoveries to come
4 A common history
5 Rethinking our ideas about Mars
6 The view from our spacecraft
7 The method of investigation
8 Early images of the planet
9 What water means for life on Earth
10 Evidence of a different past

3b Distinguishing fact from opinion **Read the information in the box below. Then look at the highlighted parts of the article. Are they fact, opinion or a combination of both?**

To increase our understanding of texts, it's important to distinguish fact from opinion. This is not always straightforward as some statements may be a combination of both.

Every time we feel close to understanding Mars, ... (opinion)

... new discoveries send us straight back to the drawing board to revise existing theories. (fact)

116

3c Find two more facts and opinions in the article.

3d Look at paragraphs A–C of the article. Find some phrases that are used to introduce information as 'fact'.

3e Do you think there is life on Mars or anywhere else in the universe?

LISTENING

4a [12.1] Listen to three people who are interested in joining a project set up to create a human colony on Mars. Complete both tasks as you listen. Choose one of the options for each gap. You do not need six of the options.

Task 1: Background and skills

Speaker 1 _____.
Speaker 2 _____.
Speaker 3 _____.

a is a pilot
b has medical skills
c is an astronaut
d is well travelled
e is single
f is in good physical condition

Task 2: Views on the Mars project

Speaker 1 talks about _____.
Speaker 2 talks about _____.
Speaker 3 talks about _____.

g stages in the colony's development
h debris in space
i the history of the galaxy
j the need for good machinery
k the importance of money
l driving over rough terrain

4b Listen again and check your answers.

5a If you had to select just one of the people in Exercise 4a for the Mars project, who would it be? Why?

5b What kind of training do you think people will need for this project?

SPEAKING AND WRITING

6a Would you join a one-way expedition to establish a human colony on Mars? Why?/Why not?

6b Write a paragraph summarising your ideas in Exercise 6a.

Looking for life on Mars

A   Since our first close-up picture of Mars in 1965, spacecraft voyages to the Red Planet have revealed a world strangely familiar, yet different enough to challenge our perceptions of what makes a planet work. Every time we feel close to understanding Mars, new discoveries send us straight back to the drawing board to revise existing theories.

B   You'd think Mars would be easier to understand. Like Earth, Mars has polar ice caps and clouds in its atmosphere, seasonal weather patterns, volcanoes, canyons and other recognisable features. However, conditions on Mars vary wildly from what we know on our own planet.

C   Over the past three decades, spacecraft have shown us that Mars is rocky, cold and sterile beneath its hazy, pink sky. We've discovered that today's Martian wasteland hints at a formerly volatile world where volcanoes once raged, meteors ploughed deep craters and flash floods rushed over the land. And Mars continues to throw out new enticements with each landing or orbital pass made by our spacecraft.

D   Among our discoveries about Mars, one stands out above all others: the possible presence of liquid water on Mars, either in its ancient past or preserved in the subsurface today. Water is key because almost everywhere we find water on Earth, we find life. If Mars once had liquid water or still does today, it's compelling to ask whether any microscopic life forms could have developed on its surface. Is there any evidence of life in the planet's past? If so, could any of these tiny living creatures still exist today? Imagine how exciting it would be to answer, 'Yes!'

E   To discover the possibilities for past or present life on Mars, NASA's Mars Exploration Programme is currently following an exploration strategy known as 'Seek Signs of Life'. This science theme marks a transition in Mars exploration. It reflects a long-term process of discovery on the red planet, built on strategies to understand Mars' potential as a habitat for past or present microbial life. Searching for this answer means delving into the planet's geologic and climate history to find out how, when and why Mars underwent dramatic changes to become the forbidding, yet promising, planet we observe today.

F   Even if Mars is devoid of past or present life, however, there's still much excitement on the horizon. We ourselves might become the 'life on Mars' should humans choose to travel there one day. Meanwhile, we still have a lot to learn about this amazing planet and its extreme environments.

SCIENTIFICA

◀▶

Comments

A I've had it up to here with all the rubbish that tree-huggers like you spout about plastic, particularly on as informed a site as this **one**. Anyone would imagine that the discovery of this wonder material marks the lowest point in human civilisation. Well, **it doesn't**. Thankfully, we're no longer living in the Stone Age, so let's make the most of the **plastic one**.

B There's no point denying that plastic is a miracle material that's more versatile, more durable and more effective than any other **substance**. We've made more advances thanks to its invention than we ever **did before** – **too many** for me to bother listing here. You'd have to be bonkers to deny that. It would be nearly impossible to live without it. Try **doing so**; you won't manage to for long.

C What about the materials plastic has taken the place of? They're hardly eco-neutral, and extracting and producing them is just as bad. How much energy goes into making glass? **Mining** releases all kinds of poisonous substances into the environment – **chemicals** like mercury. All told, do plastic-based materials cause any more problems than any **others**? I **reckon not**, and they're a whole lot more useful.

D The oil argument is often wheeled out by the anti-plastic brigade, turning a blind eye to the fact that we get most plastic from a by-product of oil refining. So, plastic is actually made from what would otherwise go to waste. How green is that?

E As for the claims that not all plastic can be recycled, well, point of fact: all types of plastic **can be**. The problem isn't the **stuff** itself, it's how we deal with it. If we wanted to recycle every last bit of it, we **could**. **Will we** in the future? I hope **so**. Anyway, biodegradable plastic (from corn, not oil!) is coming on in leaps and bounds, so, soon the waste issue may be a non-issue. On top of that, plastic makes up little more than five percent of the rubbish in your bin; that's the **same** as glass.

F So, why does plastic get all this bad press? Quite simply, you can see it and it's unsightly. Well, I'm sorry, but of all the types of pollution, the **visual sort** doesn't figure too highly on my list of threats to us. There are many dangerous invisible pollutants going into the sea that we should worry about, but **don't** because we can't see them. And besides, does it matter if a seagull builds its nest out of bits of plastic? I think **not**.

G Now, while this may be a bit of a rant, it's not an ill-informed **one** as I'm a polymer scientist working in environmental technology. So, let's all sing *Happy Birthday* to our flexible friend, polythene.

LISTENING

1 Work with a partner and discuss the questions.

1 What do you have with you today that is made of plastic?
2 There are claims that plastic is a blight upon our lives. Why?

2a 12.2 **Listen to a podcast and make notes on the speaker's main points.**

2b Which of these points did/didn't you know before?

READING

3 Read the text quickly and answer the questions.

1 What is the subject of the text? What is the writer's basic opinion?
2 How would you describe his attitude?
3 Where do you think the text comes from?

4a Evaluating arguments Read the text again and identify the key points in each paragraph. How do they relate to the points in the podcast?

4b Which of these points would undermine the scientist's argument?

1 The production of plastic from oil requires large amounts of energy.
2 Toxic chemicals leach from plastic into the environment.
3 Its comparatively low weight reduces fuel consumption during transportation.
4 The decomposition of biodegradable plastic produces CO_2.

4c Look at Audio script 12.2 on page 181. Evaluate the argument and claims. What do you think are the strengths and weaknesses of this argument?

5 With whom do you most agree, the writer of the podcast or the scientist? Why?

VOCABULARY
INFORMAL PHRASES

6 Find informal words or phrases in the text which have the same meaning as the neutral phrases below.

1 unable to tolerate more (paragraph A)
2 environmentally concerned people (paragraph A)
3 talk incessantly (paragraph A)
4 to expend time and effort doing something (paragraph B)
5 insane (paragraph B)
6 referred to and presented (paragraph D)
7 a group of people against synthetic materials (paragraph D)
8 an uncontrolled or aggressive argument (paragraph G)

7 Complete the sentences with informal language from Exercise 6. Make any necessary changes.

1 You must be _____ to want to stay here with the hurricane coming.
2 I've _____ with that racket. Turn that music down!
3 It's good to have a _____ every now and again; it helps clear the air.
4 I can't _____ to do the washing-up. Let's do it when we get back.

8 Find other examples of colloquial vocabulary in the text and make those examples more formal.

GRAMMAR
COHESION 2 (SUBSTITUTION)

9a Read the explanation and match the types of substitution (1–5) with the examples (a–e).

> **GRAMMAR TIP**
>
> In order to avoid unnecessary repetition in text and speech, substitution, whereby words and phrases are replaced by others or even omitted, can be used. This also leads to greater cohesion, or inter-connectedness, within a text.

1 Lexical substitution: replace a word with a synonym or near-synonym.
2 Nominal substitution: replace a noun/noun phrase with a word such as *one, ones, the sort.*
3 Verbal substitution: replace a verb/verb phrase with *do* or *do so.*
4 Clausal substitution: replace a whole clause with *so* or *not.*
5 Ellipsis (zero substitution): completely omit the repeated item. This often happens after words like *other, all, some, not, enough.*

a Are plastic-based materials any worse than any others we use industrially?
b There's no point denying that plastic is a miracle material that's more versatile, more durable and more effective than any other substance.
c Does it matter if a seagull builds its nest out of bits of plastic? I think not.
d Now, while this may be a bit of a rant, it's not an ill-informed one.
e We've made more advances thanks to its invention than we ever did before.

9b Look at the words and phrases in bold in the text. Which words have been replaced or omitted?

➥ Language reference and extra practice, pages 148–149

10 Rewrite the sentences using substitution techniques. Sometimes more than one answer is possible.

1 Is plastic a wonder material? I thought it was a wonder material until I listened to the podcast.
2 Poor heat resistance is a weakness of biodegradable plastic and its lack of strength is another weakness of it.
3 It is important to reuse plastic bags. If you reuse them, you are actively reducing waste.
4 Chemical leaching may be a problem caused by plastic, but I'm not sure it is a serious problem.
5 We manufacture so many things out of plastic. We manufacture carpets and clothes. We manufacture components for cars and computers. How could we live without it?

SPEAKING

11 Work in small groups and discuss the questions.

1 What do you and your country do to limit the use and consumption of plastic? How effective are these measures?
2 How would you have to change your lifestyle in order to live for a month without buying anything made of plastic?
3 What other materials have caused great change in the world?

WRITING

12 Choose one of the questions in Exercise 11 and write a few paragraphs on the topic. Try to use substitution techniques in your writing.

▶ MEET THE EXPERT

Watch an interview with professors Richard Kitney and Paul Freemont, about synthetic biology.
Turn to page 154 for video activities.

SPEAKING

1a Which insects and similar creatures do you like/dislike? Why? Work with a partner and discuss. Are there more that you like or dislike? Which do you think are the most/least important to humans?

1b What do you think this quote means?

> *If the bee disappeared off the surface of the globe, then man would only have four years of life left.*
>
> Attributed to Albert Einstein (1879–1955), German physicist

READING

2a Understanding persuasive techniques **Read this blurb from a book cover. How does it try to interest you in the book?**

A
From London to Los Angeles, from Slovenia to Taiwan, honeybees are dying. In America one in three hives was left lifeless at the beginning of 2008. In France the death rate might be sixty percent. In Britain a government minister warns that honeybees could be extinct within a decade.

If or when the world loses its black-and-yellow workers, agriculture will collapse. Civilisation itself might be the next victim. A third of all we eat and much of what we wear relies on pollination by honeybees.

What is behind the catastrophe? Viruses, parasites, pesticides and climate change have all been blamed. Some accuse beekeepers themselves of working their charges to death by shipping their hives thousands of miles every year to different monoculture sites, all in the name of agribusiness profits. In this fascinating book, two keen amateur apiarists investigate the claims and counterclaims with the scientists and beekeepers in Europe, America and beyond. And they ask the question that will soon be on everyone's lips: is there any possible way of saving the honeybees – and with them, the world as we know it?

2b Which of these words describe the blurb?

apocalyptic   apocryphal   apologetic   apoplectic

3a Read the extracts. Which parts of the book do you think they come from? Choose from this list.

1 In the beginning was the buzz (introduction/chapter 1)
2 The enemy within (chapter 7)
3 A world without bees (chapter 10)

B
The mountains of southern Sichuan in China are covered in pear trees. Every April they are home to a rare sight: thousands of people holding bamboo sticks with chicken feathers attached to the end, clambering among the blossom-laden branches. Closer inspection reveals that children, parents and even grandparents are all pollinating the trees by hand. It is a ritual they have been following for more than twenty years, ever since pesticides killed their honeybees.

C
Apis mellifera, or the western honeybee as she is more commonly known, has been revered for thousands of years for her ability to make a sweet substance that delights the human palate. The earliest record of humans' use of honey is a cave painting in Valencia, Spain, depicting a man climbing a cliff to rob a swarm of wild bees. It dates back at least 10,000 years, to just after the last Ice Age, and the love affair has continued ever since.

D
Is this what the honeybees are telling us? That our industrialised farming with its monocultures, pesticides and increasingly unreasonable demands on honeybees themselves is not sustainable? With their limited resistance to poisons and pollutants, are they the canary in the coal mine warning us that if our lifestyles are killing them, we are not far behind?

E
By the early nineteenth century, honey was no longer the standard sweetening agent in Britain. The arrival of cheap sugar meant there was no need for every household in the land to have a hive in the garden. But as industrialisation expanded, the beehive, symbol of both hard work and the acceptance of the social order, still featured in Victorian society. Many buildings of the time had bees in their decoration, like Manchester's neo-gothic town hall.

3b In which section (A–E) do we read about these things? Sometimes more than one answer is possible.

1 the function of honeybees as an early warning system
2 an example of bees no longer performing their role as pollinators
3 the possible contribution of beekeepers to the current crisis
4 the name entomologists use for the western honeybee
5 a change in diet
6 an example of the way bees provide us with more than food
7 a change in the way of keeping bees
8 the fact that the authors of the book do not keep bees for a living
9 the use of bees in art
10 the metaphorical meanings we attribute to bees

3c What do you think about the argument of this book? Do you know of any similar problems?

VOCABULARY
COLLECTIVE NOUNS

4a Complete the phrases about groups of people, animals or things with the collective nouns in the box.

bunch	flock	group	herd	pack
set	shoal	~~swarm~~		

1 a *swarm* of wild bees
2 a _____ of grapes/flowers/keys
3 a _____ of wolves/hounds/cards
4 a _____ of elephants/cattle/cows/deer
5 a _____ of fish
6 a _____ of sheep/goats/birds/geese
7 a _____ of assumptions/conditions/values/problems/tools/chairs
8 a _____ of chemicals/islands/hotels/children/admirers

4b Complete the sentences with the correct form of phrases from Exercise 4a.

1 One of the things we really wanted to see on our safari was _____.
2 While diving around the reef we saw some beautiful _____.
3 People were selling _____ by the roadside.

GRAMMAR
NOMINALISATION

5a Look at the sentences and complete the rule.

1 The *arrival* of cheap sugar meant that there was no need for every household to have a hive.
2 When cheap sugar *arrived*, it meant that there was no need for every household to have a hive.

We can make _____ from other parts of speech, very often from _____, sometimes from adjectives. We call this process 'nominalisation'.

deny – denial, argue – argument, fair – fairness

5b Find other examples in the extracts where a nominalised form is used instead of a verb. How could you express the same ideas using the equivalent verbs or adjectives?

➥ Language reference and extra practice, pages 148–149

5c Put the words in the correct order to make sentences using nominalisation.

1 diseases / by America / failed / many / the attempt / life-threatening / to keep out
2 railway / honeybees / be responsible for / could / the Trans-Siberian / the disappearance of many
3 of / is / Argentina / world's / exporter / honey / major / the
4 of embankments, / and nesting sites / roadsides / the loss / and public areas / is the result / of flowers / of excessive mowing

> **GRAMMAR TIP**
>
> We often use nominalisation in more formal situations, e.g. in formal writing.
> In nominalisation, make a note of which prepositions are used.
> *the arrival **of** the ability **to** an increase **in***
> We sometimes form a nominalisation from a verb with a similar meaning.
> *Prices go up every week.*
> *There's an increase in prices every week.*

5d Complete the pairs of sentences with a noun and any other necessary words.

1 The weather was getting better.
 There _____ the weather.
2 She got over her illness very quickly.
 She made _____ her illness.
3 He'll go into all the details later.
 He'll give _____ the details later.
4 The bombs went off all night.
 There _____ all night.

SPEAKING

6 Work in small groups and discuss the questions.

1 Bees can symbolise hard work and the acceptance of the social order. What do other insects/animals symbolise?
2 Do you think that the way we farm is changing now or will change in the future?
3 Do you eat organic food? Why?/Why not?
4 Which other insects/animals could be extinct within a decade? What kind of impact would this have on humans?
5 What could you do to protect insect or animal life where you live?

SITUATION

Ask the Panel is a current affairs and social issues discussion television programme in which a mixed panel of experts, commentators and members of the public discuss questions posed by the audience. Recent programmes have covered topics of law, the media and healthcare. This week the topic is 'science and society'.

1 Work in groups and look at the topics under discussion on this edition of *Ask the Panel*. What do you know about these subjects?

- nuclear energy
- genetic engineering
- cloning
- animal vivisection
- animal conservation
- climate change
- illegal poaching of animals
- the moral duty of science

2a Read the profiles of the members of the panel on this week's show.

> **Indira Patel: the former chair of the National Academy of Science, and a frequent media expert on science matters**

> **Bill Patterson: a high-profile member of Earthwatch, an environmental pressure group**

> **Molly Chang: an investigative journalist who recently exposed malpractice in the chicken farming industry**

> **David Perez: a school Science teacher for twenty years**

2b 12.3 The first question posed to the panel is 'Should genetic engineering, in particular the genetic modification of plants and animals that we eat, be halted due to the potential for unforeseen future dangers that it might cause for us and the planet?' Who do you think might make these following points? Listen and check your answers.

1 We can't trust the companies engaged in GM food research.
2 GM crops hold out the prospect of being able to feed the world's population.
3 We can trust the scientists and the companies concerned.
4 Research should continue, but with the correct safeguards and controls.
5 The problem is that the dangers cannot be predicted through research.
6 It is currently possible to feed the world, but politics and business prevent this.

3 Do you agree or disagree with the speakers?

KEY LANGUAGE
REFERRING TO WHAT OTHER PEOPLE HAVE SAID

4 Complete the sentences from the panel discussion using the pairs of words below (a–f). Then listen again and check your answers.

1 Well, _____ Indira _____ , this research certainly shouldn't be halted.
2 _____ David _____ about current safeguards might sound reasonable.
3 If I _____ you _____, you're saying that science-based businesses can't be trusted.
4 Could I just _____ _____ on something that Indira said about feeding the world's population?
5 She _____ that genetic engineering will enable us to feed the world, _____ that that wasn't currently possible.
6 Perhaps we should _____ to _____ the original question said, which was that there are unforeseen dangers.

a return, what   d pick, up
b as, said   e understand, correctly
c what, said   f claimed, suggesting

5 Look at different versions of the sentences in Exercise 4. Choose the correct sentence in each pair.

1 a Well, as Indira mentioned, this research certainly …
  b Well, as Indira's words, this research certainly …
2 a The things that David made about current safeguards …
  b The points David made about current safeguards …
3 a If I see you correctly, you're saying that science-based businesses …
  b If I follow you correctly, you're saying that science-based businesses …
4 a If I could just comment on something that Indira said about feeding …
  b If I could just say about something that Indira said about feeding …
5 a She stated that genetic engineering will enable us to feed the world, implying that …
  b She claimed that genetic engineering will enable us to feed the world, of the suggestion that …
6 a Perhaps we should go back to what the original question said …
  b Perhaps we should deal what the original question said …

TASK
TAKING PART IN A PANEL DISCUSSION

6a Work in groups of five. You are guests on *Ask the Panel*. Read your roleplay cards.

Student A: turn to page 156.
Student B: turn to page 157.
Student C: turn to page 158.
Student D: turn to page 158.
Student E: turn to page 158.

6b Take it in turns to be the chair of the panel. Discuss the questions in the order indicated on the producer's notes below.

Producer's notes — question running order

1 Is nuclear energy the solution to the energy crisis in the world and should all countries be able to develop nuclear power?

2 Is it right to continue testing both medicines and cosmetics on animals?

3 Do the dangers of cloning outweigh the advantages? If so, should all research into this area be halted?

4 As animals have always become extinct throughout the history of the world, do humans really have a responsibility to save animal species from that danger?

5 Should scientists ignore the moral and social implications of their research so that they can concentrate on pushing the boundaries of human knowledge without restriction?

USEFUL PHRASES

Chairing a discussion

Right, let's get the discussion under way. The question is …
Let's see what someone else thinks. David? What's your view?
Do you have an opinion on that?
Anything to say to that?
What's your response to that?
If I could just bring David in here.
I think we're going round in circles here. Shall we move on to the next question?
It's time to move on, I think. Let's look at the next question.

STUDY SKILLS
EXAMINATION SKILLS

1 Exam vocabulary Complete the sentences with the words in the box.

candidates	cheat	compulsory	cross out
invigilator	legibly	revision	

1 It is crucial to start your _____ for the exam early.
2 Your handwriting doesn't have to be perfect, but you are expected to write _____. If you make a mistake, _____ the wrong answer neatly and write the correct one.
3 In section A there is a choice of questions, but the questions in section B are _____.
4 The _____ will be looking out for _____ who try to _____ .

2 Developing self-awareness Work with a partner and discuss the questions.

1 Think about exams you have done in the past. What went well? What could you have done better?
2 Do you find exams stressful? If so, how do you try to manage the stress?

3 Comparing exam culture These points are all generally true of international English language examinations. Are they true or false for most examinations in your country?

1 Once the exam has started, if you need any help, you have to put up your hand and ask an invigilator. But they cannot tell you the answers to any questions!
2 You cannot talk to any other student; this will be viewed as cheating. Cheating is an extremely serious offence. If you cheat, your exam will not be marked.
3 In an essay question, you must answer the question that has been set. You cannot write everything you know about a topic or discuss a vaguely related topic.
4 If there is a word limit, you must keep to it.
5 At the end of the exam you must stop writing the moment the invigilator tells you to do so.

4 Preparation Here are some vital questions you should ask yourself if you're preparing to take an English language exam. Add one or two more questions.

1 How many marks are there for each section or question?
2 How long can I spend on each of the reading passages/texts?
3 In the listening exam, how many times will I hear the recording?

5a `12.4` **Listen to a discussion between a student and a teacher. What kind of exam is Thérèse going to take? What kind of tasks will it involve?**

5b Listen again and write down the advice the teacher gives Thérèse.

5c Write your own top five tips for taking exams.

WRITING SKILLS
A PERSONAL STATEMENT

6 What do you understand by a *personal statement*? When might you need to write one?

7a You are completing an application form for an Advanced Communication Skills course at a London university. One section of the application form asks you for more information about yourself. Make brief notes on these points.

1 the reasons why you want to do the course
2 your background, including previous studies
3 what you are currently doing
4 your English level and details of any English language exams you have taken
5 any work experience you have
6 your interests, hobbies, etc.
7 your future plans

7b Work with a partner and compare your notes.

7c Read the personal statement. What topics from Exercise 7a does the writer cover in each paragraph? Do you think this structure is effective?

Name: Monica Paganin

Nationality: Italian

I am applying for this course because, although I feel I have a good level of written English, I need to improve my speaking skills. I am interested in learning how to give good presentations and to participate effectively in group discussions. My pronunciation is very heavily influenced by Italian and I would like to be more like a native speaker. I know this will be difficult, but it's my dream! One of my cousins studied at your university two years ago; he had a very positive experience and recommended the course to me.

I have studied English for ten years at a private language school in my city. About three years ago, I took the Cambridge First Certificate Exam and passed with an A grade. I believe I am now at advanced level and I aim to take the CAE or IELTS exam soon. Can you advise me about that?

Concerning my background, I was actually born in India (my parents were working there for an NGO*), but I have lived in Italy since the age of three. I grew up in a small town on the west coast and this was a very significant experience for me, first stimulating my love of the sea.

When I was ten, we moved to Padova (*Padua* in English), an ancient university city near Venice, and I went to high school and university here. At school I did well in science subjects and went on to study Marine Biology at university, graduating last summer. My dissertation was on the ecological effects of the tidal barrier being built to protect Venice and it was well received. I strongly believe that our future lies in the seas and we must do everything we can to understand and protect them. After all, Earth isn't called the blue planet for nothing! I very much want to make my own positive contribution to that goal. Next year I hope to start work as a researcher in the Marine Environment Research Centre. If I am not successful, I may go abroad to do a Master's, for which English will be very important.

I am a qualified diving instructor and in my summer vacations I have helped in seaside holiday camps for disadvantaged children, taking on a wide range of responsibilities, from planning activities to consoling homesick children! This has taught me soft skills such as listening to others attentively, teamwork and leadership.

In my free time, as well as diving, I enjoy many other water sports (e.g. swimming, water polo). I also like reading, especially novels by Paulo Coelho and Haruki Murakami. My greatest love, however, is travelling and experiencing foreign cultures and civilisations. While I am attending the course, I would also like to take the opportunity to visit museums and galleries and generally soak up the rich cultural life of a great city.

I consider myself an enthusiastic and conscientious student, who will benefit from – and participate actively in – the classes. Everyone says English is important because it is the global language of communication, but for me it is also a beautiful language which I love learning!

*non-governmental organisation

8 These statements are often true of good personal statements. Are they true of Monica's? If so, why?

1 It is convincing and suggests the writer is committed and enthusiastic.
2 It shows that the writer is prepared to offer something, not merely take what they want for their own ends.
3 There are no contradictory pieces of information. It does not get itself into a tangle.
4 There are no obvious gaps in terms of coverage. No important parts of the writer's life are missing.
5 The statement has a personal dimension and the writer's voice comes through.
6 A lot of time and care has been taken over the writing.
7 The language makes the writer sound intelligent, without being pretentious.
8 There is a strong conclusion.

9 Conclusions These conclusions to personal statements were written by international students who wanted to study in a UK university. Choose the correct word/words to complete them.

1 If my application is *successful* / *rewarding* / *acknowledged*, I aim to *snatch* / *clutch* / *seize* the opportunity to take an active part in a *medley* / *variety* / *miscellany* of academic, cultural and social activities during my university life.
2 In the future I want to *play* / *partake* / *participate* a role in the development of my country of origin which, over the last *many* / *few* / *plenty* years, has been in a difficult situation and now needs good administrators. I could give back what I will *gain* / *attain* / *reap* from the UK and help my country develop its economy and *struggle* / *clash* / *fight* corruption.

10 You are going to apply for a course in an English-speaking country. Decide which type of course you are applying for, then write the personal statement that will accompany your application. Write about 400 words.

GRAMMAR

G1 THE CONTINUOUS ASPECT

Use the continuous aspect to talk about:
- an action or situation which is/was in progress at a particular time.
  He **was researching** into gene therapy at the time.

- an unfinished action or situation.
  He **had been working** in the lab when I met him.

- a temporary action.
  I**'m using** Jo's laptop while mine is being repaired.

- a trend, changing action or situation.
  Scientists say the weather **is getting** hotter.

Use the present continuous to talk about actions or situations currently in progress.
   They**'re conducting** a series of experiments into genetic mutation at the moment.

Also use the present continuous to describe future arrangements.
   I**'m giving** the lecture on Thursday.

Use the past continuous to talk about an ongoing action in the past, often unfinished.
   I **was working** on the genome project the whole of last year. (The project hadn't finished by the end of the year.)

Use the present perfect continuous to talk about an ongoing action or situation in the past that is still continuing into the present or has just finished but has a result in the present.
   The doctor **has been waiting** for you for ages.
   I**'ve been running to get** here on time. That's why I'm out of breath.

Use the past perfect continuous to talk about an ongoing action or situation in the past that is still continuing up to another time in the past.
   The researchers **had been focusing** too narrowly – that's why we stopped them.

Use the future continuous to talk about temporary actions in progress at a particular time in the future.
   We**'ll be working** on the project all next week.

G2 THE PERFECT ASPECT

Use the perfect aspect to look back from one time to another.

PRESENT PERFECT
This looks back from now to a time before now. It often focuses on completed actions or situations.
   We**'ve already interviewed** ten people for this post.

The present perfect continuous focuses on the duration of the action.
   We**'ve been interviewing** all morning.

PAST PERFECT
The past perfect looks back from a time in the past to another time before that.
   She**'d applied for** ten jobs before she got this one.

The past perfect continuous focuses on duration.
   She**'d been applying** for jobs for months before she got this one.

FUTURE PERFECT
The future perfect looks back from a time in the future to another time before that.
   Lucas **will have finished** the job by 6.00 p.m.

The future perfect continuous focuses on duration.
   Lucas **will have been working** on it for three hours by then.

OTHER FORMS
The perfect has an infinitive form: *to + have +* past participle.
   I expected you **to have completed** the questionnaires by now.

The *-ing* form is *having +* past participle.
   Having arrived at the laboratory, we were shown to Professor Dalton's office.

KEY LANGUAGE

KL STATING REQUIREMENTS, SAYING WHAT IS ESSENTIAL AND DESIRABLE

ESSENTIAL
It's absolutely essential that …
They/The candidate must have (done) …
They'll have to have (done) …
Candidates have to be able to …
That's/X is a pre-requisite/an essential requirement.

DESIRABLE
(I imagine) it would be helpful to have (done) …
It'd be a good thing if he/she had (done) …
It would be an advantage if he/she had (done) …
That/X would probably give them an edge.

VOCABULARY

V1 ISSUES IN EDUCATION
assessment, critical thinking, curriculum, dumbing down, elitism, informed decisions, interpersonal skills, knowledge base, plagiarism, rote learning, streaming, traditional teaching

V2 REPORTING WHAT OTHERS SAY
argue, claim, comment, conclude, deny, point out, suggest

V3 SUFFIXES (ADJECTIVES)
affectionate, allergic, ambitious, analytical, educational, empathetic, famous, fictional, infectious, influential, logical, passionate, persuasive, powerful, speculative, successful, toxic

V4 ABBREVIATIONS
BA, BULATS, CV, IELTS, MBA, MSc, PhD, TOEFL

G1 1 Complete the sentences with the correct continuous form of the verbs in brackets.

1 Mercedes ___ (work) as a teaching assistant since she arrived here two years ago.
2 I ___ (try) to finish my assignment all through the plane journey, but it was too turbulent.
3 The rearranged lecture ___ (take) place next Friday at 5.00 p.m.
4 Working conditions in the factory ___ (improve) before the new management started.
5 The whole family ___ (stay) with Ralph's parents until the building work is completed.
6 The security guard ___ (lock) the office when the burglars forced their way past him.
7 I know I failed the test because I ___ (not concentrate) in Professor Williams' lectures.

G2 2 Choose the correct forms to complete the sentences.

1 By the time the strike at the car plant was over, several of the workers *already found / had already found* new jobs.
2 Alan will have *negotiated / been negotiating* deals with the USA for 40 years when he retires.
3 That office block *has been / was* empty since 2012.
4 They have *closed / been closing* the production department for five days already this month.
5 We really wanted *to have / having* finished all the work by now.
6 The company had *recruited / been recruiting* graduate trainees for over 20 years when the scheme was ended.

KL 3 Read the advert and complete the sentences with phrases from KL.

University of West Hampton **UWH**

The Languages Department currently has a vacancy for a lecturer in English Language Studies.

The successful candidate must:
· be a native or bilingual speaker of English.
· have a first degree in English or Linguistics.
· have a postgraduate qualification in a related subject.

The following are also desirable:
· knowledge of at least one other language.
· experience in the higher education sector.
· interest in the development of the English language.

Terms and conditions on application.

1 _____ the applicant speaks English fluently.
2 _____ studied English or linguistics.
3 _____ completed a postgraduate degree.
4 _____ could speak another language.
5 _____ worked in higher education.
6 _____ were interested in the development of the English language.

V1 4 Complete the sentences with words or phrases from V1.

1 The subjects studied in a school/college are called the _____.
2 If you reproduce other people's work and claim it as your own, you are guilty of _____.
3 TV broadcasters are often accused of _____ because programmes aren't intellectual enough.
4 _____ is often criticised because it does not encourage independent thinking.
5 It is necessary in a language course to have frequent _____ to measure students' progress.
6 Some schools practise _____, that is, they have groups of different abilities for some subjects.

V2 5 Replace the underlined phrases with reporting verbs from V2 in the correct form.

1 The teacher put forward the idea that we might want to review the perfect aspect for the test.
   _____

2 They were about to leave when Nikki brought to our attention that we still had ten minutes left.
   _____

3 In this presentation I'll make the point strongly that we need to invest more in education.
   _____

4 The president says it is not true that he was involved in any arms deals.
   _____

5 After studying your application, we have decided after consideration that you would be the best person for the position.
   _____

6 Scientists in France state that it is true that they have found a cure for cancer.
   _____

V3 6 Complete the definitions with an adjective formed from a word in the box.

affection	ambition	empathy	infection
persuade	speculate		

1 Someone who shows you in a gentle way that they care about you is _____.
2 A theory which is based on guesswork rather than facts is _____.
3 Someone who is determined to be successful in life is _____.
4 An illness which is spread easily is _____.
5 Someone who is able to understand other people's feelings and problems is _____.
6 An argument which can make you think differently about something is _____.

GRAMMAR

G1 ARTICLES

Use the indefinite article (*a/an*):
* to introduce something for the first time.
  Madagascar is **an** island off the coast of southern Africa.

> **!** *a/an* and *one*
> *A/An* and *one* are not usually interchangeable.
> *One* + noun means 'not more than one/one only'.
> **One** egg is not enough to make a cake. (= I need two or three.)
> **An** egg is not enough to make a cake. (= I also need other ingredients.)

Use the definite article (*the*):
* to refer to something mentioned before.
  Madagascar is **an** island off the coast of Africa. **The** island is well known for …

* to refer to something obvious from the context (common knowledge).
  Can you pass me **the** pepper?

* to refer to something unique.
  Doesn't **the** moon look beautiful tonight?

* with a superlative phrase.
  It's **the best** holiday we've ever had!

* with the names of some countries and geographical features.
  The islands are in **the** Pacific Ocean.

Use the zero article (no article):
* with general plural and uncountable nouns, and abstract nouns.
  Islands often attract tourists because of the number of beaches in a small area.
  Conservation is an important issue now.

* with people's names and continents, countries, cities, mountains and lakes.
  Turkey is the only country to straddle two continents: **Europe** and **Asia**.

G2 MODAL VERBS: PRESENT AND FUTURE

ABILITY/POSSIBILITY
Use *can/be able to* for ability/possibility.
  People **can** swim from this beach.
  We **won't be able to** save Balandra Beach.

PERMISSION/REQUESTS/REFUSAL
Use *can, could* or *may* for permission and *can* or *could* for requests. Use *won't* for refusal.
  '**Can** I borrow the car tonight?' 'Yes, you **can**.'
  Could you hold my bags for a moment?
  I **won't** give up.

LIKELIHOOD/DEDUCTION
Use *can, could, may* or *might* to express a likelihood in the present or future.
  The country **may/might/could** be moving towards tourism.
  Antonia **might** be in her office.

> **!** But don't use *couldn't* to talk about a general possibility in the future; use *might not*.
> ~~The weather could not be good tomorrow.~~ ✗
> The weather **might not** be good tomorrow. ✓

Use *must* (but not *mustn't*) and *can't* (but not *can*) to express a logical deduction, for something you are certain about.
  Antonia **must** be here. Her coat's here.
  Jamie **can't** be here. He went out two minutes ago.

ADVICE/OBLIGATION/PROHIBITION
Use *should* or *ought to* for advice.
  You **should/ought to** go to bed earlier.

Use *should, must* or *have to* for obligation.
  We **should** arrange our visas soon.

Must and *have to* are stronger than *should*. *Have to* is used for rules and obligation from 'outside'.
  You **have to** pay this fine within two weeks.

Use *don't have to* or *don't need to* when there is no obligation.
  We **don't have to** wear smart clothes to the party.

Prohibition is negative obligation. Use *can't* or *mustn't* for this.
  We **can't** go in there – it's for staff only.
  You **mustn't** speak to the driver when the bus is moving.

KEY LANGUAGE

KL1 STATING YOUR POSITION
I'd like to make my position very clear (about this).
X is an absolute priority/is not negotiable.
It's vital to have X if you want to …
It simply isn't possible to …

KL2 CLARIFYING
If I understand you correctly, (you're saying) …
It seems you will/won't …
What exactly do you mean?
I understand where you're coming from …
OK, you've been very clear about …

VOCABULARY

V1 TRAVEL COLLOCATIONS
ancient monument, baking temperatures, boutique hotel, budget airline, carbon footprint, last-minute deal, local delicacy, organised excursion

V2 MULTI-WORD VERBS
avoid getting ripped off, get away from it all, get back to nature, go off the beaten track, let your hair down, live it up, lounge around by the pool, soak up the atmosphere, steer clear of the tourist traps, take in the sights

V3 THE NATURAL WORLD
archipelago, biodiversity, ecosystem, endemic, feral, lava, reserve, tectonic plate

G1 **1** **Complete the text with** *a/an, the* **or – (zero article).**
'Last year I had ¹_____ very different holiday; some friends and I went on ²_____ 'yoga retreat' on ³_____ south coast of ⁴_____ France. ⁵_____ retreat itself was fascinating – it consisted of about ⁶_____ fifty huts for two people behind a really peaceful, quiet beach. We had three hours of yoga every morning on ⁷_____ beach and then we went for ⁸_____ walks in ⁹_____ hills behind the coast in the afternoon, or just relaxed. ¹⁰_____ instructor who took us for yoga was fantastic – so knowledgeable. ¹¹_____ holiday was only a week but I felt both calm and invigorated when I got back. It's certainly ¹²_____ most relaxing holiday I've ever had!'

2 **Find and correct one mistake in each sentence.**
1 A lot of people are becoming more interested in the eco-tourism these days.
2 I'm not sure if Karen's here at the moment. Hold on a minute, and I'll check if she's in a kitchen.
3 I didn't realise you wanted to go on the excursion too. I only booked a ticket.
4 We stayed in a great hotel in Florida. While a hotel was in a built-up area, it was very quiet.
5 People are travelling less because a lot of the package holidays are more expensive this year as a result of the rise in fuel costs.
6 We've been saving up for years to go on a really special holiday – we want to go to Galapagos Islands.

G2 **3** **Choose** *two* **correct options in each sentence.**
1 As we become more aware of climate change, more people *can / may / might* choose not to fly because of the environmental damage.
2 The play has started. You *can't / mustn't / don't have to* go in until there's a break.
3 My pen's run out of ink. *Can / Will / Could* I borrow one of yours?
4 'Suki's on holiday this week.' 'That *isn't / can't be / mustn't be* true – she's got an interview on Friday.'
5 It's very likely that he will win a major tennis tournament soon but it *may / could / might* not be this year.

KL **4** **Complete the conversation with phrases from KL.**
A: I booked a holiday with you last month, but I'm afraid I can't go now. I'd like a refund.
B: That's a shame. When is the holiday for?
A: The flight leaves on Tuesday.
B: Oh, I see. If ¹___ correctly, you want your money back for a holiday departing in five days?
A: That's right.
B: Well, I'm afraid that isn't possible.
A: I don't understand. What ²___ ?
B: I'm saying that it ³___ at this stage.
A: Oh, it ⁴___ give me a refund. Is that correct?
B: I can't give you a refund. You'll have to go to your insurance company.
A: Insurance?
B: You don't have insurance? But it's ⁵___ insurance when you book a holiday.

V1 **5** **Complete the advert with collocations formed from the words in the boxes. Use one word from each box in each gap.**

ancient	baking	boutique	local	organised

| delicacies | excursion | hotel | monuments | temperatures |

Land of ¹_____, such as the Pyramids and the Sphinx
Two weeks in Egypt this summer from as little as 400 euros – one week in a(n) ²_____ on the Mediterranean coast and another sampling the ancient history of Cairo and the delicious ³_____ in its restaurants. Or, if you prefer, a three-day ⁴_____ down the Nile with one of our tour guides – what better way to escape the ⁵_____ in July and August?

V2 **6** **Find phrases in V2 with these meanings.**
1 avoid places where there are a lot of visitors: _____
2 go to a place which doesn't attract a lot of people: _____
3 relax at the hotel, sunbathing and swimming: _____
4 visit famous places: _____
5 not pay extortionate prices: _____
6 have a good time and lose your inhibitions: _____

V3 **7** **Choose the correct words to complete the sentences.**
1 One day I'd love to buy a boat and go island-hopping across the Indonesian *archipelago / reserve*.
2 Shortly after Mount Etna started erupting, *tectonic plates / lava* could be seen flowing down the side of the volcano.
3 Lime disease is *feral / endemic* to the local area.
4 The government created a nature *reserve / ecosystem* here last year to protect the local bird population.
5 This area is a thriving *ecosystem / reserve*, with hundreds of species of animal and plant life.
6 There are lots of *endemic / feral* dogs on the island which have been abandoned.

GRAMMAR

G1 SUBORDINATE CLAUSES

A sentence consists of one or more clauses. These may simply be two main clauses, joined by *and, but* or *or* .

> The contract was signed by all parties **and** the meeting ended.

The contract was signed and *the meeting ended* are two main clauses.

A sentence often consists of a main clause and a subordinate clause, joined by a subordinating conjunction such as *when, because, although, if* .

> Many people couldn't get to the conference **because** the train drivers were on strike.

When subordinate clauses begin sentences, they are often separated by commas.

> If you're ever in Geneva, let's visit CERN.
> Let's visit Cern if you're ever in Geneva.

Commas are not used before 'that' clauses.

> It's quite natural that you should be concerned about the LHC experiments.

A main clause can stand by itself. In the second example above, *Many people couldn't get to the conference* makes sense on its own.

A subordinate clause can't stand by itself: *because the train drivers were on strike* only makes sense when the main clause completes the meaning.

Subordinate clauses are dependent on a main clause; they often express a notion that explains or completes something in the main clause, e.g. a reason or a condition.

- cause/reason (*because, as, since*)
- result (*so*)
- condition (*if, unless, provided*)
- purpose (*to, so that*)
- time (*before, when, while*)
- relative (*who, which*)
- reported speech (*that*)

G2 MODAL PERFECT

A modal perfect is a modal verb + *have* + past participle.

Use *must/can't/couldn't have* + past participle to express certainty about something in the past.

> He **must have been** really happy when he found out his exam result.
> She **can't have arrived** – her coat isn't here.
> Marcel **couldn't have written** this – his English isn't good enough.

❗ The opposite of *must have done* is *can't/couldn't have done*. It expresses impossibility.

Use *may/might/could have* + past participle to express a degree of possibility in the past.

> They **might have cancelled** the class – there was no one there.
> I **could have finished** my degree but I was too lazy.

Use *should/ought to have* + past participle to express past necessity or criticism.

> You really **shouldn't have missed** the exam.
> We **ought to have called** your family in advance – they might not be in.

This can also express regret.

> I **should have taken** the job they offered me; I'd be a director by now.

Use *needn't have* + past participle to say that we did something, but it turned out not to be necessary or there was no obligation.

> I booked the tickets in advance but I **needn't have done** so as there were lots of empty seats.
> 'I've brought an umbrella for you too.' 'Oh, you **needn't have done** that. I've got my own.'

❗ Compare with *didn't need to* + infinitive. When we use this, we don't know whether the action happened or not.
We **didn't need to book** tickets as the concert wasn't very popular.

KEY LANGUAGE

KL1 STATING OBJECTIVES

Our main objective is to …
One of our main goals will be to …
Your priority is to …
Your target must be to …
We aim (also) to …
We would like to …
That/X should be a key objective.

KL2 GIVING STRONG ADVICE

It would be advisable for you to …
I think you ought to …
It's essential to …/It's vital that you …
I'd strongly advise you to …
I strongly recommend you to …
I urge you to …

VOCABULARY

V1 DEPENDENT PREPOSITIONS

ability to, fascination with, great at, love of, obsession with, passion for, proud of, reluctance to

V2 ADJECTIVES OF CHARACTER

aloof, charismatic, cultured, devious, dogmatic, emotional, hospitable, meticulous, pragmatic, self-effacing

V3 INTERNATIONAL RELATIONS

cultural awareness
diplomatic meeting/immunity/posting/crisis/negotiations/incident
international meeting/conflict/awareness/posting/community/crisis/negotiations/incident
overseas conflict/posting/community/crisis/incident
summit meeting/negotiations

G1 **1** Join the sentences using the words in brackets. Make any other changes necessary.

1 Alex joined the diplomatic service. She wanted to live in different countries. (so that)

_____

2 The people were very disillusioned. The election turnout was extremely low. (because)

_____

3 The most successful candidate was the young woman. She had the best qualifications. (who)

_____

4 I left university last June. I didn't get a permanent job until April this year. (but)

_____

5 The police searched for some conclusive evidence. The suspect was questioned. (while)

_____

6 The people in this city are very welcoming. You must respect their desire for privacy. (provided)

_____

G2 **2** Read the situations and complete the sentences (a–e) using modal verbs.

1 Robert has never had very much money. He doesn't have a very good job and he hasn't got many qualifications. Suddenly he started spending a lot of money and buying expensive things, and then it stopped.

a He _____ got a better job because he isn't well qualified and because the spending stopped.
b He _____ come into money somehow.
c He _____ won the lottery.
d He _____ inherited money from a relative.
e He _____ spent it all so fast – he _____ saved some for the future.

2 You are going to a concert with some friends and you want to eat first. Your friend Jo is late, so you find a restaurant but don't have time to eat much because you're late for the concert. You rush to get there, only to find that the concert is cancelled.

a Jo _____ arrived late – she knew we wanted to eat.
b We _____ rushed to get to the concert after all.
c We _____ spent more time over the meal and enjoyed ourselves more.
d The concert hall _____ sent a message to our mobile phones.
e Someone in the band _____ fallen ill suddenly to cancel the concert at short notice.

KL **3** Complete the conversation. Write one word in each gap.

A: We want to run a new course on cultural awareness. Our main ¹_____ is to get the students to appreciate differences.
B: That's very laudable. I think you ²_____ to consider the content carefully though.

A: Oh yes. We ³_____ to read a lot about it over the summer.
B: And I'd ⁴_____ advise you to tread carefully – people get upset about this kind of thing.
A: We know. One of our main ⁵_____ will be to reduce people's over-sensitivity. We want to get some good guest lecturers in.
B: Yes, that should be a key ⁶_____. Well, good luck!

V1,3 **4** Complete the sentences with the words in the boxes. Use one word from each box in each gap.

cultural	fascination	international	overseas
proud	reluctance		

awareness	of	postings	relations	to	with

1 My father was in the diplomatic service and had lots of _____ to interesting places.
2 I've always had a great _____ insects.
3 Many American people have a(n) _____ travel outside their own country.
4 Living in a multicultural environment, it's important to have good _____.
5 It's fine to be _____ one's country and its achievements, without being jingoistic.
6 In today's globalised world, _____ are more important than ever.

V2 **5** Complete the puzzle with adjectives. Use the clues to help you.

1 cold and distant, not friendly
2 friendly, welcoming and generous
3 someone who is sensible and practical
4 someone who is self-_____ does not push themselves forward
5 interested in art, music, literature, etc.
6 having a natural ability to attract, interest and impress other people

131

GRAMMAR

G1 COHESION 1 (LINKERS)

There are two different types of linkers: the conjunctions we use to link two sentences or clauses (e.g. *and*, *when*, *if*) and the adverbs we use to make a link across two sentences (e.g. *in addition*, *then*, *however*).

These conjunctions and adverbs perform a number of different functions.

notion/function	conjunctions	adverbs
additive	and	as well as (this), furthermore, in addition, moreover, similarly
contrastive	although, but, even though, while, whilst, whereas, yet	even so, however, in contrast, nevertheless, nonetheless, on the other hand, otherwise
causal	as, because, since	as a result, consequently, for this reason, therefore
temporal	after, as, as soon as, before, since, until, when, while/whilst	after that, meanwhile, subsequently

Notice the difference between the use of the conjunctions and the adverbs:
> Sonja was rarely ill **even though** she ate junk food and took little exercise.
> Sonja ate junk foods and took little exercise. **However**, she was rarely ill.

Linking adverbs are often used in more formal situations than conjunctions.
> We decided to have a meeting to get to know one another **while** they were putting up the exhibition.
> The exhibition was being constructed when we arrived. **Meanwhile**, we held an introductory meeting.

G2 FUTURE FORMS WITH *BE*

BE + ADJECTIVE/ADVERB + INFINITIVE

Use the following phrases to suggest certainty that something will happen: *be bound to*, *be certain to*, *be sure to*.
> Sunita **is bound/certain/sure to** pass her exams – she's studied so hard.

If you are less certain, use *be likely to* .
> Ryan **is likely to** specialise in heart surgery, but he isn't sure yet.

Use *be due to* when you expect something to happen at a particular time.
> The plane **is due to** land at half past six.

Use *be about to* when you know that something is imminent.
> Lucy is over nine months pregnant – she**'s about to** have the baby.

BE ON + NOUN + *OF* + *-ING* FORM

be on + noun + *of* + *-ing* form
Use *be on the point of/on the verge of* + *-ing* when something is imminent; it is similar to *be about to*.
> We can't stop the procedure now – the surgeon **is on the point of operating**.

BE + INFINITIVE
Use *be* + infinitive in a formal context to talk about decisions, obligations and requirements.
> The meeting **is to be held** in the boardroom and Janine **is to take** the minutes.

This can be used for prohibitions in the negative.
> The patient **is not to be given** anything by mouth.

It can also be used for events that are fixed.
> Interest rates **are to come down** to two percent.

This structure is not used in informal conversation.

KEY LANGUAGE

KL JUSTIFYING OPINIONS

One reason I favour X/doing X is …
So you can see that this …, can't you?
By this, I mean that …
That is exactly the kind of thing …
If we do X, people will inevitably …
The fact that X happens means that Y is fully justified.
While I accept that X would be …, it'd also be …
You may well ask …

VOCABULARY

V1 HEALTH COLLOCATIONS

blood pressure, chest pain, flu virus, heart attack, heart surgery, high salt intake, immune system, infant mortality, life expectancy, maternity ward, omega-3 oils, premature ageing, tanning salon

V2 HEALTHCARE

alternative medicine, conventional medicine, consultant, doctor, doctor's surgery, general practitioner (GP), have a check-up, have an operation, have a scan/an X-ray, hospice, hospital, lack of funding, long waiting lists, outdated equipment, palliative care, paramedic, pharmacist, pharmacy, post-operative infection, preventive medicine, see the doctor, surgeon

V3 THE LANGUAGE OF EMOTION

antagonised, disillusioned, disorientating, elated, exasperating, exhilarating, inspiring, invigorating, rejuvenated, relieved

G1 **1** Join the sentences using the words in brackets.

1 Jamie called for an ambulance. The ambulance arrived ten minutes later. (after)

_____

2 Sarah qualified as a doctor. She never worked in medicine. (although)

_____

3 I'm on holiday the first week of June. I can't attend the conference. (as)

_____

4 My classmates got jobs very quickly. It took me six months to get a job. (whereas)

_____

5 Joe met Maria three months ago. He has been very happy for three months. (since)

_____

6 There aren't enough people at the meeting. We can't take any votes. (since)

_____

2 Complete the sentences to make them more formal. Use a linking adverbial.

1 My family all came to my graduation and my tutor came too.
My family attended _____
_____.

2 The doctors won't operate on Mr Jacobs because he is hugely overweight.
Mr Jacobs is extremely _____
_____.

3 We were delayed for an hour on the bus while the procession went past.
The procession passed _____
_____.

4 Although I'm interested in alternative medicine, I prefer to visit my GP for serious problems.
I'm interested in alternative medicine. _____
_____.

G2 **3** Replace the underlined parts of the sentences with future forms. Make any other changes necessary.

1 These painkillers should not be taken by children.

_____

2 Your father will definitely like your present. He's fascinated by vintage cars.

_____

3 We're expecting our first guests to arrive at the church at about 3.30 p.m.

_____

4 His plane will land at any moment – look, you can see it in the sky!

_____

5 It's probable that Paul will bring the baby over at the weekend.

_____

6 Visitors should report to reception upon arrival.

_____

KL **4** Match the sentence halves.

1 The fact that your GP refers you
2 That is exactly the kind of thing
3 One reason I favour putting this to the vote
4 While I accept that a high salt intake is unhealthy,
5 So, you can see that
6 If we change the rules again,

a it's something I enjoy.
b I've told you to avoid on numerous occasions.
c we can't be of any more assistance, can't you?
d is a sign that he is prepared to admit he doesn't know.
e the people will inevitably call us indecisive.
f is that we need to know that our members agree.

V1 **5** Complete the sentences with the words in the boxes. Use one word from each box in each gap.

blood	chest	immune	infant	life
premature				

ageing	expectancy	mortality	pain
pressure	system		

1 _____ _____ is higher now in developed countries than it has ever been.

2 Constant exposure to the sun can result in _____ _____ of the skin.

3 You shouldn't take your _____ _____ reading when you are under stress.

4 Taking a vitamin C tablet every day helps to boost the _____ _____.

5 Older people need to take _____ _____ seriously as it could indicate heart problems.

6 Simple treatments like rehydrating children with stomach upsets can reduce _____ _____.

V2 **6** Find the following in V2.

1 six practitioners: _____

2 four places: _____

3 three diagnostic treatments: _____

4 three problems with a health service: _____

V3 **7** Find an adjective from V3 for each situation.

How might you feel …
1 after a day at a luxury spa? _____
2 if your blood test shows no serious problems? _____
3 if you pass all your exams with an A grade? _____

How would you describe …
4 a lecture by someone who is successful in a field you're interested in? _____
5 a cold shower on a really hot day? _____
6 a city you don't know where all the streets look the same? _____

GRAMMAR

G1 FUTURE IN THE PAST

We sometimes need to talk about the future but from a point in the past, e.g.:

two days ago: **I'm going to buy** a laptop tomorrow.
today: I **was going to buy** a laptop yesterday.

WAS/WERE GOING TO

Use *was/were going to* when the future action happened.

When I last saw Ginny, she **was going to start** her new job the next day.

But we often use it with actions that did not happen.

Michael **was going to study** law at Oxford before he had the car accident.

We can also use it to make excuses.

We **were going to get** in touch but we've been so busy.

WAS/WERE TO

Use *was/were to* in formal contexts to talk about decisions, obligations and requirements (see *be to* + infinitive, Unit 4), usually for actions that were not fulfilled.

The ministers **were to meet** at the Paris Fashion Show but it was cancelled after the bombs.

WOULD

Use *would* when the action definitely happened.

Madonna's childhood was quite poor but she **would** become one of the richest women on the planet.

We can also use phrases with nouns and adjectives that express the future (see Unit 4) with *was/were* .

They **were due to catch** the 11.20 train. I don't know if they did.
Marcus **was bound to be** chosen for the job.

G2 EMPHATIC STRUCTURES

There are different ways of changing the word order of a sentence in English to make it more emphatic.

INVERSION

Inversion means changing the position of the subject and verb to put the verb first. This is common with a number of negative adverbs, e.g. *not only*, *no sooner*, *never*, *scarcely*, *at no time*, *little*.

No sooner had the doors opened than the customers flooded in the shop.
Never in my life have I been so offended!
Little did Val know that Colin had already planned the holiday.

Note that when we use inversion with the present or past simple, we have to use the *do* auxiliary.

CLEFT SENTENCES

A cleft sentence means splitting one clause into two. We do this to emphasise part of the sentence. There are two types of cleft sentences:

It clefts emphasise the object of the clause. So, to emphasise *her dreadful behaviour* in this sentence:

I really object to her dreadful behaviour.

we can make *her dreadful behaviour* into a separate *it* clause:

It's her dreadful behaviour (that) I really object to.

Wh- clefts emphasise the verb of the clause. To emphasise *would like* in the following sentence, we can make it into a separate *wh-* clause.

We'd like to inspect your kitchens.
What we'd like is to inspect your kitchens.

With *wh-* clefts, we use *to be* to link the two clauses.

If the verb in the original sentence is in the present or past simple, we form the *wh-* cleft with *do/did* .

The companies maximise their profits.
What the companies do is maximise their profits.

KEY LANGUAGE

KL DISCUSSING HYPOTHETICAL IDEAS

Suppose we did (have a café), wouldn't that …?
It'd mean that we'd have to …
I'm not sure how (feasible) that'd be.
If we were to …, we'd …
I was wondering if we might …
We'd need to …, otherwise we'd …
(Surely,) It'd be better to …
If we (had a special range), but still …, we'd …
There'd be a chance to …
Admittedly, that'd mean …

VOCABULARY

V1 CONSUMER COLLOCATIONS

advice, boom, choice, confidence, demand, goods, issues, price index, products, society, spending, trends, watchdog

V2 COMPOUND ADJECTIVES FORMED WITH NOUNS

eye-catching, hand-made, high-quality, life-long, present-day, smoke-free, time-consuming, world-renowned

V3 SUFFIXES (NOUNS 1)

activist, consciousness, convenience, emergence, obsession, popularity, sustainability, violation

G1 **1** Choose the correct forms to complete the sentences. In three sentences both forms are possible.

1 The letter said that all new recruits *were going to / were to* report to reception on arrival.

2 The guard shouted at us to hurry as the train *was bound to / was about to* depart.

3 The Minister *was to / was due to* address the committee first thing in the morning.

4 Alice *was going to / would* join the Dior fashion house but she decided against moving to Paris.

5 It was clear from the outset that Noel *would / was to* become the President's successor.

6 Once Nadal had been knocked out, everyone felt that Federer *would probably / was likely to* win the tournament.

2 Work in pairs and discuss your answers to Exercise 1. What is the difference in meaning between the forms in the sentences where both options are correct?

G2 **3** Complete the second sentence so that it has a similar meaning to the first.

1 The staff had no idea that the company was going to close.
Little _____.

2 Steve ran the London Marathon in a rabbit costume.
What _____.

3 My accountant alerted me to the tax problems.
It was _____.

4 Nobody has ever been that rude to me before.
Never _____.

5 The humidity is really difficult to bear.
What _____.

6 The humidity is really difficult to bear.
It _____.

KL **4** Use the prompts to write sentences expressing hypothetical ideas.

1 I / not sure / profitable / that / be
_____

2 there / be / chance / attract new customers
_____

3 I / wonder / I / redesign / window display
_____

4 if we / employ / only graduates / we still / need / train them
_____

5 suppose we / have / weekly meetings / that / create / sense of involvement?
_____

6 we / need / clear / ideas with Head Office / they / not approve / funding
_____

V1 **5** Read the definitions and complete the collocations.

1 the level of satisfaction with the economy, demonstrated in how much is spent: consumer _____

2 a list of prices of products to show increase/decrease in the cost of living: consumer _____

3 questions/topics which concern consumers: consumer _____

4 the kind of things that consumers buy: consumer _____

5 the range and variety of products available for consumers: consumer _____

V2 **6** Replace the underlined words with compound adjectives. Make any other changes necessary.

1 Don't complete <u>new</u> forms for every student; it takes too long.
_____

2 <u>Famous</u> Formula 1 driver Felipe Massa announced his participation in the Monaco Grand Prix today.
_____

3 He has a <u>very noticeable</u> tattoo on his left shoulder.
_____

4 This hotel is an environment <u>where cigarettes can't be consumed</u>.
_____

5 Tissane chocolates are <u>crafted</u> by our own chocolatier, Pierre Didier.
_____

V3 **7** Complete the sentences with a word formed from a word in the box.

active	conscious	convenient	emerge
popular	violate		

1 The investigation showed that the company's working practices caused several _____ of employees' human rights.

2 The President's _____ was confirmed when the election results came in.

3 After the fall, Ben lost _____ for a few seconds, but he wasn't seriously injured.

4 A lot of people like the _____ of shopping online instead of going to the supermarket.

5 The last few decades have seen the _____ of China as a major world power.

6 During the protest, several _____ were arrested for vandalism.

GRAMMAR

G1 THE PASSIVE:

Form the passive with a form of *be* + past participle. Use the passive in the present and past continuous, but avoid other continuous forms.

> His behaviour **is being monitored**.

Form the infinitive of the passive with *to be* + past participle.

> We expect the work **to be finished** next week.

Form the passive after modals with *be* (without *to*) + past participle.

> A cure for cancer **might be discovered** in our lifetime.

There is a perfect form of the passive infinitive: *to have been* + past participle.

> The students were hoping **to have been awarded** their degrees by now.

Form the passive of *-ing* forms with *being* + past participle (e.g. after prepositions).

> We congratulated her on **being promoted**.

> ❗ Intransitive verbs cannot be made passive.
> ~~The train was arrived on time.~~ ✗

The passive is often used because the agent is obvious or unknown or unimportant. It is also sometimes used to avoid naming the agent, perhaps to avoid blame or responsibility.

> The keys seem **to have been mislaid**.

> ❗ If we want to give the agent, we use *by*:
> You will be contacted **by** customer services.

We can also use the passive to manipulate the order of information in a text. (In English we prefer to start a new sentence with something that has already been mentioned).

> This new software is revolutionary. Apex Solutions designed it. ✗
> This new software is revolutionary. **It was designed by Apex Solutions.** ✓

We can choose to put longer subjects at the end of a sentence by using the passive.

> The new software was designed **by a developer at Apex Solutions who had worked for Microsoft.**

The passive is also used to describe processes.

> The mixture **was heated** to 100 degrees.

G2 COMPLEX NOUN PHRASES

Complex noun phrases are used to describe the noun in a sentence. They either appear before the noun (pre-modifiers) or after the noun (post-modifiers).

The most common pre-modifiers are adjectives. When more than one adjective is used, they appear in a certain order: opinion → size → shape → age → colour → origin → material → purpose.

> The museum has a **beautiful old French** collection of antiques.

Form compound adjectives by using a hyphen between each word used to describe the noun.

> She has a **six-month-old** baby.

Nouns can also be used as pre-modifiers. Form compound nouns by joining two nouns, either as one word, with a hyphen, or as two words.

> pseudoscience   ex-president   address book

Use adverb + adjective collocations to give more information about the noun.

> *Scientists have announced a **newly developed** vaccine.*

A phrase introduced by a preposition can be used as a post-modifier.

> I'll meet you at the café **on the corner of 42nd Street**.

Full and reduced relative clauses can also be used in this way.

> That's the woman (**who is**) **responsible for our European sector**.

Similar to these are clauses formed with a present participle or a past participle.

> Who's the man **giving** a speech at the moment?
> Football is a popular sport **played** all around the world.

Use *that* to introduce a whole clause (subject + verb + object) after the noun.

> What do you think of the idea **that** we could all be living on another planet some day?

To introduce the purpose of a noun, use a *to*- infinitive.

> They brought in an expert **to examine** the damage.

KEY LANGUAGE

KL1 CRITICISING

But what about … ?
It's a major disadvantage.
Since when have … ?

KL2 ACCEPTING CRITICISM

That's a fair point.
I have to agree with you there.
OK, I'm not going to argue against you (on that one).
It's true that …

KL3 OFFERING COUNTER-ARGUMENTS

But really, it's up to …
That's a fact of life, you just have to …
You're absolutely right, but …

VOCABULARY

V1 DESCRIBING TECHNOLOGY

a museum piece, behind the times, cutting-edge, had its day, innovative, new-fangled, obsolete, outdated, redundant, retro, revolutionary, state-of-the-art, superseded, the last word in

V2 COLLOCATIONS

academic assessment, code sequence, complex data, diagnostic test, false results, health system, quality control, research subject, test tube

G1 1 Rewrite the sentences in the passive.

1 Technicians at our Milton Keynes factory assemble all the parts.

2 CCTV cameras are always monitoring us in this office.

3 Builders equipped the building with cutting-edge technology.

4 We require you to include all relevant documents with the application form.

5 Would you mind our cameraman recording your presentation?

6 We expected them to have made the final decision by now.

2 Choose the correct options (a or b) to complete the text.

I had an interview in the most incredible building yesterday. It's the new Department of Defence headquarters, and ¹_____. It's a high-rise building and ²_____. On arrival, ³_____ to the 'security suite', where ⁴_____ and ⁵_____ against government records. Once that is done, ⁶_____ for an appropriate level of security. From then on, when you go to particular departments, you just look into the camera as ⁷_____, and it opens automatically. If a door is not security-sensitive, ⁸_____.

1 a an architect who specialises in hi-tech systems designed it
  b it was designed by an architect who specialises in hi-tech systems
2 a it towers over the surrounding office blocks
  b the surrounding office blocks are towered over by it
3 a a guard meets visitors and takes them
  b visitors are met and taken
4 a someone scanned their eyes
  b their eyes are scanned
5 a an official checks the images
  b the images are checked
6 a officials issue a pass
  b a pass is issued
7 a you approach a door
  b a door is approached
8 a body heat alone activates it
  b it's activated by body heat alone

G2 3 Put the words in the correct order to make sentences.

1 ingredient / food / it's / is / which / used / an / most / fast / in

2 drug / potentially / the / new / side-effects / has / lethal

3 salt / needs / flavour / it / give / this / to / some / soup

4 suggestion / this / I / his / liked / that / together / all / work / we / on

5 white / vase / they / me / a / porcelain / gave / beautiful

6 restaurant / town / it's / lovely / a / the / old / in

7 bacteria / type / modern / in / most / it's / of / a / found / homes

8 woman / Sarah / the / to / speaking / who's?

KL 4 Complete the sentences. Write one word in each gap.

1 Since _____ have politicians been honest about their intentions?
2 OK, it's _____ that the product is expensive, but I think people will still want to buy it.
3 That's a fair _____ – I have to accept you're right about that.
4 All right, I'm not going to _____ against you on that point.
5 You're absolutely _____ about that, but I think you're missing the most important point.

V1 5 Find words/phrases in V1 with these meanings.

1 describes a person who is not aware of or using current ideas or technology: _____
2 based on styles and fashion of the recent past: _____
3 something new which you don't like or trust: _____
4 something so valuable or interesting it should be displayed to the public: _____
5 replaced by something new and more up-to-date: _____
6 completely new and leading to great improvements: _____

V2 6 Complete the sentences with the words in the boxes. Use one word from each box in each gap.

| academic | complex | diagnostic |
| health | research | test |

| assessment | data | subject |
| system | test | tube |

1 The sample is placed in a(n) _____ where the reaction can be observed.
2 It was an interesting theory, but after proper _____, it proved to be false.
3 The initial research threw up a lot of _____ which need to be analysed carefully.
4 Ben agreed to be a(n) _____ in trials of a new medicine.
5 Doctors carried out a(n) _____ to try and find out what was wrong with her.
6 The government was credited with making dramatic improvements to the _____.

GRAMMAR

G1 QUANTIFIERS

Use quantifiers before a noun to indicate the amount or quantity of the noun. A few quantifiers describe precise quantities, e.g. *both, no*. Most, however, describe vague quantities, e.g. *some, several, many, much, (a) few, (a) little* . Note how they are used:

+ singular countable noun	+ plural countable noun	+ uncountable noun
no, either, every	no, any, both, (a) few, a lot of, some, several, many, most, all	no, (a) little, a lot of, some, much, most, all

To talk about things in general, use quantifier + noun.
> We received **several packages** this morning.

To talk about something specific, use quantifier + of + *the/my/our/these*/etc. + plural noun.
> We received **several of the packages** you'd sent.

! With *all* and *both*, we do not need *of* :
We received **both/all the packages** you'd sent.

! We do not use *no* + *of the*. We have to use the pronoun *none* :
None of the letters arrived.

Sometimes we use a quantifier + noun/pronoun as the subject of a sentence. Most are followed by a plural verb.
> **Most** of the volunteers **are** available.
> **All** the books **have** been signed by the author.

Note that *every, much* and *little* are followed by a singular verb.
> **Every** delegate **is** expected to attend.

With *no* and *none*, we can use either a singular or a plural verb.
> **None** of the students **was/were** prepared.

G2 CONDITIONALS

These are the most common conditional forms:

ZERO CONDITIONAL
if + present, present/imperative

Use the zero conditional for actions that happen every time a condition is fulfilled, and for instructions.
> If you **press** F1, the help menu **appears**.
> If the alarm **sounds**, **leave** the room at once.

FIRST CONDITIONAL
if + present, *will/can/may/might/should* + infinitive

Use the first conditional to talk about real possibilities and for promises, warnings, etc.
> If it**'s raining** tomorrow, we **won't go** to the beach.
> If you **come** here again, I**'ll call** the police.

SECOND CONDITIONAL
if + past, *would/could/might* + infinitive

Use the second conditional to talk about an unlikely possibility in the future or an unreal situation in the present or future, and to give advice.
> If I **got** the job, I**'d have to** move away.
> If we **had** more money, we **might stop** work.
> If I **were** you, I**'d finish** my degree.

THIRD CONDITIONAL
if + past perfect, *would/could/might* + *have* + past participle

Use the third conditional to talk about unreal situations in the past, i.e. situations that are contrary to the facts, to express regrets and to criticise others.
> If I **hadn't been talking** on my mobile, the police **might not have stopped** me.
> If you **hadn't argued** with my mother, we **would have had** a nice evening.

MIXED CONDITIONALS
We use the clauses from the second and third conditionals to talk about present or past results of unreal situations.
a *if* + past perfect, *would/might/could* + infinitive
> If he **hadn't left** me, I**'d** still **be** happy now.

b *if* + past, *would/might/could* + *have* + past participle
> If I **loved** him, I **wouldn't have left** him.

KEY LANGUAGE

KL1 APPROVING IDEAS
Sounds like a great idea!
I think it's a really good suggestion.
It's a good project, in my opinion.

KL2 EXPRESSING DOUBTS
I'm not too keen on this one.
I can see some real problems.
Will it really work?
I just don't think it's feasible.

KL3 OFFERING COUNTER ARGUMENTS
It could be a very expensive option.
But X might not be such a big problem.
Some of the projects must be for the long term.
It may not cost as much (money) as you think.

VOCABULARY

V1 IDIOMS WITH *HAND*
a safe pair of hands, give someone a hand, hand in hand, have (got) my hands full, my hands are tied, on hand, time on my hands, turn my hand to anything

V2 EXPRESSIONS OF QUANTITY
a bunch of, a couple of, a great deal of, a large quantity of, a pair of, a slight majority of, a tiny proportion of

V3 IRREGULAR PLURALS
analysis – analyses, criterion – criteria, hypothesis – hypotheses, phenomenon – phenomena, thesis – theses

G1 **1** Find and correct nine mistakes with quantifiers in the report.

Creative writing course – end-of-year report
This year's presentation of the course has been the most successful so far.

Results
All of students passed the course and exam
Most them (33/40) achieved a grade 3 or better
Few (9/40) passed with a grade 1
Both the course tutors agrees that the results reflect the aptitude of the students. They agreed that most of this year's group have put in much hours and deserved their excellent results.

Student feedback
Only a little end-of-year feedback forms have been received so far (further information to follow). Of the students who have responded, several has commented that this course is the most interesting they have taken so far. Every student who have responded has praised the tutors for their knowledge and enthusiasm for their subject. No of the respondents so far feel that the course is too difficult.

G2 **2** Choose the sentence (a or b) that best describes the meaning of each conditional sentence.

1 If I were you, I wouldn't bother to read her latest novel.
   a I think you should read the book.
   b I don't think you should read the book.
2 We would have got you a ticket if they hadn't all sold out.
   a We got you a ticket.
   b We didn't get you a ticket.
3 The rubbish collectors don't see the bin if you leave it in the garden.
   a They never see the bin in these circumstances.
   b They sometimes don't see the bin.
4 If the flight to Dubai was delayed, we'd have to wait 24 hours for our connection.
   a We think the flight will be delayed.
   b We don't think the flight will be delayed.
5 The course won't take place if we don't have enough enrolments.
   a We need a certain number of students for the course to take place.
   b We can run the course with any number of students.
6 She'd probably have a job by now if she'd finished her teaching qualification.
   a She has a job.
   b She doesn't have a job.

3 Complete the conditional sentences with the correct form of the verbs in the brackets.

1 I _____ (join) an amateur operatic club if I _____ (can) sing better, but my voice isn't great.
2 The personnel department _____ (not overlook) you if we _____ (have) your details on file, but we don't appear to have them.
3 It's quite easy. If you _____ (put) the coins in and _____ (press) the green button, the machine _____ (print) the ticket.

4 We _____ (not sell) our old hi-fi if you _____ (tell) us that you wanted to keep it!
5 It's about time for a career change, so if the hospital _____ (offer) me that job, I think I _____ (take) it.

KL **4** Complete the text with phrases a–f.
Thanks for your presentation of the new organic cosmetic range. Personally, I think [1] _____, but I have some reservations. First, [2] _____ with the pricing structure. It [3] _____ for our usual market, which doesn't spend a huge amount on cosmetics. [4] _____ to expect our customer base to switch to a product that's 20 per cent more expensive, so we need to explore a different market. But [5] _____ such a big problem as we sell into some very upmarket stores. Yes, I like this idea and think we should research it further. [6] _____. What do the rest of you think?

a could be a very expensive option
b I can see some problems
c It's a good project, in my opinion
d that might not be
e it's a really good suggestion
f I don't think it's feasible

V1 **5** Replace the underlined phrases with idioms with *hand*. Make any other changes necessary.

1 Can you help me? I can't do this alone.
2 Give that to Fiona to do. She's someone we can trust to do a job without making mistakes.
3 Look, I'm not very busy. Let me finish that report.
4 Let's ask Gemma to help. She's really versatile.
5 I'm afraid I can't do anything for you because of my position. You could talk to personnel.
6 Yes, I've got one of the driving licence applications quite near. Here we are.

V2 **6** Complete the sentences with the words in the box.

bunch	great	pair	proportion	quantity	slight

1 There has been a _____ deal of speculation about who will get the manager's job.
2 When I opened the curtains this morning there was a _____ of doves sitting on the window ledge.
3 A large _____ of rain fell during the storm, which led to flash floods.
4 A tiny _____ of the people interviewed said they would be happier if their country became independent.
5 Look! I bought a lovely _____ of grapes at the supermarket.
6 Recent polls show the government is only supported by a _____ majority of voters.

GRAMMAR

G1 VERB PATTERNS

When one verb follows another, it may appear in the infinitive or -ing form.

VERB (+ OBJECT) + INFINITIVE WITHOUT TO

Few verbs are followed by the infinitive without *to*, mainly modal verbs, verbs of perception (e.g. *see, watch, hear*), *help, make* and *let*.

> We **saw the president's plane land**.
> The police **made the protestors move** back.
> My boss **let me leave** work early today.

Note the passive of *make* and *let*.

> The protestors **were made to move** back.
> I **was allowed to leave** work early today.

> With verbs of perception, the -ing form can mean either the action is still ongoing or is complete. I watched him **interviewing** the film star.
>
> The infinitive means the action is complete. I watched him **interview** the film star.

VERB (+ OBJECT) + TO-INFINITIVE

Many verbs are followed by the *to*-infinitive, often verbs of wants, desires, recommendations, (e.g. *want, need, agree, appear, promise*). There are also many that have an object (e.g. *want, allow, advise, invite, recommend, urge, tell*).

> The editor **promised not to run** the story.
> We **invited the minister to appear** on the show.

VERB (+ OBJECT) + -ING

Some verbs are followed by the -ing form, often verbs of liking/disliking (e.g. *like, enjoy*) or verbs of thought (e.g. *consider, imagine*). Most of these can have an object.

> I **can't stand having** to wait for people!
> Can you **imagine being** trapped in a lift?
> The school **doesn't mind students bringing** their own lunch.

VERB (+ OBJECT) + PREPOSITION + -ING

Many verbs are followed by a preposition. If another verb is used after the preposition, it is in the -ing form.

> The director **succeeded in raising** the money for the documentary.
> They **criticised the editor for printing** lies.

VERB + -ING OR TO-INFINITIVE

Some verbs can be followed by either the *to*-infinitive or the -ing form, with little change in meaning (e.g. *begin, continue, like*).

> I **continued to work/working** as though nothing was wrong.

G2 PREPOSITIONAL VERBS

Prepositional verbs always have an object (a noun, a pronoun or an -ing form), and the object always follows the preposition.

> The child had **broken into several houses** before he was caught.
> This is a tricky problem. Let me **look into it**.
>
> Barry can't **get over being made redundant** – he just isn't coping at all.

Adverbs of manner and degree can come between the verb and preposition, but not immediately after the preposition.

> We need to deal **quickly** with this issue. ✓
> ~~We need to deal with quickly this issue.~~ ✗

These adverbs, and most others, also can come at the end of the clause.

> We need to deal with this issue **quickly**.
> Please look into the problem **immediately**.
> I got through the course **eventually**, on my third attempt!

KEY LANGUAGE

KL BEING CAUTIOUS

We need to think this (one) through.
If you don't (get the facts straight), he could (take us to court).
If X is the case, we could be in hot water/trouble.
X is a very sensitive issue.
If we get our facts wrong, it'll have a bad effect on our reputation.
It's just speculation on our part.
We need to hold fire on this one.
It could land us in court.

VOCABULARY

V1 THE MEDIA

bias, blogosphere, broadsheet, circulation figures, citizen journalism, deadline, go viral, hit, libel laws, off the record, privacy, scoop, sound bite, source, speculation, spin, tabloid, trending, viewing figures

V2 PEOPLE IN THE MEDIA

anchor, blogger, columnist, correspondent, editor, paparazzo, producer, reporter

V3 DEPENDENT PREPOSITIONS

focus on, allow time for, feel free to, go around, begin by, sign up for

G1 1 Complete the sentences with the correct form of the verbs in brackets.

1 Working on a newspaper, I really enjoy _____ (see) the publication process from start to finish.
2 The newspaper urged its readers _____ (not vote) in the forthcoming European election.
3 The corporation will continue _____ (broadcast) controversial programmes.
4 With your health problems, you really need to consider _____ (not spend) seven days a week in the office.
5 The travellers were made _____ (empty) their bags on the airport tarmac.
6 Is everything OK with Kyle? He appears _____ (be) rather short-tempered today.
7 The minister was criticised for _____ (not reveal) the extent of the budget deficit.
8 Several paparazzi watched the two cars _____ (crash) into each other and did nothing to help.

G2 2 Rewrite the sentences using a suitable prepositional verb from the box and making any changes necessary.

come across   come up   deal with   get over
get through   look at   look into   look like

1 The error in your account has been noted. We will investigate it immediately.

2 Please observe the animal's behaviour very closely.

3 We're back and we survived the week at Aunt Doreen's!

4 Your investigators need to handle this delicate matter carefully.

5 Most healthy people recover from this illness with no adverse effects.

6 The editor's suggestion arose entirely unexpectedly – out of nowhere.

7 If you find my old reading glasses in the study, can you hang on to them?

8 Your sister really resembles Cameron Diaz! It's uncanny.

KL 3 Match the sentence halves.
1 If we don't get our facts straight,
2 Let's think about the implications of this –
3 We need to hold fire on this
4 This is just speculation on our part
5 Have you covered every possibility here?
6 We could be in very hot water

a it's a very sensitive issue.
b We really need to think this one through.
c the actor involved could sue us.
d if what you say is really the case.
e so we'd better not publish it.
f until we've heard from our lawyers.

V1 4 Complete the sentences with the words in the boxes. Use one word from each box in each gap.

citizen   circulation   go   libel   off the
popular figures

record   journalism   laws   press   viral

1 It's not easy for newspapers to print untrue stories about people because of _____.
2 The rise of social media has led to an increase in _____ used in news broadcasts.
3 The _____ always sells more than the broadsheets.
4 The journalist told me my remarks were _____, then printed the whole interview.
5 Harry never expected his video to _____, reaching over four million views.
6 Some broadsheets have increased their _____ by changing their format to a smaller size.

V1,2 5 Complete the text with suitable words from V1 and V2. Use one word only in each gap.

I started life as a journalist on a very low-quality
[1]_____ newspaper in the late 1990s. I hated it because I felt it had no principles: the [2]_____ checked every report from his journalists and he would change them to make them more sensational if necessary. The articles were often based on [3]_____ rather than hard facts, and some of its reporters had no respect for people's [4]_____, no matter who they were. The important thing was always to get the [5]_____ before the other newspapers, and to send a [6]_____ out with a camera to get the most salacious photos possible. Well, I did it for two years, but then I was lucky to get a job on a [7]_____. I'm still there, and I'm now a regular [8]_____, writing in depth about any medical stories in the news.

V3 6 Find and correct one mistake with prepositions in each sentence.
1 I'd like to begin with telling you about the project.
2 If you have any questions, feel free for interrupt with them.
3 I'm going to allow five minutes at the end to questions.
4 First, I'm going to focus at the background to the situation.
5 Please take one of the handouts going on.
6 You didn't know you were signing up at a talk on physics.

GRAMMAR

G1 ADVERBS OF DEGREE

Adverbs of degree can be used to either intensify or soften the meaning of the word they qualify. They can qualify verbs, adjectives or adverbs.

They always come directly before the word they qualify.
> The measures announced **hardly** address the problem at all.
> Your suggestion is **totally** impractical.
> This juvenile is **quite likely to** offend again.

Common intensifying adverbs of degree are: *very, really, extremely, totally, utterly, entirely* and *highly*. Of these, only *really, totally, utterly* and *entirely* can qualify verbs.
> The director is **extremely** angry at the situation.
> All the applicants were **highly** qualified.

Common softening adverbs of degree are *quite, slightly* and *fairly*. These do not qualify verbs.
> It's **slightly** inconvenient that you've changed the time of the lecture.

We do not use the same adverbs of degree to qualify all adjectives. We use different adverbs with gradable adjectives and ungradable adjectives.

Gradable adjectives represent points on a scale (e.g. *hot* and *cold*). Ungradable adjectives represent the **limits** of the scale (e.g. *boiling* and *freezing*).

The table shows common adverbs of degree used with the different types of adjective.

adverbs used with gradable adjectives	adverbs used with ungradable adjectives
very, extremely, fairly, really, slightly	absolutely, entirely, really, totally, utterly

So we say *very important* but *absolutely essential, extremely tired* but *utterly exhausted*, etc.

Many adverb–adjective combinations are quite fixed collocations, e.g. *highly qualified, completely different, fully convinced*.

The adverb *quite* has different meanings according to whether it is used with a gradable or ungradable adjective.
> It's **quite important**. = It's fairly important.
> It's **quite essential**. = It's absolutely essential.

G2 REPORTING USING NOUNS

It is possible to introduce reported speech with a noun, e.g. *claim* . The 'rules' of reported speech remain the same.
> Patrick **claimed** he had come into the country legally, but it wasn't true. (*claim* = verb)
> Patrick's **claim** that he had come into the country legally wasn't true. (*claim* = noun)

There are many nouns that can introduce reported speech, e.g. *accusation, advice, answer, argument, claim, complaint, denial, excuse, explanation, observation, point, remark, response, statement, suggestion*.
> I asked my tutor about my bad marks. His **explanation** that my work showed little independent research was fair, I suppose.

KEY LANGUAGE

KL BALANCING AN ARGUMENT

Having said that, …
Although we're here to …, I think that …
That's all fair enough but it's simply too …
Certainly X is important, but I still think that …
While accepting X, we mustn't / shouldn't …
Admittedly, X would be …
I see what you're saying, but …

VOCABULARY

V1 IDIOMATIC VERB PHRASES

bring something to a halt, draw attention to yourself, know something is amiss, make a scene, mind your own business, shirk your responsibilities, take something for granted, wash your dirty linen in public

V2 JUSTICE SYSTEMS

care system, community service, (non-)custodial sentence, deter, deterrent, juvenile delinquency, punishment, rehabilitation, young offender, youth court

V3 NOUN CONVERSION

complex, do, hopeful, international, local, mention, must, trust

G1 1 Choose the correct words to complete the sentences. In one sentence both words are possible.

1 Don't forget to send that court report. It's *very / absolutely* important they receive it tomorrow.
2 I *entirely / extremely* agree with all your points.
3 The defendant has admitted the assault so it's *slightly / highly* likely he'll get a custodial sentence.
4 We should look carefully at the final candidate – she was *highly / very* qualified.
5 I know the manager shouted at you, but don't worry, he was just *slightly / extremely* concerned about the deadline.
6 What do you think about the new project? I *really / very* believe that we should sponsor it.
7 His medication must be taken for fourteen days and it's quite *important / essential* that you finish the course or they won't be effective.
8 Let's not have an argument now. I'm *really / utterly* exhausted after work.
9 Losing those documents is *fairly / extremely* annoying, but we've got copies so it's not really a problem.
10 You're in serious trouble, so think *very / totally* carefully before you answer this question.

G2 2 Complete the reported statements.

1 'I didn't steal the bike!'
Sam denied that _____, but it wasn't true.
2 'Your music is really loud.'
Our neighbour complained that _____, and she was quite right.
3 'I'll be on time tomorrow, honestly.'
Janet insisted that she _____, but it was ill-founded.
4 'We should close early today.'
Our manager suggested that_____, which was a relief.
5 'Lucy's put on a lot of weight.'
Mark remarked that _____, which was cruel.

3 Rewrite the reported statements in Exercise 2 using nouns.

1 Sam's denial that _____
_____.
2 Our neighbour's _____
_____.
3 Janet's _____
_____.
4 Our manager's _____
_____.
5 Mark's _____
_____.

KL 4 Complete the conversation with phrases from KL.

A: Can we talk about the proposed detention centre now? A lot of us are unhappy about that.
B: Well, [1]_____ to discuss general community issues, I think we should leave that until the relevant planning officer is available.
A: Mmm, I [2]_____, but we really want to make our views known and express our concerns.
B: I understand, and [3]_____, but it's simply too early to get into discussion.
A: Yes, it's early and that's precisely why we want to discuss it now. [4]_____ is important, but can't we register our misgivings now?
B: OK, what are your misgivings?
A: Well, we really don't want criminals in our village.
B: That's a valid view, and [5]_____ opinions like these, I'm sure you'll understand we at the council mustn't listen only to your views …

V1,2 5 Complete the text with words from V1 and V2.

We've had a lot of problems with [1]_____ delinquency in our area. Young people hang around on street corners and cause problems. Only last week I saw two lads breaking things in my neighbour's front garden. I didn't want to make a [2]_____ but I equally didn't want to [3]_____ my responsibility to my neighbour. I complained to them about their behaviour, but they, of course, told me to [4]_____ my own business, so I called the police. The officer said that even if he arrested them, a [5]_____ would only give a [6]_____ sentence, such as [7]_____, which, in his opinion, was no [8]_____ at all to other young people.

V2 6 Find words/phrases in V2 with these meanings.

1 imprisonment: _____
2 a criminal under the age of 18: _____
3 punishment that prevents further crime: _____
4 punishment of working (unpaid), e.g. street cleaning: _____
5 reforming offenders: _____
6 judicial process for young people: _____

V3 7 Choose the correct words to complete the sentences.

1 The money left to Dean was held in a special *trust / complex* until he was 18.
2 If invited to dinner, talking a small present is a *do / must*.
3 If you want to know where to go out in the area, it's best to ask a *hopeful / local*.
4 I've just joined the gym at my local leisure *international / complex*.
5 The campaign did so well that we even got a *mention / do* in the national news.

GRAMMAR

G1 NON-FINITE CLAUSES

A non-finite clause contains a non-finite verb, i.e. a verb that has no indication of person or tense.

Arriving late, we failed to find a hotel.

In this example, the non-finite clause is *arriving late* and the non-finite verb is *arriving*. A non-finite verb usually relates to the subject of the main clause (*we*) and we know the time/tense from the verb in the main clause (past).

Non-finite clauses express different relationships with the main clause (e.g. time, reason, condition, result). In this case, it is reason.

Because we arrived late, we failed to find a hotel.

There are three main types of non-finite clause.

-ING CLAUSES

In these clauses the non-finite verb is active.

The company reduced its overheads, **cutting 60 jobs.** (i.e. with the result that it cut 60 jobs)

Present participle clauses can also replace relative clauses.

Did you hear the fox **calling in the garden** last night? (i.e. the fox that was calling)

PAST PARTICIPLE CLAUSES

In these clauses the non-finite verb is passive.

Handled carefully, this glassware should last a lifetime. (i.e. if it is handled carefully)

This type of clause can also replace a relative clause.

The police have identified the driver **killed in the crash**. (i.e. the driver who was killed)

INFINITIVE CLAUSES

An infinitive clause is formed with *to* + infinitive. It usually expresses a purpose or result.

They installed dim lighting **to improve the ambience in the shops**.
We came home early (only) **to find that everyone had left.**

This type of clause can also replace a relative clause.

Walcott was the only player **to score a goal.**

When an infinitive clause expresses purpose, it can come before the main clause.

To improve the ambience in the shops, they installed dim lighting.

❗ Note that non-finite clauses are usually used in formal writing.

G2 CONVERSATIONAL ENGLISH

Conversational English differs from written English in a number of ways and to the extent that we talk about the grammar of conversational English. These are the most common features of conversational English:

1 overlaps – two speakers talking at the same time, usually when one interrupts another in order to say something
2 listener responses – supportive comments such as *Really? Go on, I know what you mean*
3 hesitation and use of sounds such as *er* and *um*
4 repetition of words and phrases
5 discourse markers such as *well, you know, I mean, like*, which give a speaker time to organise his/her thoughts
6 simple clause structure, adding clauses to each other, often independent clauses with *and, but* and *or* (also called 'the add-on strategy'), or simple dependent clauses introduced by a conjunction such as *because* or *if*
7 using direct quotes, as if playing a character
8 reformulations – when a speaker starts a sentence but then either can't finish it or changes to say something else or express himself/herself in a different way

KEY LANGUAGE

KL INFORMAL PHRASES

That is, …
And as for …
But then again, …
Oh, and before I forget, …
Anyway, …
I reckon (that) …
You know, …
By and large, …
… , that kind of thing.
So, all in all, …

VOCABULARY

V1 PERFORMANCE REVIEWS: NOUNS

adaptation, bill, choreographer, company, duo, tale, venue, virtuoso

V2 PERFORMANCE REVIEWS: COMPOUND ADJECTIVES

award-winning, awe-inspiring, British-born, laughter-packed, live music-enhanced, out-of-the-way, R&B-influenced, Rambert-trained, sample-heavy, star-studded

V3 ACADEMIC VERBS

analyse, distribute, emerge, enable, erode, indicate, reinforce, reveal

G1 **1 Choose the correct form of the verbs.**

1 *Playing / To play* with the Berlin Philharmonic was James' lifetime ambition.
2 *Playing / Played* his first performance with the Berlin Philharmonic, James' felt he'd reached the pinnacle of his career.
3 *Playing / Played* by a virtuoso, the violin is truly the king of instruments.
4 We hurried to get to the theatre on time, only *found / to find* the performance had been cancelled.
5 *Found / Finding* by a nurse on the hospital steps, the baby was named Florence.
6 Luke dropped the course on the technology of music, *to find / finding* it too difficult.

2 Replace the underlined parts of the sentences with non-finite clauses.

1 The theatre raised its ticket prices <u>so that it could fund the renovation</u>.
_____

2 <u>When we arrived at the hotel</u>, we discovered that they'd given us a suite.
_____

3 We bought the tickets online, <u>then we found that we had paid twice as much as our friends</u>!
_____

4 The organisers will identify and destroy <u>tickets that have been produced illegally</u>.
_____

5 Do you remember the name of the actor <u>who was playing that role at the time</u>?
_____

6 Mario was the only student <u>who thanked me for the extra tuition</u>.
_____

7 <u>Because the show proved to be a success, it</u> was given an extended run at the Royal Theatre.
_____

8 <u>If you water these plants regularly</u>, they will provide tomatoes for several months.
_____

G2 **3 Match the underlined parts of the conversation (1–8) with the features of conversational English in the box.**

overlap   listener   response   hesitation
repetition   discourse marker   add-on   strategy
reformulation

A: I've just been reading this article about the internet changing entertainment completely, ¹<u>you know, like,</u> we download movies and that kind of thing.
B: Mmm, I'm not sure what I think about that, really. I mean, I download movies sometimes but I still watch them on ²<u>TV</u> …
C: <u>Yeah, and at the cinema</u>. At least I still watch them at the cinema. It's a better and, ³<u>er,</u> more complete experience.

B: That's right. But I ᵃ**reckon** a lot of people watch movies on their laptops and tablets, I mean, ⁴<u>if they want to be … it's just convenient</u>.
C: Sure, but it's such a small screen, I definitely prefer watching things on a big screen. ᵇ**And as for** watching movies on MP3 players, well …
A: ⁵<u>Go on</u>.
C: Well, ⁶<u>it's … it's</u> just ridiculous! They're so small, ᶜ**that is**, you can't get any nuances from the image ⁷<u>because it's too small, and it's easy to be distracted and the sound isn't great</u> …
A: Good point, ᵈ**but then again**, surely the point of MP3 players is that the sound is very good.
C: Oh, I don't know. ᵉ**Like I said**, I just know I prefer the big screen! ᶠ**Anyway**, what's on TV tonight – anything good?

KL **4 Match the meaning of the phrases in bold (a–f) in Exercise 3 with the more formal expressions below.**

as I explained earlier   which means that
moving on   with regard to   believe   however

V1,3 **5 Replace the underlined words in the text with the correct form of words with similar meanings from V1 and V3.**

Last night's performance of the Maidenhead Youth Ensemble was a marvel and has served to ¹<u>support</u> this newspaper's view that we need to invest more in the arts movement for the young. The ²<u>group</u> consists of a small orchestra and the ³<u>programme</u> included a superb solo by the young piano ⁴<u>genius</u> from Marlow, Adrian King. This was followed up by a modern ⁵<u>version</u> of Rachmaninov, which was second to none.

The ⁶<u>place</u> for the concert was a local church, which made for a very atmospheric evening, and the acoustics ⁷<u>made it possible for</u> us to appreciate the solos as much as the full ensemble pieces. With groups like this it is possible for people like young Adrian to ⁸<u>come out</u> as future stars and that is why they need local arts council funding.

1 _____   4 _____   7 _____
2 _____   5 _____   8 _____
3 _____   6 _____

V2 **6 Complete the sentences with compound adjectives from V2.**

1 The bill for tonight at the comedy club promises a(n) _____ evening.
2 With such a(n) _____ cast, the new show is certain to be a sell-out.
3 Don't miss the opportunity to see this _____ film – it well deserved its six Oscars.
4 The circus performer's abilities on the high wire are truly _____ and have to be seen.
5 The _____ singer, raised and educated in London, could perform with any of the soul greats.
6 The performance is what we have come to expect from this spectacular _____ ballet dancer.

GRAMMAR

G1 ALTERNATIVES TO *IF*

There are several different expressions that we can use in conditional sentences other than *if*.

UNLESS

Unless means *if not*, but we can only use it in 'real' conditions, not in imaginary conditions where the result is contrary to known facts:

I'll get you a ticket **unless** it's too expensive. ✔
~~I'd stay here unless I got a good job abroad.~~ ✘
~~They'd join us now unless they were so busy.~~ ✘

PROVIDED/ON (THE) CONDITION (THAT), AS LONG AS, ASSUMING

We usually use these conjunctions with the first conditional. They suggest that a condition is necessary.

I'll lend you the car **provided** (**that**) you bring it back this evening.

We often use *but for* with the third conditional. It is a preposition and so has to be followed by a noun.

But for her quick thinking, we would have had a serious accident. (= If it hadn't been for …)

SUPPOSING, WHAT IF, IN CASE

We use these mainly with the second conditional to speculate about imaginary conditions. They are quite informal.

Supposing you could take a month off work, where would you go?

We use *in case* to suggest a course of action in a possible situation. It is different from *if*:

I'll take an umbrella **in case** it rains. (= I don't know if it will rain, but I'll take an umbrella.)
I'll take an umbrella **if** it rains. (= In the situation where it is raining, I'll take an umbrella.)

We use *even if* to emphasise a condition or to suggest that it's unexpected.

Even if I passed my exams, I still wouldn't go to university. (I probably won't pass the exams.)

Whether or not introduces two possible conditions. We can use the phrase together or split it:

I'm going to become an economist, **whether or not** you think it's a good idea.
I'm going to become an economist, **whether** you think it's a good idea **or not**.

G2 PHRASAL VERBS

Phrasal verbs consist of verb + adverb/particle. They can be transitive or intransitive.

INTRANSITIVE PHRASAL VERBS

Intransitive phrasal verbs do not have an object (and can therefore not be passive). They are often used in instructions and commands.

Stand up.
Come back.
Watch out for the foxes.

TRANSITIVE PHRASAL VERBS

These have an object. A noun object can either come between the verb and the particle or after the particle.

I feel obliged to **turn down your offer**.
I feel obliged to **turn your offer down**.

However, a pronoun object has to come between the verb and the particle.

I'm sorry that I had to **point it out** to you. ✔
~~I'm sorry that I had to point out it to you.~~ ✘

Note where we can place adverbs.

Please **fill this form in** carefully. ✔
Please **fill in this form** carefully. ✔
~~Please fill this form carefully in.~~ ✘
~~Please fill in carefully this form.~~ ✘
~~Please fill carefully this form in.~~ ✘

In relative clauses, the adverb cannot come before the relative pronoun, unlike prepositional verbs.

It was your suggestion, **which I took up**. ✔
~~It was your suggestion, up which I took.~~ ✘

KEY LANGUAGE

KL1 SETTING THE AGENDA

Let's talk about …
I propose we discuss …

KL2 RESPONDING TO OFFERS

Sounds OK to me./Yeah, that's fine.
Well, I'm sorry, but that's not acceptable.
We're not happy about (the terms you offer).
We're not prepared to (invest in the project) unless (you improve your offer).
I'm sorry, we were looking for (a much higher stake).

VOCABULARY

V1 BUSINESS AND ECONOMIC TERMS

assets and liabilities, boom and slump, creditors and debtors, imports and exports, income and expenditure, mergers and acquisitions, mortgages and loans, profit and loss, supply and demand

V2 CONFUSING WORDS

affect – effect, creditor – debtor, debt – loan, lend – borrow, principle – principal

V3 SUFFIXES (NOUNS 2)

abstention, admission, clarification, collision, confusion, decision, discrimination, elimination, extension, indication, instigation, negotiation, permission

G1 **1** **Complete the conversations with alternatives to *if*. Sometimes more than one answer is possible.**

1 **A:** Can I leave early to pick up my son?
  B: Yes, _____ that you finish the urgent work.
2 **A:** Are you going to apply for the job?
  B: Yes, _____ it would mean that I'd have to move. I don't want to move again.
3 **A:** _____ you could invite anyone at all to dinner, who would it be?
  B: Oh, David Beckham, no question!
4 **A:** That agent hasn't called, and I have to go now.
  B: Leave the details with me _____ he calls later.
5 **A:** You can go to the club this evening _____ you're back by 11.00 p.m.
  B: OK, thanks, Dad.
6 **A:** How will you vote in the meeting?
  B: Against. I don't think we should sell, _____ they offer the full price.
7 **A:** I think Smiths may offer you your old job back.
  B: They needn't bother. I wouldn't go back there _____ they offered to pay me double!
8 **A:** It was lucky that the airport official was there.
  B: Yes, ___ his help, we might have missed the flight.

G2 **2** **Put the words in the correct order to make sentences with phrasal verbs. Sometimes more than one answer is possible.**

1 smoking / my father / up / recently gave
  _____
2 that road / the potholes / for / in / out / watch
  _____
3 the offer / down / you'd / turn / politely / better
  _____
4 information / interesting / that's / found / out / who / it?
  _____
5 when / played / up / the national anthem / is / stand
  _____
6 very efficiently / the meeting / up / set / assistant / your
  _____
7 the issue / bring / which / want / that's / I / up / to
  _____
8 it / you / the agenda / fit / can / into?
  _____

KL **3** **Complete the conversation with phrases from KL.**

A: Are we all here? Good. OK, first, I ¹_____ the budget for the new magazine.
B: Yeah, ²_____.
C: Actually, we'd like to suggest a different order. ³_____ about the schedule first, as in Design, we're ⁴_____ the timescale you're proposing.
A: OK, the schedule, then. We've proposed a deadline for copy on the 15th of each month and then a disc to printer date of the 29th.
C: Well, I'm sorry, ⁵_____. We can't design a 192-page magazine in two weeks.
A: I realise it's tough, but it's a current affairs magazine, so we have to produce it quickly.
B: Well, we appreciate that, but we were ⁶_____ a much longer turnaround, say 28 days. Can we look at getting closer to that …

V1 **4** **Choose the correct word for each gap and complete the sentences.**

1 I check my personal accounts each month to ensure my _____ isn't higher than my _____. (income, expenditure)
2 It's essential to reduce manufacturing output when _____ outstrips _____, and spare output can't be sold. (supply, demand)
3 A successful economy is likely to have higher levels of _____ than _____. (imports, exports)
4 Some people say the secret to a successful business is to demand payment from your _____ within 30 days but pay your _____ only after 60 days. (creditors, debtors)
5 For every economic _____ , there's likely to be a depressing _____ round the corner. (boom, slump)
6 The company has huge debts, both in the form of _____ on its properties and _____ for purchasing expensive equipment. (mortgages, loans)

V2 **5** **Choose the correct words to complete the sentences.**

1 I really need to pay off my credit card *loans / debt*.
2 I've forgotten to bring my calculator. Can you *borrow / lend* me one?
3 In case of failure to repay the loan, the *creditor / debtor* could lose their home.
4 I'd advise you to be *discreet / discrete* about this project – it's confidential.
5 The *affects / effects* of slavery lasted well beyond the 19th century.
6 We're pleased to announce the appointment of Mike Richards as our new *principle / principal*.

V3 **6** **Read the definitions and complete the words.**

1 the act of starting something: _____ion
2 a crash between two vehicles: _____ion
3 making something bigger or longer: _____ion
4 not voting for or against something: _____ion
5 being officially allowed to do something: _____ion
6 the removal or destruction of something: _____ion

GRAMMAR

G1 COHESION 2 (SUBSTITUTION)

When we construct a text, whether spoken or written, we use a number of devices to ensure that we avoid repeating things too much and also to ensure the flow of the text. Two of these are substitution and ellipsis.

Substitution means replacing one word or phrase with another. The most common form of substitution is substituting a pronoun for a noun (nominal substitution).

> **John's** arrived. **He**'s in the living room.
> We take **plastic** completely for granted. The **material** has been with us for 75 years now and **it** is here to stay. This **wonder stuff** has so many uses …

We often use different nouns for the same thing in order to avoid repetition (lexical substitution) .

We can also use words like *one*, *ones* or *the sort* to substitute nouns.

> **This course** is too expensive. I need to find a cheaper **one**.

If we want to avoid repeating a verb or a verb phrase, we use the auxiliary *do* (verbal substitution).

> I need to **write up** the experiment but I'll **do** it tomorrow. (do = write)

We can use *so* or *not* to replace whole clauses, with *do* or with other verbs (clausal substitution).

> They said we were required to complete the form, and we did so. (= completed the form)
> Can we afford to ignore this problem? I think not. (= I think we can't afford to ignore this problem.)

Ellipsis (zero substitution) means omitting something completely. We can omit nouns after words like *some*, *the other* and comparatives.

> He wants to go to **one lecture** and I want to go to **the other**.
> We were offered **two rooms** and we chose **the bigger**.

In repeated verb phrases we can usually omit the main verb rather than repeat it.

> 'She shouldn't have apologised. It wasn't important.'
> 'I disagree. I think she **should (have)**.'

G2 NOMINALISATION

Nominalisation means using a noun rather than a verb or an adjective.

> The committee **postponed** the meeting …
> The **postponement** of the meeting (by the committee) …
> The tiny baby was **perfect**. It astounded him.
> The **perfection** of the tiny baby astounded him.

Nominalisation is common in formal writing. We use it for a number of reasons:

It can combine two clauses so is more economical.

> The university decided to expand its physics department, which attracted greater funding.
> The university's **decision** to expand its science department attracted greater funding.

It can be used to avoid mentioning who does an action.

> The government closed the mine and made 300 miners redundant.
> The closure of the mine resulted in 300 **redundancies**.

It can be used to summarise a previous point.

> Protestors have prevented traffic from moving through the centre again today. **This situation** cannot be allowed to continue. (this situation = protestors preventing traffic from moving through the centre)

Nominalisations are often followed by a preposition (e.g. *postponement of, arrival at, wait for*).

KEY LANGUAGE

KL REFERRING TO WHAT OTHER PEOPLE HAVE SAID

As (Steven) said, …
What (Steven) said about …
If I understand you correctly, you're saying …
If I could just pick up on something that (Steven) said about …
(Steven) claimed that …, suggesting that …
With regard to (Steven's) argument that …
Perhaps we should return to what (Steven) said, which was …

VOCABULARY

V1 GEOLOGICAL TERMS

canyon, crater, erosion, flash flood, geyser, ice cap, meteor, reservoir, subsurface, tsunami

V2 INFORMAL PHRASES

anti-plastic brigade, bonkers, bother, have something up to here (I've had it up to here) with, rant, spout (v), tree-hugger, (be) wheeled out

V3 COLLECTIVE NOUNS

a bunch of, a group of, a flock of, a herd of, a pack of, a set of, a shoal of, a swarm of

G1 **1 Find eight examples of substitution and five examples of ellipsis (zero substitution) in the text.**

There's a lot of publicity about recycling these days and whenever I see some I wonder if it really does a lot of good. I'm all for helping the environment – of course I am – but sometimes I wonder whether all the different rubbish and recycling collections are really useful. I mean, we have a bin for household waste and one for green; we have a small bin for compost for our own garden and another that goes to council compost. We've got a box for glass, another container for plastic and a third for paper. But is all this rubbish really separated out once it's collected? Sometimes I doubt it. Then of course there's the waste that we're supposed to take to the recycling centre. I do this all the time, but then each time I go to the centre I wonder if I should have, because I use the car, and that just causes pollution …

2 Improve the texts. Change repetitions using substitution.

1 Our local council has proposed fitting microchips in all our rubbish bins. The microchips detect if the wrong type of rubbish is put in the bins. Residents would be really angry if the council put microchips in the bins, and residents have said they would refuse to comply with the proposal.

2 Apparently, incinerators are the best way of getting rid of non-recyclable rubbish so the council wants to install an incinerator here. The problem with incinerators is that incinerators can produce toxic fumes and obviously people living nearby don't like the fact they produce toxic fumes.

G2 **3 Rewrite the sentences using nouns formed from the underlined words.**

1 The images have been computer enhanced, which makes them much sharper.

2 We were amazed that Selina recovered so fast from the illness.

3 The food here is excellent, making the restaurant good value for money.

4 The hijacker threatened the flight attendant, which terrified the passengers.

5 The factory is capable of producing 1,000 cars per week, which makes it very profitable.

6 The president arrived and he was greeted by crowds at the airport.

KL **4 Complete the sentences. Write one word in each gap.**

In Questions Now, we discussed climate change. We've had a lot of phone calls on this topic.

1 If I could _____ on _____ Mr Davies said, it seems there have been no tests to check coastline erosion …

2 Mr Davies _____ this was already happening, _____ that he had reliable information.

3 Perhaps we _____ to _____ the first speaker said, connected with the warming climate.

4 With _____ the minister's argument that we aren't prepared for the effects of climate change, …

5 If I _____ you _____, you're saying that you don't think climate change is a serious issue?

V1 **5 Find words in V1 with these meanings.**

1 the process by which something is gradually destroyed by wind, rain or the sea: _____

2 a deep valley with steep sides of rock: _____

3 a very large wave caused by an earthquake or other disturbance: _____

4 a natural spring which sends hot water and steam into the air from the ground: _____

5 a piece of metal or rock that travels through space: _____

6 an artificial lake where water is stored before being used: _____

V2 **6 Replace the underlined words/phrases in the conversation with informal ones.**

A: You know, [1]I really can't tolerate any more of these [2]aggressive arguments you get in the press against taking the kids to school by car.

B: I know what you mean. I hate these people who [3]talk incessantly about parents causing congestion in the streets morning and evening, as if no one else goes out then.

A: Yeah, and they seem to think we're [4]insane driving the kids around. Don't these [5]environmentally concerned people realise that we wouldn't [6]expend time and effort getting the car out if we didn't have to because of the distance?

1 _____   3 _____   5 _____
2 _____   4 _____   6 _____

V3 **7 Match the sentence halves and complete the endings (a–f) with nouns.**

1 Jonathan gave Sue a bunch of
2 We were lucky enough to see a herd of
3 Can you bring a spare pack of
4 That farmer has a large flock of
5 The cruise takes us around the whole group of
6 We need to get a new set of

a _____ to go with the new dining table.
b _____ to the games evening?
c _____ for her birthday.
d _____ in the mid-Aegean Sea.
e _____ and they're really vicious.
f _____ on the safari.

1 EDUCATION AND EMPLOYMENT

1 You are going to watch an interview with Helen Kempster, a careers consultant. Before you watch, work with a partner and discuss the questions.

1 In what ways do you think Helen helps people find a job?
2 What do you think are the best ways of preparing for a job interview?

2 ▶ 1 Watch the interview and number the topics Helen discusses in the order she talks about them.

a what's important when writing a CV
b different ways she helps people find a job
c two main types of interview questions
d her most important advice for people looking for work
e how to prepare for an interview

3 Watch the interview again. Are the statements true (T) or false (F)?

1 The Careers Group only finds jobs for people who have recently graduated.
2 Helen helps create specialised training programmes within academic departments.
3 The most important thing for people with little experience is how they look.
4 You should create just one CV with all your skills and experience and use this for each job application.
5 You should prepare how you are going to answer certain questions in an interview.
6 Interview questions are based around what you can offer the company and your reasons for applying for the job.
7 Competency-based questions use example situations to test your problem-solving abilities.
8 When preparing for an interview, you need to do more than just finding out what the company does.

4a Match the competency-based questions with the skills in the box that they are asking about.

creativity	flexibility	independence
leadership	teamwork	

1 Tell us about a situation in which you developed a new way of doing something.
2 Tell us about a time when you worked with a group of people to solve a problem.
3 Describe a situation in which you had to guide a group of people to success. What did you do to motivate them?
4 Describe a situation in which you had to change the way you were doing something. What did you change and how did it improve the situation?
5 Tell us about a time when you went against the usual way of doing things. Why did you feel this was necessary?

4b Choose one of the questions in Exercise 4a and prepare your own answer to it.

4c Work with a partner and share your answers.

2 TOURISM AND CONSERVATION

1a Read the description of Lonely Planet and answer the questions.

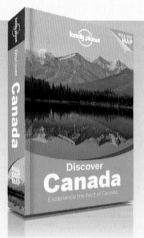

Lonely Planet is the most successful publisher of travel guides in the world. Founded in the 1970s with just one 94-page guide for budget travellers in Asia, it now produces guidebooks and apps for destinations in 195 countries, in nine different languages.

1 What qualities do you think Lonely Planet looks for in their writers?
2 What type of information do you think Lonely Planet guidebooks offer?
3 What do you think are the benefits of travel, according to Lonely Planet?

1b ▶ 2 Watch an interview with Noirin Hegarty, the Managing Destination Editor for Lonely Planet, and check your answers.

2 Watch the interview again and choose the correct answer (a, b, or c).

1 What is Lonely Planet's target market?
   a adventurous travellers on a budget
   b people going on short trips
   c all types of travellers
2 Which type of information is not mentioned as something Lonely Planet provides?
   a planning your trip
   b tips on finding work while travelling
   c what to do if you have a problem
3 Researching a book involves
   a one author and one editor.
   b an author travelling for three to nine weeks.
   c using Lonely Planet's contacts to arrange accommodation for authors.
4 What does Noirin say about collecting information?
   a They only look at new destinations.
   b They allocate more time and money to lesser-known destinations.
   c It's an ongoing, year-round process.
5 How does Lonely Planet deal with the impact of mass tourism?
   a It won't provide information on some activities, such as dolphin tours.
   b It aims to show both sides of the story and let the reader decide.
   c It avoids recommending places which are not currently tourist attractions.

3 Work in small groups and discuss the questions.

1 Do you agree that travel is a force for good? Why?/Why not?
2 How can we practise responsible tourism? Make a list of things a responsible tourist does.

3 INTERNATIONAL RELATIONS

1 You are going to watch an interview with Brendan Paddy, Head of Communications for the Disasters Emergency Committee (DEC). Before you watch, work with a partner and discuss the questions.

1 What do you think the DEC does?
2 What do you think Brendan's job involves?
3 What difficulties do you think the DEC faces?

2 ▶ 3 Watch the interview and tick the four topics Brendan talks about. Were your ideas from Exercise 1 correct?

1 Where he works
2 What his job involves
3 Successful international collaboration
4 Political problems
5 Common misconceptions about international aid
6 What he doesn't like about his job
7 What he likes about his job

3a Work in two groups. Watch the video again and make notes on the questions below.

Group A
1 What's the most important thing for Brendan when communicating with the public?
2 What types of local organisations do their member agencies work with?
3 In what situation is it especially important to involve local people in the project?
4 What two things make Brendan's job difficult sometimes?

Group B
1 What channels of communication does Brendan use when communicating with the public?
2 What's the most important starting point when dealing with cultural differences?
3 What are the benefits of buying things locally rather than shipping them from abroad, according to Brendan?
4 What impresses Brendan about people who have been affected by tragedies?

3b Compare your notes with other students in your group.

3c Work with a partner from the other group and share your information.

4 Work in small groups and discuss the questions.

1 How can other countries help those affected by disasters, apart from by sending money?
2 Would you like to work for an international aid agency? Why?/Why not?

4 HEALTH AND CARE

1 You are going to watch an interview with Neil Shah, Director of the Stress Management Society. Before you watch, discuss the questions with a partner.

1 What are some stressful aspects of modern-day life which weren't around 20 or 30 years ago?
2 What attitudes do people have towards stress in your country?
3 What are some of the health issues which may be linked to stress?
4 What can you do to alleviate stress in your life?
5 What can companies do to manage the stress their employees face?

2 ▶ 4 Watch the interview. How does Neil answer the questions in Exercise 1?

3a Without watching again, try to complete the notes.

1 Nowadays people aren't able to _____ with the amount of information they face every day.
2 Part of the problem is that we have to deal with _____ at the same time.
3 In western countries people face problems with a 'stiff _____'. They _____ their _____ up and carry on.
4 Eastern cultures have traditionally _____ well-being.
5 Stress leaves you open to illness as it harms your _____ _____.
6 _____ _____ is a good way to alleviate stress as it produces chemicals which make you feel happier and _____.
7 Employee morale, productivity, _____ and output are ways of measuring what's happening in an organisation.
8 A happy workforce will work harder, which means there's a direct _____ _____ in making their lives less stressful.

3b Watch the interview again and check your answers.

4a Which of these situations would you find most stressful? Why?

1 You have important exams soon and you're exhausted from staying up late every night studying.
2 You are constantly distracted by notifications on social networks, emails and text messages. You find it difficult to focus on anything for very long and find it hard to switch off.
3 You manage a large team of people. Staff surveys reveal that many employees in your team are unhappy and feel they need more support.

4b Work in groups and discuss the questions.

1 What measures could you take to reduce the stress caused by the situations in Exercise 4a?
2 Have you been in any similar stressful situations? How did you cope?

► MEET THE EXPERT

5 | FASHION AND CONSUMERISM

1 Work in small groups and discuss the questions.

1 What types of technology can you think of that you can wear? Do you use any of them?
2 What types of wearable technology would you like to see in the future?

2a You are going to watch an interview with fashion designers Francesca Rosella and Ryan Genz, who create wearable technology integrated into clothes. Before you watch, try to match the words and phrases from the interview with the descriptions.

1 wires
2 a conductor
3 seamless
4 an evening gown with electro-luminescent thread
5 the Twitter dress
6 an interface between you and other people

a what they didn't want to have in clothes
b what they designed for a celebrity to wear to a launch party
c how they want their clothes to look
d how they see the function of clothes in the future
e what you need to make electricity move from one point to another
f the first dress Francesca designed

2b ▶ 5 Watch the interview and check your answers.

3 Watch the interview again. Are the statements true, false or not given?

1 Francesca and Ryan design their clothes to last for 5–10 years.
2 They spent a lot of time in the beginning looking for new materials which could conduct electricity.
3 Francesca became interested in wearable technology when she was at university.
4 When they graduated, they were told there were no jobs for people researching wearable technology.
5 Nicole Scherzinger was amazed when she saw the dress functioning for the first time.
6 Most of their customers are female.
7 It's more important for clothes with wearable technology to look cool than normal clothes.
8 They believe that with wearable technology, the clothes of the future will make us feel safer.

4a Work in pairs. Design your own piece of wearable technology. Use these questions to help you.

• What type of clothing is it?
• What is its function?
• What type of material will you use?
• Who is it for?
• What special features does it have?

4b Present your designs to the class. Which design do you like best?

7 | PEOPLE AND IDEAS

1 Work in small groups and discuss the questions.

1 Which of these methods do you use to learn, share or discuss knowledge and ideas?
• watching talks/lectures/webinars online
• using Wikipedia
• reading books, magazines and journals
• attending talks/lectures
• asking questions on social media
2 Do you use any other ways of learning or sharing ideas?

2 ▶ 7 Watch an interview with Mairi Ryan, Head of Public Events at the Royal Society for the encouragement of Arts, Manufactures and Commerce (RSA). Tick the four topics Mairi talks about.

1 how they get involved with the local community
2 the types of talks they organise
3 a current project
4 taboo subjects
5 how to measure the success of a talk
6 a memorable speaker
7 the society's plans for the future

3a Watch the interview again and make notes on Mairi's answers to these questions.

1 What's the main purpose of the RSA?
2 What other events do they organise, besides lectures?
3 What three qualities do they look for in potential speakers?
4 Who do they have working on their current project?
5 What challenge do they hope to address with their current project?
6 What three ways do they use to measure the success of a talk?
7 Why was Mairi nervous about meeting Jodie Williams?
8 What was the main message of Jodie's talk?

3b Work with a partner and compare your notes.

4a You are going to talk about a subject you know well or an issue you feel strongly about. First make notes about what you are going to say. Use these ideas to help you.

• Choose a subject (e.g. something you have studied) or an issue (e.g. reducing global poverty).
• What are the current issues/most important things to know?
• What future challenges are there?
• What advice would you give to someone studying/getting involved in this area?

4b Work in groups. Take turns to tell your group about your subject/issue. Answer any questions they have.

8 JOURNALISM AND MEDIA

1 Which of these things do you use social media for? Work in groups and compare your answers. Is there anything else you use social media for?

- putting up photos of yourself having fun
- sharing links to music or videos
- sharing memes
- watching TV programmes
- gossiping
- keeping in touch with friends and family

2 ▶ 8 Watch an interview with Dr Nell Haynes, an anthropologist who studies how we use social media. Number the topics Nell discusses in the order she talks about them.

a   different ways people use social media
b   why she uses social media
c   her current research project
d   the impact of social media on mainstream media
e   the impact of social media on people's lives

3a Without watching again, try to complete the notes.

1   The current project is a(n) _____ study of how social media is used around the world.
2   They are interviewing people and _____ _____ how they use social media.
3   People round the world use social media differently as their _____ and _____ influence the way in which they use it.
4   In some countries young people use social media to start _____ _____.
5   People who live mundane lives use social media to show a(n) _____ of expensive cars and homes.
6   Social media has made mainstream media become more _____.
7   Nowadays the definition of what social media is (and isn't) has become _____.
8   Reading an article means not just _____ the _____ but also sharing it with friends.
9   The most common uses of social media are to _____ and _____ _____.
10 In an anthropological study, it's important to _____ what people _____ as well as interview them.

3b Watch the interview again and check your answers.

4 Work in groups and discuss the questions.
1   What are the benefits of social media? Do you think there are any negative effects?
2   How do you think the way people use social media will change in the future?

9 LAW AND SOCIETY

1 You are going to watch an interview with Nik Peachey, an educational consultant talking about body language. Before you watch, work with a partner and discuss the questions.

1   What kind of things do people communicate through body language?
2   What relevance, if any, do these gestures have in your culture?
    a   shaking hands
    b   tilting your head
    c   making eye contact
    d   standing in close proximity to someone
    e   kissing someone on the cheek

2 ▶ 9 Watch the interview. What does Nik say about each of the gestures in Exercise 1?

3 Watch the interview again and choose the correct answer (a, b or c).
1   What does Nik say about body language?
    a   We think about it carefully and consciously.
    b   It's the most important part of communication.
    c   We don't think about it very often.

2   Nik says that the rules of someone's own culture
    a   are not easy for them to break.
    b   sometimes mean you have to disrespect people.
    c   are easy for them to follow.

3   Nik thinks we communicate our attitude
    a   without thinking about it.
    b   deliberately.
    c   more through the things we say than the things we do.

4   Nik doesn't like people standing too close to him because
    a   he finds it aggressive.
    b   he thinks it's rude.
    c   he feels uncomfortable.

5   What does Nik say you can teach people?
    a   how to listen
    b   how to position their body
    c   nothing at all about body language

6   Nik explains some of the ways he's taught body language. Which of these things does he not mention?
    a   a TV programme
    b   a computer
    c   photos

4 Work in groups and discuss the questions.
1   What aspects of body language are most important in your culture?
2   Have you ever experienced people from another culture using different body language to yours? How did it make you feel?

12 SCIENCE AND NATURE

1 **Match the words in the box with their meanings.**

arterial disease biodegradable biomass feedstock
landfill microbe

1 a condition in which a blockage forms in one of the main blood vessels in the body
2 an extremely small living organism, only viewable under a microscope
3 raw material to fuel an industrial process
4 plant and animal matter used to provide energy
5 a place where waste is buried under the ground
6 describes material which can be broken down by natural processes

2 ▶ 12 **Watch an interview with professors Richard Kitney and Paul Freemont, Directors of the Centre for Synthetic Biology and Innovation, and answer the questions.**

1 What is synthetic biology?
  a the modification of man-made substances at cell level
  b artificially modifying the DNA and cells of living things
  c using patterns found in nature to create synthetic materials

2 Which three processes below are mentioned as applications of synthetic biology?
  a creating artificial limbs for animals
  b making something which detects a defect in the body and repairs it
  c creating microbes to produce artificial alternatives to natural resources
  d using petroleum and oil to create new substances
  e creating microbes which turn non-recyclable waste into recyclable waste

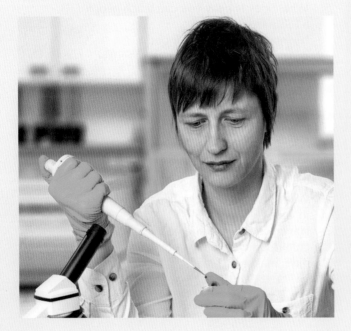

3 **Watch the interview again and complete the notes.**

1 Synthetic biology joins together _____ design and _____ biology.
2 Professor Freemont compares synthetic biology to creating _____ for your _____ _____.
3 The aim of a biosensor is first to find a(n) _____ in the body.
4 _____ _____ is responsible for 30 percent of deaths.
5 A similar device to that which helps unblock arteries could be used for the treatment of _____ _____.
6 At the moment most chemicals and plastics are made from petroleum and _____ ...
7 ... and the problem with this is that it's not _____.
8 At iGEM teams have to design a(n) _____ _____ or machine with a purpose.
9 Last year's team decided to work with something which is a(n) _____-life problem.
10 They wanted to create organisms that _____ _____ landfill waste by breaking it down and producing something new.

4 **Work in groups and discuss the questions.**

1 What benefits could each of these applications of synthetic biology have? How important do you think each one is?
  • creating biofuels (fuels created from living matter e.g. oil from sugar cane)
  • making chemicals from agricultural waste
  • making vaccines more efficient
  • cloning plants
  • creating synthetic cells

2 Do you think it's a good idea for humans to genetically modify things? What are the ethical issues which surround synthetic biology?

COMMUNICATION ACTIVITIES

LESSON 2.4   EXERCISE 6 (PAGE 23)

STUDENT A

Mayor

You lead the meeting. You should ask:

- Ricardo Hernandez to state his position regarding the project and to explain the advantages of the project to the local Granville inhabitants.
- the other members of the meeting to state their position and give their reasons.
- if anyone has any questions they would like to put to Ricardo Hernandez.

Try to have a full and frank discussion. At the end of the meeting, say whether or not you will recommend the Council to support Ricardo Hernandez's project.

LESSON 4.4   EXERCISE 6 (PAGE 43)

STUDENT A

Skin cancer

Skin cancer is caused by too much exposure to the sun: UV radiation damages the skin cells, leading to premature ageing, possibly cancer. It can be fatal. Fair-skinned people are most susceptible.

Skin cancer facts

- second most common cancer amongst people aged 20–39
- skin cancer rates rising dramatically: increased number of foreign holidays, excessive use of sun beds
- more male sufferers than female; men less likely to visit their doctor to check skin problems

Ways to lessen the risk of getting skin cancer

- avoid direct sun, especially between 11 a.m. and 3 p.m.
- avoid burning in the sun; use T-shirt and hat
- children need extra protection
- use high factor sunscreen
- report changes to your skin – such as moles that change shape – to your doctor

---

LESSON 5.4   EXERCISE 4 (PAGE 53)

STUDENT A

You think All Seasons should target the under-30s.

Why? How would you attract these people to the shops? What new facilities would be good to have? What would make All Seasons a destination store for them?

All Seasons would have to sell more up-to-date fashion. How could this be achieved? Would it be better to sell disposable fashion at low prices or quality clothes at higher but reasonable prices?

How could you use the internet? Think about online services and online presence. Would social media be of use?

In general, you think the shop should change direction radically, rather than offer special ranges aimed at particular groups, but still serving a general market.

What would the disadvantages be of targeting the family market, or the over-40s?

LESSON 11.3   EXERCISE 11 (PAGE 111)

STUDENT A

You are a Sales Representative who has recently done very well. You recently became Salesperson of the Year. You think you should have:

- a ten percent salary raise.
- a top-of-the-range new company car to impress your clients.
- to work two days a week from home (for phone sales).
- more time for training courses and staff development.

Negotiate with each other and try to get a good outcome. Begin by putting yourself in the other person's shoes.

LESSON 11.4   EXERCISE 6 (PAGE 113)

GROUP A

INVENTORS

Read the information and prepare for the negotiation. Decide:

- what your priorities are.
- what concessions you can make.
- what strategy and tactics you will use in the negotiation.

You want Ariel Capital:

Finance

- to give you at least $500,000. In return, you will offer them a thirty-percent stake in your company. You do not want to give up control of your company.

Support

- to provide and pay for a managing director to run the company during the first year.
- to recommend an accountant who can look after the financial affairs of the company.
- to offer ongoing advice on any problems which will arise during the first year.
- to agree to your partner being in charge of all the company's marketing.
- to pay for a course on international marketing for your partner.

You are prepared to offer Ariel Capital an additional five percent stake in the business (thirty-five percent in total) if they will provide ongoing management support and advice after the first year.

Facilities

- to help you find factory space to produce the device in large quantities and to hire a supervisor to manage production of the MLSD.

Long-term planning

- to help you build up your company so that eventually you will become the chairman and managing director of a major international firm, offering a range of high-tech products.

LESSON 12.4   EXERCISE 6a (PAGE 123)

STUDENT A

A senior member of the National Academy of Science

You are intensely pro-science and believe that its purpose is to expand human knowledge and to advance human society.

Look at all the discussion questions and prepare your points of view.

You are chair for the discussion of the first question.

LESSON 2.4   EXERCISE 6 (PAGE 23)

STUDENT B

Ricardo Hernandez

Try to persuade the people at the meeting that your project will be good for the island.
*   You will invest $1,000,000,000 in the project.
*   The investment will generate $200,000 annually for the island.
*   It will create 650 new jobs.
*   It will bring 400 percent more tourists to the island each year.
*   It will raise the profile of Granville Island internationally.

You can offer:
*   to build a primary school, shops and 100 houses for local residents.
*   to protect the environment where possible. You will have to cut down mangrove trees to clear the area, but will replant mango trees in other parts of the island.

LESSON 4.4   EXERCISE 6 (PAGE 43)

STUDENT B

Healthy eating
*   Healthy diet reduces the risk of heart disease and cancer.
*   'Superfoods' help fight serious illnesses, e.g. berries and tomatoes.
*   Food that contains omega-3 oils, e.g. oily fish, helps maintain a healthy brain and memory.

Facts about healthy eating habits
*   Less than twenty-five percent of the population aged 12–64 eat the recommended five portions of fruit and vegetables per day.
*   Only twelve percent of children eat five or more portions of fruit and vegetables per day.
*   Less than half of the population eat oily fish at least once a week.

What is a healthy diet?
*   at least five portions of fruit and vegetables each day
*   plenty of fibre, such as cereals and wholemeal bread
*   limited amounts of red and processed meats, e.g. ham, bacon
*   food rich in omega 3 at least once a week

LESSON 5.4   EXERCISE 4 (PAGE 53)

STUDENT B

You think All Seasons should focus on the family market and not worry about teenagers and young adults. Why?

How would you attract these people to the shops? What new facilities would be good to have? What would make All Seasons a destination store for them?

All Seasons would have to sell more up-to-date fashion. How could this be achieved? Would it be better to sell disposable fashion at low prices or quality clothes at higher but reasonable prices?

You think it would be a good idea to have special ranges aimed at particular groups, e.g. young mothers and small children, within the family market.

How could the internet be used in your strategy? Think about online services and online presence. Would social media be of use?

What would the disadvantages be of targeting teenagers and young adults or the over-40s?

LESSON 11.3   EXERCISE 11 (PAGE 111)

STUDENT B

You are the Sales Manager and boss of the salesperson. You want to keep your Salesperson of the Year, but the company as a whole has had a difficult year. You think:
*   the company can only afford a four percent increase in salary.
*   the salesperson should have a standard model car like everyone else.
*   working from home should be limited to one day.
*   there is no budget for training at the moment.

Negotiate with each other and try to get a good outcome. Begin by putting yourself in the other person's shoes.

LESSON 11.4   EXERCISE 6 (PAGE 113)

GROUP B
ARIEL CAPITAL NEGOTIATORS

Read the information and prepare for the negotiation. Decide:

* what your priorities are.
* what concessions you can make.
* what strategy and tactics you will use in the negotiation.

You want:

Finance

* to offer finance in the range of $300,000–$500,000 in return for a stake of at least forty percent. Ideally, you would like to have a controlling interest in the company (over fifty percent).

Support

* to introduce a management structure in the firm by appointing a managing director, financial director, marketing and production manager within the first year.
* to provide ongoing advice and expertise to help the company to expand and become international.

Facilities

* to outsource the production of the device either to a local firm or to an overseas manufacturer in China or India. This would reduce costs and increase profits on the product.

Long-term planning

* to persuade the inventors to focus on inventing new high-tech products to add to the firm's product range.
* to grow the company until it is large and profitable enough to be sold – in 5–10 years' time.

LESSON 12.4   EXERCISE 6a (PAGE 123)

STUDENT B
A member of the public – a taxi driver

You are generally positive about science and the improvements it makes to our lives.

You are chair for the discussion of the second question.

LESSON 2.4   EXERCISE 6 (PAGE 23)

STUDENT C
Head of the Wildlife Society

You represent the conservationists, bird lovers, farmers and fishermen in the area.

You are totally against the project because:

* cutting down the mangrove trees and clearing the waterfront area will seriously affect fish stocks.
* the eighty different species of birds in the area will be threatened. The Granville dove could become extinct.
* a rare turtle will no longer come to White Sands beach to breed.

Find out:

* what Ricardo Hernandez will do to protect the environment.
* if the ramblers will have access to the beach.

LESSON 4.4   EXERCISE 6 (PAGE 43)

STUDENT C

Physical fitness

Regular exercise helps prevent obesity. Being overweight increases the risk of heart disease and some cancers.

Physical fitness facts

* Thirty-five percent of men and forty-one percent of women are inactive.
* Obesity causes around 12,000 cases of cancer each year.
* Physical activity has declined in girls by forty-six percent and in boys by twenty-three percent in the last five years.

How much exercise should you do?

* Just thirty minutes of exercise, five days a week, will keep you healthy.
* You must balance the energy you take in from food with the energy you burn through activity.

LESSON 5.4   EXERCISE 4 (PAGE 53)

STUDENT C

You think All Seasons should focus on the over-40s. Why?

How would you attract these people to the shops? What new facilities would be good to have? What would make All Seasons a destination store for them?

All Seasons would have to sell more up-to-date fashion. How could this be achieved? Would it be better to sell disposable fashion at low prices or quality clothes at higher but reasonable prices?

How could the internet be used in your strategy? Think about online services and online presence. Would social media be of use?

In general, you think the store should change direction radically, rather than offer special ranges aimed at particular groups.

What would the disadvantages be of targeting the family market or teenagers and young adults?

LESSON 12.4 EXERCISE 6a (PAGE 123)

STUDENT C

A journalist

You speak from a personal point of view, and you always question people's arguments closely – you like strong and healthy discussions.

Look at all the discussion questions and prepare your points of view.

You are chair for the discussion of the third question.

LESSON 2.4 EXERCISE 6 (PAGE 23)

STUDENT D

Journalist

You represent the opinions of your readers. You are against the project.

Over sixty percent of your readers are against Hernandez's project.

They believe that the natural beauty of this part of the island will be destroyed, resulting in fewer tourists visiting the area.

Ramblers are particularly worried as they think Hernandez will stop them from exploring the area.

Readers fear that access to White Sands beach will be restricted or that Hernandez will make people pay to go on some areas of the beach.

Readers fear that Hernandez will lose interest in the resort once it has been built.

LESSON 5.4 EXERCISE 4 (PAGE 53)

STUDENT D

You are the Chief Executive of All Seasons.

Initially, you would prefer to offer specialised ranges of products and still cater for the general market, rather than to completely change market.

What would the advantages and disadvantages be of targeting the under-30s, the over-40s and the family markets?

What would make the shops more attractive to shoppers in those different market segments?

LESSON 6.1 EXERCISE 2 (PAGE 56)

How could the clothes be more up-to-date? What's the best way forward with the website? How could the online presence be improved?

LESSON 12.4 EXERCISE 6a (PAGE 123)

STUDENT D

A member of the public – a shop manager

You are generally sceptical of the claims made by scientists, particularly when they claim new developments will be safe.

Look at all the discussion questions and prepare your points of view.

You are chair for the discussion of the fourth question.

LESSON 2.4 EXERCISE 6 (PAGE 23)

STUDENT E

Chamber of Commerce representative

You represent business people on the island. You support Hernandez's project.

Business people believe the project will:

- help to rebuild the island's economy following the damage done by Hurricane Barbara.
- solve the unemployment problem for young people.
- completely rejuvenate this part of Granville, which has been an under-developed area on the island for many years.

Business people would like Hernandez to:

- invest more in local community projects, e.g. build a library, a cinema or a youth club.
- point out that human beings are more important than birds!

LESSON 12.4 EXERCISE 6a (PAGE 123)

STUDENT E

A member of Earthwatch, an eco-pressure group

You want science to work to benefit the world as a whole, and think that it should not harm or exploit the natural world.

Look at all the discussion questions and prepare your point of view.

You are chair for the discussion of the fifth question.

QUIZ ANSWERS

1	Score 1 for each item.			
2	a = 3	b = 2	c = 1	
3	a = 2	b = 3	c = 1	
4	Score 1 for each item.			
5	a = 1	b = 2	c = 0	d = 3
6	a = 1	b = 3	c = 2	d = 0
7	a = 3	b = 2	c = 1	
8	a = 2	b = 3	c = 1	
9	a = 1	b = 2	c = 3	

18+ You are a real technophile! However, you may be a slave to your machines!

10–17 You find technology useful, but it doesn't rule your life.

0–9 You may be a bit of a technophobe. Some aspects of technology worry you, but you still get things done!

SUPPLEMENTARY INFORMATION

LESSON 1.5   EXERCISE 4 (PAGE 14)

THE DIVER
Characteristics

- ✔ You tend to jump in and have a go.
- ✔ You like to get things over with.
- ✔ You like to see if things work.
- ✔ You like to get onto the next thing quickly.

THE LOGICIAN
Characteristics

- ✔ You like things to make sense.
- ✔ You like to know the reasons behind things.
- ✔ You are organised in your approach to study.
- ✔ You enjoy tackling complex problems.

THE DREAMER
Characteristics

- ✔ You think a lot about the subject.
- ✔ You like to research things thoroughly.
- ✔ You put off practical aspects such as writing.
- ✔ You have no idea where time goes.

THE SEARCHLIGHT
Characteristics

- ✔ You find everything interesting.
- ✔ You like to see the big picture.
- ✔ You have bits of information on lots of things.
- ✔ You find it hard to select what is relevant.

LESSON 4.1   EXERCISE 4b (PAGE 36)

MOVING TO THE COUNTRYSIDE: The environment is a key factor in determining our happiness. Noise and pollution don't do it any good at all. The rural idyll – clean air, peace and quiet – will increase your sense of well-being – but watch out for the birds' dawn chorus!

GETTING MARRIED: It's a fact – married people are happier, especially married men! Propose now.

GOING TO THE GYM: Yes, it's tedious, but physical activity can instantly boost your happiness levels. If you don't fancy building your muscles, at least build some exercise into your daily routine – a long energetic walk will do the trick.

SUPPORTING A GOOD CAUSE: There's no doubt that, in life, having a sense of purpose and helping other people lead to increased happiness. Join a charity organisation. Raise funds for disadvantaged children in developing countries or work for world peace. But you shouldn't set your sights too high all at once. Start small, with achievable short-term goals.

A RELAXING DAY FISHING: A day away from it all is great for tackling stress. And to be really happy, we have to keep our stress levels under control.

BEING SLIM: Maintaining a healthy weight is a key ingredient of health and happiness. But the road to happiness isn't lined with crash diets.

TAKING AN EVENING CLASS IN SOMETHING YOU REALLY WANT TO LEARN: How to kill two birds with one stone. You can learn a new skill, such as pottery, car maintenance or a foreign language; as well as realising a personal ambition. Both boost happiness.

GOING ON HOLIDAY WITH A GROUP OF YOUR BEST FRIENDS: Having a break will lower your stress levels, but more importantly, quality time with friends is essential for long-term happiness. But don't save it all up for a once-a-year jamboree. The more the better.

TIDYING UP YOUR ROOM, FLAT OR HOUSE: Create some living space by getting rid of all the clutter. It's not sexy work, but it'll be very satisfying and the sense of achievement is sure to raise your happiness levels.

WINNING ONE MILLION EUROS: The jury's out on this one. You'll definitely get rich quick. But will it make you happy? Some experts think no – full-stop. Others argue it will, but not in the short term – the impact on your well-being, they believe, takes one to two years to show up. The verdict? True happiness probably lies elsewhere.

159

COMMUNICATION ACTIVITIES

LESSON 4.5 EXERCISE 16 (PAGE 45)

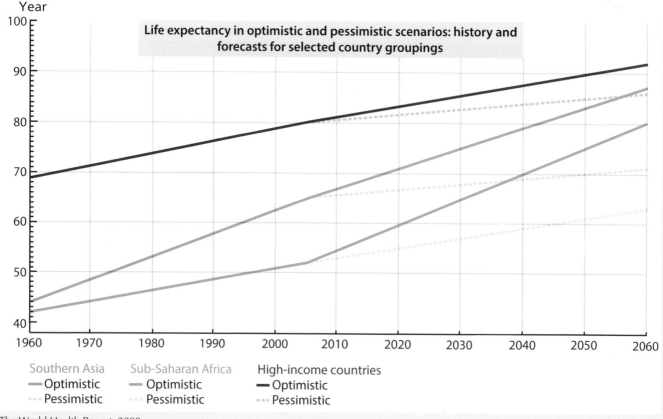

The World Health Report, 2008

LESSON 6.1 EXERCISE 2 (PAGE 56)

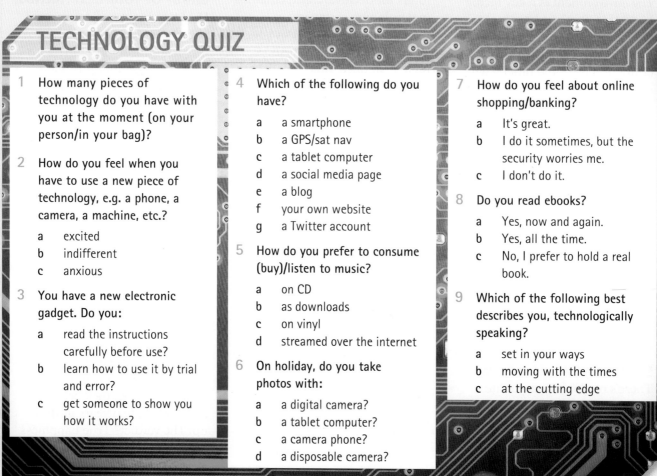

TECHNOLOGY QUIZ

1 How many pieces of technology do you have with you at the moment (on your person/in your bag)?

2 How do you feel when you have to use a new piece of technology, e.g. a phone, a camera, a machine, etc.?

   a excited
   b indifferent
   c anxious

3 You have a new electronic gadget. Do you:

   a read the instructions carefully before use?
   b learn how to use it by trial and error?
   c get someone to show you how it works?

4 Which of the following do you have?

   a a smartphone
   b a GPS/sat nav
   c a tablet computer
   d a social media page
   e a blog
   f your own website
   g a Twitter account

5 How do you prefer to consume (buy)/listen to music?

   a on CD
   b as downloads
   c on vinyl
   d streamed over the internet

6 On holiday, do you take photos with:

   a a digital camera?
   b a tablet computer?
   c a camera phone?
   d a disposable camera?

7 How do you feel about online shopping/banking?

   a It's great.
   b I do it sometimes, but the security worries me.
   c I don't do it.

8 Do you read ebooks?

   a Yes, now and again.
   b Yes, all the time.
   c No, I prefer to hold a real book.

9 Which of the following best describes you, technologically speaking?

   a set in your ways
   b moving with the times
   c at the cutting edge

3D PRINTERS

What they are
3D printers were invented in 1986 by Chuck Hull of 3D Systems. 3D printers have the ability to construct solid objects by building them up, layer by layer, from plastic or metal. Larger machines are able to print a dozen different materials to make an object. 3D printing is an important technology which is having a big economic impact.

Some of their uses
The printers are being used in a wide range of industries from industrial design to jewellery and fashion. They are mainly used:

- to make models and quick prototypes of designs.
- to make spare parts for domestic appliances.
- to provide components in complex equipment.
- to make small batches of products such as jewellery.

Examples:
- NASA recently tested a rocket with a 3D-printed fuel injector. Printing allowed it to be made with just 2 parts instead of 115.
- Printed parts are used to make pharmaceutical and papermaking equipment and aircraft turbines.
- 3D printers are being used to make replacement hips and knees in the medical equipment industry.

Criticisms
- Some people say that the potential of 3D printing to change our lives has been exaggerated.
- 3D printing is time-consuming and at present it is not a fast process.
- 3D-printed parts are not as strong as traditionally manufactured parts.

Benefits
- 3D printers have revolutionised industrial design.
- They have made manufacturing cheaper and more efficient.
- They enable spare parts to be made quickly.

SURVEILLANCE AND IDENTITY TECHNOLOGY

What it is
Surveillance and identity technology is used by governments and police forces to monitor people's movements and communications. It may also be used by companies, institutions and individuals.

Some of its uses
The NSA (National Security Agency) in the United States and security and intelligence services in many countries practise global surveillance. They collect data on foreign nationals and citizens in their own countries and share the information with security organisations in other countries.

Other uses include the following:
- CCTV cameras monitor and record behaviour in public spaces.
- Police forces keep records of an individual's DNA in order to match people to DNA found at crime scenes.
- Mobile telephone companies and internet service providers are required to keep all communications data for several years so that the police can investigate who someone has been communicating with.
- ID cards with key biometric information – for example, fingerprints – are issued to citizens in order to identify illegal immigrants and prevent ID theft and fraud.

Criticisms
- The NSA and other organisations practising global surveillance are accused of infringing people's right to privacy.
- Governments could store information and use surveillance in ways that go against the interests of the people.
- CCTV cameras mean that people have lost personal privacy in public areas.

Benefits
- CCTV cameras help identify criminals and make people feel safer.
- Camera networks provide real-time information which increases the safety of transport networks.
- Doors and locks activated by fingerprint or iris recognition increase people's security.

FRACKING

What it is
Fracking is short for *hydraulic fracturing*. It is a technique to recover oil and gas from shale rock. It is a process of drilling into the earth and using a high-pressure mixture of water and chemicals to release the gas inside. The rock is fractured (broken) apart by the high-pressure mixture. Millions of gallons of water are used to crack the underground rock so that fossil fuels can flow out.

Some of its uses
- to produce gas and oil
- to produce uranium in the future
- to increase groundwater wells
- to prepare rock for mining

Criticisms
- Fracking uses huge amounts of water which decreases water supplies.
- It produces harmful chemicals that may contaminate the area around the sites.
- It is a threat to air quality, causes noise pollution and has a harmful effect on wildlife and people's health.

Benefits
- Fracking enables firms to access difficult-to-reach sources of oil and gas.
- It has greatly boosted production of gas in the USA.
- It will produce gas for many countries in the future. The USA will have secure supplies of gas for the next 100 years.

ELECTRIC CARS

What they are
Electric cars use electric power from battery packs in vehicles. The packs are rechargeable. Well-known makes include the Tesla Roadstar and Reva, which is the top-selling electric car in Europe. Other carmakers, such as General Motors and Toyota, are producing hybrid cars. These combine petrol and diesel with an electric motor. The market for electric cars is expected to grow rapidly in the future.

Where they are used
All over the world. The top five countries for pure electric cars are Japan (twenty-eight percent), the USA (twenty-six percent), China (sixteen percent), France (eleven percent) and Norway (seven percent).

Some of their uses
- In Canada, they are allowed on city streets, but not on motorways.
- In Israel and Portugal, French carmaker Renault and Nissan, its Japanese partner, are installing recharging and battery replacement networks nationwide.
- The San Francisco Bay area (USA) will become one of the world's leading centres for electric vehicles. The plan is to switch the transport system from being powered by traditional fossil fuels.

Criticisms
- Electric cars are not as quick or practical to recharge as other cars.
- They are not really suitable for long-distance driving.
- There are problems of refuelling in remote locations.

Benefits
- They have lower carbon dioxide emissions than traditional cars and low fuel consumption.
- They are less noisy and smoother to drive than petrol-driven cars.
- They use renewable sources of power.

LESSON 6.5   EXERCISE 10 (PAGE 65)

Suggestions for dealing with cultural stress (figures refer to percentages)				
ITEMS	E	G	WC	NWC
Appoint a counsellor for each student.	36.0	28.7	22.6	12.7
Provide each student with a second-year U.S. student as a mentor.	40.2	11.5	17.6	30.7
Recommend students to share a room with a U.S. student in their first year.	15.6	9.3	18.2	56.9
Offer free, weekly English language classes for all international students.	10.7	28.3	18.9	42.1
Arrange for students to visit families in the city at weekends.	5.6	7.2	2.6	84.6
Send counsellors to places where students gather after classes and offer informal free, confidential consultations on a drop-in basis.	82.9	5.8	8.3	3.0

LESSON 7.1   EXERCISE 2b (PAGE 66)

1	in the dark
2	on the outside
3	if they are tinned tomatoes
4	in the ground
5	a leg (also: a snail)
6	one
7	His horse was called Friday.

LESSON 7.1   EXERCISE 9c (PAGE 67)

Discuss your ideas using these criteria.
- number (How many new uses did you think of?)
- originality (How unusual were the uses you gave?)
- flexibility (How many uses did you think of? (e.g. Paperclip earrings (jewellery) and bookmark (reading) are two different uses.)
- detail (How much information did you give about the new uses?)

LESSON 8.5   EXERCISE 6c (PAGE 85)

From   Charlie.Smith.@my:emails.uk
To   Friedman.B@college.network.uk

Dear Professor Friedman,

I'm sorry that I did not finish my essay on time. The reason is that I had an important exam for another subject on Wednesday and I had to do a lot of preparation for it. Because of this, I got behind with my studies. Could I please have an extension of one week so that the essay will be up to my usual standard? I hope you understand why I need the extension and that you can give me more time to get the essay to you.

Sincerely,

From   Charlie.Smith.@my:emails.uk
To   Friedman.B@college.network.uk

Dear Professor Friedman,

I sincerely apologise for not completing my essay assignment and failing to submit it before the deadline. I should explain that I had a very important examination in another subject on Wednesday. This required a great deal of preparation. As a result, I could not complete my essay for you and send it on time. I would greatly appreciate it if you could grant me an extension of one week to enable me to complete the assignment to the required standard.

Thank you in advance for taking the time to consider this request.

Yours sincerely,

LESSON 9.2   EXERCISE 2 (PAGE 88)

AGE OF CRIMINAL RESPONSIBILITY
(Below this age, children cannot be dealt with as criminals.)

7	Pakistan, the USA (in most states)
9	Ethiopia, Iran (girls only)
10	Thailand, Ukraine, the UK
12	Japan, Belize, the Netherlands, Turkey
14	Germany, Italy, Russia, China
15	Iran (boys only)
16	Belgium, the Democratic Republic of the Congo
18	Argentina

LESSON 9.5   EXERCISE 10b (PAGE 95)

Rosberg, S. (2012) The Great Depression: Key facts and figures

- following New York stock market crash (29 Oct. 1929) stock prices fell by 80% over 3 yrs
- thousands of investors ruined; some (mainly men) killed themselves (p. 8)
- in USA, crop prices fell about 60%; rural areas suffered badly – no alternative jobs (p. 12)
- 10,000 U.S. banks wiped out by 1933 (p. 23)
- 1933 – 27% unemployment in Canada (p. 41)
- Newcastle, England: collapse of shipbuilding – 70% unemployment (p. 43)

Wilkie, J. (2003) The effects of the Great Depression

- 'most serious economic depression of 20th C'; affected rich and poor countries (p. 5)
- collapse of international trade (p. 11)
- loss of economic confidence – reduced spending levels (p. 13)
- Chile and Germany badly hit; nearly 30% unemployment in Germany, 1932 (p. 109)
- led to political upheaval – growth of extreme left- and right-wing parties. Germany: Nazis came to power 1933 (p. 124)

Nguyen, T. (2011) The Great Depression in the USA

- large-scale fall in incomes and prices (p. 17)
- farming, mining and logging esp. badly hit (p. 32)
- 25–30% unemployment in 1932; people lost homes, cars, furniture (p. 46)
- high suicide rate during this period (p. 182)
- bankers very unpopular – seen as responsible for depression; bank robbers (e.g. Bonnie and Clyde) acquired 'hero' status (p. 212)
- era 'produced at least one great work of literature': John Steinbeck's *The Grapes of Wrath* (1939) (p. 263)

LESSON 10.5   EXERCISE 8 (PAGE 104)

- Make sure you know what the topic of the seminar is beforehand.
- Think about what you know about the topic – and what you don't know. Write down a few of the things you need to know more about.
- Read any relevant lecture notes you have. Read any material (articles, etc.) your teacher has given you or recommended. Research the topic in the library, on the internet, etc. Make notes of important points.
- Work out a position on the topic. What's your opinion? Are you for or against?
- Prepare some questions you can ask in the seminar.
- Consider working with another student from the same seminar group to discuss your ideas together. Or meet with other students to form a study group – you can practise participating in seminars to give you more confidence for the actual seminar.

LESSON 11.1 EXERCISE 7a (PAGE 107)

Your decisions

	(this year)	(next year)
education and training	%	%
defence (army, air force, etc.)	%	%
law and order (police, prisons and the legal system)	%	%
infrastructure (roads, railways, etc.)	%	%
healthcare	%	%
investment in industry (subsidies)	%	%
environment (e.g. recycling, traffic reduction, etc.)	%	%
social services (for children/the elderly/the unemployed, etc.)	%	%
public service jobs	%	%
arts and culture	%	%
international development (reducing world poverty)	%	%

LESSON 11.5 EXERCISE 10 (PAGE 115)

To	Karl@my.emails.uk

Dear Karl,

I've received some feedback from members of the audience who attended your recent presentation to our local distributors. Unfortunately, there were some negative comments about your presentation.

In terms of your technique, some participants mentioned that you arrived late and that you seemed to lack confidence. They felt this was possibly because you had not fully prepared your talk. Also, some people in the back row had difficulty hearing you. One person complained that you rushed your presentation towards the end; another that you failed to make eye contact.

As far as the content of your talk is concerned, some people felt they were not informed about the unique selling points of the new product. Also, I understand that you had problems with the order of your slides.

Finally, it seems that your answers to questions were not very convincing.

In view of the comments, I think you might find it useful to follow one of our short courses on presentation techniques in the near future.

LESSON 11.2 EXERCISE 2a (PAGE 108)

STUDENT B

Is Fairtrade fair?

No: other schemes are just as valuable

By Philip Booth, Institute of Economic Affairs

Private certification schemes are the unsung heroes of a market economy. They are far more effective than state regulation. It is therefore with a heavy heart that I have always had reservations about Fairtrade-labelled products. The foundation pounces on critics with its well-oiled publicity machine, always responding with anecdotes. But doubts remain.

There are many ways in which poor farmers can get better prices. They can do so through speciality brands, via traditional trade channels and using other labelling initiatives. Does Fairtrade help? The evidence is limited, but even proponents of Fairtrade would argue that only about fifty percent of the extra money spent by consumers is available to spend on social projects, and others have suggested a figure much closer to zero. No clear evidence has been produced to suggest that farmers themselves actually receive higher prices under Fairtrade.

Fairtrade cannot help all farmers. Some poorer or remote farmers cannot organise and join up; others cannot afford the fees; still others will be working for larger producers who are excluded from many Fairtrade product lines. Against that background, 'Fairtrade absolutism' does not sit well. Fairtrade schools have to do everything possible to stock Fairtrade products, but what about speciality brands produced by individual farmers? What about Rainforest Alliance products? Are poor producers to be expected to pay the costs involved to join every labelling scheme?

Fairtrade is a brand that promotes itself the way all brands do. As noted, the brand is prominent in schools. It is worrying that its PowerPoint presentation shows graphs of commodity prices that stop in 2001 and graphs of the coffee price relative to the Fairtrade minimum price that stop in 2006. The picture since then tells a different story. This is marketing, not education.

Fairtrade may do some good in some circumstances, but it does not deserve the unique status it claims for itself.

LESSON 12.1 EXERCISE 1c (PAGE 116)

1 Earth is about twice as big as Mars. (diameter of Earth = 12,756 km; diameter of Mars = 6,792 km)
2 Earth (average temp of Earth = 14 degrees Celsius; average temperature of Mars = -63 degrees Celsius)
3 Earth (Earth: 107,218 km/h; Mars: 86,676km/h)
4 Mars (Earth: 24 hours; Mars: 24 hours + 40 minutes)
5 Earth (Mars has 62.5% less gravity than Earth)
6 Mars (Mars: 2 moons; Earth: 1 moon)
7 Earth (Earth: 78% nitrogen. Mars: 2% nitrogen)

LESSON 1.1 RECORDING 1.1

P = Presenter, J = Jim, N = Nancy, B = Bob

P: OK, thank you, Miranda and the rest of the panel, for those opening remarks. And now I think we can go to our first caller, who is Jim, a salesman from Brighton. Hello, Jim. What do you think?

J: Yeah … good morning. Well, I think all formal education is a waste of time and money. It's the … it's the 'university of life' that's important – you know, learning things the hard way by doing them and making mistakes. Experience, that's what counts; that's how you learn to make informed decisions, not by reading books. I mean, obviously, you need to be able to read and write. Numeracy and literacy and all that are important, but all those subjects like Chemistry and er … Geography, how useful are they in the modern world? They don't really help anyone's career prospects. Life skills, the things that really matter, can't be taught in schools.

P: Yes, I take your point, Jim.

J: All that learning stuff by heart which I had to do at school, rote learning, just like parrots, what a waste of time! School is full of show-offs and smart alecs who want to show how many facts they know in exams, but you really learn by being out there in the world and making your own way. Everyone has the same chance in life – or at least they should.

P: OK, thank you, Jim. And now I think we can go to Nancy in Cambridge … er, who is a university lecturer, I believe. Go ahead, Nancy.

N: Thank you. I have to say that I totally disagree with the previous caller. Education is about accumulating a body of knowledge which contributes to an individual's development and helps create a sense of identity. It's really the most important thing: a broad education with a strong knowledge base. Also, if you think about it, a high-quality education system contributes to the economy as a whole. The better educated the population is, the more people go to university, the more it benefits the whole country.

P: Mmm, I think many people would agree with you there, Nancy. So a university education is important, then?

N: Yes, certainly. For me, subject knowledge and the ability to use it, er, self-awareness and mental agility are all very important qualities which are developed at university. The experience of campus life is at the heart of creating all-rounders who have the capacity for independent study and can think for themselves. That's what education is all about.

P: OK, Nancy, thank you for your contribution. And now, er, we can go to Bob, a company director in London. Hello, Bob. What's your view?

B: Good morning. I have to say I have a quite different view to the previous callers. Erm, for me, the problem with education in this country is that it just doesn't teach the right stuff – that which is actually useful for the world of work.

P: How do you mean, Bob? Can you elaborate?

B: Well, yes. Education at all levels should be much more practical, er, less theoretical. As an employer, I'm not looking for academics and eggheads. I want good team players who can write a decent letter or email – you know, people who have practical skills like meeting deadlines and the ability to prioritise tasks, people who are competent and who can be trained up. It's amazing the sort of stuff I see on application forms. I must say, I see very little of the er, the critical thinking skills which people like, er, Nancy talk about. I think we need to go back to more traditional teaching methods. I don't think any of these modern techniques actually work.

P: Right. Thank you, Bob. Well, plenty to think about there. Let's get some comments from the panel about what they've heard. Cristina, let me come to you first, because …

LESSON 1.3 RECORDING 1.2

I = Interviewer, V = Vadim

I: Thank you, Vadim. That was an excellent presentation and I was particularly interested in the marketing surveys and other marketing activities you were involved with in your job. Now, I know you're flying back to Russia this evening. Hopefully, we will have finished the interview by 3 o'clock, so you should have lots of time to catch your flight. I'd just like to start by checking some of the details on your CV. Can you tell us what you've been doing since you left your job as a financial analyst?

V: Well, since December 2013, erm I've been writing my doctoral thesis and studying at St Petersburg State University of Economics and Finance.

I: OK. I'd like to come back to that in more detail later. Having read your CV, we'd like to know more about your internship and exchange programmes, especially as you haven't had a lot of actual work experience in marketing.

V: Sure. I've been on two exchange programmes: one in Finland and one in Germany. I studied mainly business subjects and also some Finnish, although the programme was in English. One of the subjects I studied was Marketing. The programme in Germany also included International Marketing, but it was taught in German, so, if I'm honest, that was quite difficult for me. I studied German at school, but I dropped it before I had taken any exams. Luckily, my English is fairly advanced, erm and I have an 8 in IELTS, which is a really good score. I really enjoyed the exchange programme and my only regret is that I didn't study more German.

I: You mentioned your IELTS score. We know about that, but can you tell me what BULATS is?

V: Certainly. BULATS is a business language testing service, er, for people who need to use a foreign language in their work.

I: Ah, thank you. OK, could you tell us about the internship?

V: Well, my internship was actually at the place I did my work experience – the Bank of Foreign Trade – and, luckily, they invited me back to work for them after I finished my PhD.

I: Does that mean all your work experience, including your internship, has been in one place? Have you done any other work?

V: Well, I've had a number of holiday jobs. I've been a waiter and I've also worked as a shop assistant.

I: Right. I'd probably include that in your CV in future.

V: Sure, thanks for that advice. I'd applied for a number of work placements before I got the one in the bank. I'd just like to add that I'm quite proud that I was offered a job after my work placement and I really enjoyed working at the Bank of Foreign Trade. I was very happy there. But after my PhD I'm looking for a new challenge and the opportunity to use my English in Britain.

I: Mm, right, yes. Now, before we go into your current job responsibilities in detail, I need to check one last thing. I'm sorry, but I seem to have lost your references. Is it OK if we phone your referees?

V: Yes, no problem. I have their phone numbers.

I: OK, so why do you think you are suitable for this job?

LESSON 1.4 RECORDING 1.3

L = Lisa, H = Howard

L: We've got three possible candidates for the internship at UNESCO. They all have slightly different strengths, so I think it may come down to who's best at interview. Shall we run through UNESCO's requirements for this internship?

H: Yeah, let's do that.

L: OK, well, the first thing is academic qualifications. It's absolutely essential that candidates are doing a postgraduate degree. In other words, a second university degree or higher.

H: OK, so having an undergraduate degree definitely isn't enough.

L: Exactly. They'll have to be enrolled in a master's degree or already have one.

H: OK. What about languages?

L: Well, they must have an excellent knowledge of one of the working languages of the organisation – that means really good English or French, oral and written.

H: Right, so that's a prerequisite.

L: Yes.

H: How about work experience?

L: Well, they don't mention that specifically, but it's obviously an advantage to have some work experience, preferably with an international organisation.

H: Yes, that's true. You haven't mentioned computer skills.

AUDIO SCRIPTS

L: Well, candidates are expected to be able to use office-related software. That's fairly standard.

H: Anything else?

L: No, but we'll be looking for some evidence of a special cultural or scientific interest. It is UNESCO, after all.

H: Yes, quite. By the way, how long is the internship?

L: It must be between one and four months. So they're not that long.

H: OK. Shall we take a look at the candidates now?

LESSON 1.5 RECORDING 1.5

A = Anna, H = Hayato

A: I'm learning English because I love the language and I'm fascinated by the culture. When I was at school, I learnt about Shakespeare and the Queen and the Tower of London, and I dreamt of coming to England. Now I'm in London and I want to improve my English so I can understand English books, like *Pride and Prejudice* and *Sherlock Holmes*, the classics, and follow all the English films and television. I go to the theatre here twice a month. It's wonderful to see a play by Shakespeare at the National Theatre. I want to become really fluent and speak like an English person. I enjoy learning languages and travel a lot. I've visited several foreign countries.
I think I'm a good traveller because I try to fit in wherever I go. I've developed good cross-cultural skills and because of this, I always manage to integrate into the culture of the country I'm visiting.

H: What's motivating me to learn English? Simple. I work in the export department of an international clothing company. I'm attending an English course in my company to improve all my skills, so I can pass an English language proficiency test. If I pass the test, I'll get promoted and earn more money. That's my main motivation. I've never been good at learning languages and I'm not particularly interested in English or its culture, but I'm ambitious and very career-minded. I have to travel a lot in my job to visit suppliers, and I often need to communicate with customers in English. So I'm also trying to improve the level of my English to become more fluent. It'll help me to do my job better. So, to answer your question, my main goal is to pass the language test and get a higher salary, but
I also need to improve my English language skills to perform better in my work.

LESSON 1.5 RECORDING 1.6

OK then, I've told you how to organise a covering letter and what to include in it. Now let me give you some advice.

First, focus on the employer's needs and show how your qualities and skills match what they're looking for. And try to avoid starting every sentence with 'I'. I mean, you have to talk about yourself, but do try to vary the way

that you do this.
Make sure you include all your 'selling points'. They're the things you can offer which will really impress the employer. For example, you could say, 'I've had three years' experience in the newspaper industry and was voted Financial Journalist of the Year in 2006. I speak Spanish and English and can take notes quickly in shorthand.' In other words, highlight your strengths and what you can offer the employer.

Now, be careful about the length of the covering letter. If you make it too short, you'll probably leave out important information and not 'sell yourself' properly. But if you make it too long, the reader may get bored and might not read it properly. Remember that some employers have to read thousands of letters every year, so the letter needs to be concise and persuasive

And don't put the same things in every covering letter you write. Customise each letter so that the qualities and skills you mention – your strong points – are targeted at the specific job you've applied for. You may include different points, depending on the job.

And finally, sign your letter and print your name under the signature.

Well, everyone, that's about all I'd like to say about covering letters. Good luck in your job hunting. I hope you've found this talk interesting and useful.

LESSON 2.1 RECORDING 2.1

1 A holiday is all about getting away from it all.

2 I just want time away from work when I feel I can really let my hair down.

3 I just love going somewhere new and soaking up the atmosphere.

4 We live in a big city, although I grew up in the country, so getting back to nature is important.

5 I love to really live it up on holiday. I like to blow what money I have in a short time. I save all year and then have a really good time.

6 We're keen on finding unusual places – going off the beaten track.

7 Steering clear of the tourist traps is our main priority when booking a holiday.

8 I don't really like to do very much on holiday. Just lounging around by the pool is enough.

9 The main thing is to avoid getting ripped off, so I try not to look like a tourist.

10 I love seeing new things and taking in the sights.

LESSON 2.2 RECORDING 2.2

Er, I became a conservationist in part because of my family background. My father was an agricultural scientist and travelled throughout the world. One of my brothers was born in Africa. I was born in, er, British Guiana and throughout our young life we, er, were constantly exposed to my father's pictures, particularly of Africa, which were … a strong effect on me. So the first reason, I think, is that

it's the way I grew up and that attracted me to, erm, my field; and as a result of that, I went to the University of Oxford to study Zoology. I finished my first degree there. Er, after that, I was lucky enough to become a guide in the Galapagos Islands. I did that for about eighteen months and as a result of that experience, which was really quite a life-changing experience, I went to the University of Pennsylvania to study Ecology and Evolution.
Er, that took me about six years to finish that and once I had finished that, I embarked on a career almost immediately, moving straight into conservation biology and then subsequently into things like park management and research management; and that's basically how I became a conservationist.

LESSON 2.2 RECORDING 2.3

I = Interviewer, G = Dr Graham Watkins

I: What are the key threats from tourism to conservation areas?

G: I think the first thing to say about tourism is that in many situations it's a very positive thing. It can help conservation quite substantially, but there are also many examples in the world, for example in the Caribbean, where tourism also causes other … causes problems and has direct impacts on the environment. Er, many of the reefs in the Caribbean have serious problems as a result of pollution from the large hotels. So, when you have massive development of tourism, it can create substantial problems, er, for the wildlife in the particular area. There are other areas where tourism can also cause what are, you could say, are more hidden … have more hidden consequences. For example, in the Galapagos Islands, where you have a growth in tourism, an explosion in tourism that has basically resulted in more planes and more cargo ships arriving in the islands and bringing with them what we call invasive species. These are species that are not from the Galapagos that cause serious problems for the Galapagos species. It's one of the major reasons why the Galapagos is in so much trouble at the moment. So, in summary, I'd say that tourism can be positive, but needs to be managed effectively to make sure that it remains positive, er, for the conservation of the areas to which people go.

LESSON 2.2 RECORDING 2.4

I = Interviewer, G = Dr Graham Watkins

I: Should we stay away from conservation areas?

G: No, I don't think so. I think, as I've mentioned, many of, er, tourism can be very positive for conservation areas. I think it's more an issue of how we visit those areas.
I think it's important for people to see other parts of the world and also to see these incredible sights that have become conservation areas, but I also think, er, it's very important to make sure that when you

visit those areas, you minimise your impact and not just the direct impact; so you don't take away anything from the island, well, from the places you visit, you don't cause any problems for the wildlife and the places that you visit, but you also become integrated into the local society.

And so the best forms of tourism are those forms of tourism that actually contribute to what we call sustainable development, which means that you, er, contribute by making sure that the companies you're going with are … tend to be locally owned, they tend to employ local people, they intend to purchase items locally and be fully integrated into local society. If you visit under those circumstances, where you're both contributing to sustainable development of the area and contributing to conservation, I think you're having a positive impact. If you're not visiting under those circumstances, then I would suggest that you rethink your, your trip.

LESSON 2.4 RECORDING 2.5

Will Granville Island have the finest golf course in the world in three years' time? That's what everyone is talking about.

Ricardo Hernandez, Chief Executive of Hernandez Enterprises, has announced that he's made a provisional offer to buy the Roberts Estate and to develop it as a sports complex. This will be subject to the usual planning approval. Mr Hernandez plans to build a championship eighteen-hole golf course on the site. In addition, he intends to build a tennis complex, an Olympic-sized swimming pool, four blocks of timeshare apartments, forty villas and a twelve-storey hotel. There would also be housing for hundreds of staff.

Mr Hernandez is certain to meet strong opposition to his plans. The 3,000-acre estate overlooks the sea and it's in a prime area of the island. It's ecologically sensitive because it's a favourite area for ramblers and also one of the few sites for the national emblem of our island, the Granville dove, one of our most endangered species.

To build the waterfront villas, Mr Hernandez plans to remove a large number of mangroves, which will undoubtedly affect fish stocks. Mangroves are vital for the ecosystems in the area. Another problem is that the estate is close to White Sands beach, which is a breeding ground for turtles. This beautiful beach has always been a major attraction for tourists. Environmentalists say the resort will discourage tourists from visiting the beach and will have a negative impact on the turtle population.

Will Hernandez's plan become reality? Who knows? Much will depend on discussions between interested groups and the Hernandez Organisation.

LESSON 2.4 RECORDING 2.6

L = Louisa Bradshaw, R = Ricardo Hernandez

L: Let's talk about your plans for the golf course. I know that building this golf course is central to your plans, but would you be willing, if necessary, to scale down this part of the project?

R: Scale down? What do you mean exactly?

L: Well, would you be prepared to reduce the size of the course to a nine-hole course, instead of eighteen holes? Of course, we'd only ask you to do that if it was absolutely necessary.

R: I'd like to make my position very clear about this, Miss Bradshaw. The size of the course isn't negotiable, I'm afraid. It simply isn't possible to shorten its length. It's my dream to build the greatest golf course in the world here on this island. But I can't go ahead if
I have to build a shorter course. You see, it's vital to have a full-length, eighteen-hole course if you want to attract the top golfers in the world to play here. Also, I've commissioned a famous golf course architect to design the layout of the course. He certainly won't want to design anything that isn't championship length. I hope you see my point of view.

L: Mmm, I understand where you're coming from. So, it seems you won't compromise on that point, right?

R: Exactly. A full-length course is an absolute priority. I couldn't go ahead without your agreement on that.

L: OK, you've been very clear about that. I just hope it won't prevent you from realising your dream.

R: I hope not, too. But you know, there are other countries I can go to if I'm turned down here! I don't want to, but if I have to, I will.

LESSON 2.5 RECORDING 2.7

L = Lecturer, S = Student

L: OK, Erika, you have to write an essay about the effects of tourism on conservation, but you don't know how to start, right?

S: Yes, I've read the essay title, but I seem to be stuck at the moment. Just don't know how to get started.

L: OK, I think the best way forward for you is to do some brainstorming about the topic.

S: Brainstorming. OK, how do you go about it?

L: Well, there are three approaches you could use. It's up to you which one you prefer.

S: Right. Can you tell me a bit about them, please?

L: Sure. The first way is a technique called 'free association'. It's really good for generating ideas about a topic and developing supporting arguments. How does it work? Well, you list everything you can think about that relates to the topic – things you've learnt in class or from your reading, or simply ideas that come to you when you think about the topic. Even if the ideas don't appear to be very practical or realistic, you should still note them down. Er, that's free association.

S: Right, I've got that. What about the other approaches?

L: Well, some people need to see what they are thinking. And for them, 'visual thinking' is a good technique to use. It helps them to develop new ideas. This is how it works: in the centre of a bit of paper, you put some kind of picture – an image representing the topic. Then from the central image, you draw, say, five or six branches which move away from the centre. At the narrow end of each branch, you write a sub-topic of the main topic. Beneath each sub-topic, you can write data which supports your sub-topics. Er, this way, you build up a map to help you organise your essay.

S: Mmm, interesting. But I don't think the technique's good for me; I'm not really a very visual thinker. How about the third approach?

L: This approach is called 'question and answer'. It's a relatively new technique and it can help you to come up with good ideas quickly. Er, with this technique, you think of as many questions as you can about the topic, erm without worrying at this stage about the answers. The questions may help you to identify problems relating to your topic. You then choose the best questions and then are ready to start thinking about what the answers are. However, you may prefer to delay discussion of the answers to a later session. Erm one of your questions might be, 'What is the relationship between the ideas I've noted down?' This question could help you to work out a logical structure for the essay. OK?

S: Well, thanks! I'll think about what you've told me and decide which technique to use for my essay.

L: That's it, Erika, choose a technique which works for you, one you're comfortable with.

LESSON 2.5 RECORDING 2.8

As you know, many animals and plants face extinction because their habitat is being destroyed or they're being hunted by human beings. Take the example of the African elephant, the world's largest land animal. The elephant population of Africa has suffered a catastrophic decline in recent years. A century ago, there were millions of elephants, twenty years ago there were about one million, but today there may be as few as 400,000. The African elephant is an endangered species and will become extinct unless solutions are found to protect it.

Why is the African elephant population declining so rapidly? Well, most elephants have been killed for their ivory tusks, which are made into jewellery or souvenirs. Also, the tusks and bones are often ground down to make medicines. And although the sale and trade of ivory and other elephant products is banned in a number of countries, many elephants are still shot illegally by poachers. Also – and this is a very important point – increasing populations have meant that human beings are encroaching on land that used to be the natural habitat of the elephant.

LESSON 3.2 RECORDING 3.1

Many international organisations are known by abbreviations, or shortened forms of phrases. You usually say each letter separately, with the main stress on the last letter. So the International Olympic Committee, the organisation which organises the modern Olympic Games, is known as the IOC, with the stress on the final letter – C. Similarly, with the IMF, the International Monetary Fund, the stress is on the F – the IMF being the international organisation that's meant to oversee the global financial system. Some abbreviations use the first letter of each word to form a new word. And this type of abbreviation's called an acronym. Acronyms are pronounced as words rather than saying each letter. So, the United Nations Educational, Scientific and Cultural Organisation is known as UNESCO. UNESCO is a specialised agency of the United Nations which tries to contribute to peace and security by promoting international collaboration through education, science and culture. CERN, the world's largest particle physics laboratory, is another acronym. It originally stood in French for *Conseil Européen pour la Recherche Nucléaire*, or *the European Council for Nuclear Research*. However, the name changed in 1954 when the word council was changed to organisation. However, this meant the new acronym would've been OERN, which seemed rather awkward. So they decided to keep the original acronym, CERN.

LESSON 3.3 RECORDING 3.2

Most people can't begin to understand how you feel when you're sent from New York to Tokyo, to Abu Dhabi, to Moscow, without a real break. You get a strange feeling of helplessness, as if you're no longer in control of your life.

You see, when you arrive in each new place, you don't have any friends there. You feel insecure, isolated, not part of the local scene at all because you probably don't understand the culture very well. So you gradually build up a life for yourself and then, just when you've done that, you're sent somewhere else, where you have to start all over again.

Er, it's important to be positive when your partner gets a new overseas posting. It helps to remember that although you were unhappy when you arrived in the last country where your partner was posted, er, you were in tears by the time you left because you knew you would miss so much of what you liked about that country.

Our last posting was to Moscow – we'd previously been in Saudi Arabia. It would've helped if I'd been to Russia before. My husband had been there several times before we got married, but I'd always spent my holidays in France and Italy, and I'd never been to Eastern Europe before. Er, I found it really tough at first. It wasn't just the freezing cold weather in January – fifteen degrees below zero and lots of ice on the pavements – I also felt, er, really lonely at first. I know I should have learnt some Russian before we

went out there, but I didn't have time. I suppose I could have found a local Russian to give me lessons, but I just didn't have the motivation at that point.

It must have been at least a year before I felt happy in Moscow. I attended a cultural awareness course and I gradually began to understand Russian culture better, learnt more Russian words and made some wonderful friends. I created my own world and as soon as I'd done that, we were sent to Canberra, Australia, for a new posting! So, to be honest, I guess I have mixed feelings about being an ambassador's wife.

LESSON 3.4 RECORDING 3.4

O = UN Official, C = Chairperson of oil company

O: You're worried about the image of your company, Ms Leiterman. I can understand that, but at this time you need to be very clear about your objectives and how to achieve them.

C: I understand that. Of course, our image as a responsible company is important, but our main objective now is to develop a strategy to prevent the expansion of the oil flow.

O: Of course, you're right. Your priority must be to contain the oil spill, so you'll have to act quickly and efficiently. It's vital that you have a realistic plan of action as soon as possible. I know you're working on that. But there's something else you should be doing.

C: Oh yes?

O: Well, I appreciate it's a very difficult situation for you, Ms Leiterman. So I urge you to get as much outside help as you can to deal with it.

C: Of course, I realise that. I'm well aware we haven't got the expertise or the resources and labour to deal with the spill on our own. So one of our main goals will be to involve the international community.

O: You're right. It's essential to bring in some international companies for the clean-up tasks, even though it could be very expensive. And it'd be advisable to get some help from UN organisations as well as the governments of the countries that are most affected.

C: Yes, I'm counting on their support and financial help.

O: And there's another piece of advice I'd like to give you, Ms Leiterman. It would be very helpful to involve the International Maritime Organisation and MAP, the Mediterranean Action Plan group. That should be a key objective as they'll have a lot of experience to offer you. And then there's the European Union; you'll need their help as well.

C: Yes, we can't do without the support of the EU, that's for sure. We aim also to set up meetings at regular intervals to monitor progress – we're agreed that good communications are an important objective for us. We want to keep everyone in the company fully informed about what we're doing.

O: Absolutely. There's one other point I'd like

to mention. I'd strongly advise you to set up an Emergency Action Committee as soon as possible. Your top management should be involved, as well as the Ministers of the Environment in the countries along the coastline. I know you've been very busy since the spill and you haven't had much time to deal with the public relations side of things. But, you ought to organise a press conference in the very near future. I mean, as soon as you've devised a credible action plan. There are journalists from all over the world here and they're crying out for information from you. Of course, I can understand why you haven't made a statement yet.

C: Well, actually, I'm just about to issue a short statement. But I only want to talk to the international press corps when I'm fully briefed on what action we're taking. It's always a bad thing to hold a press conference before you have all the facts. You can get into a lot of difficulties that way.

O: True! Look, I know you've uh, got a lot on your plate, but all the same, I strongly recommend you visit the parts of the coastline that are most affected. It'd be good for your public relations and you might learn quite a lot from your visit.

C: Yes, that's a good idea. I'll try to organise a visit as soon as possible.

LESSON 3.5 RECORDING 3.5

How do you become an active listener? Well, I'd say there are five things you have to do – five ways to behave, if you like – when you're listening to someone.

Firstly, pay careful attention to what they're saying. You must focus on the person speaking and not be distracted in any way. Make eye contact – that's very important. Listen and try to get the message they're sending you. Secondly, show the speaker that you are listening. Use your body language to do this. You can, you can nod occasionally, and er, show by your posture that you're being attentive. You should look relaxed and receptive to what the person's saying. You can, you can use verbal signals to show interest, by saying things like 'Yes,' 'Uh huh,' 'Really?' and so on.

Next, give the speaker feedback. You're focusing on the speaker rather than your own ideas, so you may need to reflect on what is being said and ask questions. For example, you may paraphrase what the speaker has said using phrases like 'So what you're saying is …' or 'If I understand you, you're saying …'. Or you may ask questions to check your understanding, for example, 'What exactly do you mean … ?' or 'Have I got this right? You're saying …'. Now, having said that, it's important not to interrupt too often. Wait until he or she finishes. It's really annoying if you're trying to get across a message and someone keeps on interrupting you.

And finally, respond in a positive, constructive way. Show that you value the information you've received. Give your opinions, but don't be aggressive when doing so. Don't put down the person speaking, even if you don't agree with him or her. Respond in an honest and direct way.

Now then, if you put into practice the advice I've given you, you'll show that you're an active listener and this will help you to become a better communicator.

LESSON 4.2 RECORDING 4.1

We're always hearing cries for change to our national healthcare system, and right now the opposition are calling for a huge increase in expenditure on healthcare, to be financed through both increased taxation and compulsory personal private insurance. These would be huge costs for us to bear – costs which, in these difficult times, no one can afford. They claim that building more hospitals, buying the latest medical equipment and spending more on medicines will vastly improve the health of the nation. Of course, this seems to be a strong argument, but the statistics demand caution and I say that there's a better and actually cheaper way to improve the health of the nation.

The World Health Organisation health reports reveal that the connection between expenditure on health and key health outcomes is not as direct as the opposition chooses to claim. Spending more does not mean better health for the people. When we look at the United States, we see a country which spends the most per person on healthcare and which has the most up-to-date technology and medicine. However, comparative studies rank the USA at only forty-sixth in the world for healthcare success, with a spend of $6,543 per citizen.

Countries ranked more highly include South Korea, Chile, erm Venezuela and the UK. These countries spend significantly less per person than the USA. Er, for example, Chile, which is ranked much higher, at thirteenth in the world, spends $1,075 per person and Venezuela spends half this and is twenty-sixth in the world. Remember, that compares with $6,543 in the USA, forty-sixth in the world.

We must learn from this. Spending more money, while useful, I'm sure, does not actually bring the best health results. That's a fact. So just what is it about these countries, many of them in South America, and their approach towards national healthcare? How do they produce good national health at much less cost? How should we change our own system? Well, let me give you those answers.

LESSON 4.3 RECORDING 4.2

Thank you for inviting me to be with you here this morning, as you celebrate what is certain to be one of the most important days in your lives. First of all, let me say that I'm going to be nice to you, as I'm very likely to need your services one day.

You have worked hard to be where you are now and I want to congratulate you on your success. And it's fantastic to see many male graduates among you today, a huge increase on the numbers of only a few years ago. Now you are on the point of becoming members of one of the most demanding of all professions. A profession that makes a real difference to people's lives. You should treat this as a tremendous opportunity, which not everybody has. You do.

So, you'll need to be adaptable and flexible, and to think on your feet. You are going to learn that being a nurse is a full-time job – literally. You are nurses whether or not you're in uniform. Your family, friends and neighbours will call you for help in a crisis.

Erm, in the early years of your career, you'll experience uncertainty, anxiety and fatigue. For all that, these years are sure to be some of the most exciting in your life. Relish them.

New technologies are due to revolutionise the way healthcare is delivered, but you mustn't lose sight of the human dimension.

Although you'll face many challenges, you're especially well placed to deal with them. No previous generation of nursing professionals has had your level of training. You are the first generation of a new kind of nurse, with new skills, for new roles.

I've offered some advice, but I'd also like to ask you some questions. Here's one: you'll be working with people who are in pain or who are grieving. Some of these people are bound to want you to come along with them on their emotional roller coaster rides. Now, how do you intend to maintain a balance between their needs and your own? How are you going to avoid burning out? Who's going to care for the carers?

Here's another question: the longer we work, the harder it is, sometimes, to keep up our early idealism. If you're confronted with unsatisfactory working conditions and bureaucracy, if you don't get the level of respect you think you deserve from your co-workers, if the media report that you have lost your sense of vocation, how are you to keep alive that idealism that prompted you to do this work in the first place?

When the going gets tough, remember why you entered nursing. You have chosen this profession because you wanted to heal the sick and help the suffering. You are dedicated to improving health and showing concern for others. You are committed to public service. These are some of the noblest aims it is possible to have.

The qualification you're about to receive is richly deserved and a passport to a lifetime of fulfilment.

Congratulations and best wishes for the future.

LESSON 4.4 RECORDING 4.3

C = Charlie, N = Nishi, P = Peter

C: Right. Well, my proposal is that we launch a major campaign to reduce people's currently high levels of salt consumption.

N: Salt consumption?

C: That's right. One reason I favour this campaign is that eating too much salt is a significant risk factor in developing high blood pressure, which causes nearly 200,000 deaths each year.

P: OK, so is this a big problem?

C: Oh yes. The second point I want to make is that almost half of the population eat more than the daily recommended amount of salt, which is six grams a day. So you can see that this affects a large number of people, can't you? Thirdly, changing salt consumption habits has a quick and tangible effect. By this I mean that within just four weeks of reducing your salt consumption, your blood pressure will be lower. That's exactly the kind of thing that people want to see – an immediate result of their actions. Basically, a simple and slight change to lifestyle can have a dramatic effect.

N: Fair enough, and quite convincing. Have you had any thoughts about the shape that the campaign could take?

C: Yes, I have. So obviously, the main aim of the campaign is to get people to reduce their salt intake. Firstly, we need to make sure that people can find out how much salt they're consuming; and I think this means that we have to lobby the food industry for improved labelling on food packaging and, secondly, we also need to press the food companies to reduce the salt content of processed foods – you know the kind of thing: microwave meals, crisps, etc. If we do these two things, people will inevitably be eating less salt and also they'll be able to monitor their salt intake. Thirdly, we, of course, have to run a major publicity campaign to inform the public about the effects of salt. In this case, the fact that the problem's so widespread means a TV advertising campaign's fully justified. Whilst I accept that it'd be expensive, it'd be the most direct way to reach such a large target audience. A key part of the strategy here would be to have a humorous approach to make the message memorable.

P: OK, and I guess you'd have a poster campaign as well, and an internet presence of some sort, wouldn't you?

C: Absolutely. And on the internet we'll provide fact sheets and have some blogs written by people who are reducing their salt intake. You know the kind of thing: weekly updates about the changes in their diet, how their health is improving, etc. Finally, the whole campaign would be tied together by our main campaign tool – Sid the Slug!

N: Sid the Slug? Do you mean an animated slug?

C: Exactly. You may well ask why a slug, and the answer is that salt kills slugs. And so Sid the Slug will highlight that direct link between eating too much salt and the increased risk of fatal heart attacks. And also, this gives us the all-important humour that I talked about. We can have Sid being tempted by all those things which are high in salt, only to see him fall ill as a consequence. Or we could have him turning his back on that kind of food, telling us why he always goes for lettuce over a packet of crisps. Of course, we'll need a slogan – perhaps 'We're all Sid at heart.' I like that because it makes the connection with blood pressure. Oh, and on the website, Sid'll host the site and answer user enquiries and so on. So what do you think?

LESSON 5.1 RECORDING 5.1

P = Presenter, M = Mika Ando,
C = Caroline Ishikawa, J = Jun Tanaka

P: Japan is one of the most highly developed consumer societies in the world. Some people even call it a hyper-consumer culture. And for a long time brands, especially luxury brands, have been important to the Japanese. Even in the current economic climate and after the devastating tsunami of 2011, Japan is still responsible for nine percent of the world's luxury purchases. Mika Ando has her own advertising agency, TokyoMA, located in the trendy Omotesando district of central Tokyo. She explains why brands are so important to the Japanese.

M: You have to look as if you come from a middle-class family. Erm, but one of the problems we have here, especially in large cities like Tokyo, is that the value of land is astronomically high. So most people, even those with good jobs, live in very small apartments. So people want to show their status by means of clothes, shoes and bags. This is really where brand value comes from.

P: Critics of this consumer society – many of them Japanese – believe it's far too materialistic. But how did Japan get to this point? Professor Futaba Ishikawa is a historian from Ueno Gakuen University.

C: After the devastation and defeat of the Second World War, Japan was determined to rebuild. By the 1980s, it had become extremely successful at developing advanced manufacturing techniques in a wide range of industries. The growth rate was phenomenal. The Japanese had money to burn and consumerism became a sport, a hobby. But it wasn't to last. The spending excesses of the 1980s were brought to a sudden halt when the bubble burst in the early 1990s.

P: From the mid-1990s, however, Japan began to recover and conspicuous consumption bounced back. But not all consumers were equally influential. By the mid-noughties, one group in particular had emerged as the most important of all – young women aged between eighteen and thirty. They maintain their spending power by living off their parents. Jun Tanaka is a sociologist who is concerned by this phenomenon.

J: Men's earnings have decreased, so these days women don't want to get married. It would mean a lowering of their standard of living. This has profound implications for family life in Japan. What we are seeing now is a situation in which consumerism outweighs having children. It's actually more attractive to be a consumer than to have kids. A parallel phenomenon is affecting men. In recent years, people have started using the term 'herbivores' to describe young men who don't want to get married or even have a girlfriend. Instead, they prefer to spend their money on personal grooming and manga.

P: The consequence of all this is a population that's ageing and shrinking. What are the solutions? Some Japanese are suggesting a move away from this rampant materialism to more traditional Japanese cultural values, with a greater emphasis on the family. But others just want to get on with some more retail therapy.

LESSON 5.3 RECORDING 5.2

N = Narrator, M = Mark Hambling

N: In India, in a hot, airless factory and for the sixteenth hour today, Amitosh carefully sews some tiny plastic beads onto the blouse he is making. No sooner has he attached one than he picks up the next from the thousands in the bag. The blouse bears the label of an internationally famous fashion chain. Amitosh, whose name means *happiness*, is only ten years old. In Paris, the shockingly skinny male model walks moodily down the catwalk. Little does he realise that he is about to spark a huge debate about fashion, models, men and anorexia. Not only has the use of thin models long been controversial, but it has also been revealed recently that men account for twenty-five percent of all eating disorder cases. In London, the cash tills ring incessantly as shoppers grab the latest bargain outfits to replace the ones they bought only a month ago. At no time are they aware of the effect this fast fashion is having on the environment.

M: Three different snapshots of the fashion industry and in each one you have a victim. All of which begs the question, does the fashion industry do enough to be socially responsible? To discuss this, I have with me in the studio Sarah Maitland from the campaign group Making Fashion Better and Diana Spooner from the Fashion Industry Association.

LESSON 5.3 RECORDING 5.3

M = Mark Hambling, D = Diana Spooner,
S = Sarah Maitland

M: So Diana, that's a fairly damning introduction to the workings of the fashion industry. What's your response?

D: Well, it may have been damning, but it's the fairness of your introduction that I question. I think you'll find that the fashion industry as a whole has been taking steps to improve things.

M: Such as?

D: Well, to take the example of sweatshops, almost all major fashion chains now make their suppliers and manufacturers sign agreements which detail the rules for fair employment, concerning everything from child labour to working hours.

S: If that's the case, how come we still keep hearing about the appalling conditions that workers face all over the world when producing products for multinationals?

Surely, it's because these agreements are not worth the paper they're printed on. It's the enforcement of these rules that fashion chains have to focus on and companies are not doing enough on that front.

D: In defence of the industry, it's not easy to check working conditions in small remote factories all over the world.

S: Yet they seem to be able to check the quality of their displays in their shops all over the world! What the companies do is maximise their profits, not improve their workers' lives.

D: Yes, but remember, the suppliers are independent companies who have a contract with the fashion house. We can't be held so responsible for the way they treat their staff; technically, they're not our workers.

M: OK, well, er, perhaps we should move on and deal with the whole size zero question. Sarah?

S: Indeed, and not only is this about the health of the models, but also about the psychological health of young women – and men, all over the world. The continual use of very thin models is harmful to young people. It leads to both men and women having a very poor body image and, I believe, directly leads to the ever-increasing prevalence of anorexia and unhealthy dieting.

D: Well, that has always been a hard thing to prove. You mustn't forget that the slimmer look is both attractive and popular. Our own research shows that people feel more positive towards clothes that are modelled on such models rather than on people with fuller figures. Also, the clothes hang much better on a thin model – designers want their work to be shown as well as possible, you know, and a thinner model is perfect for that. Many designers see themselves as artists and, you know, you wouldn't expect to see a Picasso in a gallery with the lights turned off, would you?

S: That's just so irresponsible. Fashion isn't art; it's a global industry and its imagery directly affects people's health and sense of self and identity, and at the moment the industry's creating unreasonable and dangerous expectations in both women and men. What's even more dangerous is the immediate effect this has on the models. It's widely recognised that models frequently ruin their health in order to suit the whims of the designers and the industry.

D: Well, on that point, the industry's taking steps to help models look after their health. For example, we make sure that healthy food is always available at shoots and shows and some agencies are providing health check-ups, and I should say, not all thin models are unhealthy; many of the girls are naturally just built that way.

S: But that's just missing the point again – what's important is not providing a few carrots at a photoshoot. I mean, it's not that kind of shallow change that I'm talking about. What you need to do is change the whole approach of the industry towards body size.

M: Well, on that point about deeper changes, perhaps we should now consider the effect fashion, particularly contemporary fast fashion, has on the environment.

LESSON 5.4 RECORDING 5.6

C = CEO, M = Mandy, S = Sean

C: First of all, I'll run through the feedback from the consultant's report, which basically divides into four main areas: our shops and their facilities, the product range, our key markets and our internet presence.

It seems that our shops are seen as dull and dated in appearance. Basically, they don't offer a pleasant shopping experience. For example, bookshops often have cafés inside them nowadays, whereas we don't even have seating areas for people to rest in. All of this is exacerbated by poor standards of customer service. Overall, shopping in our stores is not an uplifting or relaxing experience. Now, any comments?

M: That all has a ring of truth, but I think we should be careful how we change things. Suppose we did have a café, wouldn't that just reduce our sales space? And also, it'd mean that we'd have to have food storage and preparation facilities. Most of our shops are in restricted high-street locations – I'm not sure how feasible that'd be.

C: Indeed, but we'll leave such discussion till later in the meeting. Right ... erm moving on to our product range, on the positive side, our clothes are seen as good quality. The fabrics are good and the clothes are long-lasting. However, they're not seen as up-to-date in terms of look and design, and they're not cheap, although this is balanced by the impression of quality. Oh, and er, our accessories and homeware ranges are clearly limited.

S: Can I just say something here?

C: Sure.

S: Well, if we were to copy new designs by major designers rather than use our own in-house designers, we'd certainly be more up-to-date. Mind you, we'd need to produce the clothes quickly then, otherwise we'd still be behind the times.

C: Well, we'd need to look into that carefully. OK, moving on to our markets, at the moment we cater for everyone; we aim our clothes at all ages and at a very general market. The consultants wonder if this market really exists anymore; exactly who are our customers? Yes, Mandy?

M: Just on that point, I was wondering if we might introduce an element of specialisation rather than make a total change.

C: How do you mean exactly?

M: Well, if we had a special range, say one for kids, but still offered a wide general range for customers, we'd differentiate ourselves from other stores without losing our current customer base. There'd be a chance to market the special range and use this as a way to get people into our shops.

S: Erm, Mandy, I think a special range is an interesting idea, but surely, it'd be better to target one part of the market much more aggressively. Admittedly, that'd mean taking a big risk and possibly losing some of our traditional customers. But then we'd have to think about how we go about how we go about ...

C: OK, save those thoughts for later. I've got just a couple more points to make. Firstly, our website is extremely limited, with just basic store information, a limited selection of items featured and a store locator. It's so outdated. We must focus on our web strategy and do much more with, and over, the internet. You know, would social media be useful? Whatever, we need to develop our online presence and services. In a way, that connects to the final point, which is about the shops' brand identity. As you know, we currently are ...

LESSON 6.4 RECORDING 6.1

Good afternoon. Today I'm going to talk about mobile technologies. In my opinion, they're the modern technologies that've brought the most benefits to mankind. I'll start by mentioning some interesting statistics which I think support my case. After that, I'll take a closer look at the impact of these technologies on developing countries and on business. Finally, I'll answer any questions you may have.

OK, there's no doubt that mobile technologies have become widespread throughout the world. I mean, look at the facts – they speak for themselves, don't they? The global population is roughly seven billion and the total number of mobile phone subscriptions globally is 5.4 billion. Impressive? Incredibly impressive, I'd say, and it's happened in a fairly short time period. And that's not even counting all the pay-as-you-go phones in circulation.

Right ... here are some other amazing figures. Mobile phone penetration in low-income countries is almost forty-five percent; it's over seventy-six percent in lower middle class countries and almost one hundred percent in middle- and upper-income countries.

And I'll finish with the words of one commentator who said: 'No other technology has been in the hands of so many people in so many countries in such a short space of time.' That's food for thought, isn't it? And you can't argue against it.

OK, let's look at some specific examples. Mobile technology has brought countless benefits to all of us, but for the purposes of this presentation I'm focusing on the benefits to developing countries and to business people. In developing countries mobile technologies are now used to communicate information about healthcare, weather conditions and natural disasters, like hurricanes and flooding. People get this kind of information quickly nowadays thanks to mobile technology. Another example is in Kenya, where there's a very successful system called M-Pesa for transferring money via mobile phones. It's incredibly useful because lots of people don't have bank accounts in

that country. I also want to point out how important mobile technologies are in business and education. Just think about how much salespeople use mobile technology. They make presentations from their laptops or tablets, or remotely using WebEx. They check stock levels and place orders from their phone while they're on customer sites. They can even make sure they get to appointments on time using apps which help them avoid traffic delays en route. And as you all know, in education, mobile technology has greatly improved communication between students and teachers. What is certain is that in the years to come, mobile technologies will play an increasingly important role in the economic growth of developing countries.

LESSON 6.4 RECORDING 6.2

P = Presenter, K = Katherine, R = Ricardo, M = Marie

P: Are there any questions? Yes, Katherine?

K: You've made a good case for mobile technology. But what about the bad effects of the technology? You know, you just can't get away from it. Lots of business people check their emails late at night. Young people constantly check Facebook and other social media. It's a kind of social pressure, I think.

P: Mm, that's a fair point, Katherine. It's certainly the downside of mobile technology.

K: It's a major disadvantage, I'd say. Also, it's great working on your laptop or tablet or whatever, but they're expensive to buy and are often stolen. I lost my laptop a week after I'd bought it. Some guy stole it while I was in the cinema. That's happened to a lot of my friends, you know.

P: Sorry to hear that. It's true that mobile devices tend to attract thieves – that's a fact of life, you just have to be super careful. Any other questions? Yes, Marie?

M: Well, you know, I think Katherine's got a point about the bad effects. I don't think mobile devices are good for children and teenagers. They spend far too much time on their mobile phones and tablets, they chatter away for hours when what they should be doing is getting outdoors and doing a sport or, I don't know, going to a gym, whatever.

P: Mm, yeah, I have to agree with you there, I suppose. But really, it's up to the parents to step in if their children are spending too much time on their phones.

M: You think so? Since when have teenagers listened to their parents?

P: OK, I'm not going to argue against you on that one. Yes, Ricardo? You have a question?

R: Yeah, I'd like to ask you about poor countries. You think the increased use of cell phones – mobile phones – in those countries is a good thing – that's what you said. But is it true? I disagree with you on that point. Surely, what most poor countries need is cleaner water, better sanitation and more medical centres, more schools – that sort of thing, not more

mobile phones, laptops and iPads.

P: You're absolutely right, Ricardo. They do need things like better sanitation very badly, but good communications are part of the infrastructure of a country and more mobile phones are a quick and cheap way of building up their communication networks. You know, some studies recently have suggested that there's a link between increased mobile phones and economic growth.

R: Really, I must say that surprises me. I'd like some references to the studies later on.

P: I'd be glad to give them to you. OK, thanks for your questions. I hope I've made a good case for mobile technologies! Please vote for my technology!

LESSON 7.1 RECORDING 7.1

Good morning, everyone. Our topic today is creativity – a topic I know many of you have been looking forward to. So what is creativity? Well, I think we can say that it is a mental process connected with the generation of new ideas or concepts. It's also a way of approaching issues, solving problems and exploiting opportunities. It's been studied in a variety of disciplines, from business to psychology, from design to philosophy. However, there is no unified single definition of what it is or a standardised measurement technique.

So, how do you spot a creative person? Well, creative people are constantly asking questions and challenging ideas and assumptions. They're able to make links easily and see relationships between things. They explore possibilities, are flexible and open to alternatives and they reflect critically on ideas, actions and consequences. Creativity has also often been linked to genius, mental illness and humour, and while some argue it's a character trait people are born with, others claim it can be taught using simple techniques. Although the idea of creativity is, these days, generally associated with the arts – art and literature – it's also extremely important in innovation and invention, and therefore important in business, music, design, er, engineering and science as well. It seems that sometimes the term *creativity* is preferred in the context of the arts, whereas the term *innovation* is sometimes preferred in business, when, really, they're probably the same thing, although the latter is considered to be both the generation and application of creative ideas. Within organisations, *innovation* is the term used to describe a process where new ideas are generated and then converted into commercial products and services.

LESSON 7.1 RECORDING 7.2

Finally, I'd like to take a look at the work of Graham Wallas in psychology and his pioneering theory which attempts to explain the creative process. This model is often the basis for many creative thinking training programmes available today. Wallas, working with Richard Smith, presented one of the first models of the creative process in the 1926 book *Art of Thought*. Here, they outlined a five-stage model. So they argued that creative thinking goes through five phases. I'd like to take a brief look at each stage.

The first stage they found is, perhaps not surprisingly, the 'preparation stage', which means a person or individual does preparation work which focuses their mind on the problem. They may also be exploring the limits of the problem.

Secondly, they were able to find an 'incubation stage'. What this means is that the problem is brought into the unconscious mind, but nothing seems to be happening. The idea is that perhaps a break from the problem may, in fact, help to find a solution.

The next stage they identified is perhaps difficult to imagine. This is the 'intimation stage', where the creative person gets a feeling that a solution is on the way.

Following this – I hope you're still with me because it's about to get exciting – is the fourth, or 'illumination stage', sometimes called 'insight', where the idea develops from its preconscious processing into conscious awareness or the moment when the new idea finally emerges. In other contexts this might be known as the '*Eureka!* moment'.

The final step, or stage, they give is 'verification'. At this point the idea is consciously verified, expanded and then applied. Since ideas or solutions don't always work out in practice, this final stage is crucial to the success of any project; it's the 'checking-it-out phase'. Now, are there any questions before we move on to look at some examples …

LESSON 7.2 RECORDING 7.3

P = Presenter, K = Professor Kotov,
D = Dr Petrakis

P: Welcome to the last programme in the series *Extraordinary People and Ideas*. Here with me again today are our regular panellists. Professor Kotov, would you like to begin?

K: Certainly, Joanna. As an economist, I'm biased, but I'm a great fan of John Maynard Keynes, and he's so topical at the moment. Keynes was the first economist to come up with an answer to what happened in the Great Depression of 1929.

If the goal of **many** economists is to secure full natural employment without inflation, then Keynes' interventionist policies hold up well. In simple terms, Keynes said that government spending, on **many** things such as construction and transport, was the key to managing the economy. This means that in an economic downturn, governments should spend a lot more, not cut, in order to stimulate the economy.

So, in general, by adjusting government spending properly, a government should be able to set consumption and investment and government spending at just the right level to produce full natural employment without inflation.

Keynes' theories lost their popularity when Monetarism became the flavour of the nineties – when the state was cut back and most things were privatised. Competition became the deciding factor, really. And I suppose all of this contributed to out-of-control banking and finance sectors creating the credit crunch, as they were driven by the pursuit of profits for shareholders – and without **any** consideration of the wider impact on communities and society as a whole. And this is where a re-evaluation of Keynesian policies, whereby society's needs are seen as an organic whole, began. Keynes went out of fashion, but now he's back and it will be interesting to see whether the financial community will re-embrace **some of** his ideas – and in **some** cases, I think they will.

P: Thank you, Professor Kotov. And I'd now like to bring in Dr Petrakis.

D: Well, Joanna, as I said last week, I think the greatest thinker of all time was either Aristotle or Karl Marx. And as last time I talked about Marx, today I'm going to talk about Aristotle. His works had largely been lost in the West and were rediscovered in Arabic translation in the twelfth century. Within a few years his ideas had spread across Europe, contributing to the intellectual renaissance. Aristotle spent his whole life trying to understand and explain the truth about the world around him. He was the student of Plato, and Plato was interested in what peoples' lives ought to be, but Aristotle thought more about what they were actually like and about how to solve **some of** the problems that people find in their lives. He looked at the facts of the real world that he could see and then tried to work out new ideas from those facts. You could say that logic began with Aristotle. What was really impressive about him was his vast intellectual range covering **almost every** science and **many of** the arts. He wrote on **many** subjects, including physics, poetry, theatre, philosophy, music, public speaking, politics, government, ethics, biology and zoology. I think it's true to say he is one of the most important founding figures in Western philosophy. It's fascinating as so much of Western civilisation was actually re-introduced to the West via Islamic cultural thinkers, philosophers and scientists. Fortunately, **some of** the knowledge of the Greeks was preserved by the Arabs in Alexandria and reintroduced to the West via Moorish Spain. Our modern concepts of maths, science and medicine were heavily influenced by Islamic thinkers and they contributed massively to the expansion of classical Greek thought.

P: Thank you, Dr Petrakis.

LESSON 7.4 RECORDING 7.6

D = Director, M = Mayor, C = Councillor

D: Well, we've done a thorough analysis of the city's problems, Mr Alves, and also conducted a survey to get the opinions of members of your community.

M: Thank you for your hard work. Please go ahead and let me know what you've found.

D: Uh, there are quite a few things that need changing, we think. Everyone seems to agree that there are not enough green spaces in the city, not enough trees, plants and vegetation, and that's one reason why there's a pollution problem here.

M: I see. Go on, please.

D: You've also got a problem with your downtown shopping district. There are too many cars there, constant traffic jams and a lot of accidents with pedestrians. The whole area's overcrowded – something needs to be done about it.

M: You're right, of course. It's a nightmare for many people when they do their shopping there. I know you're worried about this, Manuela.

C: I am. Very worried. The number of traffic jams per month has increased by almost twenty percent in the last three years.

D: There's another transport problem: your inter-city transport system. There are too many small buses and taxis and they simply can't cope with the number of people wanting to come into the city or cross it. The trains need modernising, they're often late and the stations are, well, let's say, not very well maintained. Also, people in the survey told us it's dangerous to walk in the streets later in the evening.

C: All that's true. Also, there is a lot of petty crime on the buses because of the overcrowding. We've got to find an answer to that.

M: Well, transport is one of our greatest problems. No doubt about it.

D: There are other things we could mention: the flooding after heavy rain, especially at the edge of the city, and the large number of children who live on the streets. They're certainly a social problem. We need to get them off the streets and into schools or jobs. And there are other problems mentioned in our report.

M: Well, thanks for highlighting some of the problems. Could we talk first about the lack of green space in our city?

LESSON 7.4 RECORDING 7.7

D = Director, M = Mayor, C = Christina, CA = Carl

M: We've talked in our council meetings about the need for green spaces and lack of trees and come up with an idea. I would like to know what you think of it.

D: OK, go ahead.

M: Well, we think the neighbourhoods in the city should be given trees to plant. There are areas for development where they could do this and it would be possible to plant trees at the side of the roads in many cases. We have estimated we'll need to distribute at least half a million trees, maybe even more. They would really improve the environment in so many ways. What do you think?

D: Sounds like a great idea. What do you think, Christina?

C: I like the idea a lot. It's a very creative solution to an environmental problem. I can't see why it wouldn't work. How

about you, Carl? Do you think it's a good idea?

CA: I don't know. I'm not too keen on this one. I think there'll be some real problems with the scheme.

C: Oh? In what way?

CA: Well, for a start, it would be a very expensive option – major investment. And I wonder who would look after the trees – it'd cost a lot of money to take care of them. Also, the city wouldn't see the benefit of the tree planting for quite a long time. I'm not sure it's a good option.

M: Mm, you've raised some important issues, Carl. But looking after the trees might not be such a big problem as you think. Our idea is that each neighbourhood in the city would be responsible for planting the trees and taking care of them. And the job could probably be done by unemployed youngsters, once they'd had a bit of training.

D: I must say, I think it's a really good suggestion, planting trees. It would involve the local communities – something you believe in – and it could have a big impact on the environment of the city in the long run. You can't change everything quickly – some of the projects must be for the long term. Carl, you're still shaking your head.

CA: I don't know. Will it really work? I just don't think it's feasible. I think it relies too much on cooperation from the local community. And you can't depend on that. You could spend a lot of money and not get much in return.

M: I can't agree. You know, you have to trust local people and give them responsibility. I'm certain it will work. People will participate because they know it'll make their area more beautiful. It'll create jobs and get some people off the streets, and it will have a good effect on pollution.

D: I like the idea, too. It's a good project, in my opinion. I support it. And it may not cost as much money as you think. You could probably get a grant from a United Nations environmental agency to help you finance it.

M: Mmm, that's an interesting thought. I will look into it.

LESSON 7.5 RECORDING 7.8

The first question I'm sure you'd like me to answer is: what is critical thinking? Well, when you read, critical thinking involves not just taking things at their face value. When you read critically, you should evaluate the writer's ideas and think about the implications and conclusions of what the writer is saying. When you read an academic text, you need to approach the text critically. First, you should try to identify the argument and work out the writer's main line of reasoning. Next, try to analyse and criticise the argument. Has the writer given reasons for his or her views? Are the reasons valid? Is the argument presented in a logical and coherent fashion? Is the writer being objective or trying to persuade you by using emotive language? Then look at the evidence the writer gives you. That may be in

the form of statistics, the results of a survey, erm, opinions of influential writers with, references you can check or the findings of reports or experiments. When you look at the evidence, it's essential to evaluate it and to decide whether it's weak or strong.

Now, after considering the evidence, study the writer's conclusions. Ask yourself if they're supported by the evidence. Has the writer given good reasons for the position he or she has taken? In some cases, you may feel there could be other explanations for the conclusions the writer has reached. For example, the writer may have been asked to present a particular point of view in return for a payment. Really, the key to critical thinking is to read actively and ask yourself questions all the time about what you're reading rather than just accepting, without questioning, the opinions or ideas of the writer.

Critical thinking is certainly a skill that is highly valued in business nowadays. A major study of business people in the USA has identified four skills that students need to learn if they want to succeed in today's world. The skills are called 'the four Cs': critical thinking, creativity, cooperation and collaboration. The development of these skills is generally a major objective of courses in business schools at tertiary level.

LESSON 8.1 RECORDING 8.1

1 Well, I have to make sure we hit the deadlines. There's a lot of emphasis on hits on the online version as well as circulation figures these days, what with all the competition. Although we do sometimes pay for feature stories from reliable sources, we have to be very careful because of the libel laws. It can cost a lot if someone decides to sue over something we've written. The other big difference these days is people's short attention span – they want less reading and more infographics. It's extremely gratifying when it all works and it's put to bed and we can start working on the next issue.

2 You really do have to be able to work under pressure, especially when you have some breaking news on the evening bulletin and someone is screaming in your earpiece from the gallery. Sometimes I have to interview politicians – they're so evasive, beating around the bush. It's all sound bites. They never give a straight answer to questions and are always trying to put a spin on things. It's very competitive. We're constantly involved in ratings wars and we're all expendable. It seems that more and more airtime is given over to celebrity stories to get the best viewing figures, which is a bit frustrating.

3 I started out on my own and then ended up doing it for a big media organisation. It's great! I write more or less what I want, although I have to do quite a lot of updates as things move fast these days. We do get some negative comments. There are a lot of internet trolls out there ready to attack you, and each other. Luckily, the moderators are usually good and take

upsetting or offensive stuff down pretty quickly. It's great when what you write starts trending on social media or you start something which then goes viral. I have a lot of Twitter followers, so it happens quite a lot. Or the other way round: I pick up on other stuff on social media, often through the hashtags people use. What's now called 'citizen journalism' is becoming more and more important to us. It really helps us get stories first, which is very satisfying. TV is much slower these days.

4 Everyone's looking for a scoop – you know, that one really big story or a real exclusive, but mostly it's quite mundane stuff. When something new comes up, it's good to be able to get a feature out of it. There's a lot more user-driven content around these days because of social media. You can get leads on stories from the blogosphere. There's also still a lot of chequebook journalism around though in the tabloids, and there are so many so-called press conferences which are anything but. It's just a prepared statement with no opportunities for questions. I don't know, maybe people want more infotainment rather than hard news. I think media bias is much worse in the broadcast media, though.

5 I've been posted all over the place. Last year I spent six weeks with the army. The conflict got a lot of media coverage. I was filing reports at all hours. There are tight deadlines and sometimes you have to file copy under some difficult conditions. I've also had to do some live broadcasts, which can be a bit tricky sometimes – you know, problems hooking up with the satellites. On the whole, though, it's a terrific way to make a living.

6 We get a bad press – if you'll excuse the pun. I usually sell my stuff to the popular press, the red tops, the glossies, and there's a lot of online stuff now. So, you know, even some of the broadsheets are now getting in on the act. Sometimes it's really easy just to doorstep someone, but other times I have to stake places out for days just to get one shot. The problem for us these days is everyone has a camera phone – they may get the best shots and we lose out. People will go mad for the right snap. People who go on and on about invasion of privacy make me sick. The celebs love the exposure. Any media coverage is good for them. I have a few good sources who let me know who's in town – and then off I go. It's easy money. They're all fair game, these people.

LESSON 8.2 RECORDING 8.2

I was delighted when you **invited me to talk** to you this afternoon about what I have learnt in thirty-five years as a journalist and I'd like to **congratulate you on receiving** the 'Best Student Newspaper' award.

First of all, I'm not going to **apologise for being** a journalist even though we're not flavour of the month. Journalists report what people want to read. It is the public who stop

to look at a traffic accident, not journalists. I can't stand listening to complaints about sensationalist reporting from people who buy sensationalist papers.

I think the advice I can give those of you who **want to go** into journalism is best summed up in the words of Joseph Pulitzer. He said, 'Put it before them briefly so they will read it, clearly so they will appreciate it, picturesquely so they will remember it and above all, accurately so they will be guided by its light'. Many of you here today started writing stories and poems when you were very young. The crucial thing about a story is that other people must want to read it – and you don't want them to **stop reading**. A well-written introduction will encourage the reader to stay with you. Always treat the reader with respect and don't **make them feel** inadequate. Try to imagine who the reader is and put yourself in their place.

After giving you a few hopefully interesting stories from my career as a journalist, including my first attempts on our student newspaper, I'll be happy to answer any questions. Finally, I'll look at a current issue in journalism, namely invasion of privacy.

LESSON 8.3 RECORDING 8.3

For this session, I'd like to focus on social media and why Chris Hadfield succeeded in connecting with people. I'll speak for ten minutes, to allow time for questions. But please feel free to interrupt if you want to make a comment … or even better send me a tweet from your tablets. There won't be any handouts going around as the transcript will be posted online after the talk. I'd like to begin by telling you why I'm focusing on Commander Hadfield, an astronaut, when you thought you were signing up for a conference on social media.

LESSON 8.3 RECORDING 8.4

1 To be honest, I just don't trust information in blogs and tweets as much as information in newspapers because the information isn't always backed up by sources and checked properly. Unfounded rumours such as the deaths of celebrities and political leaders can be spread in seconds all around the world and the information is simply unreliable.

2 I'm a newspaper journalist. For my newspaper columns I spend a lot of time rewriting them and getting them edited and checked. However, I enjoy writing my blogs the most. I suppose I like the more conversational style of writing blogs. It's almost like writing an email to a family member. I write them quickly and sometimes post them from stations or airports without getting them edited. In summary, I like the immediacy, the connection with audiences and the style of blogs.

3 Twitter is more fun and more flexible than blogging, which is too time-consuming. It's the fastest way you can interact with anybody. It's very mobile and gives me

something to do in the ten minutes between things. It's become a crucial tool for journalists and plays a central role in the way stories are sourced and distributed. Twitter's speed when it comes to breaking news is unrivalled. I think Twitter is the most positive thing to have come out of the internet.

4 I accept that social media such as Facebook, YouTube and Twitter have a big role to play, but I think that TV news and newspapers still drive the news agenda because it's only when they pick up on a Twitter story or a YouTube video that it reaches everyone. The news itself may emerge first with Twitter, but it's the mass media that picks it up and packages it for a mass audience. Mainstream media content is the lifeblood of topical social media conversation and still provides the vast majority of news links that are shared.

5 I think the internet is taking us back to the conversational culture of the coffee house in the seventeenth century, where news was exchanged and discussed in a lively atmosphere. For many people, Twitter and Facebook have become the meeting places of the twenty-first century, new hubs for the creation and spreading of news. These virtual coffee houses now have a global reach and individuals can create and move information with a power to bring down governments and shame big companies at a very high speed. Sometimes I prefer quality over quantity of information. Sometimes I prefer speed. But I cannot say whether I prefer social media to mainstream media. I don't think social media is replacing mainstream media. I think they live in a symbiotic or dependent relationship feeding off and amplifying each other.

LESSON 8.4 RECORDING 8.5

D = Dan, M = Margaret

D: We'd really like to run this story, Margaret. I don't think the asking price is high. What's two hundred thousand dollars when you think of the increased circulation we'll get if we publish the story? I mean, the coach is a household name and no one's aware that he's unhappy at his present club. It'll be a huge story when we tell the readers that he's planning to join another team. We've got to go for it.

M: We need to think this one through, Dan. You're right, it could be a great story, but we've got to be very careful. If you don't get your facts right, he could take us to court and get substantial damages. And I don't want another court case.

D: OK, but we have to take risks. That's how we've increased our circulation, you know that. I suppose the emails could be fake, but we could check them out. We can't miss this opportunity, Margaret – it'll make a terrific feature article. It's the kind of reporting our readers love.

M: Hold on, Dan. There's a problem with this material. We have no idea how our source got the information. Maybe he did something illegal and if that's the case, we could be in very hot water. I don't need to tell you, the coach is a popular guy; he's a legend in the sporting world. I don't think our readers will thank us for running the story. It's a very sensitive issue. If we get our facts wrong, it'll have a bad effect on our reputation. We wouldn't be able to say where we got our information from, so it'd look like pure speculation on our part.

D: OK, so you won't approve payment for the emails?

M: No … no, sorry, we need to hold fire on this one. I've got a bad feeling about it. It could land us in court if the emails are not genuine. I think you ought to try to interview the coach. He might let slip that he's not happy with the performance of his team. Then you could sound him out, maybe suggest he'll be looking for a new job if the team performance doesn't improve.

D: OK, I'll do that, but I'm really disappointed. I thought you'd support me.

M: Oh, sorry about that.

D: OK, I'll try to get an interview with the coach. It won't be easy, but I can probably persuade him to see me.

LESSON 8.5 RECORDING 8.6

Good morning, today I'll be talking about formal and informal writing. OK, there are indeed significant differences between formal and informal writing. I'll consider these first of all, then in the second part of my talk I'll say a few words about a neutral style of writing and also about the language of social networks.

Right, as you all know, I'm sure, there are different ways of using words in different situations. The way we write for academic and scientific purposes, for instance, is very different from how we write to a friend or close colleague. The tone, the vocabulary, the grammar, all change according to the situation, the purpose of the communication and who's receiving the message. Basically, we're talking about the difference between formality and informality, between formal writing and informal writing. OK, what are some of the differences?

Well, one obvious difference is our choice of vocabulary. In informal written English, we often use colloquial words such as *guy, kid, lots of, awesome, gonna* and so on. In formal English, instead of those words, we'd probably use terms like *man* or *woman, child, a large number of, remarkable, going to* and so on. We generally avoid colloquial language in a formal piece of writing.

We also avoid contractions if possible. For example, we say *cannot*, not *can't*, and we say *should* not instead of *shouldn't*. You get the point.

Another important difference between the two styles of language is that we prefer to use longer, more complex sentences – ones with subordinate clauses and linking words or phrases – in formal written English. In informal English sentences tend to be shorter and use simpler language.

It's an important point, the sophistication of the language. In written English the vocabulary tends to be more sophisticated and wider in range. For example, in an academic essay in this college, one of you might write *The arguments support the view that phone hacking is a serious problem*. The verb *support* is probably a more suitable verb to use than the phrasal verb *back up*. Another example: a sentence such as *A considerable amount of research has been conducted into attitudes to privacy* is an example of using vocabulary well. The student could have written *They've done a lot of research into attitudes to privacy*. But the verb *done* is not as suitable as the word *conducted*. This verb is more formal and you should note that the student used a passive form. Passive forms rather than active forms are a feature of formal academic writing.

So, there are many language features that differentiate formal writing from informal writing. However, I'd like to make the point that there are some informal language items that can be found sometimes in formal writing, depending on the context. For example, phrasal verbs like *come up with* and *bring about* do appear in formal writing, but they are less common than single verbs. So, for *come up with*, which sometimes appears in formal writing, you will more often find verbs like *create, produce, develop, discover* and so on.

Similarly, if you're writing an opinion-led essay for an academic tutor, you might use the personal pronoun *I* to express your opinion in the first and last paragraphs of that essay. In that context, it's perfectly acceptable to use the personal pronoun. Passive forms can be found in both styles of writing, but they're particularly common in formal writing, perhaps because formal texts, on the whole, need to be more objective and to avoid an overly emotional tone.

Right, so there are many differences between the two styles, though some features appear in both.

I'll move on now to the second part of my talk: neutral English and the language of social websites.

LESSON 8.5 RECORDING 8.7

I'd like to say a few words now about a third style of writing. In the first part of my talk, I discussed the differences between informal and formal English. There's also a third style, which is called a neutral style of writing. This style is not specifically formal or informal. It's often used when a writer wants to present the facts of a topic in a non-emotional way. It's also a common style of communication when people do not know each other very well. It might be used, for example, when someone is communicating with a colleague on the same level in a company by email. Writing in a neutral style will often involve deciding which is the appropriate word or phrase to use in order to express your idea simply and clearly. For example, here are three sentences. Which sentence do you think is written in a neutral style? OK?

The economic situation has got worse.
The economic situation has become worse.
The economic situation has deteriorated.

Yes, the style of the first sentence is informal, the last formal and the second sentence is written in a neutral style.

Are there any questions you'd like to ask? Yes?

LESSON 9.1 RECORDING 9.1

1   It's impossible to overstate the importance of privacy in English culture. Jeremy Paxman points out that 'the importance of privacy informs the entire organisation of the country, from the assumptions on which laws are based, to the buildings in which the English live.'
    Hover above any English town and you will see that the residential areas consist almost entirely of rows and rows of small boxes, each with its tiny patch of green. The English all want to live in their own private box with their own private little green bit.
    I would add that a disproportionate number of our most influential social rules and maxims are concerned with the maintenance of privacy: we are taught to mind our own business, not to pry, to keep ourselves to ourselves, not to make a scene or a fuss or draw attention to ourselves and never to wash our dirty linen in public.

2   English drivers are quite rightly renowned for their orderly, sensible, courteous conduct. My foreign informants noticed well-mannered customs and practices that most of us take for granted: that you never have to wait too long before someone lets you out of a side road or driveway and that you are always thanked when you let someone else out; that all drivers stop for pedestrians at zebra crossings, even when the pedestrians are still standing waiting on the pavement and have not set foot on the crossing. I met one tourist who found this so astonishing that he kept repeating the experiment, marvelling at the fact that he could single-handedly bring streams of traffic to a deferential halt without the aid of red lights or stop signs.

3   In restaurants, as elsewhere, the English may moan and grumble to each other about poor service or bad food, but our inhibitions make it difficult for us to complain directly to the staff.
    Most English people, faced with unappetising or even inedible food, are too embarrassed to complain at all. Complaining would be 'making a fuss' or 'drawing attention to oneself' in public – all forbidden by unwritten rules. They will not go back to that establishment and will tell all their friends how awful it is, but the poor publican or restaurateur will never even know that there was anything amiss. Some slightly braver souls will use method number two: the apologetic complaint, an English speciality. 'Excuse me, I'm terribly sorry, erm but, er, this soup seems to be rather, well, not very hot – a bit cold.' 'They look at the floor and mumble, as

though they have done something wrong!' an experienced waiter told me.

4 The most noticeable and important 'rule' about humour in English conversation is its dominance and pervasiveness.

In other cultures, there is a 'time and a place' for humour; it is a special, separate kind of talk. In English conversation, there is always an undercurrent of humour.

It must be said that many of my foreign informants found this aspect of Englishness frustrating rather than amusing: 'the problem with the English,' complained one American visitor, 'is that you never know when they are joking – you never know whether they are being serious or not'. This was a businessman, travelling with a female colleague from Holland. She considered the issue frowningly for a moment and then concluded, somewhat tentatively, 'I think they are mostly joking, yes?'

The English may not always be joking, but they are always in a state of readiness for humour. We do not always say the opposite of what we mean, but we are always alert to the possibility of irony.

5 When asked to compare English working and business practices with those of other cultures, all my foreign and immigrant informants commented on the English sense of fair play and specifically on our respect for the law and our relative freedom from the corruption they felt was endemic and tacitly accepted – albeit in varying degrees – in other parts of the world. Many felt that we were not sufficiently aware or appreciative of this fact. 'You just take it for granted,' a Polish immigrant complained. 'You assume that people will play fair and you are shocked and upset when they do not. In other countries there is not that assumption.'

Fair play, with its sporting overtones, suggests that everyone should be given an equal chance and that people should conduct themselves honourably, observe the rules and not cheat or shirk their responsibilities. At the same time, 'fair play' allows for differences in ability and accepts that there will be winners and losers – while maintaining that playing well and fairly is more important than winning.

LESSON 9.2 RECORDING 9.2

If we are to assess programmes aimed at the punishment and, more positively, the rehabilitation of juveniles involved in antisocial behaviour, drug addiction and crime, we must first accept that teenagers are psychologically different to adults. Teenagers are not yet fully developed and, even when they have committed very serious crimes, adolescents have different needs to adult criminals. From this we can conclude that the juvenile justice system needs to take these differences into account if we are to provide effective punishment and rehabilitation. The programmes that are most effective will surely be those which do not violate the basic

principles of adolescent development. If they do violate these principles, it can only lead to an ever-deepening rejection of society and its laws by the teenagers in question.

LESSON 9.2 RECORDING 9.3

So, what are these particular psychological traits of the teenager?

Firstly, all teenagers, even lawbreakers, have a strong sense of fairness. They will be moralistic and intolerant of unfairness.

Secondly, they are looking for respect from the world and their peers.

Thirdly, they respond best to encouragement rather than punishment. Harsh punishment may temporarily alter behaviour, but their attitudes and deeper behaviour seldom change.

Fourthly, they reject imposed structure and outside control. Teenagers do benefit from limits, like children, but, unlike children, they do need to have some kind of voice within that structure, or in the determination of that structure.

Also, whilst young people need help, advice and guidance, they will reject it when it comes from people or institutions that are felt to be unfair, disrespectful, punishing or, or that impose limits and structure.

Youths also have a need to feel competent at something and to achieve success, and, alongside this, they need, at times, to be in charge and to make their own choices.

In addition, there is also a need to belong, on equal terms, to groups and communities.

And finally, settled youths appreciate and value the strengths of their families.

LESSON 9.2 RECORDING 9.4

While the wilderness camps are particularly strong with regard to counselling and therapy, the boot camps hardly address juveniles' psychological problems.

Because the boot camps principally operate on a punishment basis, the teenagers are quite likely to reject any advice or guidance that is offered by the adults there.

In a sense, boot camps partly meet teenagers' expectations of fairness, in that good behaviour is rewarded and bad behaviour is punished. However, as the teenagers utterly lack the chance to determine the structure and limits, they are fairly certain to see things as unfair.

It is extremely important that families are involved in the process, and this certainly occurs at wilderness camps, while it seems to be entirely absent at boot camps.

The suggestion that boot camps don't respond to the teenage desire for success is slightly unfair, as the physical military training offers plenty of challenges. However, wilderness camps are extremely focused on success, from the building of a campfire to the taking on of a leadership role.

The highly complex range of tasks and skills required at wilderness camps means teenagers are almost certain to feel that they belong to a group, get respect and to make their own choices. In contrast, the range of tasks at boot camps is rather limited and they completely

lack chances for people to make their own choices.

LESSON 9.3 RECORDING 9.6

P = Presenter, C = Carlos Jimenez

P: Our next speaker in tonight's debate on global migration is Carlos Jimenez. Carlos is Director of the International Migration Trust and he's going to be looking at migration myths. Carlos.

C: Thank you very much. International migrants are very much in the news these days and often generate quite a lot of negative press. Claims that migrants are taking our jobs, pushing up the crime rate and taking advantage of our public services are easy to find in the media. Some political parties are using this for their own ends. So, is any of this really true? Or are we just looking at a set of migration myths? Tonight I'm going to attempt to debunk some myths about international migration. As we'll see, they just don't stand up to the evidence. So here we go.

Myth number one: a very frequent comment people make is that international migration is on the increase. Well, actually, the number of international migrants has grown, but only relatively slowly, from 154 million in 1990, to 175 million in 2000, and about 232 million today. However, the reason for this is principally down to population growth, so the number of migrants as a percentage of the world's population has remained pretty stable at around three percent.

Myth number two: another common complaint is that the majority of migrants are illegal. Of course, it's difficult to get reliable data on this, but it appears that in the United States, for example, about twenty-five percent of migrants are undocumented. The figure in Europe is lower – perhaps around ten percent. Let's not forget, though, that some of these migrants will be fleeing persecution and so they'll often be crossing borders without any documentation. Actually, even if you're not a refugee or asylum seeker, entering another country without the necessary documents is usually considered a civil rather than a criminal offence, so the frequently used term 'illegal immigrant' is something of a misnomer, and some media organisations – that were previously very fond of this term – have now stopped using it.

Myth number three: a further argument that has gained some currency is that migrants take our jobs, jobs that otherwise would go to local people. The experts' response to this is that the relationship between migration and labour markets is complex, but in developed countries, especially in times of economic growth, the kinds of jobs migrants do tend to be low-skilled and low-paid, jobs that the local populace don't actually want to do. Also, immigration can help create economic growth. For example, a business run by a migrant may employ local people. Furthermore, these developed countries have ageing populations which will create increasing demand for long-term care services – a gap migrants can fill.

Myth number four: the accusation that migrants are a drain on public services is one of the most forcefully argued points by those who are against immigration. In fact, in a lot of countries, migrants can't access services like healthcare, housing and education. And where they can, they're less likely to use these services than local people because many of them are young adults without significant health problems or educational needs. A recent study in the UK found that migrants were, and I quote, 'forty-five percent less likely to receive state benefits or tax credits than natives.' The observation that migrants pay a great deal more in taxes than they receive in social benefits was also made.

Myth number five: the suggestion that migrants are in some way responsible for an increase in antisocial or otherwise …

LESSON 9.4 RECORDING 9.7

O1 = Official 1, O2 = Official 2, O3 = Official 3

O1: So, let's look at the law concerning truancy. Obviously, we want to cut the levels of truancy, partly to reduce juvenile crime and also to improve the education of our country's lowest achievers. Having said that, this law is not solely about children. In a sense, it's more about making parents take responsibility for their children's education. Too many parents ignore their role in education, and particularly their role in discipline. Now, although we're here to amend this law, I think that one of its current strengths is its clarity; there's no room for doubt and confusion. Basically, if your child doesn't go to school, and they don't have permission to be absent, then you will be punished. Also, the law applies to everyone, without exception.

O2: That's all fair enough, but it's simply too inflexible as it stands. If a child's absent for only one day, then the parents will be punished. Surely, this kind of punishment should be used only for serious repeat offenders?

O1: Perhaps, but wouldn't it then be unwieldy and cumbersome as a law? As I said, its current strength is its clarity and the strong message that it sends out.

O2: Well, certainly it's important that the law sends out a strong message, but I still think there must be some built-in flexibility. People's lives are not straightforward. I mean, what if a child's being bullied at school, but can't tell anyone about it? In that case, missing a day in order to escape the bullying would then result in their parents being punished, which would only increase the child's sense of shame.

O3: Well, obviously, in that case the punishment wouldn't apply.

O2: You say that, but as it stands the law's very clear that the punishment's immediate and direct. I think we need to show that there's built-in flexibility and room for manoeuvre.

O1: Well, whilst accepting that as a fair principle, we mustn't make it too complicated.

O3: Er, Can I just point out that there's another aspect we need to consider.

O1: Oh yes? What's that?

O3: Well, the punishment, particularly the fines, may not be the best thing. I mean, I think that many truants come from poorer families and many of these behavioural problems stem from this poverty. Surely, fines will only increase the level of poverty. And then, will wealthier families be concerned about fines? Admittedly, imprisonment would be a deterrent, but, overall, I'm not sure that this particular punitive response is best. Perhaps parents and children should do some kind of community service, in the field of education – they could help out at schools for children with special needs, for example.

O1: I see what you're saying, but one thing I like about the current proposal is that it's easy to enforce. Community service would require special organisation and management. A fine's much more straightforward.

O3: Well, I think there's more to say on that, but I think we should get some amendments agreed now; we know we've got to change this law in some ways. First of all, how can we address …

LESSON 9.4 RECORDING 9.8

O1 = Official 1, O2 = Official 2, O3 = Official 3

O3: First of all, how can we build some flexibility into this law?

O2: How about a three strikes and you're out kind of rule? You know, the first two times there's a warning, and the third time leads to punishment of the parents.

O3: And what about replacing imprisonment with community service – I think that'd be much more appropriate and would still act as a deterrent.

O1: I think I can agree to those suggestions. I think the law will still serve its original purpose. So, how shall we phrase it for the minister to look at? Let's see … What about 'Parents are responsible for ensuring their children's attendance at school. When a child has been absent three times without permission, the parents are liable to a fine or a community service sentence.'

O2: That's great.

O3: Erm, hold on a minute.

O1/2: What?/Hmm?

O3: Well, when we say 'three times', do we mean in their whole school career? In a year? In a term?

O1: Oh, good point. We'd better clarify that. Any thoughts?

LESSON 9.5 RECORDING 9.10

Thanks for downloading this podcast. I'm going to be talking to you about literature reviews, what they are and how you should go about doing them. University students, especially at the higher levels, are often required to write a literature review. The term is potentially confusing, as it suggests reading Shakespeare or Tolstoy. In fact, a literature review is a survey of what has been published in a particular field – your field – be it Astrophysics or Business Studies. It's a synthesis of what's known about a subject. To carry out such a review obviously involves extensive reading, and by doing this you'll learn a great deal about the subject, and become – to some extent – an expert on that subject. As you prepare the literature review, you'll clarify your own ideas on the topics you read about, and form your own opinions about what specialists in the field have written. You'll be able to see how the subject – and the research on that subject – has developed over time. When you finish your reading, you'll be in a position to identify half a dozen key pieces of research on the subject and see how each piece has influenced the others.

Doing a literature review also helps to identify existing gaps in the knowledge about the subject, gaps that your research can fill. You can see how your work will follow on from the work of others, and how it might answer some unanswered questions. It's a bit like a jigsaw puzzle with one or two missing pieces. When you've assembled it all, you can see where there's a gap to be filled.

As with any kind of synthesis, organisation is the key. Some students find it helpful to …

LESSON 10.1 RECORDING 10.1

1 It was OK, but, well, the music is rather dated. I mean, the musical's over twenty years old now and it was always very much of its time, wasn't it? But er, still, I was pretty impressed by the sets and it's such a lovely romantic story.

2 Astounding! What more can I say? I completely forgot that the characters weren't real animals and the tale was quite magical. Great stuff. Well worth the cost of the ticket.

3 Experimental music isn't really my kind of thing, but I guess these guys created a good atmosphere with their music. I liked the clips from the old movies, but, well, it probably went on a bit long for me, to be honest. Not quite my thing.

4 Well, it lived up to the hype, mainly because those guys are so talented. You really can't go wrong when you're seeing people like that – I mean, they're legends, really. The venue's good as well – not too big and a great atmosphere, although it took ages to get there. Top marks all round, I'd say.

5 Well, it could've been better. Mind you, his performance is certainly up there with the best, but, I don't know, in the end the

production doesn't really hold up. Perhaps I'm too much of a fan of the original movie. They just didn't get the atmosphere of the New York docks over very well. But, that's not to say it's not worth seeing, just that it's not the best. And you can't always have that, can you?

LESSON 10.3 RECORDING 10.3

S1 = Student 1, S2 = Student 2, S3 = Student 3

S1: I think a lot of people do seem to be addicted to, to surfing the internet, and I think, erm, er, I think in some ways it can be really good 'cause you can, you can, er, I don't know, you can find out loads of stuff that you weren't – you know, initially planning on finding out. You might have gone on to look for information about one thing and then you're like, oh, followed the link to, to this next thing, and, and on like that.
But then the bad side of it is people who look up illnesses and symptoms and things like that …

S2: Yeah, Doctor Google.

S1: Yeah, exactly.

S3: I do that.

S1: Do you?

S3: Yes. I buy all my medicine off the internet as well.

S2: Do you?

S3: Yeah.

S1: Do you?

S3: Yes. It's much cheaper.

S1: But I mean 'cause the thing is, symptoms are so, you know, symptoms could relate to anything, and the symptoms for you know, like a brain tumour could be very similar to symptoms for just headache or something like that, so it can really sort of cause a lot of panic, I think.

S2: Well I think I am one of those people who is actually addicted to the internet. Erm, and I …

S3: I've seen you at work, yes.

S2: Yeah, you can see my screen, erm. 'Cause, erm, I'm one of those people who I get home from work, I put the TV on and I get my laptop out, so I sit watching a film or TV and I'm constantly surfing the internet at the same time. So if there's an actor or someone that turns up on screen – ooh, I wonder what else he was in, so …

S1: Yeah, yeah, yeah.

S2: Erm, yeah and it just means that you never, you never really fully concentrate on any one thing because I'm constantly doing several things at the same time, and I'm sure the internet is to blame for that. But I wouldn't be without it, that's for sure.

S1: Oh no, erm …

S2: It's enriched our lives, surely. I mean it's not without its problems, but I certainly – I mean, everything depends on it now, so at work we couldn't do a lot of our work without the internet now, because we use email. So …

S3: Yes, if the internet goes down we, we'd stop working.

S2: You'd have to actually talk to people!

S3: Yeah, have to play solitaire with actual cards.

S2: Well I actually, I actually left, I left Facebook for about three years because I got so irritated with people putting what they had for dinner, or …

S3: Food pictures are the worst, yes.

S2: Oh, what is the point? Erm, and just moaning about their lives when it was something really minor, and they just put 'Oh, I feel really sad today.' And then all their friends go and comment 'Oh, what's wrong, what's wrong?' 'Oh, I can't say on here.' And you just think what on earth was the point in you saying, and it was all about getting attention from people.

S1: Erm, I think it's quite scary how, how companies sort of get hold of your data on just through monitoring your sort of, your internet usage. So you could be looking on, on a department store's website for, you know, you could be looking at sofas and you log into Facebook and then er, on the ad bar down the side it's like oh, looking for a sofa? Well try this at – you know, try this shop or whatever, I think that's quite scary.

S3: It is scary but then I also think I would rather have something that's relevant to me than something that's completely irrelevant.

S2: That, that sort of thing doesn't bother me too much. Erm, I'd be, I try to be quite careful about not having my full name with my date of birth together in the same place, and that sort of thing. But it doesn't bother me if I get sent adverts for something, because like you say I'd rather have an advert that I'm actually, I might be interested in rather than something completely random, so …

S3: And as long as it, it's automated and it's not, say … the way they read it, it's … not really a person looking into your browsing history, it, it's just automated. But I, I guess it is a fine line because you don't always know how much of your personal data they have. But then I don't have anything that's worth money so what are they going to steal?
Think, you know, there's a healthy level of paranoia but also shouldn't be too paranoid about it.

LESSON 10.4 RECORDING 10.6

1 Hi! I'm Tony and I'm from Scotland. I guess there's only one way to describe what I am and that's a natural-born winner. That is, all my life I've come top in everything – you know, sports at school, my studies at uni, in my banking career. I work with people from all over the world, clients and colleagues, and I'm good at languages, so I'd probably be a bit of a leader on the island. And as for surviving on the island, well, I reckon that won't be an issue, as I'm fit, strong and healthy – I play squash three times a week and I never take days off sick. But then again, that doesn't mean that I'm perfect. Just almost perfect! What I mean is, I don't suffer fools

gladly, so I guess I can seem rude or impatient – perhaps arrogant. But then again, is that really so bad? Well, anyway, trying to win *The Global Village* will be a challenge that'll fire me up to even greater efforts and it's a challenge I want to take on. And when I take something on, I come out on top. Always.

2 Hi. I'm Roberta. I'm from Australia and I'm a builder, which is why I reckon I'd be good to have on the island. Need a rain shelter? No problem – I'll knock one up in under an hour. Awesome. Seriously, a builder is a must-have on the island, surely? One thing though, I'm totally terrified of spiders. Euurgh, sends shivers down my spine! Apart from that, I guess you could say that, by and large, I'm pretty laid back – you know, I'm a tolerant kind of a girl, I've got mates from all over the world and I don't get wound up much by people. Mind you, I've got no time for laziness, especially when everyone needs to pull together to get things going. Oh yeah, and another thing is, I reckon my hobby'll come in pretty useful: I love fishing. I've done it from boats and everything. So, all in all, I reckon I'd be a great choice for *The Global Village* and it'd be a great chance for me, to be part of an awesome global community like this. Like I said, the island needs a builder.

LESSON 10.4 RECORDING 10.7

M = Mel, D = Danny, L = Lucy

M: Right then, what do you think?

D: Well, I reckon they're both pretty good, but with weak points. Overall, I'd go for Tony.

L: Really? I'm not so sure. Tony seems rather too full of himself. I really don't know that he'd be a good team player.

D: Ah, but Lucy, that's why I think he'd be good. It could be good to have someone who might challenge the group. And, you know, perhaps the group will have an effect on him. We might see him become more collaborative – you know, less competitive.

M: OK. Well, anyway, let's look back at the criteria before we go off track. All in all, I don't reckon Tony meets that many of the criteria points. He hasn't particularly shown collaboration skills, but then again, his job will involve some for sure. As for practical skills, I'm not sure what he offers.

L: Exactly. And he seems too focused on the show as a competition. That is, he doesn't show much interest in the cultural experience – about learning about other people and so on.

D: Fair enough. Like I said, I did think they both had some weak points. What about Roberta? She's obviously got great practical skills, what with the fishing as well as the building.

M: For sure. And she comes across as quite smart.

L: Sure, although not sure how smart it is to go to a deserted island when you're scared of spiders!

D: Indeed! Although I guess that means she's someone who's up for fun and stuff.

L: Yes, and all in all, she has a positive attitude towards the concept of the show, doesn't she?

M: Yeah, she does. And Danny, you talked about how Tony might challenge the group, but, you know, so would Roberta if others are a bit lazy. That could be interesting to see – you know, how people from different cultures regard what is and what isn't laziness.

D: That's a good point. You're right, cultural difference should come into play there. That'll be interesting to watch.

M: OK then, so let's decide. I reckon Roberta would be a good choice and Tony wouldn't be right for this show. Maybe he'd be better on that business show – you know, the one which is more about conflict and competition. Lucy, I think you agree with me. Is that right?

L: Yeah, it is. I think it's a straightforward decision.

D: Yes, well, it seems Tony doesn't meet enough criteria, really, so let's go for Roberta. Right, who's next?

M: We've got someone from Iceland and someone from Mali. First up is this one, who I think is quite interesting because …

LESSON 10.5 VIDEO RECORDING 10.1

S = Shanice, J = Jane, F = Felipe, N = Natasha, B = Ben

S: Hi, everyone, so **I'm leading the seminar today.** Er … **we're going to be looking at the language of drama** and trying to answer the question 'How real is it?' To start with, **I thought we should confirm what we mean by** *drama*, **so that we're all clear about that. We're thinking about drama in quite a broad sense.** Obviously, we're including plays in the theatre, Pinter or Mamet or whatever. But we're also thinking about TV drama, stuff like *CSI*. Soap operas like *EastEnders*, *Coronation Street*. And, of course, screenplays of films – *Pulp Fiction*, and so on. So those are the parameters of the discussion. **Is that alright?**

J: **What about radio drama?**

S: Yeah, obviously, that's part of it, too. OK? Hopefully, everyone's done the reading. And the conversation analysis task. Yeah? **Did everyone record a minute or two of conversation and try to transcribe it?**

ALL: Yes/Yeah.

S: OK, so, **first**, we're going to look at the features of real conversation and then we can compare real conversation with the language of drama and see how similar or different they are. So, what are the features of real conversation? What did you find from your research? **Would anyone like to start?** Silence. No one wants to be first! Felipe, I know you spent some time on the task. **Do you want to kick off?**

F: Yeah, I'm happy to do that. Well, in real conversation you get a lot of repetition.

People say the same stuff again and again. But as well as the topic, they also repeat the language, too. So you hear the same words, the same phrases over and over. Also, in real conversation, the sentences are usually very short. Much shorter than when we write …

J: **Sorry, but can we really call them sentences, though?** I mean, aren't sentences something we only use in writing – you know, capital letters at the beginning, full stops at the end? Isn't speech more of a continuum?

F: OK. Maybe *sentences* is the wrong word. Perhaps I should've said *utterances*. But it's true they tend to be relatively short.

S: **Right. What else?**

B: The language is pretty informal. In the one I analysed, I noticed a lot of idioms, expressions, phrasal verbs, quite a bit of swearing, too. There's also the speaker's accent or dialect. I recorded a conversation with my Scottish flatmate. He's got a really strong accent. And he uses words like *lass* and *fitba*.

N: Fitba? What's that?

B: Football.

N: Oh.

J: Well, everyone's got an accent of some sort, haven't they? I mean, some people have got regional accents, some people have got class accents.

F: True. Something else we get in real conversation is a lot of, um, hesitations, false starts, fillers, overlaps, pauses …

N: **Can you repeat that, please?** I'm taking a few notes.

F: Yeah. Hesitations, overlaps, pauses, fillers, false starts, I mean these are really common.

S: Alright, **is everyone happy with these terms? Do we need to clarify anything?**

N: **What do we mean by fillers exactly?**

F: Well words like *er*, *well*, *you see* – you know, those kinds of words and phrases. Things we use when we don't know what to say and we're thinking – playing for time.

N: OK. Thanks.

J: Um, I don't think it matters if conversation is like this, anyway.

S: **Sorry, what do you mean by that?**

J: Well, conversation is only really for those people who are involved in it.

S: **Yes, go on.**

J: That's why we often can't understand other people's conversations. If we listen to them on the bus, for example. The participants can often understand one another because of shared background information or from non-verbal behaviour. I think this has implications for dramatic language. You see, when we look closely at dramatic language, what we find is that…

S: **OK, that's interesting. Let's come back to that later** when we look at the language of drama.

N: **Sorry, can I cut in here?**

S: **Go ahead, please.**

N: Well, we're all talking about conversation as if it's all the same – you know, there's only one type – but it's well known that

men and women talk in different ways.

B: But how do you mean?

N: A lot of research has been done by people like Deborah Tannen. Men are always trying to compete with each other, even in conversation; you know, one guy tells a story, then another guy tries to tell a more interesting story, then the third bloke tries to beat them all by telling the best story of all.

S: **Does Tannen actually say that?**

N: I don't know, but women don't talk like that. The way they talk is much more collaborative; they support each other.

B: What? I don't think that's true at all!

N: It is though!

S: **Alright. Wait a moment … hang on. I think Natasha has a point, but maybe we can generalise, too.**

J: Yeah. You're right. A lot of conversation *is* cooperative. Doesn't matter if you're a man or a woman. If we didn't cooperate, conversation couldn't happen. The way we take turns, for example.

B: **Sorry, does anyone know why they're called soap operas?**

S: **Sorry, what?**

B: Yeah, soap operas. Does anyone know why they're called that?

S: Right, OK … **We don't want to get off track here,** but does anyone know the answer?

J: I heard it was because when they first started in America, they were sponsored by soap manufacturers.

S: Right. Thanks. OK, **let's try to stay focused. We were talking about** how real conversation is cooperative. Er, had you finished what you were going to say?

J: Ah, er, well, almost. Except maybe to mention Grice's maxims.

N: Sorry, whose maxims?

J: Grice. Paul Grice, a linguist. Grice called it the cooperative principle.

S: **How many of us are familiar with this?**

F: I am.

S: OK. So not all of us. Jane, could you explain?

J: Well, Grice claimed that there are four maxims or rules of conversation. Basically, and I'm paraphrasing, we should be true, be brief, be relevant and be clear.

S: Alright. **I'm going to try to summarise what we've said so far.** We said that real conversation is repetitive, full of short utterances, false starts, pauses, hesitations. The speakers may have a particular accent or dialect. But perhaps this isn't important if … if the speakers can understand each other. We recognised that there may be some differences between the way men and women speak, but that conversation is basically a cooperative activity.

LESSON 11.2 RECORDING 11.1

R = Rachel, S = Susan

R: Welcome to tonight's programme. This week we'll be looking at the pros and cons of microfinance. My guests tonight are Dr Susan Filer, who works for an MFI, or Microfinance Institution, and Professor Ali

Hadad, Professor of Economics at Stanford Business School. Dr Filer, could we begin with you, please? Could you tell us what microfinance is?

S: Thank you, Rachel. And please call me Susan, OK? Well, according to Kiva, the world's first lending platform, *microfinance* is a general term to describe financial services to low-income individuals or to those who do not have access to typical banking services. I think the principle behind it is that it is a sustainable means of alleviating poverty leading to lasting development and changing lives. And I think there are a number of other terms, such as *creditor* and *debtor*, that we need to be clear about from the start. A lender or creditor provides credit to a borrower or debtor. The creditor provides the loan and the debtor receives the loan. Right, back to looking at the pros and cons of microfinance.

I think there are five main reasons why microfinance is successful and, and has had a huge impact on helping those in poverty. Firstly, access. Banks simply won't lend money unless it is profitable for them to do so and they won't extend lending to those with little or no assets.

Microfinancing works on the idea that even small amounts of credit can help get people out of poverty. There are a number of success stories like the Grameen Bank in Bangladesh, started by the Nobel Prize winner Professor Yunus, where incomes of Grameen members were forty-three percent higher than the incomes of non-programme villages. Or in El Salvador, where the weekly income of FINCA clients increased by 145 percent, FINCA being a charitable microfinance institution. Or in India, where half of SHARE clients, SHARE being another microfinance institution, graduated out of poverty.

Secondly, microfinance often targets female borrowers as they are statistically less likely to default on their loans than men. So, microfinance is a good tool for empowering women.

Thirdly, with regard to education, it seems that families receiving microfinance are less likely to remove their children from school for economic reasons.

Fourthly, microfinance often leads to improved health and welfare, for example, access to clean water and better sanitation. And also better access to health care.

And finally, job creation. Microfinance can often help create new employment opportunities, which has a beneficial impact on the local economy.

Overall, I think there is enough evidence to show that microfinance works. It helps very poor households meet basic needs and protects against risks such as serious illness.

And I'll finish with something the founder of Kiva said. Suppose you see somebody on the street who is begging as you approach them. Imagine how that affects you. And what if you see somebody with a story of entrepreneurship and hard work who wants to tell you about their business? Imagine how you feel then.

LESSON 11.2 RECORDING 11.2

R = Rachel, A = Professor Ali Hadad

R: Thank you, Susan. Can I turn to Professor Hadad: do you agree with Susan?

A: Well, Rachel – and you can call me Ali – yes, microfinance can play a role in the battle against poverty and I accept some of the points that Susan has made. But, Susan, I think the picture you have painted is too rosy. As long as repayment rates are not unreasonable, then microfinance can work in the short term. However, sometimes interest rates are a lot higher than many people think and I think there should be more regulation of the industry as not all the microfinance institutions are as reputable as Kiva or Belgium's Alterfin. Moving on to repayments, unless the client is meeting scheduled repayments, they risk being pushed into debt problems. And I really don't think there's a lot of solid evidence that microfinance makes a significant impact on poverty levels. Susan mentioned earlier the Grameen bank which pioneered the microfinance model. But the bank relied heavily on subsidies from the Bangladeshi government to keep its interest rates low.

I think we have to accept that microfinance is not always the most appropriate method. It might not be suitable for populations that are geographically dispersed. Or where there is a high incidence of disease. Or a reliance on only one agricultural crop, or if there is hyperinflation. In these cases sometimes small grants, infrastructure improvements or education and training programmes can have more of an effect. Another problem may be that some microfinance institutions might focus excessively on profit and move away from poorer clients to serve better-off clients who want larger loans.

I'll finish by saying that even if there are a number of success stories, microfinance should never be seen as the only tool for ending poverty.

LESSON 11.4 RECORDING 11.3

W = Woman
M = Man
K = Kenneth Carter, I = Ingrid Carter

W: Thanks for your interesting presentation. We'd like to ask you some questions now.

K: Go ahead.

W: There are quite a few marine life-saving devices on the market. What's so special about your product?

K: Erm, we think it's got a lot of advantages compared with competitors' products. It emits a very loud alarm signal, erm, it has a very wide coverage, a wide range, up to, er, four kilometres, and it constantly monitors the position of the person who's fallen overboard. The battery's rechargeable – that's a big advantage over our competitors – and the device is ultra-light and easy to attach. Oh yes, er, one other very important point: the product will be sold at a very competitive price. The whole package will cost approximately $1,800 – that's less than most other devices on the market.

W: Mmm, interesting. What about patents? Is the technology fully protected?

K: Yes, it is. We've taken out worldwide patents on the technology, the device and the receiver.

W: Good, that's very reassuring. How many of the devices have you actually produced?

K: We've made four working prototypes. They've been tested here and in international waters. We've got written confirmation from several international marine associations that the device works and can do what we claim it does.

W: Right, just four prototypes. So you're not really set up as a business yet.

K: No, that's why we've come to you. We need finance. The cost of bringing the product to the market and marketing it will be considerable. We have a couple of personal loans, but they're not nearly enough. Also, we need advice and support.

W: OK. Let's see if my colleague has any questions. John, over to you.

M: Thanks. Er, I've got two questions at this stage. Er, firstly, who would you say is your target consumer? Who do you think will buy your product?

K: I'll let Ingrid answer that. She's got some good ideas about how we should market our device. Go ahead, Ingrid.

I: OK, well, erm, we'll aim at several segments in the market. Owners of seagoing private boats and yachts is one segment, sea rescue crews is another one, and, erm of course, there are the river boats. There could be plenty of demand from commercial companies hiring boats to inexperienced customers. Naval training boats – that's another segment that could be very profitable. Er, so our target consumer is really anyone who owns a boat and is concerned about their own security or that of their crew.

M: Mmm, plenty of scope then for selling the product. A final question: where do you think you'll be in five years' time with this device?

I: Erm, it's early days now, of course, but we're both very ambitious and committed to the product. We think we'll have a multi-million dollar business in the future, selling and licensing our products all over the world. Our greatest asset is our ability to invent new products. We have other projects in the pipeline; we could talk about them later.

LESSON 11.4 RECORDING 11.4

W = Woman
M = Man
K = Kenneth Carter, I = Ingrid Carter

W: Let's talk about the agenda for this afternoon. I propose we discuss three specific areas: the amount of our investment in your business, the stake you can offer us and other projects you're working on. How about that?

K: Sounds OK to me.

I: Yeah, that's fine.

W: OK, how much would you like us to invest?

K: We think we'll need $500,000 to market the product successfully, and for that we can offer you a stake of fifteen percent in the business.

W: Well, I'm sorry, but that's not acceptable. Investing half a million for a fifteen-percent stake wouldn't interest us.

I: If I can come in here, let me remind you of the benefits you'll get from investing in our device. Don't forget it's a state-of-the art product and several marine associations have tested it and found that it works. Also, it's got an international patent. MLSD will generate a lot of income for any investor. You'll get a very good return on your $500,000.

M: We can't be sure of that. It's a risky investment. There are competing products on the market.

I: Ah, but not with our advanced technology.

W: Maybe. But we're not happy about the terms you offer. We're not prepared to invest in the project unless you improve your offer.

K: How about if we offered you a bigger stake? Would you be willing to give us $500,000?

W: We might consider it. What can offer us?

K: Supposing we give you a twenty-percent stake for the full amount, what do you say?

W: I'm sorry. We were looking for a much higher stake.

K: Well, that's our final offer. It looks as if we can't make a deal.

W: I'm afraid not. The numbers just don't add up for us.

K: OK, then, thank you for your time. I'm very sorry we couldn't reach an agreement.

W: Well, that's too bad. We wish you the best of luck finding an investor. But, to be honest, you may find it difficult to get the terms you want.

I: We'll see. Thanks very much for meeting us.

LESSON 12.1 RECORDING 12.1

1 I did my first degree in molecular biology and now I'm doing a PhD in the same area. What's driven me in my research is the desire to break new ground, to discover something new, and the Mars project is quite similar. Getting public support will be crucial as the costs are astronomical. But if everyone donates something, we can make it a success. To be honest, er, space enthusiasts and scientists may be the hardest people to convince because of their knowledge of the difficulties. I know a one-way ticket to Mars may not appeal to everyone, but to me it sounds like the greatest adventure of all time! I'm very fit as I do a lot of outdoor activities, especially mountaineering, so I think I'm ready in all respects.

2 I was interested in applying to NASA to be an astronaut, but Mars isn't one of their destinations at the moment – I mean, not for humans, anyway. I think I've got both the technical and the people skills. Once we're there, we'll need to make better vehicles for exploring the surface and my engineering knowledge will come in handy. Also, I've visited a lot of foreign countries and gained good intercultural skills. That'll be important when you're cooped up with relative strangers for long periods of time. I'm convinced the long-term solution to the survival of our species lies in deep space – outside our solar system – but to get there, you've got to have stepping-stones. That's where Mars comes in.

3 I think this project's the most historic thing ever to happen in our galaxy. Because of that, it's something I'm prepared to risk my life for. My experience will obviously help. I currently fly commercial jets, but before that I was in the United States Air Force. In the early years on Mars staying safe will be a priority and everyone will need to have good medical skills. We'll need to reduce the risk of radiation and make the base as self-sustaining as possible. The scientific stuff will come later. My husband really supports the project, but he's not so keen on the idea of me never coming back!

LESSON 12.2 RECORDING 12.2

Today is something's birthday, something which we probably all use every day, but, er, I'm afraid that this isn't a happy day of celebration. This is a sad birthday, a birthday which would be better if it wasn't, because today's the birthday of the plastic bag. Erm to be exact, it's seventy-five years since polyethylene was discovered, by cruel chance, by two scientists in the UK. Polyethylene, more commonly known as polythene, is the basic constituent of plastic bags. So, why shouldn't we celebrate its birthday? Allow me to explain.

Erm, well, first of all, polythene, and most other plastic, is made from oil, and it's all part of our dependence on this raw material, and that's a dependence which leads to pollution and the destruction of the natural environment. The oil industry's one of the most polluting industries that we have, and our excessive use of plastic only encourages that industry. We should aim for an oil-free society.

Secondly, plastic simply doesn't go away or, at least, it takes an incredibly long time to do so, with some estimates that it takes 1,000 years for a plastic bag to decompose. This causes untold numbers of problems. Plastic waste takes up valuable space in our landfill rubbish disposal sites, but more importantly, it has a direct effect on wildlife. Animals and birds eat plastic by mistake or get caught up in plastic cables and bags and suffocate to death. There are so many depressing images of dead birds that have been cut open to reveal guts that are filled with plastic. What right do we have to inflict this harm on animals? We share this world and we need to share it responsibly. This problem though is no better exemplified than in the middle of the Pacific Ocean, where there is a floating island of plastic trash, but this island is twice the size of the state of Texas. That's right, twice the size of Texas. This is only the most extreme example as all of our oceans are teeming with plastic waste. And furthermore, some of this stuff slowly breaks down into tiny micro-particles which either are ingested by marine animals, animals that we then later eat, or gather on our beaches as plastic sand. So, we're actually eating plastic and we'll soon be sunbathing on plastic beaches. We have done this to our lovely planet and we need to stop.

So, stop using plastic bags, stop using coffee cups with plastic lids, stop buying over-packaged food. If we all do so, perhaps we'll no longer see the depressing and heartbreaking images of birds building nests for their young out of plastic or, or turtles mistaking plastic bags for food as they look like jellyfish. This is all too sad and it needs to stop.

LESSON 12.4 RECORDING 12.3

C = Chair, I = Indira, D = David, B = Bill, M = Molly

C: So, the first question is, do the panel agree that genetic engineering, in particular the genetic modification of plants and animals that we eat, should be halted due to the potential for unforeseen future dangers that it might cause for us and the planet? Well, certainly, this matter still raises a lot of controversy. GM foods are banned in many countries and the science is probably still relatively young. Indira Patel, what are your thoughts?

I: Well, you won't be surprised to hear that I disagree with the basic tenet of the question, that is this research should be halted. Genetic engineering may mean we can actually feed everyone on this planet, something we are significantly failing to do at the moment. Rice that requires less water; cows that produce higher yields of milk; potatoes that are resistant to disease. That's what genetic modification means and
I believe that is something we should strive for. How many more children do we want to see on our TV screens dying of starvation?

C: David, what do you have to say?

D: Well, as Indira said, this, er, research certainly shouldn't be halted, although, although, I mean, that's not to say that it shouldn't be heavily controlled and carefully managed. Which is, which is really the situation we have now and I think that if those safeguards continue, well, er, we, erm, we have little to, er, worry about, really.

C: OK, I imagine you might have a different view, Bill. Am I right?

B: What David said about current safeguards might sound reasonable, however, he seems to be forgetting that not all countries engaged in GM food production have exactly the same standards as us. And don't forget, genetic engineering of food is really about business, not science and not academia. This means that profit is the driving force and we all know that profit causes a blindness when it comes to potential dangers. Can we really trust scientists who are working for profit-driven multinationals?

I: Hold on, hold on a minute. If I understand you correctly, you're saying that science-based businesses can't be trusted. That is patently absurd. You trust pharmaceutical companies, don't you? They're just as driven by profit as an agrochemical company. It would hardly be good for profit if they did produce something that was a danger to human society, would it?

C: Before you respond to Indira, Bill, could I just bring Molly in here?

B: Well, I'd like to give an immediate answer, actually.

C: I understand, but I think we should hear from Molly first. Molly?

M: Thank you. First of all, could I just pick up on something that Indira said about feeding the world's population? She claimed that genetic engineering will enable us to feed the world, suggesting that that wasn't currently possible. Well, erm, while it may be true that many millions of people are suffering from starvation or poor diets, that isn't because there isn't enough food. It's because the world's food is divided unequally. We could feed everyone now if there was the political and commercial will to do so. And I would predict that the current inequality would continue even if we had GM food. The whole thing is merely another attempt by big business to make bigger profits And another thing regarding Indira's argument that we trust pharmaceutical companies, so therefore we can trust agrochemical or bio-engineering firms. I'm not sure that that's a fair argument and perhaps we should return to what the original question said, which was that there are unforeseen dangers. The problem is that we don't know what will happen once genetically engineered organisms co-exist with natural ones. Will they inter-breed to produce defective species, making the food situation even worse? Will one cause the extinction of the other? These kind of issues can't be answered in the lab, but they are real, fair and important questions. And so, can we really go on with this research?

LESSON 12.5 RECORDING 12.4

D = Don, T = Thérèse

D: Right, I don't think we've got time for any more today, so that's it – and see you Thursday. Have a nice afternoon! Enjoy the sunshine while it lasts.

T: Er, Don?

D: Yes, Thérèse?

T: Well, I was wondering if, er ... Could you give me some advice?

D: Some advice?

T: Yeah, about exams. What's the best way of doing them? Could you tell me what I should and shouldn't do?

D: Er, well, it's pretty difficult just to give general advice like that. Erm, I suppose, I mean, you've looked at some past exam papers?

T: Yes, but I don't feel very confident.

D: Well, don't worry if you feel a bit nervous. It's a good thing and will actually sharpen you up a bit – as long as it's kept under control. Oh, and, erm, check out the exam centre in advance. You're doing it at Westminster, aren't you?

T: Yes.

D: Well, do you know the best way to go, how long it takes?

T: I went to register there.

D: OK, well, basically, just allow plenty of time. You know what the Tube's like. Erm, oh, this is an important one. Don't just start writing. If you're doing an essay, that is. I don't know how many times I've seen that. You have to make a plan. If you've got forty minutes to write the essay, spend at least ten minutes on the plan. If you do that, it's much easier to write quickly afterwards.

I always say this to my classes, but it's amazing how many students just start writing. It's the pressure, I guess. What else? Oh, don't watch other students. Just focus on your own work. And, read the whole text before you try to answer a question. You know, if you're doing an exercise filling the blanks, always read the whole text quickly first before you do anything. Then you can see the context. Again, lots of students just start filling in the gaps without having any idea what the text is really about. Ah, this is another important one. Take a long-term view. You may need to do the exam more than once. I know it's expensive, but basically, the first time is often just about getting the experience, so you know what it's like. Then the second time you can really go and get the grade that reflects your level. Erm, and don't expect everything to be perfect. A few years ago, we had a student who complained that she couldn't concentrate during the listening test because the invigilator, who was wearing high heels, kept pacing up and down and making a load of noise. You have to be ready for stuff like that and not let it faze you. The oral examiners are usually friendly, but you may get one who isn't or who's tired. So, don't be afraid to ask them to repeat the question or to clarify it if you don't understand. Students sometimes complain about traffic noise from the street. Ah, you just have to focus, concentrate.

T: Thank you very much, Don.

D: I'm not sure what else I can say. Oh yeah, make sure you attempt all the questions.

Especially in the reading test. One of the problems many students have is that they can't finish all the reading passages – they run out of time. They spend too long on one or two passages and don't have time for the rest. But you need to keep going. If you meet a tricky question, think about it for a minute. If you can't find the answer, move on. Come back to it later if you have time. You have to try to get through all the passages. If there are three passages and you only do two, you automatically lose a third of the marks. Er, I can't think of anything else at the moment.

T: Thank you so much.

D: Does that all make sense?

T: Yes, I understand. You've given me a lot of good tips.

D: Well, if I think of anything else, I'll email it to you. Anyway, good luck. I'm sure you'll be fine! And don't forget to treat yourself to something nice afterwards!

Elementary, Pre-intermediate and Advanced levels

Gareth Rees studied Natural Sciences at the University of Cambridge. Having taught in Spain and China, he currently teaches at the University of the Arts, London. As well as teaching English, he is an academic English course leader, and unit leader on courses in cross-cultural communication for the London College of Fashion. He has also developed English language materials for the BBC World Service Learning English section, and he makes films which appear in festivals and on British television.

Ian Lebeau studied Modern Languages at the University of Cambridge and did his MA in Applied Linguistics at the University of Reading. He has thirty-five years' experience in ELT – mainly in higher education – and has worked in Spain, Italy, Japan and the UK. He has directed and taught on a wide range of programmes including foundation, IELTS and general English. Among his pedagogical interests are curriculum design, Content and Language Integrated Learning (CLIL), and critical thinking and writing skills.

Intermediate, Upper Intermediate and Advanced levels

David Cotton studied Economics at the University of Reading and did an MA in French Language and Literature at the University of Toronto. He has over forty-four years' teaching and training experience, and is co-author of the successful *Market Leader* and *Business Class* course books. He has taught in Canada, France and England, and has been visiting lecturer in many universities overseas. Previously, he was Senior Lecturer at London Metropolitan University. He frequently gives talks at EFL conferences.

David Falvey studied Politics, Philosophy and Economics at the University of Oxford and did his MA in TEFL at the University of Birmingham. He has lived in Africa and the Middle East and has teaching, training and managerial experience in the UK and Asia, including working as a teacher trainer at the British Council in Tokyo. He was previously Head of the English Language Centre at London Metropolitan University. David is co-author of the successful business English course *Market Leader*.

Simon Kent studied History at the University of Sheffield, and also has an MA in History and Cultural Studies. He has over twenty-five years' teaching experience including three years in Berlin at the time of German reunification. He has spent the majority of his career to date in higher education in the UK where he has taught on and directed programmes of business, general and academic English (including IELTS). Simon is co-author of the successful business English course *Market Leader*.

Far left: Simon Kent
Centre left: David Falvey
Centre: Gareth Rees
Centre right: Ian Lebeau
Far right: David Cotton

Pearson Education Limited
Edinburgh Gate
Harlow
Essex CM20 2JE
England
and Associated Companies throughout the world.

www.pearsonelt.com

© Pearson Education Limited 2015

First published 2015
ISBN: 978-1-4479-6143-7
Set in Optima 10/12 pt
Printed in China (Golden Cup)

Acknowledgements

The Publisher and authors would like to thank Anita Gera for her contribution to the material.

The Publisher and authors would like to thank the following people and institutions for their feedback and comments during the development of the material:

Brazil: Ray Shoulder; **Germany:** Dr Elisabeth Gilbert, Deidre Junghanns; **Poland:** Piotr Święcicki, Piotr Szymończyk; **UK:** Mark Heffernan, Adrian Grose-Hodge, Elzbieta Klim, Branka Visnjic

We are grateful to the following for permission to reproduce copyright material:

Images

Book cover on p.86 *Watching the English: The Hidden Rules of English Behaviour* by Kate Fox, Hodder & Stoughton, 2005. Reproduced with permission from Hodder & Stoughton Limited.

Figures

Figures on p.44 & p.160 from 'WHO causes of death' from The World Health Report 2008 *Primary Health Care – Now More Than Ever*, Figure 1.8, p8, http://www.who.int/whr/2008/whr08_en.pdf, accessed March 2014; and *Projections of global health outcomes from 2005 to 2060 using the International Futures integrated forecasting model* by Barry B. Hughes et al, Bulletin of the World Health Organisation 2011: 89: 478-486, accessed March 2014, copyright © World Health Organziation; and Figure on p.105 from *Reflective model in Reach, Touch and Teach* by Terry Borton, McGraw Hill, Inc., 1970. Reproduced by permission of The McGraw-Hill Companies, Inc.;

Logos

Logo on p.12 from UNESCO, copyright © UNESCO 2014. Used by permission of UNESCO; Logo on p.108 from FAIRTRADE®, copyright © Fairtrade Foundation 2014. Used by permission of Fairtrade Foundation.

Text

Extract on p.7 adapted from 'Learning by rote in the digital age', 10/10/2013, http://www.quipper.com, copyright © Quipper. Reproduced with permission; Extract on pp.10-11 adapted from the CV of Vadim Kufenko. Reproduced with kind permission; Extract on p.12 adapted from UNESCO Activities, copyright © UNESCO 2014, available at https://en.unesco.org/about-us/introducing-unesco. Used by permission of UNESCO; Extract on p.20 from "The beach that turned back the commercial tide", *The Guardian*, 27/05/2008 (Robert L. White), copyright © Guardian News & Media Ltd, 2008; Extract on p.27 adapted from "Moaning, drinking and queuing are what make us British", *The Telegraph*, 10/11/2008 (Matthew Moore), copyright © Telegraph Media Group Limited; Extract on pp.28-29 adapted from "After the Higgs hype, Cern still has as much purpose and passion as ever", *The Guardian*, 08/11/2013 (Suzanne Moore), copyright © Guardian News & Media Ltd, 2013; Extract on p.30 from an interview with Yingfan Wang http://www.un.org/cyberschoolbus/modelun/resp_wang.asp. Downloaded 2009. Reproduced with permission from the United Nations; Extract on p.30 adapted from an interview with Gillian Bristol. Reproduced with kind permission; Extract on p.38 adapted from "First world results on a third world budget", *The Guardian*, 07/09/2007 (Rory Carroll), copyright © Guardian News & Media Ltd, 2007; Extract on pp.40-41 adapted from "Are nurses angels? I don't think so", *The Daily Mail*, 18/07/2006, copyright © Solo Syndication, 2006; Extract on p.60 adapted from "DNA testing: should you worry about the state of your genes?", *The Telegraph*, 02/01/2014 (Dr Phil Hammond), copyright © Telegraph Media Group Limited; Extract on p.64 adapted from *Intercultural Business Communication* by Robert Gibson, Cornelsen Verlag, 2002, pp.43, 48. Reproduced by permission of Cornelsen Schulverlage GmbH; Extract on pp.70-71 from "50 great ideas for the 21st century", *The Independent*, 06/08/2006 (Stephen Bayley), copyright © The Independent, www.independent.co.uk; Extract on p.78 from "Hot off the press", *The Guardian*, 25/09/2008 (Simon Jenkins), copyright © Guardian News & Media Ltd, 2008; Extract on p.87 adapted from *Watching the English: The Hidden Rules of English Behaviour* by Kate Fox, Hodder & Stoughton, 2005, copyright © Kate Fox, 2004. Reproduced with permission from Hodder & Stoughton Limited, Lucas Alexander Whitley Ltd, and Nicholas Brealey Publishing and by kind permission of the Author; Extract on p.90 adapted from Statistics in 'international migration', http://esa.un.org/unmigration/wallchart2013.htm, copyright © United Nations. Reproduced with permission; Extract on p.91 adapted from the biographical introduction for Fleur Adcock and Grace Nichols from The Poetry Archive website at www.poetryarchive.org, copyright © The Poetry Archive; Poetry on p.91 "Immigrant" by Fleur Adcock, from *Poems 1960–2000*, Bloodaxe Books. Reprinted with permission of Bloodaxe Books, on behalf of the author, www.bloodaxebooks.com; Poetry on p.91 "Like a Beacon" by Grace Nichols, from *The Fat Black Woman's Poems*, Virago, 1984. Reproduced by permission of Little, Brown Book Group Limited; Extract on p.96 from 2011 Scottish Household Survey in *Scotland's People Annual Report*, http://www.scotland.gov.uk/Publications/2012/08/5277/13 © Crown copyright, The Scottish Government; Extracts on p.97 adapted from "Public Service Broadcasting" 16/11/2012, http://www.timeout.com/london/music/public-service-broadcasting; "Amused Moose Soho" 31/01/2009, http://www.timeout.com/london/comedy/amused-moose-soho-10; "Kenny Wheeler/Stan Sulzmann/John Parricelli/Chris Lawrence/Clive Fenner", 03/02/2009, http://www.timeout.com/london/music/kenny-wheeler-stan-sulzmann-john-parricelli-chris-lawrence-clive-fenner; "Nobody Rides the Unicorn", 18/12/2013, http://www.timeout.com/london/theatre/nobody-rides-the-unicorn; "Haim", 01/06/2012, http://www.timeout.com/london/music/haim-2; and "Thomas Noone Dance", 2009, http://www.timeout.com/london/dance/thomas-noone-dance, 06/02/2009, copyright © Time Out Digital; Extract on p.98 adapted from Musical Instrument Museum press release details, http://mim.org/ and http://mimmusictheater.themim.org. Reproduced with permission; Extract on p.100 adapted from "Kids with cameras lead the way in giving web users their daily Fred", *The Independent*, 28/07/2008 (Andrew Keen), copyright © The Independent, www.independent.co.uk; Extract on pp.100-101 from *Digital Performance: A History of New Media in Theater, Dance, Performance Art, and Installation* by Steve Dixon, MIT Press, 2007, copyright © 2007 Massachusetts Institute of Technology, by permission of The MIT Press; Extract on p.108 from "Fairtrade: Is it really fair? YES: It puts people back at the heart of trade NO: Other schemes are just as valuable", *The Independent*, 06/05/2012 (Harriet Lamb, Fairtrade Foundation and Philip Booth, Institute of Economic Affairs. Ed Sarah Morrison), copyright © The Independent, www.independent.co.uk; Extract on p.117 from "Fourth Planet from the Sun, overview", http://mars.nasa.gov/programmissions/overview/, copyright © NASA; Extract on p.120 from *A World Without Bees* by Alison Benjamin and Brian McCallum, Guardian Books, 2008, back of book blurb and pp.3, 28, 239, 262. Reprinted by permission of The Random House Group Limited; Extract on p.159 from *The Study Skills Handbook, 3rd edition* by Stella Cottrell, Palgrave Macmillan, 2008, p.59, Reproduced with permission of Palgrave Macmillan; Extract on